URBAN ENCOUNTERS

URBAN ENCOUNTERS
ART AND THE PUBLIC

Edited by Martha Radice and
Alexandrine Boudreault-Fournier

McGill-Queen's University Press

Montreal & Kingston • London • Chicago

© McGill-Queen's University Press 2017

ISBN 978-0-7735-5005-6 (cloth)
ISBN 978-0-7735-5006-3 (paper)
ISBN 978-0-7735-5007-0 (ePDF)
ISBN 978-0-7735-5008-7 (ePUB)

Legal deposit second quarter 2017
Bibliothèque nationale du Québec

Printed in Canada on acid-free paper

This book has been published with the help of a grant from the Canadian Federation for the Humanities and Social Sciences, through the Awards to Scholarly Publications Program, using funds provided by the Social Sciences and Humanities Research Council of Canada.

McGill-Queen's University Press acknowledges the support of the Canada Council for the Arts for our publishing program. We also acknowledge the financial support of the Government of Canada through the Canada Book Fund for our publishing activities.

Library and Archives Canada Cataloguing in Publication
Urban encounters : art and the public / edited by Martha Radice
and Alexandrine Boudreault-Fournier.

(The culture of cities)
Includes bibliographical references and index.
Issued in print and electronic formats.
ISBN 978-0-7735-5005-6 (cloth).–ISBN 978-0-7735-5006-3 (paper).–
ISBN 978-0-7735-5007-0 (ePDF).–ISBN 978-0-7735-5008-7 (ePUB)

1. Public art–Canada. I. Radice, Martha, author, editor
II. Boudreault-Fournier, Alexandrine, 1978–, author, editor
III. Series: Culture of cities

N8846.C2U73 2017   701'.030971   C2016-908270-9   C2016-908271-7

CONTENTS

ACKNOWLEDGMENTS

Such an interdisciplinary book could only have come out of the kind of project where people say, in the tradition of improvisational theatre, "yes, and!" *Urban Encounters: Art and the Public* was, first, the name of an innovative international colloquium held in Halifax in 2013, which brought together artists, academics, and members of the public for three days of conversation and collaboration stimulated by academic papers, roundtables, artists' talks, exhibitions, installations, and art performances. Many more people participated than are represented in this book, but we would especially like to acknowledge here the commentators in a roundtable on public art, whose discussion contributed to the arguments and structure of the introduction: Alison Bain, Peter Dykhuis, Eleanor King, and Jamie MacLellan, who were skilfully interviewed by CBC radio journalist Stephanie Domet. The colloquium would not have been possible without the hard work of Tonya Canning, who coordinated the conference side of things, and Michael McCormack and Annie Onyi Cheung who coordinated the art exhibitions and performances. We would also like to thank the student assistants at the colloquium, especially Brenden Harvey and Brenna Sobanski, for taking notes on the roundtable and research-creation workshop. NSCAD University and the Khyber Centre for the Arts graciously hosted the event's urban encounters.

The colloquium itself was a crucial part of a broader research-creation project, *Tracing the City: Interventions of Art in Public Space,* funded by a grant from the Social Sciences and Humanities Research Council of Canada that also supported this publication (award no. 848-2010-0019, 2011–15). Principal investigators Solomon Nagler, Kim Morgan, and Martha Radice started delving deep into interdisciplinary research-creation when they met in 2009, later inviting collaborators Christopher Kaltenbach, Ellen Moffat, and Erin Wunker to join in too. The colloquium, this book as a whole, and in particular the chapters by Bird and Nagler, Moffat and Morgan, and Radice, Harvey, and Turner, are the fruits of a collaboration that was as exciting and productive as it was challenging. The *Tracing the City* team would like to thank NSCAD University colleague Bruce Barber for his unflagging support for the project, as well as Nethra Samarawickrema for her early research assistance in gathering in its intellectual strands.

Working together on this book has been a real pleasure for us. We would like to thank all the contributors for their patience, diligence, and rapid response times but most of all for their stimulating, creative ideas. Will Straw, coeditor of the Culture of Cities series, and Jonathan Crago, editor-in-chief at McGill-Queen's University Press, have been champions of the book since its beginnings and offered wise counsel at all stages. We also thank the anonymous reviewers whose astute comments strengthened many parts of the book. Emily Fraser provided invaluable research assistance and eagle-eyed skills in manuscript preparation. We are grateful for the McGill-Queen's production team's help during the final steps toward publication. Dalhousie University's Faculty of Arts and Social Sciences granted Martha Radice a Burgess Award, which gave her precious extra research time in winter 2015 for editorial work. We both appreciate the general support of our departments and colleagues at Dalhousie University and the University of Victoria, as well as the fertile field of anthropology in Canada, which keeps both of us inspired.

URBAN ENCOUNTERS

Martha Radice and Alexandrine Boudreault-Fournier

INTRODUCTION:
ENCOUNTERS WITH ART IN THE URBAN PUBLIC

Art installations and interventions are increasingly being created and used to open up new lines of inquiry into the socialities of urban public space. As cities strive to be indexed as culturally dynamic and "creative," the stakes of artistic production in public space are raised ever higher. Yet there has been little rigorous research into how interactions between art and the public actually play out in the urban social context. This book directly engages with the relationship between art and the public by exploring how artworks in diverse media and genres can shape the urban public – the patterned and unpredictable encounters, events, and flows of city life – and, conversely, how the urban public can shape artistic production. The volume raises questions such as: What forms are artistic engagements with the city taking, and how do they influence the city's people and places? How does the urban public encounter art in the city, and how do these encounters affect the structure and content of the work? What kinds of urban social relations and publics are brought into being through art? How can we investigate and interpret encounters between art and the public in urban spaces? *Urban Encounters* addresses these questions by testing the productive tensions between "creation" and "research" and by seeing how artistic practices and production can interweave with social-scientific investigations of public life. Each chapter explores particular art projects in Canadian cities, analyzing them in their public context to make or critique claims about how art interacts with everyday urban life.

Artworks in public space have the potential to change the ways in which members of the public experience their cities. Artworks that fit into the interstices of the city – the parking lots or alleyways, the gaps between buildings – open up these spaces for new explorations. Artworks that appropriate central urban places, like main squares or monuments, can reframe or subvert their dominant meanings. Art can reclaim the streets. Art can alter the fabric of the city by projecting images or sounds onto its architectural surfaces or wrapping the city in new layers of surfaces. It can use new media technologies to create circuits for the urban to flow from "real" to "virtual" and back again. It can insinuate itself into existing urban institutions and infrastructures. In short, art can disrupt and rework the social and affective spaces of the city.

Moreover, while all art is interactive, in the sense that it calls for a reaction, many artists are experimenting with work that exists only through explicit engagement with the public in some form. This can mean attending carefully to the structures and rhythms of public spaces such that their surfaces or sounds, for instance, are built into the piece. It can mean creating art that is activated by participants' gestures *in situ* or accessed through the medium of individuals' mobile devices. Art can be crowdsourced, with conduits set up for incorporating textual or visual contributions from members of the public. More rarely, viewers' perspectives on art might be directly integrated into the work itself in an instant feedback loop. Art in the city can consist of performances that involve members of the public, either on a planned basis, through calls for participation, or spontaneously, as people pass by the art or as it comes to them. Still other kinds of public art are generated in dialogue, through more or less long-term collaborations with groups of people investigating specific urban social properties or problems in creative ways. Artistic engagement with the urban public can thus generate many kinds of encounters.

This introduction draws out the key terms and parameters of how art engages, reworks and disrupts the urban public in the Canadian contexts covered in the book. To set the stage for the chapters that follow, we situate the artworks in the book in relation to forms of public art, we tease out three useful ways to think through the word "public," we propose a definition of the city and show how its distinctive features can emerge in art, and we point to certain debates about how public art is framed and encountered in Canadian cities today. We take examples from this volume to illustrate our arguments but discuss each chapter in more detail in the section introductions.

The artworks presented in this volume are made of a variety of media and emerge from a wide range of artistic practices, many of them collaborative. Some of the chapters focus on performances, from the formally organized kind, such as contemporary dance (Matthias), to the organized yet informal or even "guerrilla" kind, like flash mobs (Shawyer), as well as in-between kinds – like Robert Bean and colleagues' participatory happening that was a sort of expanded creative workshop and the organic yet expected weekly drum gathering of the Montreal tam-tam (Vernet). Several contributions deal with media art, including the production or projection of audiovisual recordings (Bird and Nagler; Boudreault-Fournier and Wees; Moffat and Morgan; Radice, Harvey, and Turner) and the use of locative media and virtual networks to uncover new traces of the city (Moffat and Morgan; Johnston; Bean et al.). Artworks in the form of material installations of objects in urban spaces are also analyzed, including examples of architecture or industrial design (Bird and Nagler; Radice, Harvey, and Turner) and sculpture (Bain and Rallis; Vernet). Two of the chapters take up curatorial projects combining many forms of art, much of it performative or gestural, and with a dialogic, relational, or littoral (Barber 2013) aesthetic that called for responses from the public (Migone; Johnston). Some kinds of public art are notably absent from this volume, including graffiti and other uncommissioned visual street art (Bengtsen 2013; Seno 2010), and the kind of participatory, socially ameliorative projects known as community art (Crehan 2011).

Understandings of what makes public art "public" have always oscillated between the physical – art is public when it is in open, publicly accessible space – and the social – art is public when it engages pertinent public issues. As Johanne Sloan (2007) makes clear, any public artwork will touch on both these poles. Even the traditional "hero on a horse" statue, whose main function may seem to be to embellish a central place, embodies commemorative values that were important to the social group that put him there. Conversely, while counter-monuments might have social commentary as their key purpose, they are often very carefully sited. An artwork can be understood as physically public because it aesthetically enhances its site or represents some phenomenological sense of place or unpacks the implicit social relations that produce that site (Kwon 2002). Public artworks that emphasize the social might invite participation in the creative process from the local community, trigger public reactions and interactions when the art is presented, generate activism over crucial issues, or spark dialogue between different social factions (Hall 2007; Lacy 1995). Whether the publicness of public art is articulated through place or people, the concerns that it addresses might be superficial (fulfilling "per cent for art" stipulations), instrumental (improving the design of a place), or momentous (remembering victims of political oppression). Public art can placate crowds or ignite controversies. In these ways, "the field of public art is informed by a productive tension between permanence and impermanence, between monumentality and ephemeral traces, between the material weight of history and the fleeting signifiers of everyday urban experience" (Sloan 2007, 221–2).

Interestingly, only the first chapter of this book (Vernet) discusses public art in its most conventional sense: the imposing permanent monument, which acts as a landmark in a public square or plaza – the kind that proponents of "new genre" public art (Lacy 1995) dubbed "plop art." The art discussed in all the other chapters is time-based (film, dance, soundscape) or time-limited (by the parameters of a festival or exhibition schedule or participation instructions). If it produces permanent material artifacts (a pavilion, drawings, prints), then these are only impermanently placed in the public realm before passing into storage or private possession. Even the monuments in the first chapter – which are themselves altered materially and symbolically by the passage of time – are put into relation with time-limited, weekly gatherings or "scenes" (Blum 2003) revolving around them. This temporality points to the potential that ephemeral public art creations offer for experimentation, which Patricia Phillips urged the art world to consider more than twenty-five years ago. When "the work is part of the urban fabric for short periods of time, there is freedom to try new ideas, new forms, new methods of production. Perhaps there is also the willingness to engage difficult ideas and current issues in ways that more enduring projects cannot" (1989, 334–5). However, it may also point to a lack of resources available at this time to channel into longer-term projects that produce permanent public art. While "slow food" and "slow cities" movements have caught on, we have yet to hear about a return to "slow public art."

We hesitate to call all the artworks that feature in the following chapters "public art" if we understand this term in its strongest social sense to mean art that invites the negotiation of diverse social identities (Massey and Rose 2003, 19) or that "take[s] the idea of public as the genesis and subject for analysis" (Phillips 1989, 332). Rather, we consider these works to be art *in public*. "The public" is a rich, knotty concept, pulled in different directions by different disciplines and for different purposes; three lines of thought help smooth out the threads for what we need to do here. We shift now to conceiving the public not in material form (places, things) but as patterns of social relations. First, we can think about the public as constituted in relatively accessible spaces or places where strangers are brought into contact, if not direct communication, with each other. The contact can be of the most minimal kind – Goffman's glance of "civil inattention" – but it acknowledges that the strangers are copresent and visible to each other. This is the public realm in a concrete, immediate sense, broadly but not exactly coincident with public space, in that private or hidden spaces can sometimes host public modes of relation, and public spaces can be appropriated for private purposes (Lofland 1998). In other words, the public realm emerges from the kinds of relations that are made in public spaces but is not the same thing as those physical public spaces. Vernet's and Matthias's chapters, among others, investigate the patterns of interaction between strangers at this level of the urban public; the monuments and choreographies that these two authors analyze modulate those patterns in particular ways.

Second, we can think about the public in a less spatial, more discursive sense, as the arenas where private actors come together to discuss matters of mutual concern and to influence or take political action. This is the public sphere, "a sociopolitical collective that is constructed through dialogue and action" (Staeheli et al. 2009, 634), which is distinct from but (ideally) shapes and steers the state and market apparatuses and institutions that govern our lives. It is also, we suppose, the kind of public that Phillips (1989, 332) would like to see engaged in public art. This second kind of public is not immediate like the first; it takes shape over a longer time-period, in many dispersed but connected places. Lawrence Bird and Solomon Nagler's discussion of how cinema and architecture influence urban forms evokes the public sphere of city-building. The Artifact Institute's "investigation" of electronics rejected by the Halifax municipal garbage collection service, curated and discussed here by Wes Johnston, engages directly in the public sphere by initiating local debates about what counts as refuse. Bean, Le Blanc, Lilley, Lounder, and Luka's Narratives in Space+Time Society has been exploring and re-presenting the events of the Halifax Explosion of 1917 in a series of guided walks-with-performances, similar to the event at the Hippodrome described in this volume (figure 0.1). Their research-creation reworks another facet of the public sphere by replenishing and often challenging the city's collective memories of this traumatic event. So, this second kind of public is where ideas about the distribution and value of material and symbolic resources are put up for discussion, perhaps to converge, probably to be contested.

Third, we can think about the public as audience (a meaning underlined in French, where "an audience" can be translated as *un public*). This mode of publicness seems particularly pertinent to art. This is the public that "exists *by virtue of being addressed*" (Warner 2002, 50, emphasis in the original) and that therefore emerges in relation to the texts, or artworks, that address it. The public mode of address not only transmits information to but also constitutes its audience; it activates its public. This kind of public can be the mass-mediated collective imagined as the nation-state (Cody 2011), among other iterations; it is not necessarily copresent either (although it can be, as at a live dance performance for instance). Many of the artworks created for Christof Migone's curated series, *Door to Door*, interpellate the public in this sense. Addressing the Canadian settler legacy in her work *Not From Here*, Nancy Nowacek seeks to buy the goods offered in exchange for land in the purchase of Mississauga in 1788, while Micah Lexier's piece takes up a page of the *Mississauga News*, turning the newspaper's audience into a new kind of public by giving them some unexpected art to read. Susanne Shawyer's chapter points to the tension between two layers of such interpellated publics: the participating public addressed by "Steve" that carries out his instructions for the MP3 experiment and the bystanding public addressed by the participants' performance. These three modes of the public – spatialized realm, discursive sphere, and addressed audience – are closely related, and it is very easy (and sometimes desirable) to slip from one to another when talking or writing or indeed reading about them. This book raises questions about what art does to, or for, the urban public at all these levels.

What has perhaps emerged most strongly in the last few decades' production of scholarship on the public is the recognition of the fragmentation of "the" public into multiple publics and counterpublics. As Nancy Fraser's (1990) reworking of Habermas's (1989) foundational theory of the public sphere demonstrates, conditions of social inequality, not to mention the effectively nonneutral terms of engagement, mean that "the public" should not be understood as universal. There are many publics and relations between them, configured by social differences such as class, gender, race, ethnicity, religion, immigration, indigenous/settler status, rural/urban outlook, professional or kin roles, and so forth. Public institutions like libraries (Newman 2007) and art galleries have had to address this issue as they react to – or indeed, strive for – the diversification of their publics. All three modes of the public that we have drawn out here are inflected by diverse social identities, although in different ways; for instance, spaces in the public realm are theorized to function best when social differences are politely minimized (Simmel 1950, Tonkiss 2003), whereas the latter need to be explicitly recognized in the public sphere. Moreover, we would argue that all three modes of the public are especially concentrated in cities, even when they do not take the form of publics copresent in space.

Cities are defined by social heterogeneity, density – of people, resources, buildings – and mobility or mutability – of ideas, aspirations and affiliations as well as objects (Wirth 1938, Remy 1972). While cities are clearly where strangers come into contact (public realm), they are also – by virtue of concentrating people and resources – the hubs of the discursive public sphere and often the stages from which public audiences are most loudly addressed. Indeed, at this point in time, so many key political, social, economic, and environmental questions are being refracted through an urban lens that it is not surprising that art practices, too, are exploring "the urban" with vigour, as Canadian cultural theorist Saara Liinamaa explains (2014). She argues that the thread running through "art's diverse urban actions ... is the recognition that urbanization represents the dramatic concentration of everyday inequality" (2014, 536). Overall, the contributions to this volume do not address the social inequality and diversity inherent in the urban public in a strong way, with the exception of the chapter by Alison L. Bain and Nicole Rallis. They show how art is implicated in the gentrification and rebranding of James Street North in postindustrial Hamilton, Ontario, at the expense and exclusion of the working-class, immigrant, low-income publics who once predominated in the neighbourhood. Other chapters give glimpses into the multiplication of publics, offering perhaps what Liinamaa calls "soft solidarity" in recognition of the implicit social inequality between them. Thus, Martha Radice, Brenden Harvey, and Shannon Turner identify "lay" and "expert" publics at the Situated Cinema, and Alexandrine Boudreault-Fournier and Nick Wees's research-creation leads to encounters with the hidden and potentially marginalized social worlds of Vancouver's back alleys. We encourage this book's public to look for other examples.

The cultures of cities are strongly shaped by density and mobility as well as social heterogeneity. Art in the urban public enters into systems of flows, exchange, and interaction that are more far-reaching and less predictable than those in which it is embedded when it stays in a studio or gallery (Boutros and Straw 2010). Immersing themselves in those circulatory systems, Ellen Moffat and Kim Morgan choose commercial and transit hubs for their audiovisual research-creation that attends to the movement of the body in the city. The qualities of their movements and the resulting video/audio are greatly affected by the density and im/mobility of people in each hub: the artists are jostled in Paris, they have space to play in the more loosely occupied centres of Regina and Saskatoon, and they are left to roam on their own through the port of Halifax at night. Art in public leaves the art gallery, the theatre, the cinema, the studio, the conference, or the university; the container dissolves and the art institution melts away to be gossamer thin. Wes Johnston curated performative and documentary work by artists who engaged with the urban at the scale of the entire regional municipality (although, being Halifax, it hugs the rural tight and is dotted with the "little lakes" that Anne Macmillan swam round). In contrast, Marriott and Kraven each used the postal service to carry their artistic interventions into the homes of Mississauga residents in Migone's *Door to Door* series, creating a public in the domestic realm. Johnston's and Migone's projects, like Bain's recent monograph (2013), challenge the notion that art can only come out of the heart of the city. Even at their very edges, the suburbs, too, furnish material for new artistic projects and practices (Archer 2011), and also provide art publics, although these are likely to be differently configured – more dispersed, more mediated – than the copresent audiences of the public realm in urban cores. The potentially contested contours of what counts as "urban" public art run parallel to debates in the social sciences about tentacular processes of urbanization or whether everywhere is urban now (Brenner 2013). Art in public plays out in all kinds of urban places, at all kinds of scales.

Art can also be either made or shown in public – or both. Moffat and Morgan and Boudreault-Fournier and Wees used the properties of urban spaces to make their art, recording video and sound to edit into original representations of the embodied experience of urban space. We don't know, however, if their media artworks might be exhibited in public space. Bean and colleagues made or rather prepared their art over the Internet, through what has been called Hertzian space (Dunne 2001), at some 1,200 km from the Montreal Hippodrome, where their event came together as a participatory performance that itself incorporated a mediated layer of "virtual" urban space. The MP3 experiments that Shawyer analyzes were similarly primed over the Internet but executed (and again mediated by mobile devices) in public places. At the other end of the spectrum, even though they are inspired by and partly shot in the urban public, the films shown in *Brief Encounters* (Bird and Nagler) and the Situated Cinema (Radice, Harvey and Turner) really only met the public when they were projected. The publicness of art can thus relate variably to its creation and/ or its consumption.

Among the questions we can ask about encounters between art and the urban public are how is the art framed? Does it trumpet its arrival or sneak up by stealth? Does it creep into back alleys or crowd onto the soccer field? Is it a one-off intervention or part of a multisited, multiwork series such as an arts festival? These questions are particularly relevant when the work of art, or at least its passage in public space, is not permanent, and they are important because they raise further questions about the instrumentalization and regulation of art. Anthropological, sociological, and geographical research on festivals identifies a useful conceptual tension between the carnival and the spectacle (Cohen 1982, Bélanger 2005, Waitt 2008). The carnival is the vernacular, bottom-up, potentially subversive festive event, while the spectacle is the top-down strategic pageant orchestrated by the powers that be. Artists perhaps most often want to create on the side of the carnival, cracking open the everyday to turn it into a thing of wonder, by means of interventions that may be

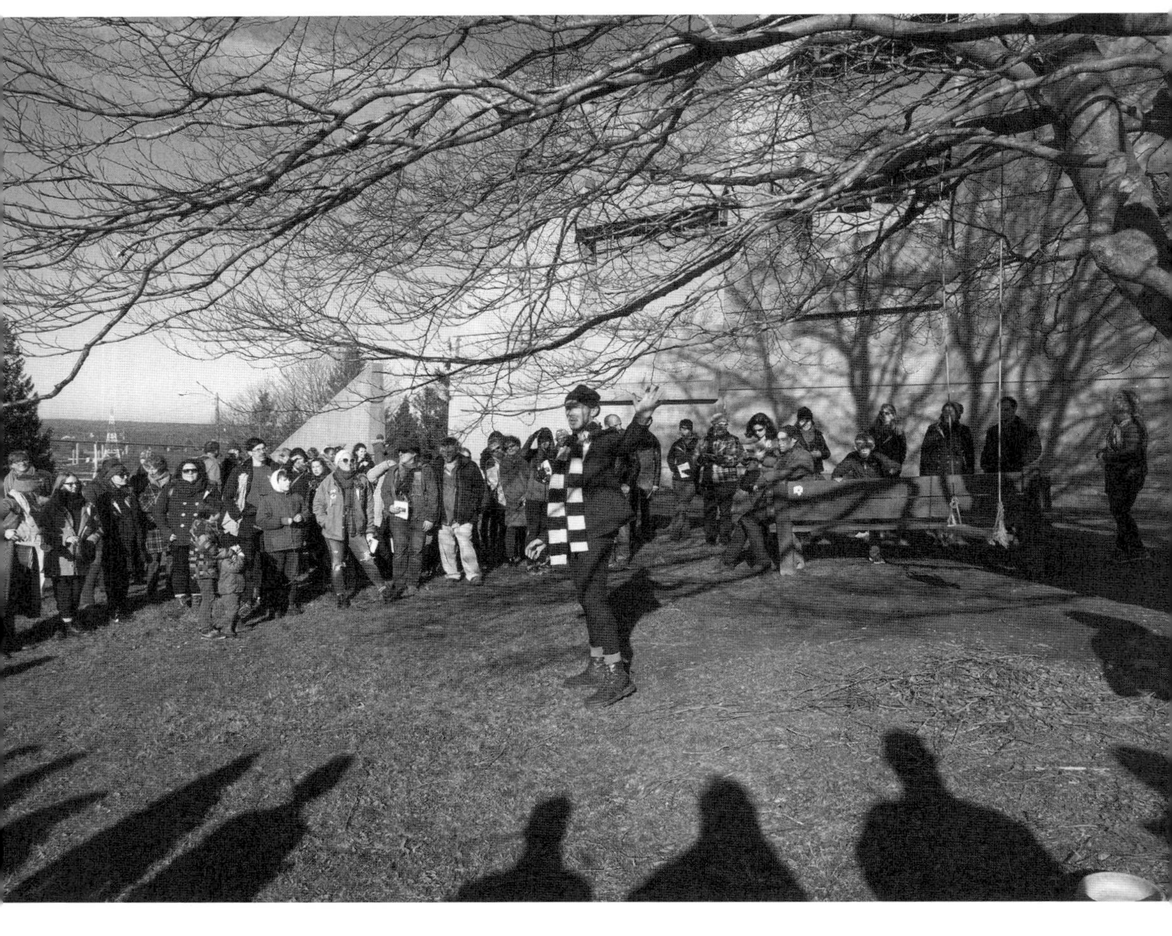

0.1 *Walking the Debris Field: Public Geographies of the Halifax Explosion, December 6, 2015.* Narratives in Space+Time Society. Photo: Robert Bean.

boisterous, like the MP3 pranks studied by Shawyer, or furtive (Loubier 2001), like the placards, signs, and stickers placed by Irving, Quagliotto, and Plotnikoff in Migone's *Door to Door* series. But in the current economic and political context, artists often find themselves and their works corralled into city-boosting spectacles, like the Supercrawl analyzed by Bain and Rallis. The risk is then that the spectacular festive framework overdetermines the structure of the artwork. Bureaucratic regulation is one problem: the curator of Halifax's Nocturne in 2013, Eleanor King, had to negotiate her way around the city's reluctance to let artist Lucy Pullen's swings *(Interval for Halifax)* go up with anything less than two security guards watching each one. Bean and colleagues tried and failed to obtain permission to use the disused Hippodrome for their happening (which was framed by an urban studies conference on mobilities), but the lack of municipal endorsement did not seem to spoil the day. The Situated Cinema's first site, in a parking lot, was simply secured by feeding the parking meters (and making a courtesy call to the restaurant next door). Discreet noncompliance is thus one possible solution, allowing one kind of public to circumvent another.

Although arts festivals are one of the primary ways that the public encounters art, not all festivals are the same (and in any case, as Cohen points out, can potentially articulate both hegemonic and oppositional ideologies at once). As Radice, Harvey, and Turner's chapter demonstrates, the same creative piece is likely to be experienced in one way in the context of an independent experimental film festival and in another way by the crowds of a nightlong citywide one. Drobnick and Fisher's (2012) special issue of *Public* on "Civic Spectacle" shows that many artists feel conflicted about these larger kinds of festivals; on the one hand, they suck up great quantities of resources, while on the other, they generate new publics in terms of not only the myriad actual encounters with artworks and among viewers but also the way that the city subsequently imagines itself as a site for cultural production. Art in the urban public often teeters between carnival and spectacle. The trick may be to foster works of art that are, as it were, multi-purpose, rewarding both fleeting and in-depth engagement. However, in order to gauge those rewards, research has to be conducted to investigate how members of the public actually feel about the art they encounter in urban settings.

In addressing the multiple articulations of art and the public in Canadian cities – Halifax, Montreal, Toronto, Mississauga, Hamilton, Winnipeg, Regina, Saskatoon, Vancouver – this volume brings together authors from a range of academic disciplines and fields of practice. Among them are artists, architects, and curators, as well as anthropologists, geographers, and urban studies scholars. They approach their objects of study from a variety of angles – as creators, curators, observers, or participants – and with a range of methods, some of which are more associated with arts scholarship and others with the social sciences. This interdisciplinary mix perhaps reflects cultural conversations that are peculiarly Canadian, given the relatively stable infrastructure that supports the many creative acts of making and talking about art in public. This includes artist-run centres like Dare-Dare, Montreal (see Johnston, this volume), institutions like the Canada Council for the Arts and regional arts boards, and new streams of funding like the Social Sciences and Humanities Research Council's "research-creation" grants. In collaborations that arise from the latter, when artists and social scientists come together, it can be hard to figure out who gets to be a researcher or creator and how to adapt to each discipline's ideas of what counts as research or what value is placed on creation. Yet, far from accentuating the dichotomy between arts and social sciences, we think that this book makes a unique contribution to scholarship on art in public. This is because every chapter presents a hands-on engagement with public art based on original empirical research, creation or research-creation – as distinct from purely theoretical or interpretive work.

Urban Encounters: Art and the Public is divided into three parts. The first, "Performing Art Publics," deals with art in public in the form of creative performances or events. These are not only held *in* the public realm, they also illuminate the sociospatial patterns, properties, and connections *of* the public realm. Part 2, "Making Art, Making the City," situates the production and consumption of art in the context of urban political economies (and vice versa). It shows how art has the potential to make, or unmake, the city. Part 3, "Meeting Art in Public," discusses what happens when art is offered up to the urban public and when curators' and creators' intentions rub up against audiences' reactions, bringing new art publics into being.

Overall, the book builds upon and further develops the substantive project of the Culture of Cities series. As rich in scope as earlier volumes, it likewise aims to understand how cultural forms and the city reciprocally intervene in and constitute each other, in an era when increasing value is placed on arts and culture by institutional and commercial actors in the urban symbolic economy. The contributions to this volume treat public art not just as an aesthetic object to be installed or encountered within urban space but also as an agent that participates in the ongoing social and cultural evolution of the city. The encounters that art in the urban public generates have the potential to transform the city itself – and the ways in which people relate to it.

Part One

ALEXANDRINE BOUDREAULT-FOURNIER
AND MARTHA RADICE

: Performing
Art Publics

This section deals with events and performances in which artworks or artists engage with urban public spaces. In the following four chapters, performance implies provoking the encounter; it is about engaging with public spaces, through various means such as dance, music, walking, and theatre, in order to disrupt or transform normal everyday life and provide an alternative use and vision of urban space. Performing the public implies a conscious interference in the normal activities or uses of a space, in order to better reflect on the presence of people and their relationships with these spaces. In her chapter, Susanne Shawyer looks at the flash mobs or urban pranks called *The MP3 Experiments* in public spaces in Toronto, organized by a prank collective based in New York City, Improv Everywhere. She argues that these experiments, which use humour to disrupt or breach normal everyday life, have the potential to be a form of political art in the vein of Rancière's dissensus. *The MP3 Experiments* described by Shawyer incite antagonistic reactions; they are a reminder that public art can disturb and shock. Because of this, these performances offer an alternative engagement with public spaces during which both the participants and the passersby are called to critically explore the impact of art in public.

Whether politically driven or not, these provoked encounters offer a momentary experience of alternative patterns, rhythms, relations, and copresence in and with urban public spaces.

In performing publics, the provoked encounters become part, for a moment, of social space. Performing publics is about the meeting of bodies that are placed together temporarily, bodies that are in contact with each other, with objects, obstacles, and different materialities that facilitate or inhibit those performances. The movements and flows of connections created and disrupted emerge through the act of performing; the groove of the dance floor acts as a springboard for spontaneous body interactions, sequential rhythms and gazes, as Sebastian Matthias suggests. Monuments also work as magnets around which strangers temporarily come closer to listen, dance, and share, in the chapter by Laurent Vernet.

Performing publics contribute to "making visible" what is normally taken for granted – or invisible. Let's take the metaphor of a mirror to explore this idea further. Performing publics is about what becomes visible through the conscious act of real-izing what is reflected in the mirror and what remains invisible – what is excluded, outside the frame. In "making visible," the artist highlights the relations and networks that connect (or not) the elements that are part of a public and of an urban mise-en-scène (more on this point below). Matthias's chapter shows how dance can reflect the patterns of social interactions in urban public spaces. His participatory choreography at the *Champ de pixels* in Montreal's Quartier des Spectacles stimulated coincidence and mimesis between dancers and passersby, which Matthias later explored in *Danserye*, a choreography performed in venues that were reconfigured to mirror public spaces (no seated audience for instance). Even when people do not engage with their reflection in the mirror of art, they still contribute to the performance of the public. This is also strongly expressed in Shawyer's chapter: passersby might not want to take part in the flash mobs, but their participation is demanded by their mere presence.

Yet, like all metaphors, the one of the mirror is not flawless. What is represented in the mirror is not a perfect copy of the public; it is transformed and altered. The public becomes a mise-en-scène, performed by various actors, a performance that is in some ways influenced by the intentions and presence of the artists and/ or of their work. In organizing a creative participatory mobile workshop in the old Blue Bonnets Hippodrome in Montreal, Bean, Le Blanc, Lilley, Lounder, and Luka give new life to this abandoned site. With the workshop participants, they contribute to the creation of alternative meanings, stories, and experiences in dialogue with the remaining materialities and enacted memories of the site. In addition to interacting with the workshop's stations or "pin drops," the participants' actions combine the history of the site, its present life, and its uncertain future in novel ways. This site, the authors write, is full of tensions between what is present, what is off the radar (the absent horses, crowds, sulkies, etc.) and what is planned for the future, and, as a consequence, the Hippodrome can be approached as a nonsite, a heterotopia, where the absences have left traces, some more visible than others. The workshop at the Hippodrome organized by the Narratives in Space+Time Society (NiS+TS), a locative media group based in Halifax, generated an alternative experiencing of the site. In their case, the digital also served as a way to mediate this experience, bringing another layer of meaning through which the participants can interact with the space. This research-creation-in-practice shows that mediated art offers various possibilities of copresence and "telecopresence" (Zhao 2005) that can potentially bridge distinct spatial and temporal dimensions as well as reshuffle the notion of what "being together" means.

Public space is replicated through performance but not like a mirror; it is enacted through the presence of the artists and/or their work. In intervening in public spaces, the artist is involved in the "staging" of mise-en-scènes in which various elements interact. Richard Freeman (2001) approaches the public spaces of Buenos Aires in this way. He explains that although mise-en-scène means "staging in action," it does not refer only to "staging"; that is, it means more than mere background. He writes: "In theatre and film, the director has complete control over setting. Despite a lack of control in real life, we can see players in society attempt to do precisely what film and theatre directors do – control the set" (2011, 38). The artist's intention might be to control the set, even momentarily, but many aspects of the performance depend on improvisation and serendipity. In the case of Bean and his colleagues, who had only acquired a remote and mediated representation of the Hippodrome before they actually visited the site with the workshop participants, the unexpected dimensions of the performance (not to mention the weather) also directed the experience of the site and the landscape. Performances in many ways echo the unpredictability or, rather, semipredictability, of public spaces. Yet, the artist and/or the work of art might have an effect other than echoing public spaces; they might also create a new setting that redirects the circulation and movement of people and objects.

The opening chapter by Vernet, on the weekly urban musical and social gatherings that spring up around two public monuments in Montreal, explores this dimension. In comparing two musical events that take place at the base of two imposing permanent sculptures, Vernet suggests that the interactions between artworks and passersby produce contrasting cases of public encounters. More specifically, he describes the tam-tam, a popular musical gathering that takes place near the *Monument to Sir George-Étienne Cartier* in the Parc du Mont-Royal, as more organic than the more programmed Piknic Électronik, a music festival organized at the foot of Alexander Calder's *Man, Three*

Disks on Île Sainte-Hélène. Quite provocatively, Vernet argues that the types of relationships strangers have with one another during each of these events is replicated in their interactions with the sculptures. Here again, we notice the distorting effect of the mirror of performance offered by public art.

In these ways, performing the public through art becomes a dialogical experience that permits a momentary reconfiguration of the urban public.

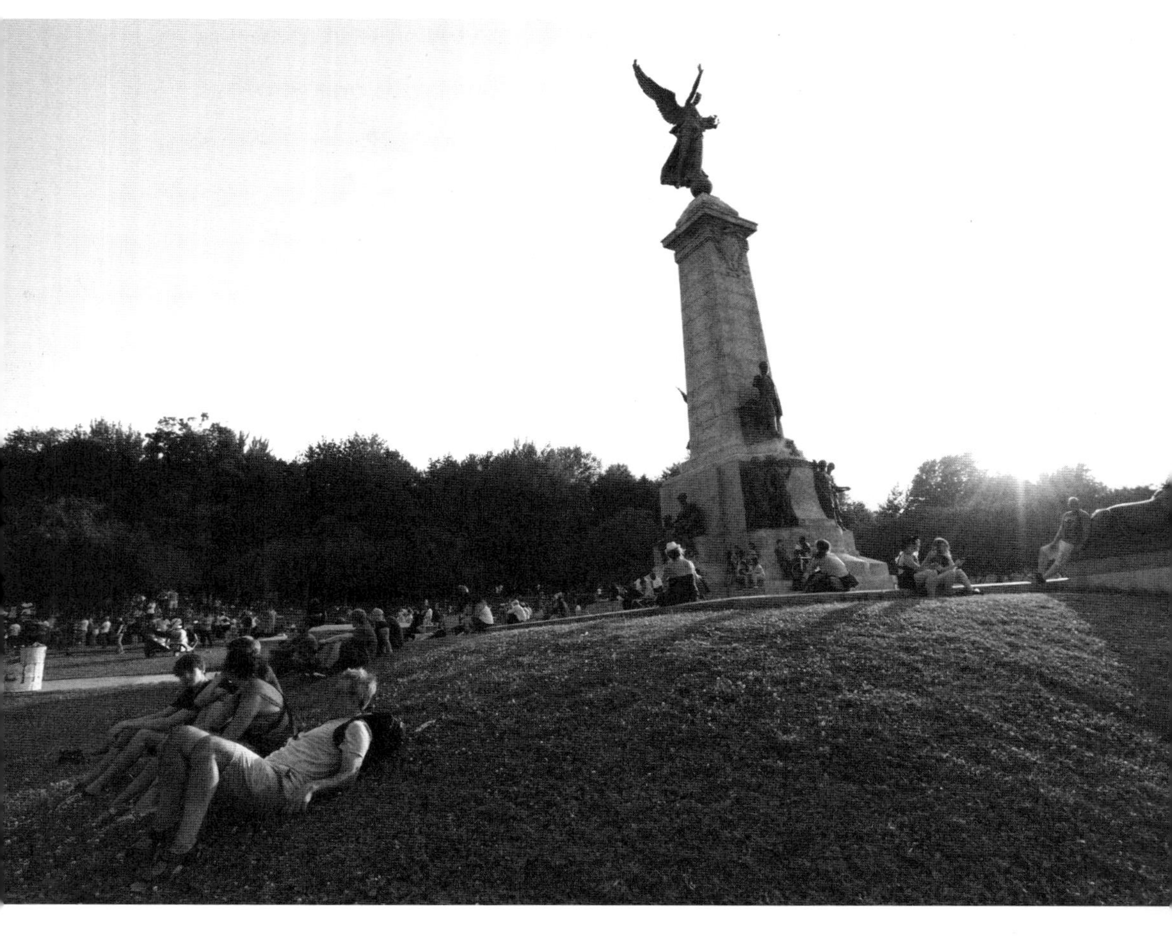

1.1 The *Monument to Sir George-Étienne Cartier* during the tam-tam.
Photo: Thibaut Larquey, 2014.

Laurent Vernet

1

—

ARTWORKS AS STRANGERS? ENCOUNTERS WITH TWO MONUMENTAL ARTWORKS IN MONTREAL

It is just another Sunday afternoon in Montreal; the summer weather has finally returned after months of snow, slush, and freezing temperatures. Around George William Hill's 1919 *Monument to Sir George-Étienne Cartier*, in Parc du Mont-Royal, and Alexander Calder's 1967 sculpture *Man, Three Disks*, on Île Sainte-Hélène, two popular gatherings are taking place. With music at their centre, these social events offer a unique perspective on the present-day impact of artworks that have been installed in public spaces for decades. On the east side of Parc du Mont-Royal, in the great open space at the foot of the mountain (Mount Royal) along Avenue du Parc, up to four thousand people come together every week throughout the warmer months. This event is called the tam-tam, which means drums in French: at its core is a drum circle, made up of thirty to fifty percussionists, which forms near the monument to Cartier (figure 1.1). Off the pathways circumscribing the artwork's site are fifty craft vendors – another key component of the gathering. This is to say that the monument is an intrinsic part of the event and its identity, even though its intended meaning has nothing to do with the tam-tam itself. The thirty-metre-high composition, featuring eighteen bronze figures, is a tribute to a French-speaking Father of Confederation (the founding of the Canadian state in 1867). Facing east and west around the base of the monument are allegorical figures representing the first nine provinces to join Confederation; on the north and south sides are two groups representing "education" and "law," two domains to which Cartier contributed. On a higher level of the monument, linked to the representation of the provinces, are statues of the man himself and of a patriotic soldier holding a standard. The pyramidal column is crowned by what is commonly assumed to be an angel but which is actually a winged figure of "Renown" holding a laurel branch. This complex assemblage is installed on architectural components designed by brothers Edward and William Maxwell, which include a terrace and stairs that are part of the monument. Four lions at the corners of the terrace, added later, complete the composition; these symbols of the British Empire are the work of Belgian sculptor Louis François Étien. (This description of the monument is based on Gubbay 1979.)

In another public park – this one on an island in the middle of the St Lawrence River – a different gathering takes place on summer Sunday afternoons. Created in 2003 to make electronic music accessible to a bigger audience by taking it out of its habitual context of the rave and the after-hours club, the Piknic Électronik is a weekly festival presenting local and international DJs, taking place between 2:00 p.m. and 9:30 p.m. from mid-May to the end of September (figure 1.2). There are two stages at the Piknic, but the main dance floor is located under Alexander Calder's "stabile" (a term coined by Jean Arp to designate Calder's airy monumental artworks that touch the ground at a few points, as opposed to his mobiles) entitled *Man, Three Disks*. The work was commissioned by the International Nickel Company of Canada for the 1967 Montreal World Fair, known as Expo 67, and it was later given to the Ville de Montréal. Its title is a reference to the Expo 67 theme, "Man and His World," and so the abstract sculpture can be seen as a symbol of unity and equality in difference. At twenty-two metres, it is the second-tallest work by Calder in the world (after one in Mexico City) and the tallest that is unpainted. It consists of five overlapping arches sitting on six legs, topped with three discs and two points. The work was moved from its original location in 1991 to the belvedere created specifically for it; this site offers a spectacular view of the downtown core and the mountain in the middle of the city (Ville de Montréal, Public Art Bureau 2015). *Man, Three Disks* is without question part of the Piknic: the image of the work has been used in advertisements for the festival as well as on various products such as glasses and t-shirts.

In this essay, I take advantage of the similarities between the two events mentioned above to propose an urban sociological perspective

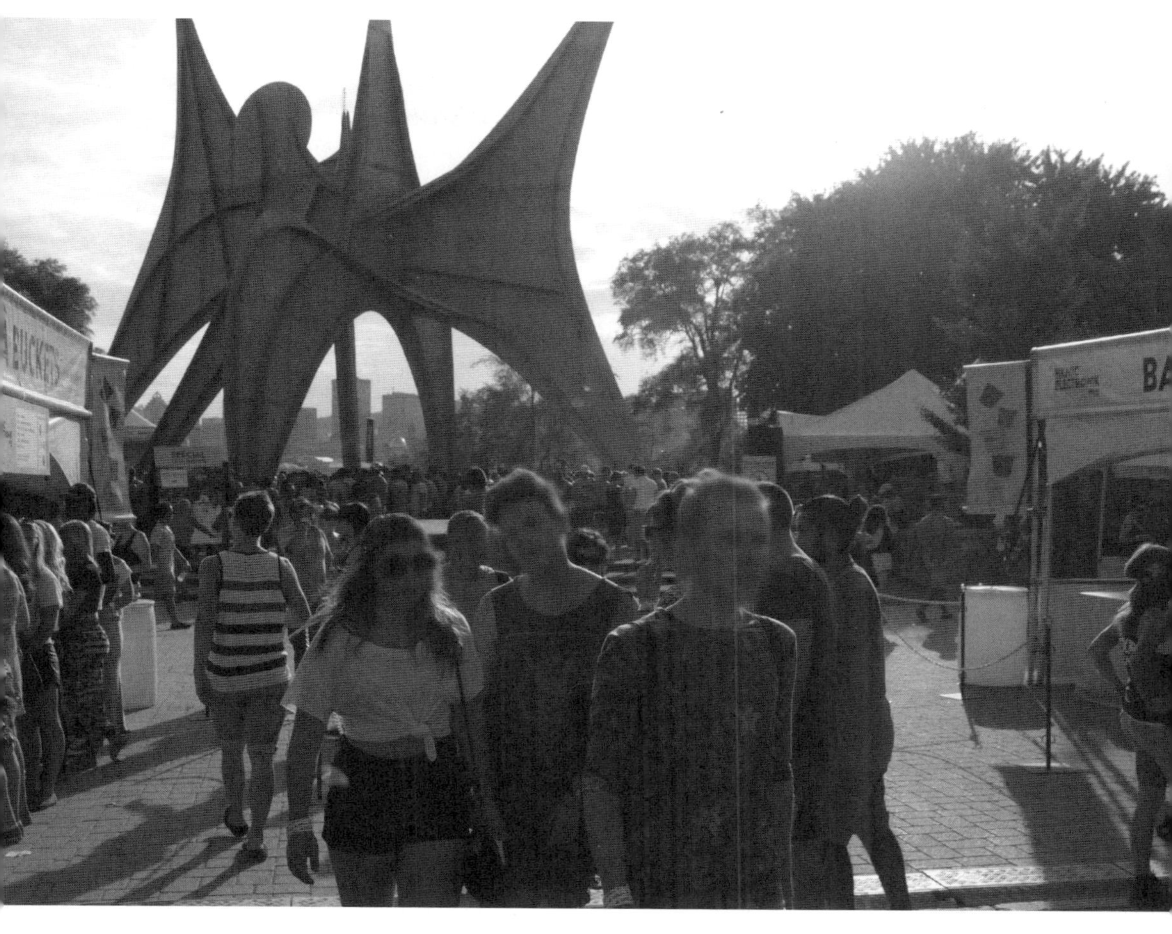

1.2 *Man, Three Disks* during the Piknic Électronik.
Photo: Thibaut Larquey, 2014.

on the notion of publics for artworks in public spaces.[1] As a point of departure, the tam-tam and the Piknic Électronik offer starkly contrasting cases of publics' encounters with monumental artworks. My study of these gatherings is based on filmed and participant observations conducted both during the Sunday afternoon gatherings and during the rest of the week. I use Lyn H. Lofland's (1998) principles of stranger interaction as an analytical guide to better understand the relationships of publics with art objects. First, I look at the Sunday events as contexts for intense public sociability: even though they are different in nature – one more organic, the other more programmed – one of the reasons that people take part in them is the pleasure of being in a public space with strangers. Then, I develop the idea that the relationship that these strangers have with one another in these public parks is replicated in the relationship that people have with the monumental public artworks found there. I cite key ideas from scholars working with pragmatic sociology, including Bruno Latour's actor-network theory, for the pertinence of these authors' approaches to associating people with objects (notwithstanding Latour's reservations about the concept of sociability). Finally, the social experience of these artworks feeds into a reflection on the cultures of public spaces in Montreal and on the contribution of artworks to the social life of large public parks.

BETWEEN STRANGERS

As this book shows, there has been growing academic interest in the outcomes and effects of various forms of public art. This is especially true in disciplines such as geography and anthropology, which offer the theoretical and empirical tools that enable practitioners to conduct fieldwork in the city. By concentrating on users' interactions with and perceptions of the art objects, recent contributions have produced a shift in the discourse on art in public spaces, displacing the focus from the artwork itself to the individuals that interact with it. In their introduction to *The Uses of Art in Public Space*, Julia Lossau and Quentin Stevens observe, "'Use' moves the locus of attention and power to the public, who find their own purposes in the aesthetic objects and experiences presented to them" (2015, 5). An example of this shift would be cultural geographer Martin Zebracki's (2012, 2013) work on the perceptions and representations of artworks by users and residents. For my part, I have described publics for artworks in public spaces by looking at how individuals use them (Vernet 2015) and by establishing the different degrees of relationship that publics have with the art object (Vernet 2014). My intention is to create a break with the usual art-historical discourse, which, following Rosalyn Deutsche's (1996) definition of public art based on Jürgen Habermas's (1974) public sphere, has typically considered the site of the public artwork to be one of debate and political discourse, leading to confusion between discursive and physical sites. Instead, I argue that artworks should be looked at within the specific context in which they are experienced: public spaces, which include parks, plazas, squares, and streets (see, for instance, the typology by Carr et al. 1992). In these sites, strangers coexist with one another in a mingling process that is called public sociability, defined as weak and ephemeral social interactions (Grafmeyer and Authier 2008).[2]

Here, I pursue this exploration of the question of the publics for artworks in public spaces by transposing well-established vocabulary and research methods specific to the study of the city, both as a form and as a social space:[3] I propose that the vocabulary of public sociability – more precisely, Lofland's five principles of stranger interaction – can help to elucidate the concept of publics (see also Matthias, this volume). As we will see, we need to adjust certain theoretical considerations and vocabulary before applying human-to-human patterns of interaction to human-to-object relations. For the moment, I shall introduce the general patterns that, as Lofland reminds us, work in combination with each other. These patterns were established through systematic observations, based on fundamental work by theorists of social relations including Erving Goffman, Jane Jacobs, and William H. Whyte. The first pattern is cooperative motility, which is described as the somehow cooperative, uneventful movements of individuals through public space, in which objects may also intervene. The second is civil inattention, meaning respect for the other's presence in the same space without interfering in his or her actions or personal space, although one might cast a glance at him or her. Considering this as a form of social relationship, Lofland notes, "Civil inattention suggests that when humans in the public realm appear to ignore one another, they do so *not* out of psychological distress but out of a ritual regard, and their response is *not* the asocial one of 'shut down' but the fully social one of politeness" (1998, 30; italics in the original). Third is audience role prominence, which takes place when our attention is directed toward someone else's actions such that watching them is our predominant role. Fourth is restrained helpfulness, which can be exemplified by asking for a simple bit of information (such as the time), without it leading to a more substantial relation. Fifth is civility toward diversity, expressed by tolerance for each other's differences, which usually only becomes visible when it is not respected, when incivility arises.

As my fieldwork has shown, all five of these patterns come into play at events such as the tam-tam and the Piknic Électronik, where strangers have to deal with the presence of hundreds of others. The analysis of each event in terms of experiences of public sociability, presented in the following section, helps deepen our understanding of publics' interactions with artworks in public spaces. Such a systematic approach is not so much the result of this specific research as it is integral to the method of a broader experiment: it feeds into my inductive process and builds on my intention to transpose the vocabulary of these types of festive experiences onto the interactions that occur between publics and artworks – this time in an everyday situation.

FRIENDS, CAMERAS, AND A BLANKET: LEARNING FROM THE FIELD

I conducted my observations at both the tam-tam and the Piknic Électronik in the manner that the events should be experienced: in a participatory way, my fieldwork took place with the help of friends, a picnic, and a blanket spread out so we could sit on the ground. A still camera was used to record specific actions or elements, and a video camera was used in an impressionistic manner, as a *flâneur* or a tourist would do, to capture ambiences, rhythms, and general dynamics. One of the limitations of this research method lies in the fact that it allowed me to classify users only according to easily recognizable social categories (age, phenotype, clothing style, and other traits).

Four extended observation sessions were conducted at the tam-tam on Sunday afternoons in 2013 and 2014. A first look at the crowd allows for general statements about its composition. The event attracts mainly young adults aged eighteen to thirty-five. There are no barriers around the tam-tam and there is no charge for attending it, so it attracts a wide variety of individuals. For instance, we recognized several homeless people whom we had encountered in our everyday activities who were there to enjoy their day like any other participant, illustrating the degree of civility toward diversity. The most popular activity at the tam-tam is sitting back and relaxing in order to eat, chat, drink, and, to some extent, enjoy the drumming, depending on where you choose to hang out. This instantly puts hundreds of strangers in various situations of interaction. This mass of individuals does not form a coherent whole: it is composed of small groups of people who have chosen where to sit according to how far they want to be from other people and which of the different atmospheres in the subsections of the site appeals to them. In terms of cooperative motility, even though the grounds are crowded with participants, their trajectories never interfere with the activities of others; people make sure that they walk around the groups. Interactions among the different groups are governed by civil inattention: they do not have contact with one another, even though they are in great proximity, but they may glance at each other, as people watching is a popular activity.

Even though no one is responsible for organizing the tam-tam and very little control is exercised on the site, there is no apparent tension. Indeed, the tam-tam is a spontaneous event that started in the 1980s. Because of its organic origins, it is impossible to say exactly who started it and when, although there are urban legends on the subject (Germain 2003; Handfield 2008). Even today, there is no official organization in charge. This self-regulation is the result of a social compromise that happened in 1994, after a conflict that lasted almost a year. The event had become very popular the previous summer, which had led to negative consequences such as a great quantity of litter left by the participants, including broken bottles (Bonhomme 1993; Dion 1993), and graffiti on the monument (Baillargeon 1993). Once the municipal authorities became involved in the situation, they started to find other infringements of bylaws: the sale of alcohol, drugs, and food prepared in unknown conditions and without a permit (Paquin 1993). At first, the police were sent onsite to manage the situation, which, unsurprisingly, was not appreciated by the participants (Poussart 1993). Instead, a forum was set up by the city to discuss the situation, involving all parties (including musicians, vendors, and the authorities). A consensus was reached: food and alcohol would not be sold onsite, but participants would be allowed to bring their own, and the city would issue fifty permits a week to people who wanted to sell arts and crafts – the main form of official control and programming of the event (Hachey 1994; Pelchat 1994). Today, given the festive character of the gathering, the municipal authorities responsible for the park tolerate alcoholic beverages on site, when they are brought to accompany a picnic (as per general city policy). To show the extent of this modus operandi, here are two more examples of civility toward diversity. First, we saw a man and two women openly selling pot brownies out of wicker baskets. Their action did not shock anyone on site – to the contrary, it seemed to be appreciated by some. Second, a few individuals patrolled the site to collect refundable cans and bottles; they not only checked garbage cans but also directly asked people who had just finished their beverages if they could take them. For what I could observe, far from being bothered, people seemed to be happy to not have to carry these containers back home. This case also highlights restrained helpfulness, since the refundable cans were worth five or ten cents.

Although the tam-tam is a mainly organic event, the same activities occur in the same subsections every week, without any form of obligation or official mobilization. The site is divided into three main areas: the area around the monument at the centre; a large, open, sunny space south of the artwork, along the street; and a space to the north, stretching toward the forest that covers the mountain. Although activities are more homogeneous in the open space (representative of what I described above), a wider range of possibilities opens up in the wooded area. A surprisingly broad mix of activities can be performed in the context of a spontaneous musical gathering: the tam-tam's evolving nature allows for the emergence of new sorts of happenings. In and around a glade, some people play volleyball and hacky sack, and others perform yoga and circus-inspired acts (slacklining, juggling, devil sticks, hula hoop, and aerial silks). The trees obviously come in handy for activities such as silks and slacklining. Musical groups perform, and spiritual activities take place (for instance, Hare Krishna members sing mantras). Some participants clearly appreciate having an audience, as exemplified by a very popular role-playing game that has been played at the tam-tam for fifteen years: medieval battles. In a dusty glade that marks the northern border of the tam-tam, contemporary knights fight their opponents, showing their skills and demonstrating their tricks. Passers-by stop and gather around them, and some curious spectators even ask to borrow equipment to try it out (Cauchon 2007; King 2011; *La Presse* 2001). The tension between looking and being seen is an incentive to come to the tam-tam for all participants. In recent years, a new musical gathering has even been established on the same site, at the same time. At the south end of the site, a resourceful DJ now brings his own equipment every Sunday afternoon to offer his own free version of the Piknic Électronik: the music in this space is "harder" and generally attracts a slightly different crowd than the tam-tam, but it does not interfere with it.

At the centre of the tam-tam event and its site is the *Monument to Sir George-Étienne Cartier*, which has four interrelated functions in this context. Its first function is to be the core of the tam-tam, in a historical, social, and economic sense: it hosts the greatest concentration of activities (music and commerce) and the greatest density of participants (musicians, dancers, spectators, sellers, and buyers), elements that define the essence of the gathering. Today, the percussionists are on the slope just behind the monument. Up to 2005, when the artistic and architectural components of the artwork underwent restoration, they used the terrace and the steps around it as their stage: during the renovations, they had to temporarily move a few metres west, to a site that became their permanent one, even though one might have expected them to return to their original site. (Although I found no explanation for this relocation, one could hypothesize that the new site provides better acoustic conditions because it is more distant from the street and that the monument may act as a sound barrier.) The musicians, who usually number about fifty, attract a large audience composed of curious spectators and a few hard-core dancers: civility toward diversity may also enter the picture here, as exemplified by an intoxicated dancer who was intensely active but easily called to order by one of the musicians during one observation session. The fifty vendors continue to use the same location: they set up their wares by the three paths around the monument. Near the site, at the edge of the forest, illegal drugs can be purchased, which reinforces the idea that the tam-tam's most historical components can be found in this subsection, as the availability of drugs at the event is something of a tradition. Second, the monument functions as the element around which the space of the whole gathering is organized. If the tam-tam were a city, the monument would be its downtown core and neighbourhoods with specific identities and functions would be laid out around it. This function is different from the first in that the first function is centripetal, attracting activities to the centre, while the second is centrifugal, generating dynamics that move outwards. Its third function is to act as a landmark not only from within the space of the park but also within the cityscape. Although this role is not specific to the tam-tam, it takes on a particular significance on Sunday afternoons. Facing the west end of Rue Rachel, Avenue du Parc, and Parc Jeanne-Mance (which is right across the avenue), the *Monument to Sir George-Étienne Cartier* occupies a strategic site – which is why it was installed at this location in the first place. With its exceptional height and size, it is visible from a distance, indicating a destination and gathering point (people can also hear the drumming from adjacent neighbourhoods). The fourth function of the monument is also not event-specific: it is a gateway to this section of Parc du Mont-Royal. When the gathering takes place, many people enter the site – whether to go to the tam-tam or not – via the monument's terrace. It is therefore common to see individuals who came by bike or on foot waiting for their friends to join them on the perimeter of the monument, alone or in groups, sitting or standing, watching the crowd and checking their cell phones.

On an island in the middle of the St Lawrence River, *Man, Three Disks* fulfils very similar functions during the Piknic Électronik. Two observation periods were conducted at the event in 2014 – data saturation occurred more quickly than at the tam-tam because the range of activities at this programmed event was less broad. As the general director of the festival confirmed in an interview, when the Piknic started, participants were mainly between twenty-five and thirty-five years old, with significant numbers of families with children, gay men, and lesbians; these groups are proportionally less important today, and eighteen- to twenty-five-year-olds now form the core audience. The Piknic also became popular rapidly; in its first year, about 300 people attended each week; now, up to 5,000 are expected. Interestingly, the festival's mission, as stated on its website, includes programming of both electronic music and public sociability: "With electronic music at the core of its mission, Piknic aims to open up the genre by offering an immersive social experience" (Piknic Électronik 2014). Whereas music seems to be less important than public sociability at the tam-tam, at the Piknic, the two are of at least equal importance. The Piknic's mission is conveyed by the way the site is physically organized: practical functions frame the social experience. Participants reach the site after a five-minute walk from Jean-Drapeau metro station or the parking lot and must go to the main and only entrance for two reasons. First, they have to pay their admission fee: admission costs $10 before 3:00 p.m. and $15 after that time. Attendees are given electronic bracelets that employees at each entrance scan to control access to the site. Second, their bags have to be checked: they are allowed to bring picnics, even though there are many food options on site, but alcoholic beverages must be purchased at the bars set up for the event. After passing through this area, they arrive at the main dance floor under Calder's stabile. The sculpture has four functions. The first is to be the core of the Piknic, in the sense that many of the key elements that define the event are gathered there: a DJ, the dance floor with the abstract sculpture as a roof and a spectacular view of the city as a background, large drinks bars, designated sitting areas formed by artificial turf carpeting in front of a low wall, a spot for sponsors, and bleachers. This furniture, as its original function implies, is an indicator of audience role prominence and of the general programming of public sociability. Although the artwork is not really a gateway into the Piknic, its second function is to be a signal within the space of the park, marking the gathering point: you hear the beat as you leave the metro, and the Calder sculpture emerges from the treetops as you walk toward the site. Its third function is an acoustic one: the sculpture absorbs and retains sounds, creating reverberation (Lamarche 2003). Its fourth function is to act as a spatial organizer, because all of the other subsections of the site are connected to it, as we will now see.

There are two pathways branching off from the main site. The one on the east side leads to a quieter seating area (chairs are installed for participants) that ends with an exit into the rest of the Parc Jean-Drapeau. The one on the west side leads to the second stage, which features different programming, to broaden the musical range offered on site. This pathway works as a commercial street: there are food trucks, a snack bar, a wine bar, sanitary installations, and promotional booths for the event's sponsors. The middle of the "street" has a high volume of pedestrian traffic – people going from one stage to the other – and the shops and services are on the sides; it is a form of cooperative motility that generates efficient movement through the site rather than opportunities for people to meet. At the second stage, the ambience is usually more relaxed, and there is ample seating available in the form of bleachers and chairs. This is where my co-observers and I undertook what I call the blanket test. In the early years of the Piknic, we used to bring blankets to sit or lie on; once a common practice, this now seems obsolete. Given the movable furniture installed in this area, unfolding the blanket required some thinking and manoeuvring around other individuals already in the space. Using the blanket revealed a certain lack of flexibility, which can be attributed to what Karen Franck and Quentin Stevens (2007) call "tightness" of the space. In their conceptualization, space becomes loose through people's gestures of appropriation, opportunities for which vary depending on the type of space. It can be argued that the space at the Piknic is, to borrow the authors' vocabulary, only *apparently* loose – a concept they define by referring to the shopping mall experience: "Many loose occasions and places can be seen as merely licensed 'safety valves,' harmless ways to release tension which are carefully regulated in time, space and intensity. But controlled and pre-programmed 'looseness' is not loose; people can only appropriate space for their own uses if they have full access and freedom of choice" (2007, 24–5).

Indeed, the event's "immersive social experience" presents its own version of public sociability. In relation to civility toward diversity, the cost of admission clearly affects the composition of the crowd; compared to the tam-tam, the participants are more socioeconomically homogeneous, with no homeless people or individuals collecting refundable cans and bottles to be found. In other words, the Piknic brings together, and consequently puts into contact, people from particular social strata who appear to appreciate this context. All aspects of the social experience are organized to some extent. For instance, alcoholic beverages not bought on site stopped being allowed in 2012, following some unfortunate incidents of excessive drinking; the restriction reduces the likelihood that such incidents happen again, thereby helping to guarantee a friendly, hedonistic atmosphere (Agence QMI 2012; Doyon 2012; Renaud 2010). In terms of "original" (non-dance-related) activities, we observed hula-hoop and hacky-sack only in the early hours of the Piknic, when there were not many people on site. In fact, the organizers orchestrate happenings to create new social contexts, such as special offers for men with long beards and a special international students' day. In general, a large proportion of participants seem to be conscious of their appearance, playing directly with civil inattention: well-coiffed hair, fashion accessories including the almost-mandatory sunglasses, little clothing (fit women in bikini tops, shirtless men with good physiques). Flirting is also part of this: we witnessed people exchanging phone numbers. With an apparently loose space and what tends to be a relatively programmed form of public sociability, the Piknic Électronik attracts a clientele, and therefore publics, with a clear taste for this type of overall creative environment. Perhaps a study of other factors, based on interviews with participants, would show less homogeneity in nonobservable factors such as occupation, place of residence, and values.

Setting aside considerations of public sociability for a moment, in order to expand the way we think about these cultural practices we could interpret them as scenes. Alan Blum (2003) has analyzed this complex notion not as community or social circle but as an imaginary structure that is part of the social life inherent to a city. He shows that scenes put collective life into play and lays out what he calls their grammar, which includes, for instance, the notion of theatricality. Described as seeing and being seen and characterized by the reciprocity implied in the voyeur/exhibitionist logic, it applies to both the tam-tam and the Piknic Électronik. Intimacy is also crucial in scenes: "The scene makes sharing enjoyable as if it is a private experience, and it makes the very private orientation to quality and discrimination something to be shared" (Blum 2003, 179). The notion of "being private in public" is embodied in both events by the fact that groups of friends socialize in a sea of strangers with whom they entertain interactions of a weaker order. Finally, as scenes are informed by cities just as much as they inform them, Blum adds to his conception that it "connects the space to time through the idea of making it an occasion. This occasioning of the space is part of what we mean by its emplacement, its making space into a place" (Blum 2003, 187). In this context, the *Monument to Cartier* and *Man, Three Disks* link their scenes to the city: they define the place where these occasions occur. That said, to go further into our study of the interactions that participants in both events have with the artworks, we have to take a closer look at notions of public sociability.

ARTWORKS AS STRANGERS: PRAGMATIC AND PRACTICAL CONSIDERATIONS

To what extent can participants in the tam-tam and the Piknic Électronik be considered publics of the monumental artworks around which the events take place? Although the functions described for the artworks are valid at the scale of the crowd, they cannot explain how individuals might appreciate them. Generally, although the events cannot be dissociated from the artworks, it seems safe to say that the objects will not be conceptualized in the same way and to the same degree by everyone there. It is actually possible to not look at, and even more possible to not give any thought to, the *Monument to Sir George-Étienne Cartier* or *Man, Three Disks* during the tam-tam or the Piknic Électronik; as casual conversations with various individuals revealed, some people do not even notice that they are there. Moreover, there is a disparity between the relatively generic functions that I have identified, which could be valid for many monumental artworks in various contexts, and the singular experience of public sociability specific to the tam-tam and the Piknic Électronik. To counter this discrepancy, I propose to explore a similarity: if people take part in these events because they enjoy each other's presence without generally engaging with them, can the same then be said of their relationship with the artworks? If civil inattention is the main relationship observed during these Sunday gatherings, is it possible to use the same principle to describe participants' main relationship with both artworks?

The inclusion of objects in social interactions can be justified by referring to pragmatic sociology: indeed, this approach, which includes Bruno Latour's (2005) actor-network theory (known as ANT), has reintroduced objects into the study of social relations. Rather than taking social relations for granted and presuming society to be a complete and definite whole, ANT is based on reconstructing associations among actors by following them through their various situations. More importantly, ANT considers objects to be actors when they influence those associations, and even when they do not they are still conceived as "actants" with the potential to influence associations. Thus, objects are seen not as passive but as active parts of relationships. Antoine Hennion's (1993) sociology of mediation, and specifically his work on music lovers, is a translation of this approach into the study of arts publics. In Hennion's pragmatic definition, publics are understood in interrelation with the art object: they can be discerned by looking at what people do with art objects, as well as what artworks make people do (Hennion 2005). That said, Latour is critical of face-to-face interactions and sociability because in his view they are ends in themselves; they do not redeploy the action. Because his sociological project consists of identifying how collectives are assembled and transformed, he is not interested in weak and ephemeral interactions such as public sociability, which do not allow for the study of redistribution of the social. In spite of this, the Latour-inspired idea of publics interacting with artworks in public spaces is pertinent to my argument because it spatializes these interactions into specific situations, demonstrating that all content actually matters. In this context, using the vocabulary of public sociability shows that artworks are part of our experience of public spaces, just as strangers are.

In this light, Lofland's principles have to be slightly adjusted, or at least further explained, in order to be applied to artworks as strangers. First, cooperative motility is seen as how our trajectories can be influenced by art objects or can put us in contact with them. Second, civil inattention is identified when people passing by an artwork cast an impartial glance at it, giving it enough attention to show that they recognize its presence. Third, audience role prominence is when individuals in public spaces look at others who are engaged with an artwork; this can have the effect of enlarging the audience through a domino effect, when individuals consciously or subconsciously reproduce someone else's actions. Fourth is restrained helpfulness, which cannot be applied literally, since artworks do not talk: instead, we could reconceive this principle as art objects acting as a prop or support for actions or gestures for which they were not necessarily intended. Taking pictures would be a variety of this principle (when in relation with the fifth principle), because artworks indicate the space that the photographer was in or serve as a stage on which the person photographed acted. Using the artwork as a meeting point, in the sense that it helps people locate each other, would also fit this definition. The fifth principle, civility toward diversity, can here be renamed recognition of the artwork's singularity. Artworks are conceived and installed to be looked at: this is a contradiction of the original principle, which is based on the notion of *not* acting on or reacting to someone else's difference. Below, I will use this heuristic set of principles to better understand the concept of publics.

Filmed observations of the artworks that we conducted during the week provided material for testing the hypothesis that artworks are strangers, and for close analysis of how Lofland's five principles relate to monumental artworks. Inspired by sociologist and urban planner William H. Whyte's 1988 documentary film *The Social Life of Small Urban Spaces*, for the past few years I have been using filming in my research to document how people act and interact with artworks in public spaces. This has proven to be an effective data-collection method because careful consideration of the seemingly trivial actions performed by the publics requires detailed descriptions, which in turn rely on accurate recordings. Because I can pan and zoom in on the video footage after it is shot, and because they show the general dynamics of the site, the footage obtained is well suited to the present line of inquiry. Six and five forty-five-minute observation periods were conducted, respectively, at the Cartier monument and the Calder stabile at different times of day and week, between 2011 and 2014. Field notes taken by the on-site observer-camerawoman had several uses: they were a point of comparison to validate my own observations, they could point out an action in the background that I had not noticed in the first place, and they could supply additional information about an action that started beyond the camera's field. The number of observation periods was determined according to a principle of saturation: filming at a site stopped when analysis of the footage yielded no new information. For each artwork, we found spots for the camera distant enough from the artwork that it would not interfere directly with everyday activities. The camera angle also needed to be wide enough to see how actions evolved within each site, and both camera and observer were visible on site. The observations of everyday life (as distinct from special events) that were recorded during this phase of fieldwork can also be interpreted according to interaction patterns, as I explain in the following two sections.

A FLEXIBLE, POPULAR PLAZA: THE *MONUMENT TO SIR GEORGE-ÉTIENNE CARTIER*

It is useful to set our observations of the *Monument to Sir George-Étienne Cartier* in context by looking at how it is connected to the city (figure 1.3). It faces Avenue du Parc, a busy north-south thoroughfare that defines the park's eastern border and can, therefore, be seen by people in vehicles and on public transit. Although the artwork is highly visible in this context, because it is in the middle of a cleared space (the only trees around the monument are there to show it off), these individuals have a relationship of civil inattention with it. Our observations focused on dynamics of a different scale and were centred on the monument and its direct perimeter, for which the interface with the street is still very important: most users

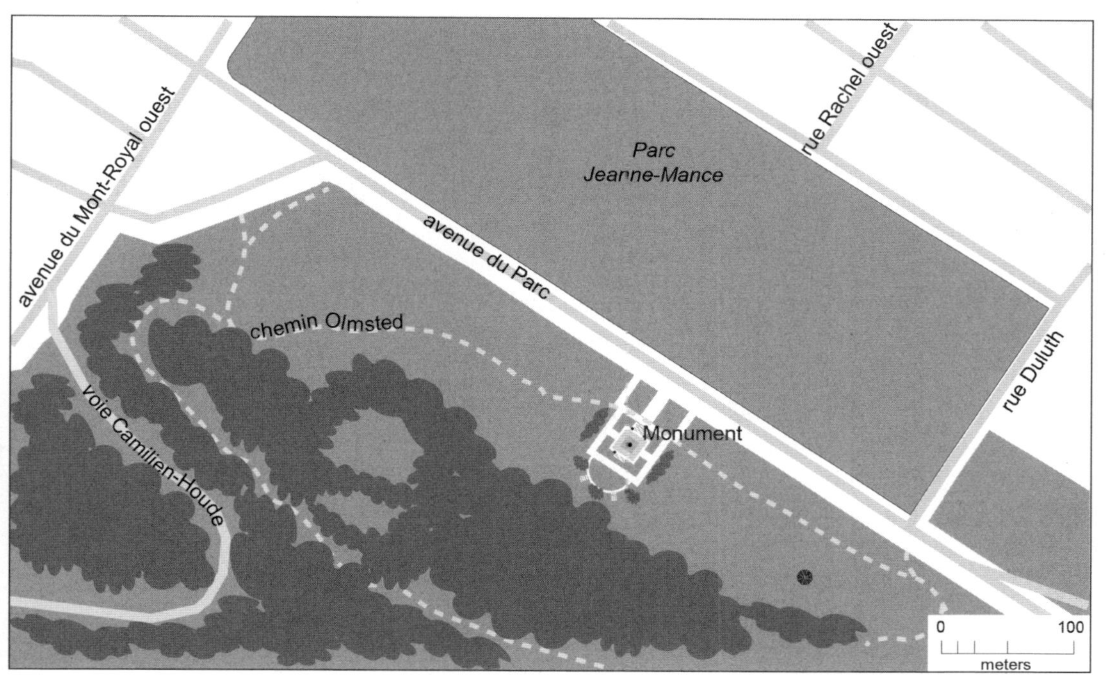

1.3 Map showing the context of the *Monument to Sir George-Étienne Cartier*.
Credit: Nathalie Vachon, Institut national de la recherche scientifique, 2015.

enter the park from Avenue du Parc; Rue Rachel, on an east-west axis, also provides access to the monument via Parc Jeanne-Mance from the local area. Therefore, this section of the park is well connected to the adjacent residential neighbourhoods and is a very popular location for everyday leisure and physical activities – biking, jogging, dog walking, and strolling (with or without companions or baby strollers) – bring users to the park via these streets and put them into contact with the monument.

Cyclists' and joggers' trajectories around or on the monument's terrace highlight a conscious choice based on cooperative motility. The great majority of these people choose to go around the terrace to avoid climbing the steps or disturbing the crowds that gather there; by doing so, they themselves frame and thus emphasize it. In contrast, a few joggers choose to challenge themselves by running up the steps, and occasionally bikers riding down the hill also make use of them. As we will see, actions such as the latter, which were not intended when the monument was created, "loosen" it as a space, to borrow Franck and Stevens's (2007) term. Many pedestrians entering and leaving the park choose to walk along the terrace of the monument, showing by their east-west trajectories that the artwork does actually act as a gateway to the green space. In addition to cooperative motility, in the sense that the artwork supports their actions and that they move around its components, civil inattention is the main relationship that they develop with its various sculptures: they will, at most, take a quick look at them. That said, some people walking near the monument may slow down or walk around the pedestal to look at its components: this illustrates recognition of the artwork's singularity, which occurs less frequently. Looking at the artwork only from a distance is another option and a form of civil inattention made possible by the scale of the artwork, as exemplified by pedestrians walking on Avenue du Parc.

Some users stay in the space around the monument, such as joggers who stop there to stretch. The bases of the lions and the steps descending toward Avenue du Parc are handy because they allow for a variety of uses. An individual can put one foot on the base of the monument to stretch a leg, and someone who wants a deeper stretch can use the steps. The steps occasionally replace the apparatus found in gyms: one man was seen doing push-ups with his feet and hands on different levels. Cyclists offer a similar example. We observed a couple who stopped at the monument to wait for a friend (who arrived eight minutes later). While the woman sat on a bench, the man practised bike tricks on the steps and the terrace, hopping from one step to another and then moving to another section of the monument in the middle of his practice session. Although his use of the steps produced a loosening through both restrained helpfulness (the monument is the prop for this exercise) and recognition of the work's singularity (no other element in the area could support this activity), the fact that it was a meeting point also refers to both principles. The monument plays its role as a landmark, defined as a distinctive object in this large park (recognition of its singularity); it is also the obvious answer to the question "Where should we meet?" which enables friends to find each other in the park (restrained helpfulness).

In fact, the monument proved to be a highly popular meeting point. Its various components allow different possibilities for performing activities while waiting for the other person – it seems to be the rule that one of the parties is always early or late. One may linger on the terrace or sit on a step: in fact, the steps facing the street, and especially those around the base of the sculpture, are useful because they are elevated and offer a better view of who is coming. More generally, the steps are a very popular place to sit and take a break while in the park.

Another very common activity is taking photographs of the monument. This activity is often a prelude to a longer stay in the vicinity of the artwork: for instance, it may lead to a more careful examination (by walking around its base to look at more than one of its sides) or to sitting down. Taking photographs brings into play both restrained helpfulness (the artwork is the "where") and appreciation of the monument's singularity. More than one individual may take pictures at a time because of the monument's grand scale and multiple components. Indeed, people may take photographs from a distance, in order to get the entire composition into frame (or because the photographer simply does not perceive the monument to be singular enough for a closer look). Taking a picture of someone on the steps shows that the person shared a moment with the monument as a whole; the human figure helps show the large size of the artwork. On a smaller scale, the lions are great props for humorous snapshots: for instance, some adults sat on a lion and raised an arm in the gesture of riding a bucking bull. Thus, the singularity of the artwork is brought into play by these individuals' creativity. In fact, all kinds of publics appreciate the lions, from children who like to climb on them (under the eye of a more or less enthusiastic parent) to pedestrians who touch them in passing. They also encourage original gestures of appropriation: one man was observed lying on the back of a lion to sunbathe for 20 minutes while waiting for a companion (illustrating both restrained helpfulness and recognition of singularity).

Finally, although individuals usually keep their distance from one another on the terrace, the monument has also proven, on rare occasions, to facilitate public sociability. A couple walking around the monument to look at it carefully was imitated by another one, illustrating audience role prominence engendering a domino effect. The two couples (who did not know each other before) then exchanged cameras to photograph each other with the monument, showing restrained helpfulness between themselves, as well as with the artwork. Overall, the interactions with the monument show that it acts as a popular, flexible plaza within the space of this large urban park, which also benefits from its connections to nearby neighbourhoods. By contrast, the publics we observed for the Calder sculpture in Parc Jean-Drapeau are dependent on the nature of the park and the specificity of its management.

COMPULSORY ATTENDANCE: *MAN, THREE DISKS*

Île Sainte-Hélène and Île Notre-Dame form Parc Jean-Drapeau, a public space managed by a paramunicipal organization, the Société du parc Jean-Drapeau. The organization's mission statement says, "Parc Jean-Drapeau stages many recreation-tourist attractions that make it a unique site in Canada ... This outstanding park, which was created at the time of the world's fair, Expo 67, attracts sports enthusiasts, young families, culture aficionados, nature lovers and visitors who attend its international events. Its areas of attraction are enlivened by concerts, sports events and major festivals that contribute to its diversity" (Société du parc Jean-Drapeau 2015). Arguably underused for decades, Parc Jean-Drapeau has been the focus of rehabilitation efforts since about 2000. For instance, in 2005, the Ville de Montréal decided to relocate the ethnocultural festivals that used to happen in urban neighbourhoods to the Parc (Germain et al. 2008). Probably because they and their infrastructure are temporary, the various special events (concerts, festivals) seem to have no discernible impact on everyday

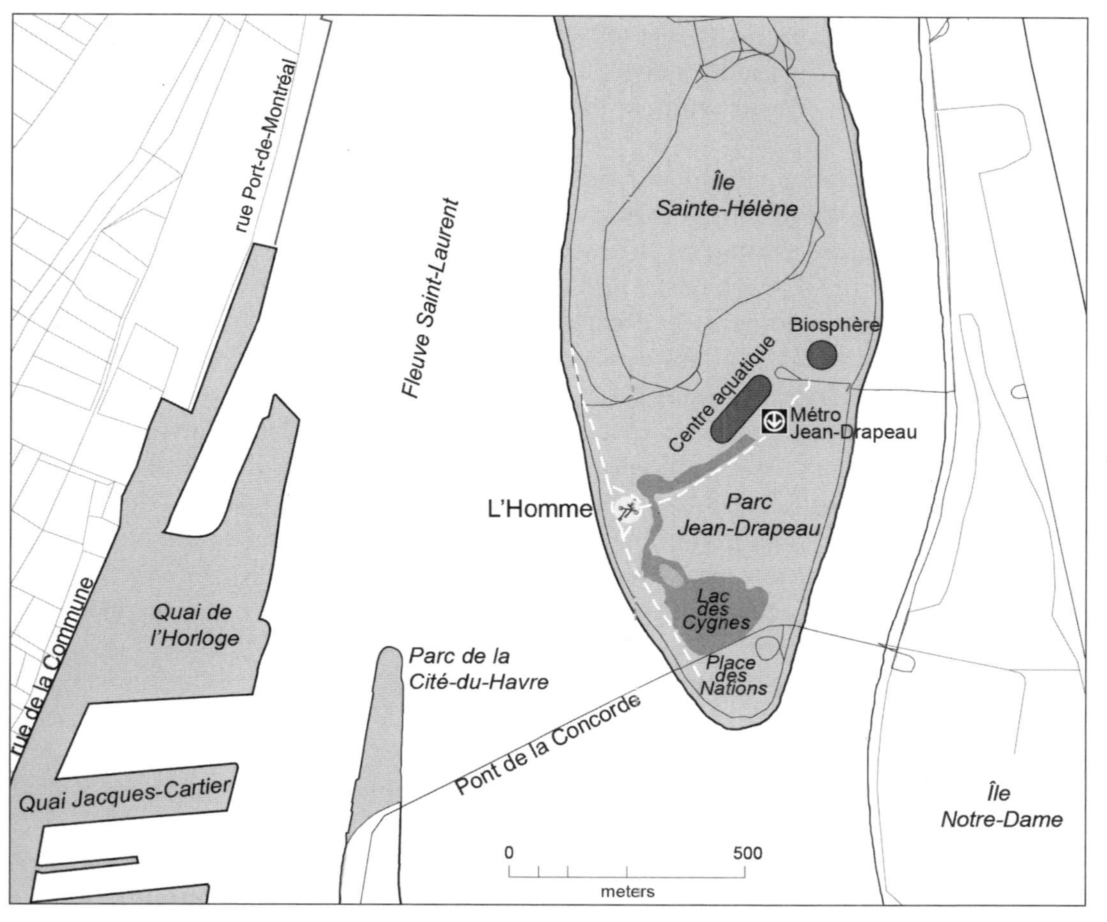

1.4 Map showing the context of *Man, Three Disks*.

Credit: Nathalie Vachon, Institut national de la recherche scientifique, 2015.

use of the park, except in that they restrict access to certain areas, including the site of the Calder stabile, for the duration of the event. They may, however, have helped promote the park as a destination to Montrealers and visitors.

On an everyday basis, park users who might eventually entertain a relationship with Calder's stabile come to the islands to enjoy what they have to offer: recreation (at the casino, amusement park, or sports infrastructures, including a beach and a swimming pool), cultural activities (there are two museums and various heritage sites), and special events (car races, concerts, and festivals). This explains the relative homogeneity of users (compared to users observed at Parc du Mont-Royal) and their patterns of attendance: there are fewer users in the belvedere containing the Calder sculpture in the mornings because the park's other institutions and facilities are not yet open. Individuals come to the Calder stabile while they are jogging, walking, or biking through this remote park (another transportation mode that we observed once was the Segway, used during organized tours of the park) (figure 1.4). Users generally come to the belvedere where the stabile is located because it is a major point of interest. They tend to stay for at least two minutes, appreciating the magnificent panorama to the north of the river and the downtown core with the mountain as a backdrop. Some people picnic in this spot and take pictures of the cityscape, others just sit on the north-facing benches for a while. In fact, when people enter this space, they tend to look at the breathtaking view first, before turning around and looking at the monumental sculpture. In summer, users cannot look up at the sculpture as they enter the space at midday because the sun is usually blinding: it is the view of the city, at eye level, that attracts them first. So although users generally express civil inattention to the artwork when they enter the site, some discover the singularity of the object when they turn to look at another section of the park: they may express their appreciation by taking pictures of the artwork or having someone take a picture of them with it – adding restrained helpfulness.

Like the *Monument to Sir George-Étienne Cartier*, *Man, Three Disks* has a direct impact on individuals' trajectories. Touching the ground at six points, so people can go under it, the artwork organizes the entire space of its plaza as well as the circulation around or through it: everybody who enters this space has a mandatory cooperative motility relationship with it.

The plaza is an enclosure surrounded by a low wall and dense vegetation, and people have to enter it via pathways that act as funnels; thus, users practically become captive audiences of the sculpture. On the one hand, some people, especially cyclists, choose to go around it without looking at it, which serves to highlight its presence and illustrates civil inattention. On the other hand, many choose to walk in a straight line and pass under it: their presence is thus framed by the artwork. Even if they do not look at it, or barely give it a glance, people seem to appreciate the sculpture's presence because many walk or bike very close to it, reinforcing the impression that they give it civil inattention while experiencing cooperative motility. Park employees driving pick-up trucks to collect garbage or mechanical brooms to clean the surface of the plaza also have to deal with the fact that the artwork organizes the space: as we observed, they have to drive their vehicles very carefully and cooperatively around the sculpture.

People often engage with the stabile from a distance: because of its large scale and great height, this is the only way to take in the whole sculpture (there is no detail to examine at ground level). This explains why some people stop to look at the sculpture or take a picture of it (recognizing its singularity) but do not enter the site. In contrast, a commemorative plaque installed on the ground, right in the centre of the space, attracts many individuals' attention. In fact, this plaque, the only element at human scale within the plaza around the artwork, sometimes creates a domino effect: audience role prominence is involved when people, seeing others reading the inscription, approach it themselves and follow suit. In general, even though it is common not to establish direct contact with *Man, Three Disks*, its scale and its placement in the space make it impossible not to interact with the sculpture and thus not to become a public for it.

ENJOYING THE PRESENCE OF STRANGERS: NOTES ON MONTREAL'S CULTURES OF PUBLIC SPACES

The analysis of encounters with these two monumental artworks, both during events that draw large crowds to them and during regular day-to-day use leads us to two kinds of conclusions. First, it is productive to think about banal, everyday gestures with and around art objects in terms of interactions with them, combining the vocabulary of public sociability with the idea of artworks as strangers. The most common interaction that users have with the art objects are somehow at the same level as the associations that they have with strangers in public spaces. In this context, the five principles that I have used show that users are publics for the artworks to greater or lesser degrees: the works influence their behaviour in different ways, which generates different interactions with them. Indeed, as we have seen, an artwork's materiality (including its components and its relationship with its site) clearly impacts how publics interact with it and is an active component of its public space. We can conceive of these interactions as being along a spectrum. At the low end is the common action of passing near an artwork without looking at it. In this weak kind of relationship with the artwork, considered as civil inattention, very little association is created between the artwork and the user. As we move up the spectrum, the principles tend to be combined; at the top end are original but relatively rare gestures of appropriation, such as the singular case of the man who used one of the lions in the Cartier monument as a chair for sunbathing. Although observations cannot replace interviews in determining how users perceive and think about the artworks that they encounter, observation and analysis of the social life of artworks in my research indicate that users can indeed be considered publics when their behaviours justify it. This is precisely why pragmatic sociology, which seems not to have been applied before to the question of publics for artworks in public spaces, can be of help: publics should be considered as such according to their interactions with art objects and not only with regard to their knowledge or perception of them. While the concept of public sociability may not be strictly speaking compatible with aspects of ANT, it does not mean that this type of interaction should be dismissed. On the contrary, as I have illustrated throughout my descriptions, these interactions are meaningful, as they define the publics' specific experiences of public spaces and also redefine the meaning of the artworks involved.

Second, reflecting on Montreal's cultures of public spaces, it should be noted that the observations of social dynamics both during the events and the rest of the week correspond to the functions and management of the respective parks. On the one hand, the Parc du Mont-Royal has proven to be very flexible and open, both spatially and socially – a truly "loose" space. Just as the tam-tam eloquently demonstrates a persistent activity that arose organically from a gathering, the range of publics for the *Monument to Sir George-Étienne Cartier* is characterized by diversity and original activities. On the other hand, Parc Jean-Drapeau is managed as a destination and a venue for popular events. The Piknic Électronik, as a programmed "immersive social experience" that is loose only at first glance, reflects this type of management, as do the users who frequent the park in general: they are relatively homogeneous both socially and in their interactions with *Man, Three Disks.*

The events themselves also speak to two very different definitions of collective cultural practices as they are experienced in public spaces. The tam-tam is a free celebration of being-togetherness in public spaces; the Piknic Électronik is an example of the increasing commercialization of public spaces and public sociability – in essence, their privatization – which, in turn, reduces the experience of diversity. If both tendencies coexist, it is because each has an appreciative public: in fact, quite a few people enjoy both events, so there is some overlap in their different "crowds." The tam-tam and the Piknic Électronik have contributed to shaping Montreal's reputation as a culturally exciting city, and they offer two of the many opportunities that Montrealers and their guests have to celebrate the city's eagerly awaited, too-short summer: they are local scenes, as they are moments or events in the social life of Montreal that take place in specific places defined by singular artworks. In this context, it seems important to consider the diversity of publics that these coexisting events create. Similarly, we should appreciate finding a diversity of artworks, representing the history and plurality of artistic expression, in public spaces.

Notes

1   I would like to thank Nicolas Cournoyer, general director of the Piknic Électronik, who granted me an interview for this research project. I am grateful to my research assistant, Cecilia de la Mora, for undertaking the fieldwork for this study, and to photographers Denise Caron and Thibaut Larquey, who accompanied me during follow-up observation sessions during the week and at the events, respectively. Käthe Roth's precise and intelligent eye on my written English is, as always, extremely valued. Special thoughts to my friends who, at some time in

the last decade, have shared my passion for music and people watching at the tam-tam and the Piknic Électronik – they know who they are.

2   Many urban scholars throughout the twentieth century have discussed notions of anonymity and strangers' interactions as fundamental conditions for the civilizing functions of the city; see, for instance, Simmel ([1903]1950), Jacobs (1961), and Sennett (1974).

3   The form of the city is described using vocabulary reminiscent of Kevin Lynch's (1960) functionalist vocabulary of urban planning, which, even though it is static, serves the purpose of anchoring social interactions in an urban setting.

Susanne Shawyer

2

—

URBAN PRANKS AS ACTIVIST PERFORMANCE

One sunny summer day in 2008, about 400 people converged on a grassy hill at Toronto's Riverdale Park East. They wore brightly coloured T-shirts and earphones or headphones attached to MP3 players. At some unseen signal, the crowd separated in two, with red and yellow shirts on one side of the lawn and blue and green shirts on the other. Each person inflated a balloon. Most of the balloons were the simple latex kind popular with children, although tubular rubber balloons, some twisted into the shapes of swords by dextrous participants, dotted the crowd. The two sides charged, flailing and striking with their makeshift weapons of sword and sphere. This good-natured mock battle raged for a few minutes, and then the participants began to mime dramatic deaths. Limbs jerked and shuddered. Faces contorted. One by one, people fell to the ground. Soon there was only a sprawling mass of frozen bodies scattered across the field: silent, except for the occasional giggle.

This event was one of many annual MP3 *Experiments*, participatory mass performances in public parks organized by Improv Everywhere, a New York–based comedy group who call themselves a prank collective and who organize surprise performances in urban environments for audiences of passersby. Improv Everywhere exploits the public spaces of parks, streets, subway cars, and train stations as well as the open spaces of retail food courts and shopping malls to create unexpected comedic performances in cities in the United States, Canada, and across the globe. Many of these prank performances involve crowds of participants using humour to disrupt conventional uses of public space: the playful balloon battle in the park upsets a community league soccer game, and the hundreds of participants standing still in a busy train station interrupt the bustling rhythm of urban transportation. Although these pranks intervene in the use of public space and thereby open up room for critical discussion of urban environments, founder Charlie Todd states on the Improv Everywhere blog and in media appearances that Improv Everywhere's pranks are not meant as political commentary. "Even if it's a noble cause we personally support," he writes, "Improv Everywhere does not stage missions to draw attention to an issue. We are focused on creating comedy for comedy's sake and staging events that purposefully have no explicit reason behind them, other than the goal of spreading chaos and joy throughout the world" (Todd 2014a). Although Todd is correct that the group's pranks are not explicitly political, urban prank performances like *The MP3 Experiments* nevertheless raise questions about the everyday politics of how people interact in urban spaces, how they experience the urban environment through artistic expression, and how these kinds of surprising creative encounters engage in critical social and political discourses.

To encourage participants to engage with urban spaces, *The MP3 Experiments* draw on participatory theatre and performance forms. Coloured clothing, balloons, and soap bubbles offer a playful and carnivalesque aesthetic, while the heightened physicality of the crowd's movements evokes the affective power of mass spectacle or what theatre theorist Antonin Artaud called the "poetry of festival and crowds" (1958, 85). In addition to encouraging a carnivalesque atmosphere, *The MP3 Experiments* use theatrical improvisation exercises to promote engagement with others and the urban surroundings. Activities like forming groups according to the colour of one's shirt, filling the space as evenly as possible, or working together to create an enormous image are the kind of ensemble-building warm-up techniques commonly used by theatrical improvisation troupes like Toronto's Bad Dog Comedy Theatre or The Second City. As part of a yearly performance tradition that repeats and transmits these performance practices around the globe,

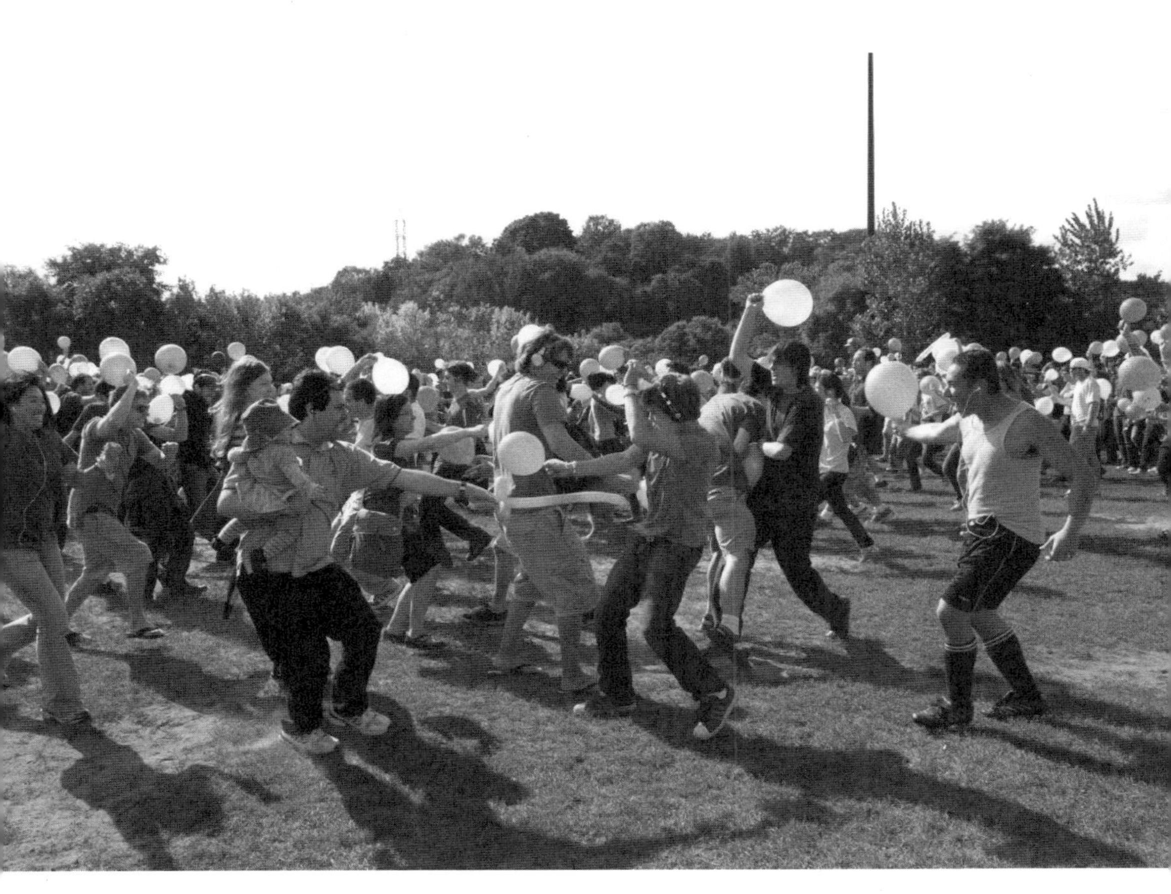

2.1 Participants in Improv Everywhere's *The MP3 Experiment Toronto* engage in a balloon battle. Photo: Ian Watson, 2008.

these prank performances also perpetuate a social and aesthetic ritual that is both symbolic and reflexive, akin to what performance theorist Richard Schechner calls "restored behavior" (1985, 35). In his foundational performance studies work *Between Theater and Anthropology*, Schechner defines "restored behavior" as a performance ritual that either through continual rehearsal or the repetition of the performance process takes on social symbolic meaning outside of the individual participant or action (35–7). In other words, "restored behavior" is both repeatable and contains, or stores, social meaning. Thus while Todd argues that Improv Everywhere's participatory mass performances are "comedy for comedy's sake" and "purposefully have no explicit reason behind them," a performance studies approach argues that *The MP3 Experiments* have, as Schechner writes, "a life of their own" as artistic creations (1985, 35). They are symbolic performances that both live in and engage with the urban landscape and also allow participants and audiences to critically explore art and the public.

In answer to the question "why do you do this?" on their website, Improv Everywhere responds that "it can simply be about making someone laugh, smile, or stop to notice the world around them" (Todd 2014a). This last phrase, "stop to notice the world around them," suggests that, while not expressly political, *The MP3 Experiments* have social utility and potential as political performance. French philosopher Jacques Rancière (2010) argues that politics is a process of noticing spaces and moments where political ideology does not correspond with political reality. In other words, challenging everyday assumptions to reveal gaps or fissures in the social landscape is a political act. A prank becomes a political performance if it can do this kind of political work or, as Rancière suggests, "make visible that which had no reason to be seen" (38). With the ability to make participants and audiences "stop to notice," *The MP3 Experiments* and other urban prank performances have activist potential. While Improv Everywhere clearly does not intend *The MP3 Experiments* as social commentary or political performance, this mass participatory performance form nevertheless has political potential not only because it can challenge social norms and question the use of public space but also because of its carnivalesque nature, its affective power, and its power to perform Rancièrean political dissensus.

URBAN PRANKS AND THE CARNIVALESQUE

A prank is a joke, made up of actions rather than words. A prank is inherently performative, a doing that creates amusement for the participants and observers but that also draws attention to social constructions. The unlucky victim of a whoopee cushion on April Fool's Day is made to look foolish as the unexpected sound of flatulence inserts the scatological into spaces governed by social rules of civility. In his book on college pranks, Neil Steinberg writes that "a prank makes a statement. It is instructive" (1992, xi). The whoopee cushion instructs that despite our complex social codes for polite behaviour, we cannot escape our animal nature and the physical processes necessary to sustain life. When student engineers perched a Volkswagen Beetle on the top of the University of British Columbia's clock tower in 2014 (Rosenfeld 2014), their prank juxtaposed the seemingly ordered institution against the supposed carefree creativity of youth, while at the same time disrupting these stereotypes because it was the institutional knowledge of the Engineering Department that enabled the prank to succeed and allowed the students to hoist a car up the tower. Pranks walk a line between the comedic and the serious by using humour to instruct and challenge the way that observers think about the world around them.

Urban pranks are mischievous acts that take place in a public space and for a public audience. The website of the Urban Prankster Network, a loose organization of provocateurs including Improv Everywhere who use flash mobs and guerrilla theatre to poke fun at contemporary society, lists several types of urban pranks: hacks, culture jamming, participatory and interventionist art, and "other creative endeavors that take place in public places in cities" (Todd 2011b). Urban pranks include hacking electronic highway construction information signs to read "Zombies Ahead" (Wolfson 2009) or painting over illegal street advertising with community-created artworks (Schiller 2009). By changing the highway sign, pranksters not only provide drivers with a laugh but also remind them of the life-safety importance of reading these omnipresent information signs. By painting over illegal street advertising, pranksters challenge unlawful practices, offer visual markers of local crime to the community, and critique the ubiquity of legal advertising that floods the urban landscape with consumerist messages. Recent Canadian "yarn-bombing" pranks place knitted scarves on trees, lampposts, and statues, not only to brighten up the winter gloom but also to offer warm winter wear to those without the means to keep warm (Wiebe 2013). In 2014, cheerfully coloured scarves left draped around the sculptures of Laura Secord and Sir Isaac Brock in downtown Ottawa criticized how we celebrate these historic national heroes even as we overlook poverty in Canada today (Chan 2014). The work that urban pranks perform is similar to the effect of sociologist Harold Garfinkel's breaching experiments, which explored how unexpected actions in social settings can reveal unspoken and unexamined expectations of behaviours. Garfinkel argues that if a person is "a stranger to the 'life as usual' character of everyday scenes" (1967, 37), they can expose the underlying assumptions that structure and determine everyday situations. Altering construction signs and creating unexpected art in the urban landscape make the surrounding environment strange, rather than the person inside it. Yet the end effect is similar: as it uses art to change the local environment, the urban prank interrupts and comments on community activities and invites passersby to become "a stranger" to the everyday.

Culture jamming and interventionist art creations are not the only kind of artistic urban prank: mass performances like *The MP3 Experiments* or flash mobs also have the potential to estrange the everyday for the purposes of social commentary. *The MP3 Experiments* share some formal similarity to the flash mob, in which participants gather nonchalantly in a public space, perform a simple preplanned activity, and then disperse quickly afterward. The flash mob was first designed by Bill Wasik, senior editor at *Harper's Magazine*, in 2003 as an attempt to exploit and resist the ennui of young urbanites in Manhattan (Wasik 2006). It has since become more widely known as a type of choreographed dance performance staged for corporate conventions or advertising purposes: for example, Montreal's FM102.3 radio station staged a "KPOP Gangnam Style" flash mob in the city's Chinatown in 2012 as a publicity stunt (MontrealFM1023 2012). Flash mobs have also been used by social protest movements to raise awareness. In December 2012 demonstrators from Idle No More, a Canadian grassroots movement supporting Indigenous treaty rights, blocked the intersection of Yonge and Dundas Streets in Toronto. Protesters joined hands and performed a simple round dance, moving in a spiral pattern around the intersection (WorldTruthNow 2012). As drummers provided a steady rhythm from the centre of the intersection, the dance continued for about ten minutes before demonstrators dispersed. Video of the event appeared on YouTube within hours, promoting the Idle No More mission "to honour Indigenous sovereignty and to protect the land and water" (Idle No More 2015). In urban prank performances like these, the unexpected actions of a crowd turn participants into strangers of "life as usual" and also estrange everyday urban scenes of shopping and traffic. Whether through unexpected art, surprise dance, or other interventions in the public landscape, urban pranks disrupt, however briefly, everyday behaviours and norms and can use this disruption to raise questions, make a political statement, or offer alternative ways of doing, thinking, and consuming. It is this intervention that gives urban pranks activist potential.

Perhaps the most well-known urban pranks in the United States and Canada today are created by Improv Everywhere. The group's pranks can be simple: in 2006 Improv Everywhere and comedian Colton Dunn set up a booth where locals could *Meet a Black Person* in the predominantly white town of Aspen, Colorado (Todd 2012a). Improv Everywhere's pranks can also be complex, such as musical theatre numbers needing rehearsal or large-scale actions requiring careful coordination, such as the group's most famous performance, 2008's *Frozen Grand Central*, which boasts over 34 million views on YouTube. In this prank, two hundred participants stopped still, or froze, for five minutes in the middle of New York's busy Grand Central train station (Todd 2008a). While Improv Everywhere's pranks can consist of just one actor, as is the case in *Meet a Black Person*, they are most famous for large-scale pranks like *Frozen Grand Central* or *The MP3 Experiments* that rely on hundreds, even thousands, of participants creating a mass performance in a large open public space.

The popularity of Improv Everywhere's pranks has spread around the world. Inspired by *Frozen Grand Central*, in 2008 pranksters in Montreal created their own frozen train station at Berri-UQAM, the busy central hub of the Montreal Metro (Brigade SnW 2008). Improv in Toronto, a member of the Urban Prankster Network, organizes repeated mass prank performances like *Canada's Biggest Water Fight*, *Toronto Pillow Fight*, and *Subway Dance Party*, and members participated in the 2008 Toronto MP3 *Experiment*. Improv in Toronto is also one of the many international organizers for the annual *No Pants!* subway ride, a prank instigated by Improv Everywhere that simply asks participants to ride the train in the winter without pants, meaning, in principle, in their underwear (Todd 2015). This prank is so successful that in 2014, *No Pants!* subway rides were held in sixty cities, including Toronto, Montreal, Calgary, and Vancouver, and in twenty-five different countries (Todd 2015). This prank comments on the social norms for users of public transportation in the modern metropolis: on a crowded bus or subway car, personal space shrinks, and riders reduce eye contact and social interaction. The incongruity of riders wearing no pants on a winter day, like a breaching experiment, encourages both participants and passing subway riders to consider the underlying rules and expected norms of social interaction on public transportation.

Improv Everywhere's pranks are carnivalesque in nature: they are short-term comedic inversions of the norm. In order to get participants and audiences to "stop to notice the world around them," urban pranksters depend on the carnivalesque subversion of the chosen performance space, its structures, and its sometimes hidden ideologies. The potential for ideological intervention derives from the temporary disruption of the public space's normalized activities and behaviours; for example, as the frozen commuters stilled the hustle and bustle of the train station, they inserted the static and fixed into a place of dynamism and movement. Carnivalesque performances, as literary critic Mikhail Bakhtin writes, offer "temporary liberation from the prevailing truth and from the established order," while also imagining new possibilities in social or political structures (1984, 10). The frozen participants in Berri-UQAM temporarily liberated the Metro station from its people-moving purpose and imagined a meditative urban space untouched by the pressures of the capitalist rat race. Outside Toronto's Eaton Centre mall, the dancing Idle No More demonstrators stopped holiday shoppers in a sudden rejection of Christmas consumption. Comedian Colton Dunn's presence in Aspen upset the racial privilege of skiing and other winter sports, reminded holiday-makers of the historic link between racial and economic privilege, and also implicitly imagined an Aspen without racial privilege, a place where it wouldn't be necessary to "meet a black person" as part of a vacation novelty experience.

Carnivalesque performances are temporary: participants in Grand Central Terminal and the Berri-UQAM Metro station froze for about five minutes before continuing on their way, and *The MP3 Experiments* typically take between thirty minutes and one hour to perform before participants disperse back into the city. In Toronto, rules for urban social interaction were only briefly overturned as strangers mingled and played in Riverdale Park East. The short balloon battle forced social interactions and encouraged heightened awareness of the playful possibilities of the park space. And as participants in Toronto *The MP3 Experiment* frolicked on the park's soccer fields, they disrupted a community league soccer game, walked across the field, distracted players, and drew the ire of a referee. As the participants challenged an existing and accepted use of public space and offered their own alternative use of the space, they drew attention both to the local policies that govern the use of public space and also to how these rules police the movement of bodies in those spaces.

Bakhtin (1984), writing about Medieval pre-Lenten carnivals, notes that carnivalesque performances end with the reestablishment of the old social order and the reinstatement of prevailing political structures. Improv Everywhere organizers participate in the reestablishment of social norms by both clearly defining the end of their prank performances and reminding participants of the normal rules for the performance spaces used. For *The MP3 Experiments*, they use the length of a downloadable audio file to define the performance's beginning and end, caution participants to pick up any garbage left behind, and warn participants to be polite to locals in both the audio files and on their webpage. Although Improv Everywhere's performances are short, they are carefully archived on the group's website. Descriptions, first-hand accounts, photographic images, and videos of the events survive online long after the live prank ends. These detailed records offer inspiration to other pranksters, publicize the activities of Improv Everywhere, and also provide an archive for scholars investigating the event. For each *MP3 Experiment*, Improv Everywhere founder Charlie Todd posts descriptions and images gathered from observers and participants. A comment section at the end of each blog post offers another way to engage with the prank: typically participants reminisce about the fun they had, while blog readers express a desire to become pranksters too. The brevity of carnivalesque prank performances and the ultimate reestablishment of norms may seem to undercut the activist potential of urban prank performance; however, the lingering online presence and affective power of *The MP3 Experiments* suggests that, combined with the comedic inversions of the norm, pranks retain activist potential after the performance ends.

The MP3 Experiments pranks combine embodiment, music, costume, and theatrical improvisation. Participants download a specially created audio file containing a series of instructions set to music, synchronize watches with an atomic clock, meet at an appointed place, press "play" at the appointed time, and follow the instructions as each listens to the audio file on their own mobile device. Each year the performance takes place in a different park in New York; some years the performances go "on tour," as in Toronto in 2008. According to descriptions posted on the Improv Everywhere website, participants might be asked to form a giant conga line or walk like zombies through a park (Todd 2006, 2005). Sometimes they are required to dress like a tourist or wear a specific colour of shirt (Todd 2013, 2007, 2008b, 2008c, 2009) or bring simple props like a camera, an umbrella, a balloon, soap bubbles, or a plastic grocery bag (Todd 2007, 2008b, 2008c, 2013, 2014b). Because participants, also called Agents, wear headphones, the performance is relatively silent to observers, barring participant snickers and giggles. While the goal is unison, the inevitable fumbling of human fingers on mobile devices means that the action is slightly staggered as some participants start ahead of or lag behind others. This adds to the overall anarchic comedic effect and is perhaps why Improv Everywhere does not stream the audio file online. Nonparticipants cannot hear the instructions and therefore cannot anticipate what the crowd is going to do next.

The events at *The MP3 Experiments* may appear to follow a random sequence to observers; however, archived evidence posted on the group's blog reveals that each performance of *The MP3 Experiments* proceeds according to the same structure: first a warm-up, then a challenge in which participants must work together to solve a problem, next an interaction with nonparticipants, and finally some kind of conflict that is quickly resolved. *The MP3 Experiments* thus follow the basic structure of Western drama with a beginning and exposition (warm-up), middle and rising action (working together), and finally a crisis and ending (conflict and resolution). Participants perform tasks similar to theatrical improvisation, or improv, exercises, not surprising considering that Improv Everywhere organizers perform at the Upright Citizens Brigade Theatre, a New York-based improvisational comedy venue. In fact, *The MP3 Experiments* depend

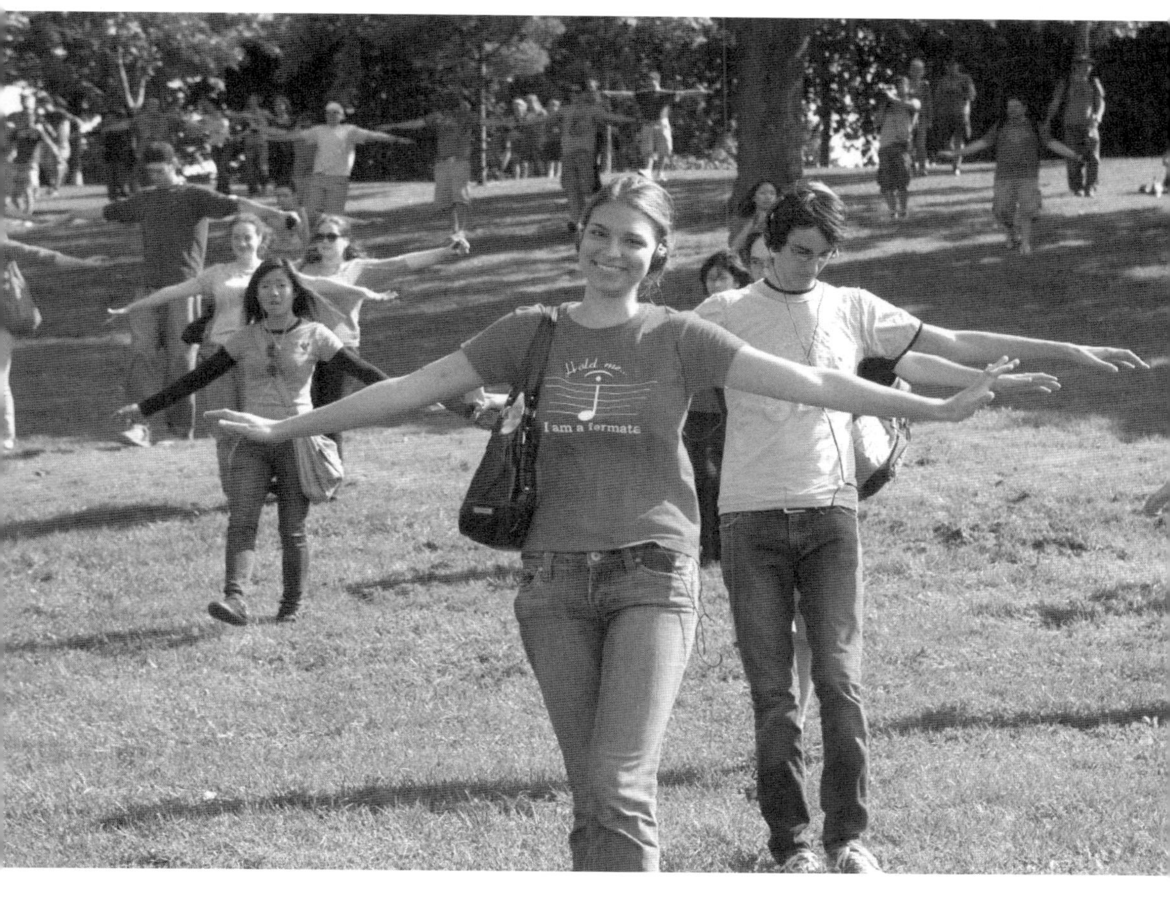

2.2 Participants in Improv Everywhere's *The MP3 Experiment Toronto* warm up with a mock police sobriety exam. Photo: Ian Watson, 2008.

first and foremost on the foundational improv tenet of accepting an offer. Improv gurus Viola Spolin and Keith Johnstone call this idea respectively "Yes! And," and "acceptance" (Spolin 1999; Johnstone 1981). Performers in *The MP3 Experiments* must accept or say "Yes! And" to Improv Everywhere's ideas: synchronizing watches to an atomic clock, pressing "play" at the designated time and place, and following all instructions from "Steve," the "Omnipotent Voice from Above" (Todd 2006). Charlie Todd's blog descriptions of the events reveal that Steve's first instructions tend to be common improv warm-ups that get participants accustomed to accepting his demands, for example, simple stretching and games of "Enemy/Protector" or "Simon Says" (Todd 2006, 2012b). Steve led listeners of *The MP3 Experiment Toronto* through a test similar to a police sobriety exam, asking them to walk in a straight line and touch their noses (Todd 2008c). Once prepared to fully accept Steve's instructions, the crowd works together to solve a problem. This can take the form of the theatre game known as "Line Up" or "Data Processing," which asks participants to arrange themselves in some order, typically without using verbal communication. Tasks might include finding the tallest person, dividing into concentric rings according to shirt colours, or forming a spectrum based on shirt colour (Todd 2006, 2007, 2014b). In Toronto, Steve asked the participants in similarly coloured shirts to form the shapes of Tetris blocks and then try to fit together with other groups in a human-sized version of the popular computer game (Todd 2008c). The culmination of participant interaction at *The MP3 Experiments* is a conflict. In each performance participants separate into groups and engage in a contest: a water gun or balloon battle, a game of "Rock, Paper, Scissors," or a game of tag (Todd 2008c, 2012b, 2005, 2007). The contest is good-natured and has no winner: the crisis is resolved by the recorded voice of Steve, always acting as *deus ex machina*. In Toronto, Steve ended the performance by instructing the participants to mime dramatic deaths and then finally reminding them to collect any balloon debris on their way out of the park.

In addition to its carnivalesque nature, a prank's potential for ideological intervention also stems from embodied community, the shared physicality of the participants. This is the highlight of the event. *New York Times* technology blogger David Pogue, a participant in 2009's *MP3 Experiment*, writes that he "couldn't stop laughing" throughout the event because of "the weirdness of seeing 3,000 people acting in perfect unison, even though externally, there wasn't a sound" (2009). While Pogue was perhaps exaggerating about the "perfect unison," his affective experience exemplifies the kind of pleasurable communal physicality that stems from an intensified physical awareness. Dance and performance scholar Susan Leigh Foster, writing of her experience marching in the 1999 Seattle demonstrations, argues that there is a "heightened sense of physicality that results when the body steps outside the quotidian routines of daily life and into non-normative action" (2003, 412). In an Improv Everywhere blog comment, an Agent who participated in 2005's *MP3 Experiment 2.0* notes the excitement of interacting with strangers: "it was truly amazing to see all those unfamiliar smiles" (Todd 2005). This heightened and shared physicality produces sensory pleasure. Another commenter, a participant in the first *MP3 Experiment*, noted that "[t]here were times when I felt so happy during it that I giggled like a little schoolboy" (Todd 2004). In *Performance Affects: Applied Theatre and the End of Effect*, James Thompson argues that performance's transformative power to change a mind or alter a course of action is rooted in the physical and pleasurable experience of the performance (2011, 7–8). The affective power of a prank creates a community of pleasure even as the prank's performative action disrupts and comments on community hierarchies and behaviours.

The *MP3 Experiments* are clearly designed to be affective. The recorded voice of Steve instructs participants when to be quiet, when to jump around with abandon, when to hug an animal, when to hug a stranger (Todd 2008c). These instructions encourage a range of moods and physical expressions. Thompson (2011, 7–8) posits that the transformative power of political performance stems not only from its message but also from affect: the experience of performance, the emotional and sensory responses, the aesthetic and physical pleasure. In a successful activist performance, an affective response to the performance experience works together with the content, or argument, of the performance. Foster makes a similar case about the transformative power of mass demonstrations. She contends that mass protests "call forth a perceptive and responsive physicality that ... deciphers the social and then choreographs an imagined alternative" (2003, 412). In other words, affect and message work together. Like a mass demonstration, *The MP3 Experiments* have an affective and potentially transformative power inspired by the pleasurable physicality of nonnormative action, as comments on the Improv Everywhere blog attest.

"Eddie Mazz" reminisces that "[t]he party atmosphere was Awesome! [...] With everyone cheering and all" (Todd 2008d); while "Elspeth" notes that "the spirit was infectious [...] it was fantastic" (Todd 2008b). "Suzanne Zazou" comments that "[i]t was great fun to act silly with a bunch of friendly strangers" (Todd 2008c). Theatre scholar John Muse notes that mass participatory performances like *The MP3 Experiments* "mourn and mock the ironic dearth of communal activity in an overconnected age," as they also "stage a digitally enabled in-your-face revolt against the erosion of face-to-face interaction in a digital nation" (2010, 12). Participants respond to the affective power generated by social interaction, shared physicality, and communal sensory experiences.

The affective power of *The MP3 Experiments* both disrupts and models community, critiquing community structures and expectations while also offering another mode of action and interaction. Although admittedly self-selecting, comments from Pogue and other positive responses on the Improv Everywhere blog suggest that many participants find pleasurable kinship through their participation in the prank and find an "imagined alternative" of affable social interaction in public spaces that can often be isolating or alienating. Yet the improvisational and participatory nature of the prank performance can also create unpredictable and unexpected affective responses. Asking participants to partake in improv games does not guarantee that they will follow Steve's instructions precisely or even at all. For example, when the character of Steve made a physical appearance in the *MP3 Experiment III*, some participants broke rank and stopped following directions in order to cluster around Steve and worship him as a deity (Todd 2006). In his description of the Toronto event, Todd notes that several participants walked through, rather than around, the soccer game in the park. Photographs posted on the Improv Everywhere website indicate that the soccer game was in session and visible to performers before the prank began and that there was plenty of room in the park for the hundreds of *MP3 Experiment* participants who did not need to use the same physical space as the soccer players (Todd 2008c). Here some participants created an antagonistic relationship with others using the same space. Their "imagined alternative" did not include room for other understandings of the public space. The audio file of instructions from Steve offers some affective guidance to participants. Yet by relying on participant improvisation, the performance creates an environment that encourages unruly affective response. This affective openness, combined with the use of public spaces, also challenges audience reception.

Although Improv Everywhere aims to make strangers "laugh, smile, or stop to notice the world around them," there is no guarantee that audience members of mass performance pranks like *The MP3 Experiments* will react with the desired emotional affect. For example, the soccer referee yelled angrily at participants who pranced through his game (Todd 2008c). Posted photographs of the referee do not show him laughing or smiling in response to the pranksters. *The MP3 Experiments* use as performance spaces the public parks of New York, Toronto, and other cities. Images on the Improv Everywhere website reveal that these public spaces tend to be already occupied: by picnickers, sunbathers, park rangers, athletes, dog walkers, and uninterested passersby. The parks are already in use in multiple ways, and the prank imposes the layer of a performance space onto that mix of uses. At each *MP3 Experiment* Agents are required to interact physically with the audience of passersby and observers who happen to be at the same physical location at the time of the performance. This interaction draws witnesses into the performance. Audience interaction may take the form of a high-five (Todd 2007, 2008b, 2009, 2011a, 2012b, 2013) or using an unsuspecting stranger in a game of "follow-the-leader" (Todd 2009). In addition to giving high-fives to observers, Toronto participants were also asked to hug an animal, which resulted in large crowds surrounding the few dogs present in the park (Todd 2008c). These live audiences have not accepted the premise of the performance. They did not sign up to be a part of a prank or theatrical event. They did not download the audio file. Yet this audience of observers is explicitly asked to accept, to say "Yes! And" to the Agents wanting to use them for high-fives and "follow-the-leader." Demanding that the audience accept their premises, Agents determined to follow Steve's instructions are not open to audience refusals to play. Although Improv Everywhere on its webpage and Todd in media appearances reiterate that the group's goal is to "make people smile" and have "organized fun," the fun may be aggressively one-sided during the performance event.

Despite Improv Everywhere's official position that "a prank doesn't have to involve humiliation or embarrassment" (Todd 2014a), a performance like *The MP3 Experiment* does contain an element of hostility. It may be considered what Freud calls a "tendentious joke," that is, one with a hostile purpose ([1905] 2003, 85–95). Freud argues that three people are required for a tendentious joke: the one who tells the joke, the one who receives the joke with pleasure, and one who is the butt of the joke and object of aggression. Here the joke-makers and receivers are the Agents participating in the prank, while the unsuspecting passersby who function as an impromptu audience become the target of the joke. The prank positions them as outsiders. Without the insider knowledge of the MP3 file the audience for *The MP3 Experiments* are framed as confused, clueless rubes excluded from the exuberant community of the participants. This framing is a central part of the prank. The word "Agents" underscores this insider/outsider dynamic: not only are the participants agents in the sense of active performers rather than passive bystanders, they are also agents in the sense of a secret: they enjoy knowledge that passersby do not. Comments on the Improv Everywhere website, from Todd and Agents, demonstrate how strangers and passersby are positioned as the target of the prank. In his description of *The MP3 Experiment Six*, Todd (2009) writes "part of the fun of the MP3 Experiment each year is seeing the looks on the faces of those who happen upon us and have no idea what is going on." A commenter identified as Agent Y-Bot complained about the isolated location for the *MP3 Experiment 5*, posting that "when I do weird things in public, I want people WATCHING" (Todd 2008b; emphasis in the original). Another comment from Siobhan agrees, pointing out that "doing weird stuff is way more fun when there's hapless bystanders around" (Todd 2008d). These comments highlight how an audience of outsiders is essential for the prank to work. The prank revolves around participants behaving foolishly or unexpectedly by playing improv games in the park, yet it is in fact the "hapless" passersby, called into being as astonished and ignorant audience members, who receive the prank's hostility.

Passersby become audience members, but they also become performers too. Muse explains that audiences of mass participatory performances, who witness pranks "without their consent or even their knowledge become unwitting performers who complete and validate the event" (2010, 15). As participants like Agent Todd and commenter Siobhan note above, part of the pleasure for participants comes from watching the reactions of the incidental audiences of *The MP3 Experiments*. This pleasure feeds into the affective experience of the performers. But bystanders are also necessary to validate the surprising behaviour of the pranksters by providing

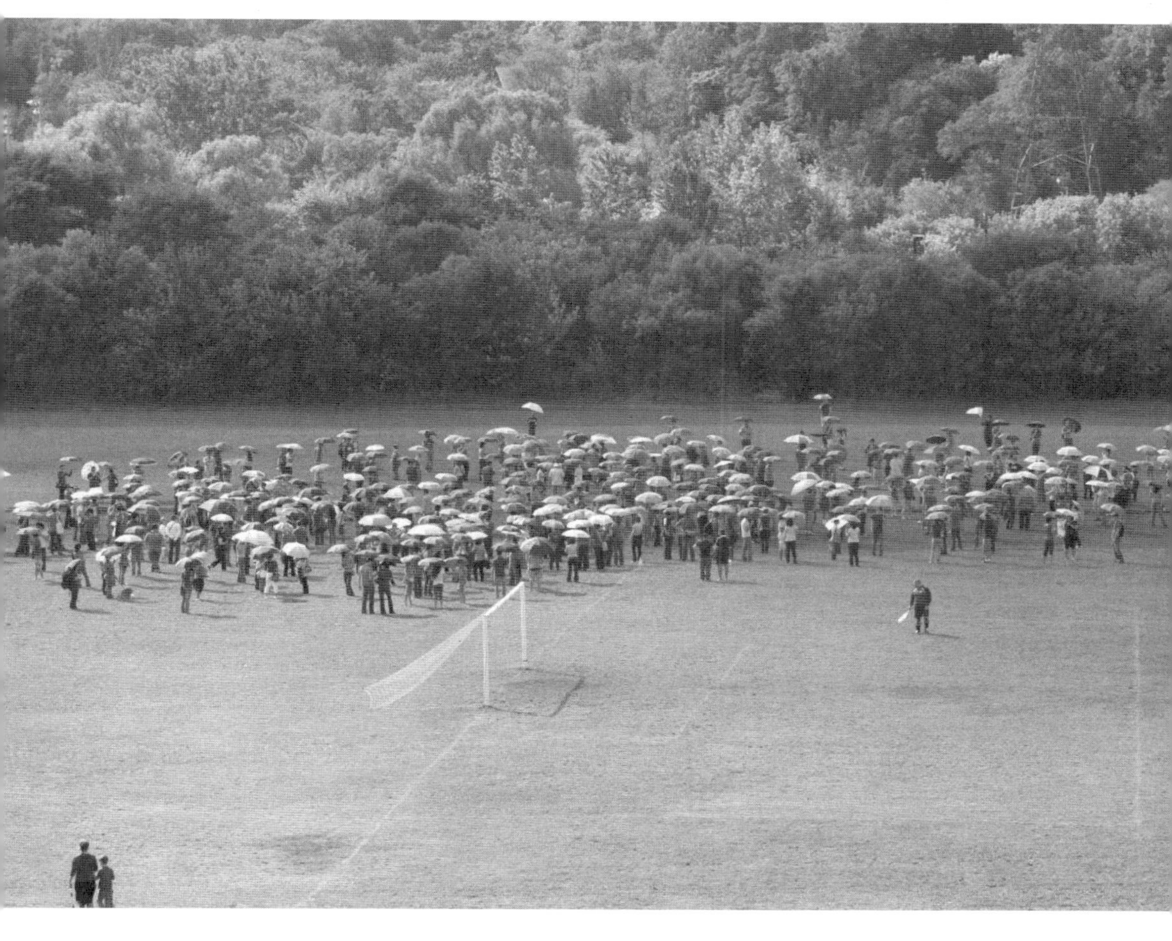

2.3 Participants in Improv Everywhere's *The MP3 Experiment Toronto* disrupt a soccer game in Riverdale Park East. Photo: Ian Watson, 2008.

contrasting conventional behaviours. Agent Y-Bot's frustration with the lack of passersby at *The MP3 Experiment 5* echoes this need for validation. Without the sunbathers, picnickers, dog walkers, tourists, and locals filling a public space, a mass participatory prank may make the participants laugh and smile, but it won't make a bystander "stop to notice the world around them." Pranks work best when both participants and witnesses are present and offer contrasting experiences of the public space. Thus what can seem initially like a tendentious joke is in fact mutually agonistic. The conflict between both performer and audience is needed for the prank to do its performative, disruptive, and instructional work.

POLITICAL DISSENSUS AND ACTIVIST POTENTIAL

The inherent "antagonisms of public space" allow the audience of *The MP3 Experiments* to become both the unwitting target for the prank and also an unwitting participant who contrasts and reflects behaviour back to the pranksters (Thompson and Sholette 2004, 18). Public space is bound by ideology: it negotiates concepts of freedom, notions of access, regulations for behaviour, and ideas about who belongs to a community and who belongs in the public sphere. It serves as a locus of social tension and political dissent. Creative performances in public spaces are answerable; that is, they happen in the context of a conversation with others who can react and respond to them in predictable or unpredictable ways and through a variety of languages or forms of discourse (Bakhtin 1990). Improv Everywhere's MP3 file is answerable both to the audience of passersby and to the *The MP3 Experiment* participants who may follow Steve's instructions in different ways or refuse to follow directions at all. The event in Riverdale Park East placed musical and embodied languages in conversation with discourses of freedom, competition, and publicness. When Agents disrupt normative uses of the park with performative play and interact with bystanders, they encourage audience members to join their alternate social behaviour. But like the Toronto soccer referee, upset at the disruption of the game he was responsible for officiating, some audience members resist the carnivalesque performance and offer other responses. In these varied answers to the performance, social conflicts emerge. Bakhtin scholar Ken Hirschkop argues that social conflicts represent "a struggle over the context, narrative or otherwise, which will embody the development of some languages at the expense of others" (1999, 266). When does the will of the group over-rule the wish of the individual? When does a special event trump a community tradition? Who is permitted to use the space when and in what way? Website accounts reveal that some bystanders do not want to high-five strangers. Some want to keep sunbathing or watching the sunset (Todd 2007, 2011a). Some want to continue their birthday picnic in the park (Todd 2006). For some, the prank performance does not offer an "imagined alternative" or affective transformation but instead a moment of dissent, a disruption of the use of public space.

Because *The MP3 Experiments* can create moments of dissent as well as imagined alternatives, they present potential for political dissensus. Prank performances that can encourage both participants and audiences to "stop to notice the world" are doing the work of dissensus by pointing out unspoken expectations, invisible rules, and hidden assumptions that govern public space. As Hirschkop notes, "modern societies are over-producers of language and narrative, and, rather than throw all their efforts into one arena, they spread them around at various levels and institutions of the social structure. Competing languages thus do not struggle on the level surface of the city square, as Bakhtin imagined, but in the urban maze of an unevenly structured linguistic world" (1999, 266–7). By using the image of an "urban maze," Hirschkop argues that public space is a tangle of conflicting discourses. For example, an Agent at *The MP3 Experiment 2.0* noticed a Central Park groundskeeper calling for reinforcements due to a fear that the performers would drop litter at the Sheep Meadow and disrupt what is meant to be a natural green space in the middle of an urban environment (Todd 2005). The groundskeeper's first reaction was to keep order and maintain the illusion of the Sheep Meadow as a natural space, rather than to allow the pranksters to reveal its affinity with the littered city streets beyond the park. In Toronto, a participant or audience member might ask why organized team sports have privileged space in the park or how the history of urbanization has left dogs as the most convenient nonhuman animals in the park to hug. A performer might pause to think about their daily encounters with strangers as they move through the urban landscape or why the pleasurable affective experience of being part of a prank performance crowd feels different from the rush hour crush on the subway. A passerby might wonder how such a crowd was organized and why it is unusual to see large crowds moving together in near unison in the urban landscape. From the experience or observation of *The* MP3 *Experiment*, questions arise that may lead to political dissensus.

The move from descriptive to hypothetical language here is purposeful. *The* MP3 *Experiments*, as Improv Everywhere claims, are not political performances meant to argue a point of view or communicate an ideology. But as performances with a life of their own, they do suggest activist potential. Urban pranks like *The* MP3 *Experiments*, with their temporary carnivalesque disruption, their affective power, and their room for political dissensus, offer room for theatrical and political activists to ask how they might harness this activist potential for social commentary, political action, innovative pedagogy, or community engagement, and space for art and performance historians to consider how mass performance pranks work as political art.

Political art, according to Rancière, expresses a contradiction or conflict. He argues that art is not "political because of the messages and sentiments it conveys concerning the state of the world. Neither is it political because of the manner in which it might choose to represent society's structures, or social groups, their conflicts or identities" (2009, 23). It is not the representation or subject matter that makes art political but rather "the very distance it takes with respect to these functions"; in other words, it is the ability to displace perception and challenge sensibility that makes art political (23–4). In creating his definition of political art, Rancière bypasses art that is conventionally thought of as political or art that directly engages with politics. An example of art that is traditionally considered political is Invisible Theatre, created and designed by Brazilian director and theatre theorist Augusto Boal. In *Theatre of the Oppressed* Boal describes how actors in Invisible Theatre infiltrate a public space or private space: "a restaurant, a sidewalk, a market, a train, a line of people" to stage a didactic play (1985, 144). The actors are prepared with a script, fully rehearsed, and ready to improvise with the witnesses and observers, "those who are there by chance" (144). Despite its similarities with an urban prank like *The* MP3 *Experiments*, Boal's Invisible Theatre of the 1960s had an explicitly political purpose: he used it to draw attention to poverty, income disparity, and the precarity of service workers under the capitalist system (144–7). Invisible Theatre is polemical and didactic with a targeted message and, therefore, not political art as conceived of by Rancière. Mass urban pranks like *The MP3 Experiments*, on the other hand, are suggestive rather than polemical and instructive rather than didactic. They offer participants a means to displace perceptions of everyday life in the city and question the rules and discourses that govern the urban landscape. They do not demand Rancièrean politics but instead offer its potential.

How might this potential be activated? One possibility is through pedagogy: using mass performance pranks to teach students about the expectations and rules that shape their movements and behaviours on university campuses and in urban environments. Pranks like flash mobs, *The MP3 Experiments*, and other unexpected performances can both engage and disrupt campus communities. For example, in the spring of 2004, I introduced the then relatively new phenomenon of flash mobs to my Theatre History students at a large public university. They were studying twentieth-century explorations of the nature of performance, and I thought that the example of flash mobs (a popular craze in 2003–04 and before the flash mob's choreographic turn) would provide a relevant, contemporary example we could compare and contrast to historic Dada exhibitions, 1960s happenings, and Invisible Theatre experiments. The students, however, were most interested in comparing urban prank activities to their own experience rather than to historical actions. They saw parallels to the pranks they had pulled in high school: simultaneous sneezing on cue or the synchronized dropping of textbooks to startle the teacher. While they understood the historical broadening of the definition of performance and rise of early performance theory, and could relate the flash mob to that historical narrative, their focus was less on theatre history and more on the exciting and subversive nature of the prank.

The students pranked the very next class. When a certain student's mobile phone alarm rang, students stood up. The prank embraced the simplicity of early flash mobs: the students who received an email sent through the course website were told to stand for one minute in silence, and then sit back down again. About half the class had checked their email before the early morning class; the others looked on in confusion, amazement, and dawning glee as they realized that their peers were flash mobbing the class. After the minute was up, the participating students quietly sat down, and the lecture continued. The simple act of standing drew attention both to the embodied academic hierarchy of the lecture classroom – students trapped and still in desks, professor free to move about – and also to the lecture classroom's privileging of intellectual work over embodied practice. It was a minimalist performance, and hardly disrupted the class at all, yet afterwards, the students talked with great enthusiasm about the affective pleasure of the prank, the fear of being the only one to stand, the excitement of group participation, and the looks on the faces of witnesses. It was obvious to the entire teaching team that the affective experience of the flash mob provided a means not only to animate a large lecture class but also to spur discussion about how the campus landscape regulates bodies and reproduces hierarchies.

In Canada, University of Toronto engineering students and faculty have used prank performances to disrupt and relieve the stress of examinations. During exams in 2011 and 2012, the tense silences of large lecture halls exploded as students burst into song, stood on their desks, and rapped or sang about test anxiety and the pressures of academic performance and assessment (Skulenite 2011, 2012; Bellemare 2012). Astonished students watched as their instructors joined the performance, participating in several minutes of unexpected musical fun before the exam continued. In this carnivalesque performance, the formality and order of the lecture hall was briefly overturned as students danced on desks and on the stairs. The affective power of the prank is clear in the video evidence: students who were previously hunched over their exam papers with grim and serious expressions relax their shoulders, grin, laugh, cheer, clap hands, and move their bodies to the rhythm of the music. Some record the prank on mobile devices to enjoy again later. The prank performs its immediate work of inserting a moment of levity and relaxation into the stressful environment of the exam hall. It might also perform the more lasting work of tempering the anxiety of future University of Toronto engineering students, especially as the online video of the 2012 event enjoys about four million views. But through its disruption of the serious exam hall, the prank also raises broader questions about the efficacy of pedagogy in large lecture classes, the pressure to succeed in a competitive environment, and the value placed on an undergraduate degree in the neoliberal capitalist economy.

There is no guarantee, however, that the participants and audiences of the University of Toronto prank asked these broader questions. Likewise, there is no guarantee that witnesses to and participants in *The MP3 Experiments* consider issues of public space, social conventions, and their relationship to the urban landscape. Mass pranks in university classrooms or urban environments cannot definitively be said to be political art, in either the conventional or Rancièrean understanding. But with their carnivalesque disruption, affective power, and ability to instruct audiences about the world they live in and suggest possible alternatives, mass prank performances do have the *potential* to be Rancièrean political art. They have the potential to explore and critique people's relationships to the ideologies that govern their behaviour and their relationship to urban environments. Now it is up to pedagogues, artists, and activists to harness that potential and use urban pranks to make political critique and stimulate political discussion.

Sebastian Matthias

3

—

DANCE ENCOUNTERS: PERFORMING ARTS AS AN EXPERIMENTAL PLATFORM FOR URBAN PUBLICS

In 1959, Erving Goffman adopted for his theory of the presentation of self in public life an idea that was already inscribed at the entrance to the Globe Theatre in London: "all the world's a stage" or "the whole world acts as an actor." For him, the theatrical perspective offered a productive socio-logical viewpoint on how people behave in public (Goffman 1959, xi). The argument I develop in this chapter extends this method by utilizing the perspective of dance as a performing art to gain a deeper understanding of how peoples' movements engage with and affect each other in public places. It builds upon my artistic research as a choreographer and PhD candidate, investigating participatory modes of perception in the groove phenomenon in club dancing. In this research I oscillate between two perspectives to explore what actually happens between people when they dance together in clubs to electronic dance music: the perspective of an artist in creating and testing the effect of choreographic situations and that of a dance scholar in analyzing movements and experiences. The vast quantity of movements and the fluctuation of encounters pose a real chal-lenge to analysis. In my PhD project I propose a conceptual framework for how communication and relations between dancers are organized and structured to provide the sensation of groove, understood as the collective movements that facilitate each individual dance improvisation. In clubs it seems much easier to dance in a group on the dance floor than to be the first one to start moving in an empty space.

For this chapter I extend the conceptual framework and methodology of my artistic research to public encounters in urban places, drawing on my dance performances *installation chorégraphique participative* at the *Champ de pixels* (Montreal, 2009) and *Danserye* (on tour in Germany, Switzerland, Belgium, and the Netherlands, 2013). I aim to offer insight into how differentiated modes of perception are necessary to create different forms of encounters, which can reconfigure audience-performer relations. Specifically, entrainment perception – the perceptual processing of durational information through body movements, which I will explain in more detail below – can create a system of interrelated negotiations that I call "choreographic groove." This perspective offers a new line of inquiry into the sociality of urban public space. The choreographic installation at the *Champ de pixels* site at Place des Festivals in downtown Montreal and the performance space of *Danserye*, created for theatres, can both be considered experimental platforms for the constitution of urban publics. They provide examples that help construct a hypothesis on the performativity of how we encounter dance movements and what kind of dynamics that creates.

TAKING DANCE INTO THE PUBLIC REALM

Amidst the bright red lights reflecting in the snow I stroll carefully into the center of the blinking field of the Place des Festivals. Leaving behind the crowd of people who came to watch the performance, I am entangled by the crossing paths of the performers who are contracting on every other step or the trajectory of other passersby who are crossing the space on an errand. Children copy the tiptoeing movement of one of the dancers, creating a caravan of movement not unlike the luminous canon of the small LED cylinders that turn on when you pass them and switch off three seconds later. I decide to follow one other dancer, making my way up the slight hill to the other end of the plaza. The more we leave the busyness behind, the emptier the space gets. Only some dancers make it all the way up. When one dancer turns her path to return, our gazes meet and I feel I meet her personally, alone in the huge white open space with only two illuminated lights around us.

The *Champ de pixels* is an interactive light installation by Jean Beaudoin and Erick Villeneuve that was installed on the Place des Festivals in the Quartier des Spectacles in Montreal in the winter of 2009–10. It was made up of 400 LED lights arranged perpendicularly on wooden planks and spread over 40,000 square feet of pavement covered in snow. Conceived like a gigantic "Lite-Brite," *Champ de pixels* was equipped with motion sensors on each light to detect passing movements, so the sensors changed the illumination of the pixel from red to white and back again when pedestrians crossed the Place des Festivals, from the main downtown axis of rue Sainte-Catherine and the central business district north toward the buildings of McGill University and Université du Québec à Montréal. The organization team of the Quartier des Spectacles invited me to create a performance for the installation during my residency at Les Ateliers de danse moderne de Montréal Inc. (LADMMI, known since 2012 as the École de Danse Contemporaine de Montréal). I worked with twenty-four students on this choreographic installation, which was supposed to be a durational performance but was cut into three slots of fifteen minutes due to the -17°C weather so that the dancers could warm themselves between slots. Due to its public setting, the performance was comprised not only of the dancers and guests coming to see the announced performance but also pedestrians accidentally passing the "stage" on their way through the city. A nice side effect of the extreme cold was that everyone present was wearing thick winter clothes, putting their bodies into similar shapes, which made it hard to distinguish who was a dancer and who was not. Moreover, as the light installation had been running already for a couple of weeks and downtown regulars had become used to the site being populated by people playing with it, the performance was not obviously a special event. Passersby didn't pay attention to the performance as an exceptional art space; rather, they treated the installation as a normal kind of public street meant for connecting different parts of the city. The ambiguity of this situation created the possibility of overlapping a performance art space, with its dancers and audience, with an urban public space and its users and behaviour patterns – creating a dance performance as urban public art. This mixture of people with different intentions, different backgrounds, and different interests created diverse choices in behaviours. The *installation chorégraphique participative* at *Champ de pixels* hence created a public realm with the experimental properties of an art space and offered a platform on which to test practices that push the limits of public behaviour, generating multiple interactions between art and the public.[1]

> Surrounded by attentive audience members crouched on the floor, I sit and watch guitarist Paul Norman and dancer Lisanne Goodhue share a little stool back to back in a yellow wash of light. The delicate pauses in between the musical phrases of the melancholy renaissance melody "Mille regretz" played by the guitarist become tangible for me as a collectively created silence. Into these silences, the echoes of rhythmic footsteps fall in the phrasing of the pavane dance step. A dancer in a sci-fi renaissance costume presents himself in the space and addresses each person as he passes by. As other performers – musicians and dancers alike – join the collective step, the sounds of his steps are joined by the ringing of little bells that emphasize the rhythm. The shared moment created in the silence gets transformed into a shared dance as some audience members join the step-touch, step-touch, step, step-touch. As I walk rhythmically through the space I meet the gazes of still standing spectators, walking spectators, and passing performers. The divide between audience and performer is blurred as people meet people.

In contrast to the *Champ de pixels*, the dance performance *Danserye* created a platform that was experimental from the perspective of theatre. The setup in the theatre generated ambiguity in order to open up encounters between audience members, performers, and other audience members that were similar to those of the public realm.[2] When the audience entered the performance space of *Danserye*, they found themselves in a dimmed light installation consisting of three suspended sculpture-like illuminated semicircles (figure 3.1).

Each audience member was handed a wristband with two golden bells to be wrapped around a wrist or ankle. The contrast to what one expects when entering a dance performance was heightened when clarinetist Jack McNeill greeted the guests at a row of music stands, identifying himself as the caller of the dances to come and explaining their specific dance steps. Jack's instructions, however, did not match the performed dance

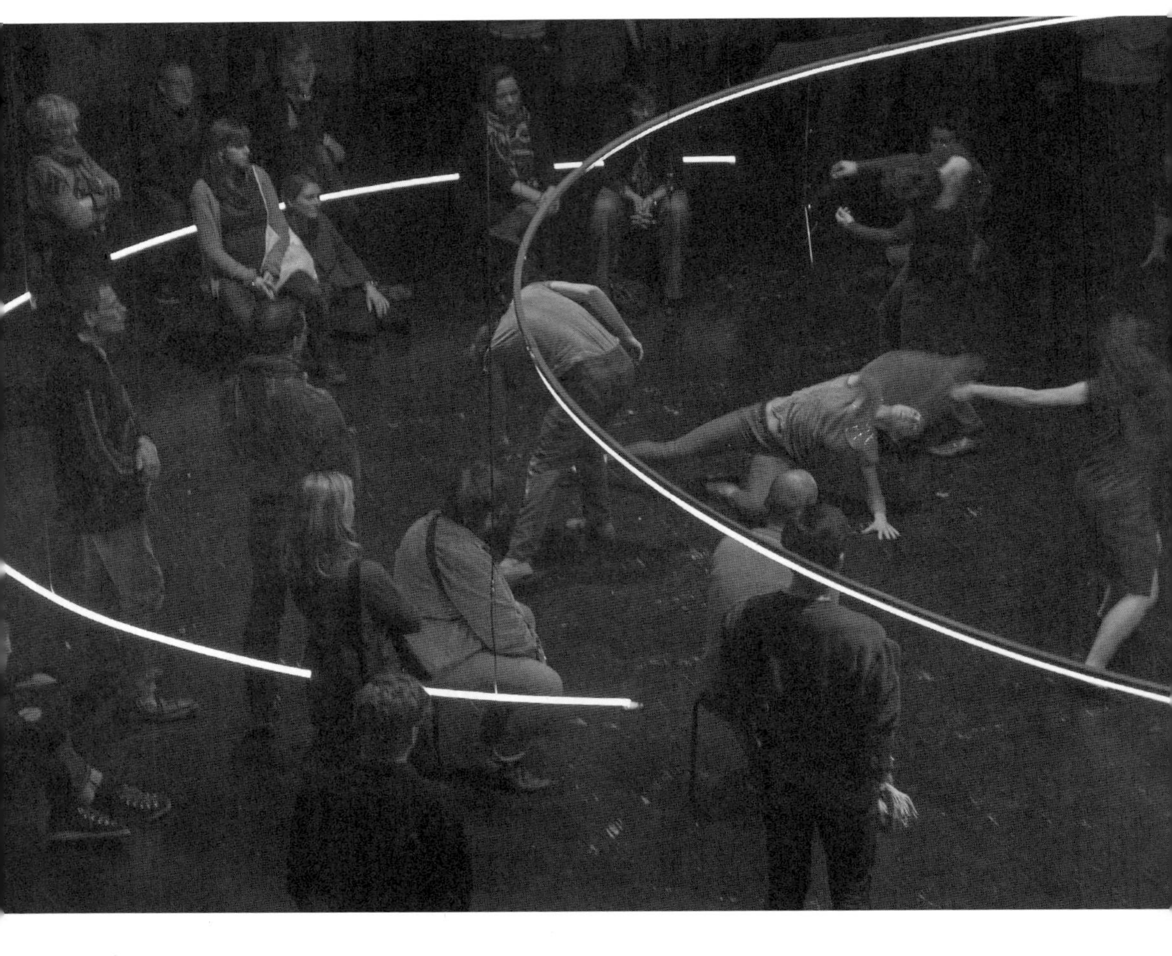

3.1 *Danserye* at Sophiensaele, Berlin, 2013. Photo: Arne Schmitt.

and were thus ambiguous information that forced people to make their own decisions about what was going on and how to respond to it.

To create the choice of multiple perspectives of observing (like watching the dance from inside or outside the semicircles) and different forms of participation (like acting as a musician using the bells provided or dancing by following the instructions of the caller) were indeed the goals of *Danserye*, which was a collaboration between composer Michael Wolters, visual artists Awst and Walter, and myself. I expected the various performances to be quite different due to peoples' choices and was surprised to see distinct patterns of behaviour emerge in the course of thirty-five shows in venues in four European countries.

It became clear that audiences used behavioural knowledge from other public contexts, while dancers needed to combine their performance mode with a more urban social attitude to facilitate the establishment of something like an urban public space. Although theatres are semipublic places, where one needs to buy a ticket to enter, it seems that by removing the theatrical conventions of seats and proscenium the behaviour pattern of immersed observation that was established by the bourgeois theatre (Wiles 2003, 229) is destabilized. In the dark theatre, the spectator is supposed to sit motionless so that he or she can be isolated from other spectators and engrossed in the aesthetic experience of the performers' bodies undisturbed and hence forgetting his or her own body (Eikels 2013, 119). In contrast, *Danserye*'s open performance setup offered individuals who do not necessarily have a relation to each other (apart from occupying the same space) the opportunity to encounter each other in a public manner (Goffman 1963, 35). *Danserye* amplified its publicness through its bright lighting, which meant that everybody present could see each other without exposing the audience in an intimidating way. Such visibility is necessary to transform dance from a privately immersed experience into a public art.

Sociologist Lyn Lofland (1998, 26) defines the public realm as a space in which interaction occurs between people who are strangers to one another. Lofland has defined five overarching principles of stranger interaction, all of which I was able to identify during both dance installations, at the *Champ de pixels* and in *Danserye*: cooperative motility, civil inattention, audience role prominence, restrained helpfulness, and civility towards diversity (see also Vernet, this volume). *Cooperative motility*, which Lofland defines as how "strangers work together to traverse space without incident" (29) could be observed when people formed an orderly line so as to have a better view, positioning themselves parallel to the action of the dancers or when audiences followed the performers' paths at an even distance through the installation. Following Goffman's idea, Lofland understands *civil inattention* as what "makes possible copresence without commingling, awareness without engrossment, courtesy without conversation" (30). This was evident in *Danserye* and at the *Champ de pixels* in the acknowledging but disengaging glances of audience members passing by each other as they moved through the space. It was even used by audience members toward the dancers and musicians when the latter were not intentionally being "available as a source of embodied information" (Goffman 1963, 15), for instance, when they were moving in a more pedestrian way to position themselves in the space between and during scenes.

Audience role prominence is Lofland's idea that "inhabitants of the public realm act primarily as audience to the activities that surround them" (1998, 31). It was constituted in the *Champ de pixels* by newcomers who preferred to join other viewers to create crowds of bodies in the otherwise empty space. In *Danserye*, it could be observed when audiences did not move during the whole performance and decided to sit close to others or stand in the very back for the entire piece. For Lofland, "specifically targeted and clearly limited requests for mundane assistance and a response of *restrained helpfulness* … are a constant feature of life in public places" (32, emphasis added). This principle was demonstrated in *Danserye* when one of the music scores was pushed off its stand by a passing audience member. A witness to the incident only hesitantly picked it up to return it to its proper place but in such a restrained manner that the score was placed on its stand upside down. In the *Champ de pixels*, newcomers asked other people in the audience about the nature of the performance. Following the principle of restrained helpfulness, they were answered with a short explanation, which would not have been possible (or necessary) during a proper performance in a theatre.

The principle of *civility towards diversity* needs to be adjusted to be applicable here. As Lofland explains, this principle "specifies that in face-to-face exchanges, confronted with what may be personally offensive visible variations in physical abilities, beauty, skin color and hair texture, dress style, demeanor, income, sexual preference, and so forth, the urbanite will act in a civil manner, that is will act 'decently' vis-à-vis diversity" (1998, 32). For me, the term "offensive" is misplaced and requires redefinition. I believe this urban code of social conduct could better be labelled as "indifference" or "universality of treatment" (33) in situations of obvious breach of the normative matrix. Passing pedestrians showed civility towards diversity in the *Champ de pixels* when they moved close to the performance situation with only a short glance, as if this kind of performance of forcefully contracting people in the snow at the Place des Festivals were the most normal thing in the world to see on the streets of Montreal. In the performance situation of *Danserye* the principle was not obvious, since an audience expects the theatre to be a place where diverse actions can be performed that are not possible or acceptable in a public space. However, the wrist or ankle bells, which could perhaps make you feel a bit like a sheep, were rarely refused when they were handed out at the shows. Audiences always eyed them sceptically but then handled them as if it were an accepted practice to have a bell attached to your hand that makes every step you take audible.

Drawing on these five principles, I would like to claim that the choreographic installation in the *Champ de pixels* and the performance *Danserye* both create spaces that are similar to the public realm and at the same time offer platforms to play or experiment with perspectives on public behaviour and different interactions between art and the public. Can the social dynamics that regulate urban spaces be also found or investigated in these platforms?

Since Georg Simmel ([1903]1950), urban life has been described as the close assembly of differentiated social relations and actions. Urbanist Edward W. Soja further developed Simmel's notion, describing the dynamic processes of urban copresence that provide a constantly evolving source of stimulating social synergy with the term *synekism* (2003, 274). Deriving the term from *synoikismos,* Soja defines it as "the conditions that derive from dwelling together in a particular home place or space" (273). Used in biology to refer to "an association of species to the benefit of at least one (but no harm to the others)" (273), one can apply it in the urban context to mean living together creatively and supportively. Can the mere physical copresence of audience and performers enable *synekism* in a performing arts context as well?

As dance performances, *Danserye* and the *installation chorégraphique participative* focus attention on the body, giving us the opportunity to explore the performativity of physical movements to create patterned encounters and their potential to constitute group dynamics. These patterned encounters create different ways of addressing people copresent in spaces defined above as public realms. Following Michael Warner, a public "exists by virtue of being addressed" (2002, 50, emphasis removed). Hence, describing dance encounters in both cases can shed light on the constitution of urban publics through movement. The interaction of people copresent at the performances provides insight into the kinds of social synergy that can be created through different types of encounters.

I now use Lofland's categories to take a closer look at three dance encounters in which specific ways of relating to and experiencing other bodies in space were observed:

(1) the performative body as an object of inquiry in the context of audience role prominence;

(2) audiences and performers structuring the performative space as a landscape through civil inattention;

(3) a feedback loop in which the movements of both performers and audience members create a basis for the emergence of the choreography as a principle of cooperative motility.[3]

DANCE ENCOUNTER #1: THE PERFORMATIVE BODY IN THE CONTEXT OF *AUDIENCE ROLE PROMINENCE*

In *Behavior in Public Places*, Erving Goffman claims that copresence enables face-to-face interaction "with a richness of information flow and facilitation of feedback" that results in various kinds of encounters (1963, 17). Goffman further defines encounters or "face engagements" as "all those instances of two or more participants in a situation joining each other openly in maintaining a single focus of cognitive and visual attention" (89). As mentioned above, Lofland argues that in public spaces people engage easily in a single focus of cognitive and visual attention within an audience role, which can be described as a static positioning of oneself across from the event, within the "interactional territory" (Streeck and Knapp 1992, 5), yet at a certain distance that is often decided by the first person who takes up the audience role.

This behaviour pattern was clearly practiced and further refined in the *Champ de pixels*. Because the installation took up such a vast space, one could engage as an audience member from any point of its periphery – meaning the outermost row of lights – and have a clear and uninterrupted view of the entire event. However, people who joined the audience mostly chose a position parallel to the rows of lights, taking a position within the interactional territory, rather than choosing to stand at a corner of the square in order to maximize their field of vision. Yet another pattern appeared in the *Champ de pixels* that further defined audience role prominence: people joining the audience gathered into a group, clump or row with other audiences who had already positioned themselves. This urge to group together was so strong that when entering the installation, people made the long trip along the space to join the other peoples' perspective on the dancing bodies, rather than positioning themselves at the point where they had entered the Place des Festivals. Their entry into an aesthetic encounter in public space was guided by grouping up as a crowd.

Jacques Rancière points out that the subject of an aesthetic experience is "not the population in its entirety, the intermingling of all classes, but a subject without particular identity, whose name is 'anybody'" (2006, 78). Placing oneself within the group creates a safety zone into which one can vanish, losing one's singularity and position as a body. Rancière's aesthetic *anybody* is not about equalizing differences but rather disappearing as a subject. This is only possible in the intermingling of one's singular body with a number of people making up the group. At the *Champ de pixels*, a single viewer would be marked as part of the choreography, since it used the whole surrounding urban environment, including pedestrians, as a physical frame for the dancing. In addition, the body shape made by winter clothes resulted in an abstract identity that was an integral part of the scene. Only the clusters of audience became "black holes" that were excluded from the arrangement of moving and static bodies, differing from the rest of the situation and creating an opposition between performers and audience that was coded with reference to traditional performance practices in theatres.

In the theatrical context, the most common encounter in a dance performance is the collective observation of a dancer's body executing a dance. In *Danserye,* when audiences first entered the space they stayed by themselves or with their companions, keeping a respectful distance from people unknown to them without creating the group that marks the audience role. Without exception one could observe people moving closer together when the performers started to dance. Once a dancer exhibited a virtuosic and nonpedestrian movement, audiences turned to face that movement, marking it as a performance. The out-of-the-ordinary event triggered the role of the audience, dividing the group into active performers and visibly static observing audiences in an instant. The composition of groups could change quite quickly, and the performers were included in the audience group by moving into a pedestrian body posture and by addressing their gaze toward the same dancing body or bodies.

In figure 3.2, we see individuals not known to each other – dancer and audience – become a group as part of an encounter with a moving body intentionally made available for the observing aesthetic gaze due to its virtuosic movement. As theatre scholar Kai van Eikels (2011, 5) succinctly puts it, "Aesthetics sets up collectivity by providing a symbolic economy that enables, and eventually motivates, individuals to imagine themselves as belonging to a community of art appreciators." Drawing on the work of philosopher and playwright Friedrich Schiller, Eikels points to a political pedagogy that emerges from the egalitarian potential inherent in aesthetic pleasure, which consists in "making [audiences] become *familiar with an anybody-ness* ingrained in subjectivity [of art appreciation], an in-difference of subjective self-appreciation against its outside where the I appears as one more example of a human being" (2011, 5, emphasis in original). The privilege of being this aesthetic "anybody" offers a security that shields the individual from being exposed and therefore having his or her differences exposed (as would be the case for the single body seen across the *Champ de pixels* outside the group). Although the dancer wears a costume and clearly differs from the audiences, addressing the gaze to the aesthetic body of the dancer creates a collective or, following Warner's definition, an urban public with an inherent egalitarian potential. However, the synergy of that potential undermines interaction among the art appreciators and implies a different type of engagement with the event. Even though they are grouped close together, the interaction between people does not become intimate, resembling a situation in an elevator where nothing personal is revealed. It was rare that audience members stepped out singularly from the group, to engage with the light installation or to follow the dancers as they made

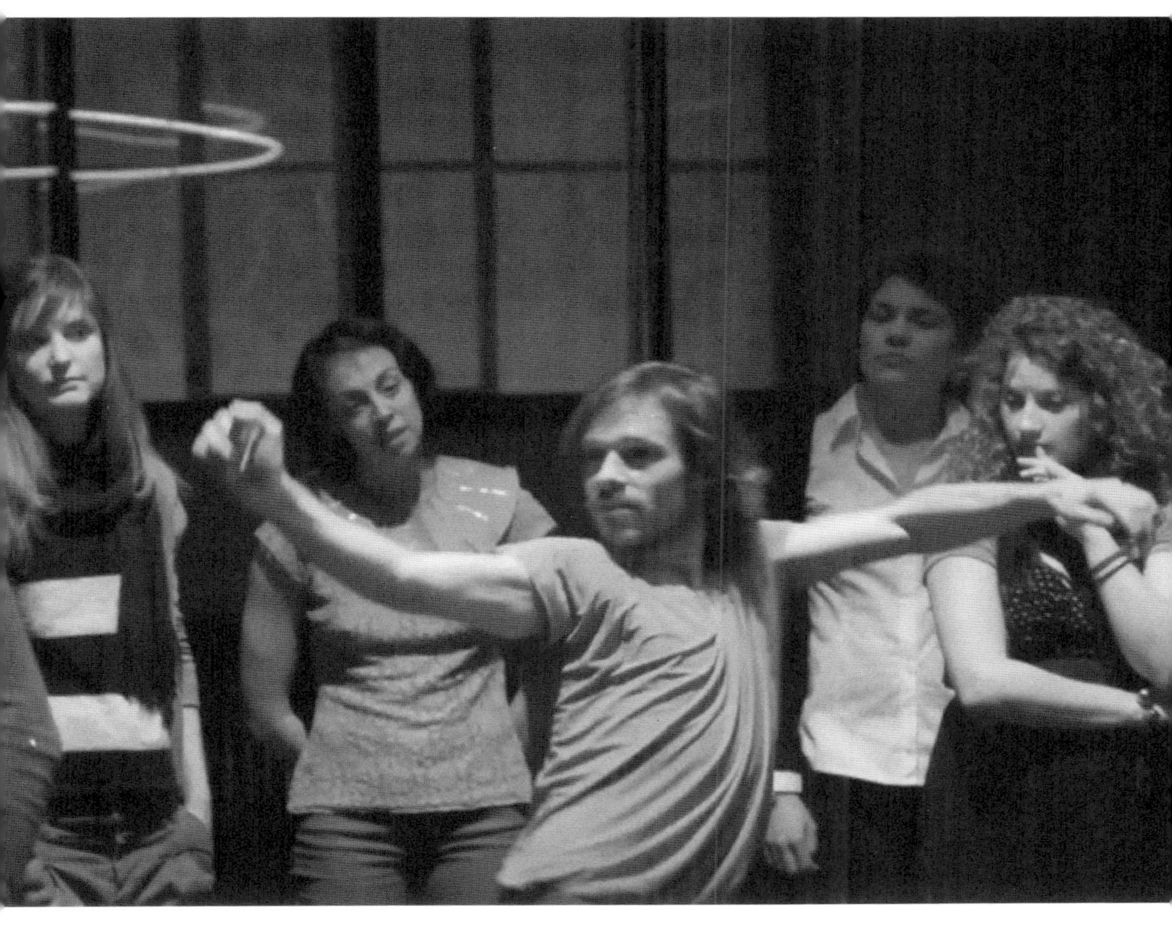

3.2 Lisanne Goodhue watching Isaac Spencer dance in *Danserye* at Dampfzentrale Berne, 2013. Film still: Oliver Clarke.

their way through the installation, once their audience position had been established. Audience role prominence when constituting an urban public mutes their choices to act. Only as smaller groups or if personally invited did people move out into the space from their place of security. This dance encounter therefore cannot offer a collective development of the event, as the visitors stay outside of the action and its assembly produces a passive group dynamic rather than the stimulus through interaction that Soja claims for synekism in urban spaces.

DANCE ENCOUNTER #2: THE PERFORMATIVE SPACE AS A LANDSCAPE OF *CIVIL INATTENTION*

In contrast to the behaviour patterns typical of the theatre performance, where there is a single collective focus, knowledge of aesthetic encounters in the museum or gallery context was utilized in both the *Champ de pixels* and *Danserye*. While the *installation chorégraphique participative* was framed by a preexisting visual art installation (the interactive light installation), it was the enormity of the space that gave people the impulse to move out of the audience groupings to follow the dancers as they danced towards the distance, thereby establishing another dance encounter. As there were twenty-four dancers in the choreography, one could not follow a single group as they danced across the space but rather had to choose an individual performer and share his or her trajectory in one's movement patterns. This created a situation similar to a gallery space, where visitors choose their own path through the exhibition, deciding on their own points of interest and duration of engagement. Some audience members/participants stopped to play with the lights while disregarding the performers, treating the latter like passing pedestrians with the appropriate attitude of civil inattention: that is, with a glance of recognition and maybe a fleeting smile but without engrossment, in a way not meant to foster focused attention. During the dancing in the furthest reaches of the space, audience members and performers found themselves alone with each other. In those moments, individuals were not shielded by a group anymore and could meet the performers on an individual level in a face-to-face unit of interaction. Following Karen Prager (1995, 21), this can be understood as an intimate interaction where something personal is revealed: in the face-to-face unit interaction the *anybodyness* peeled off and the audience member was addressed, making it a personal matter. On the side of the performer, the isolation in the huge space undermined the performance attitude and for a moment let the dancer step out of the representational mode. Civil inattention then allowed the dancer – after a short smile and eye contact – to continue the choreography without ignoring and distancing the person. It offered courtesy and respect in this intimate situation without requiring either participant to stay longer and gave the performer the option to dance away dynamically. The use of civil inattention between performers, viewers, and other pedestrians thus created a respectful and inviting space for everybody to be in. Everybody had their space and position within the installation no matter what choice they made. By combining the wandering of a gallery and the respectful social codes of an urban environment with civil inattention, the *installation chorégraphique participative* created a collective landscape of bodies that constituted the choreography.

Similar to the collective landscape of bodies in the *Champ de pixels*, the section called "musical map" of *Danserye* led all musicians and dancers to spread out into different areas of the room, engaging in independent and interchanging improvised scenes of solos, duets, or trios. Dancers moved next to standing or seated musicians, danced with each other, or danced entirely alone, with or without anyone watching them.

Audiences here also needed to choose where or what to observe and when to disengage from the event. They could choose a new location or position or move further away in order to take in the space in its entirety. When a dancer is left alone with a single audience member, the *anybodyness* of the aesthetic encounter again loses its effect. But due to the relatively stationary position of both performer and audience, the encounter becomes even more intimate than the ever-traveling dances in the *Champ de pixels* and hence creates individual scenes within the meta structure of the musical map. This "intimate capsule" of face-to-face interaction including both dancer and audience member in the performance can become for a third audience member or group the main focus of the choreography, as in figure 3.3.

Similarly, theorist and curator Irit Rogoff (2005, 129) suggests exchanging the privileged moment of an encounter with an art object with a single focus of attention in the exhibition space, for the experience of divided attention towards its surrounding contexts and multiple perspectives.

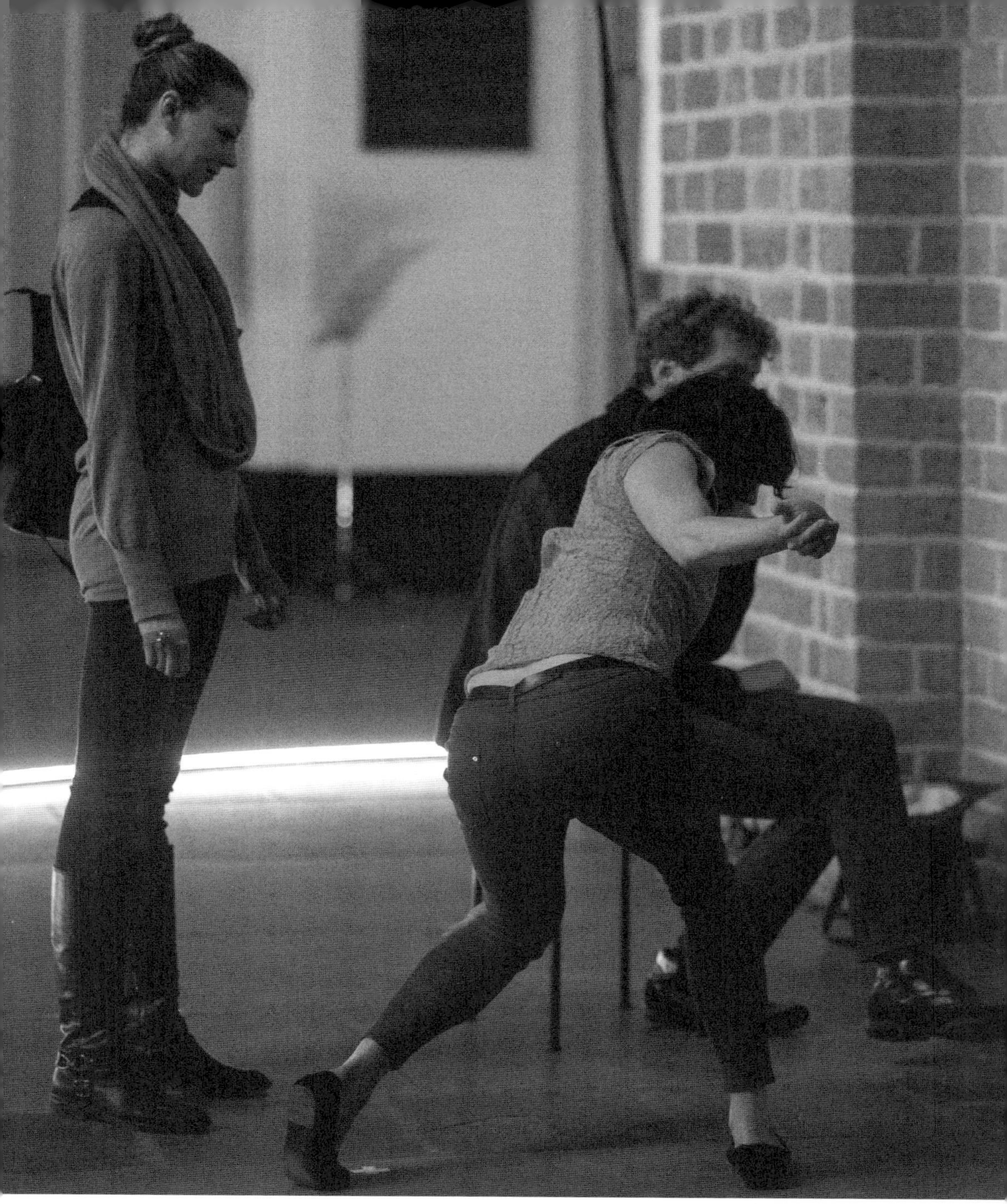

3.3 Lisanne Goodhue dancing in an "intimate capsule" with an audience member during *Danserye* at the Spring Festival in Utrecht, the Netherlands, 2013. Photo: Arne Schmitt.

She describes how a fellow visitor in an art exhibition turned out to be a TV star and how the excitement of meeting her added another layer to the space. In following her around, being mesmerized by her beauty and speculating on her relationship to her companion, Rogoff's attention in the exhibition was divided between the interpellation of the art of Jackson Pollock and that of the star. "Not only was one mythic structure [that of Hollywood celebrity] mobilized in relation to another one, that of the exhibition, but the viewing position, an alternate of imbricated fan as opposed to reverential spectator was put into play by this disruption" (130). The attention divided between the star and the art objects offers a different perspective on Rogoff's own position as a spectator of the art event, bringing her role and the regimes here at play into question. Following Rogoff, dividing my attention in *Danserye* among those who are present while moving around the little dance scenes, past them, in between them, causes my physical presence to erupt into the experience of the choreographic art event for everyone present in the space and into its very constitution. Questions of one's own position, one's role, and the condition of one's body in the moment of the performance are mobilized by the conjunction of the realm of audience and performers for the viewer witnessing the intimate capsules of face-to-face units.

The short glances and smiles between performers and audience members, recognizing each other lightly in a form of civil inattention, are crucial for the mobilization of divided attention. It marks a distance from one another within the intimacy of the scenes that are constituted by the physical presence of both and signals that either the performer or audience member could disengage from the other without being disrespectful. These encounters of disengagement allow performers and audiences to leave the other in their respective activity of dancing or observing without pressuring them with the responsibility to continue constituting the intimate scene. The mode of civil inattention is thus essential for the functioning of fluctuations in the choreographic landscape, as the direct gaze as a mode of address nails audiences (and performers) to a position from which they can hardly escape, denying them the choice of where to direct their attention. Through the freedom of choice provided by civil inattention, audiences can let their attention be divided from the single perspective of the aesthetic body towards a network of standing, sitting, and walking bodies between distributed dances, composing a random choreographic landscape of independent yet interrelated bodies. This in turn highlights one's own body positioning as intrinsically choreographic.

Without the ability to be openly inattentive in a respectful manner towards another person, one cannot divide one's attention among other layers of the performance event. With art objects this is not so problematic but for an open dance encounter this is crucial. Hence, the freedom of disengagement that civil inattention offers aids in distributing attention and pushing the audience out of being "anybody" into participating as "somebody" in this network of events, all the while without expecting this somebody to act in any particular way. This dance encounter functions through the division of attention and enables the audience member to participate with self-directed engagements, physical as well as intellectual, wandering from interaction to interaction in a coproduced matrix of interrelated bodies. Addressing an audience member as "somebody" in the performance gives them a conscious perspective on the constitution of the event and an awareness of their own role in its formulation. This dance encounter thus has the potential to open up an awareness of the constitution and production of urban public space. The intervention and disruption that is created through fluctuating engagements in the performance can generate critical viewpoints. That said, the constant (re)addressing of the gaze to different situations without committing to them creates a space that is dynamically static. The interaction in this kind of urban public will stay isolated, distant, and divided; given that it can hardly develop a creative and supportive group dynamic, it cannot be described as Soja's synekism.

DANCE ENCOUNTER #3: A FEEDBACK LOOP OF COOPERATIVE MOTILITY

The *installation chorégraphique participative* gave a glimpse of how a developing interaction between dancers and audiences could function as a supportive group dynamic when a line of dancers following each other moved parallel to the walkway, going in the same direction as passing pedestrians (figure 3.4). Their choreographic material and body posture were similar to a walking action, with a bit more forceful momentum or thrust forward than a normal walking stride. In between steps each dancer contracted their trunk arhythmically. Coincidentally, it happened on a few

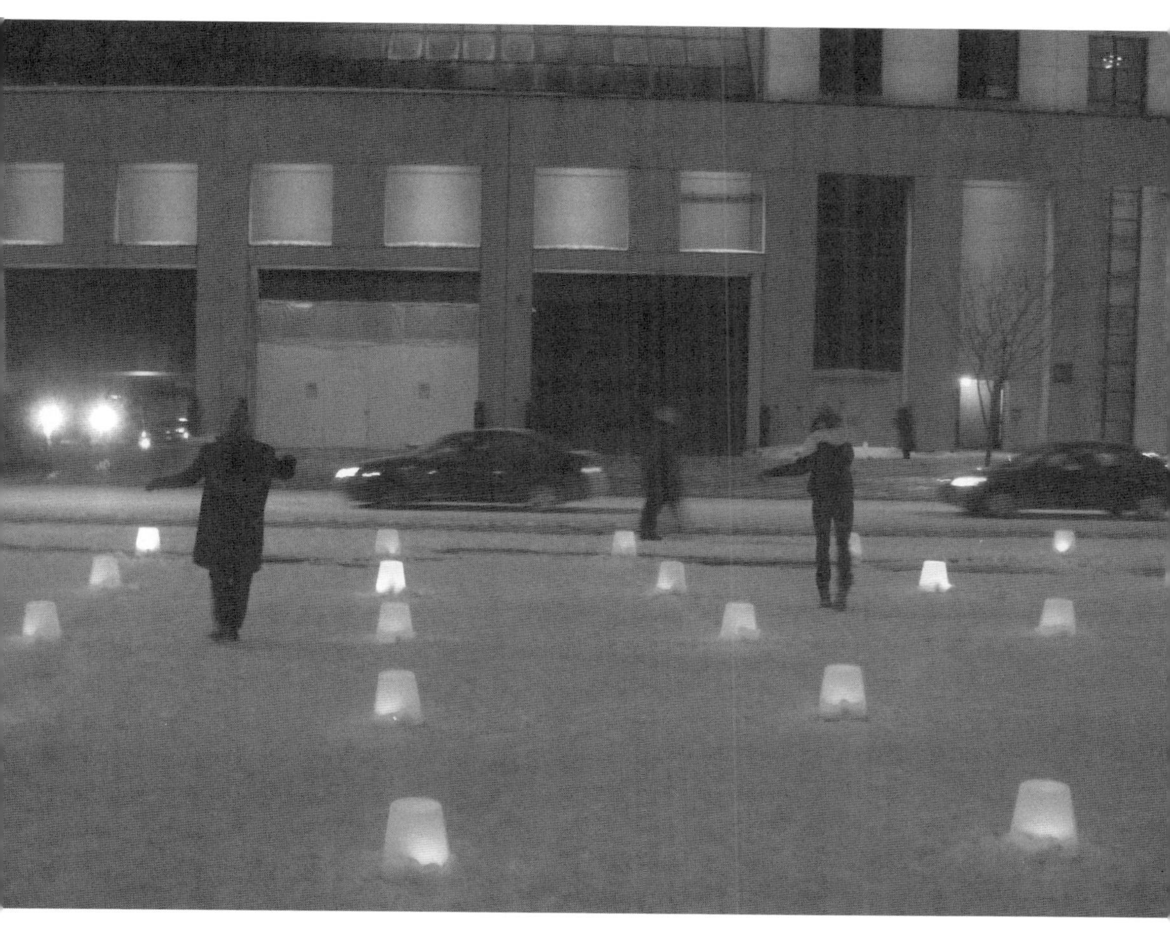

3.4 Two dancers in formation in the *installation chorégraphique participative* at the
Champ de pixels at the Place des Festivals, Montreal, 2009.
Photo: Sebastian Matthias.

occasions that the dancers came level with passersby, and they walked for a few paces with each other. When a dancer passed one pedestrian with this thrusting stride forward, the pedestrian seemed also to speed up a little, synchronizing their momentum with the dancer. With the next dancer passing right behind the impulse from the thrust forward continued, even though the first dancer had already passed. Together, the group of pedestrians and performers had a momentary baseline of physical trajectory from which the contracting trunk movements developed like ornaments. Only after the last of the dancers had distanced himself from the walkway did the synchronizing movements of the pedestrian noticeably slow down. Although it was difficult to observe from a distance, it seemed that in at least one such coincidence the pedestrian maintained the induced speed. From this observation, we can infer that certain dance encounters can affect the movements of other bodies in proximity, such that the assembled bodies can support each other in a choreographic effort. This choreographic engagement can usefully be understood as an urban encounter that follows the principle of cooperative motility. It is quite similar to situations at a busy train station when you slip in between people in the crowd, matching and sensing their flow of movement in order to pass more easily through the space.

This principle could even be observed in a choreography that does not *a priori* imply an audience in motion. The section "Allemande" of *Danserye* uses a movement improvisation system that we call a "movement quality." In this continuous periodic movement system, the dancers try to endlessly unravel an instigating impulse of momentum in their bodies. They take the momentum from an arc into the air, letting the curve pass through their body without letting the thrust of the impulse be interrupted. The limbs of the body seem to be expanded or filled locally, and then this filling travels through the dancer's whole body, letting the dancer "ride" its momentum continuously. If it is too slow, the movement needs more effort; if it is too fast the filled body cannot be sustained.[4] While observing the dancers, I could sometimes detect that audience members moved their bodies along with the dancers' bodies, apparently subconsciously following their momentum. The most obvious example was a female audience member in a performance in Freiburg, Germany who moved circularly along with the dancers without seemingly trying to perform. In the same section of the performance, one could observe other audience members keeping their eyes unfocused and not directly on the dancers. One audience member in Basel kept his arms spread in this unfocused encounter, as if sensing his own body. He later explained in the discussion after the show that he could physically sense "dance" for the first time. How can this encounter be understood? How can the movement of some bodies physically affect other bodies?

In my research on nightclub dancing, I have come to recognize the potential of periodic "bouncing." A "bounce" is the most common movement pattern in a club, when you drop your knees a little to let the elasticity of your legs bounce up, jolting against gravity. The force of tension brings the weight of the body back to straight legs where they left off. A bounce is inherent in the famous "step-touch" when club dancers sway from one leg to the other, tapping their foot on each side while bending or rather bouncing their knees with the beat on each step. Bounce as a movement quality is very potent to stimulate entrainment and to activate an interactive rhythmic matrix of moving bodies on the dance floor. For Jessica Phillips-Silver et al. (2010), *entrainment* is a mode of perception of rhythms or periodic stimuli. The perception of visual, acoustic, or tactile rhythms is for her coupled across these modalities with motor synchronization. Entrainment, from "to entrain" or French *entraîner*, means being carried away or swept along. It implies a certain unintentional action that is also found in the idea of information processing of entrainment. Bobbing one's head to a groove or dancing can be understood as entrainment to music; "being carried away by the music" is a common experience of how perception relates with acoustic information processing. Entrainment also hints at "to train" with its implication of repetition and learning. The process of perception, being a "technique of the body" (Mauss 1978, 202), implies a system of internalized cultural practices, which, following Pierre Bourdieu (1977, 124), are learned, not natural. This sensory motor feedback facilitates the perception of complex temporal structures (Phillips-Silver et al. 2010, 4), which are trained repetitively as cultural practices.[5]

In clubbing, dancers don't relate only to the music but also to other dancers. The periodic stimuli of surrounding bouncing bodies offer targets for entrainment, which will generate new bouncing stimuli. Through entraining, each receiver of rhythmic visual information will extend and sustain the information flow as a sender. A group of dancers on the dance floor bouncing with each other to the beat are paradoxically rarely dancing in unison. One can observe that the heads move arhythymically in the crowd, while their knees seem to be quite musically on the beat. Each dancer has a different anatomical structure, which, depending on the tension in the joints, the length of the spine or variation of the distribution of the movement impulse from the knees, will produce different durations until the bounce impulse manifests in a visible movement in the neck. Visual synchronization with dancing can thus be targeted at different parts of the body wave that comes up from the bounce in the knees. A dancer can for example entrain to the wider arc of the chest with his hips, varying the movement material that keeps the dance floor moving and changing for as long as the quality of the movement keeps the same synchronizing capacity. Synchronizing dance movements in clubs function like other synchronizing mechanisms, only between independent oscillating systems, which in this situation are individual moving dancers. If one dancer holds still on the dance floor, he interrupts everybody else's dancing process and usually gets irritated glances. For the feedback loop to function, each person must act independently. In synchronizing mechanisms, rhythms will never be identical due to their constant readjustment, so one could call this transmission of rhythms an "irreducibly collective performance of reciprocal measuring of time" (Eikels 2013, 170).

Furthermore, the bouncing body affects our awareness of our own physical sensations. The concept of proprioception, put forth by Brian O'Shaughnessy (1995, 183), suggests that our "postural and kinesthetic sensations" depend on nerve endings all over the surface of the body. Every change of relation of body parts to each other generates a difference in proprioceptive knowledge, bringing those body parts into awareness. Through constant shifts in posture, our physical awareness is amplified. The amplified kinaesthetic sensations that are produced by the bounce will be adjusted and influenced within the entrainment mode of perception by the rhythmic matrix of movements surrounding the dancer in the club, thus creating an experience of "vibe," "connectedness," or "collective groove" as a primary experience of going clubbing. I call this dynamic process that provides a constantly evolving source of social synergy "choreographic groove."[6]

To a certain degree, what functions in the club also seems to work in the performance context. Dancers in the "Allemande" section of *Danserye* claim that it is easier to dance the periodic patterns of its movement system when in proximity to other bodies moving with the same movement quality. It seems that the periodic movement pattern of "Allemande" has the same entrainment capacities as a bounce and can produce its own choreographic groove. The production of motor synchronization in audiences, as well as a change of sensation in the body through the movement that was described above, would be the outcome of these entrainment capacities. The dance encounter in a choreographic groove changes the relation of performer and audience in *Danserye* into a matrix of (rhythmic) autonomous interrelated bodies that can create synekism through their copresence. The assembly of moving bodies opens up the possibility of reciprocal support for each other, as well as being a source of innovation and variation.

In the context of the *Champ de pixels*, the choreographic groove raises the question of self-awareness and intention among the assembled people. The pedestrians walking next to the installation did not intentionally participate in the choreography. Maybe they were not even aware of the group of dancers next to them. Yet in this instance, it didn't matter if they were audience members or not: their determined movement was enough to support the group. Body parts interacted with body parts and not people with people. In the club context, Phil Jackson (2004, 93) claims that a techno party is only successful in creating the emotional surplus of groove if everybody present is determined to take part in the event: "The party arises from people's determination to participate. It must become visible on the surface of the flesh." In a club, interaction with face-to-face units is not required for an encounter with the choreographic groove. One interacts mainly with the other dancers without their awareness; addressing a direct gaze or even civil inattention toward them is distracting. When one dances in front of a DJ booth and then turns around, the gazes of the dancers behind can be intimidating. In this cultural context, one usually entrains to movements that surround the dancer rather than to movements in face-to-face positioning. When dancing in the crowd only certain aspects of each person's dancing become visible. A head movement can interact with an arm movement, which doesn't need to be recognized by the other person. In this scattered information exchange of visible stimuli dancers interact intensely with each other but more with body parts rather than as subjects. In this perspective I want to frame this communication process as *a*-subjective rather than personal or intimate. Dancing here is a different form of communication that is mediated not through a directed reading of gestures with a single focus of attention but by letting the visual qualities of movements on the "surface of the flesh" enter, unguided, into the visual field. The pedestrian in the *installation chorégraphique participative* doesn't need to be aware of the dancers; peripheral perception of their movement in the field of vision is enough to facilitate his or her own strides. The urban public that creates the choreographic groove is thus not determined by intention but by mere copresence – simultaneously occupying the same space. Through entrainment, the movement that one makes while in the presence of others can affect them. If we take entrainment as a mode of perception as our starting point, then the mechanisms of the urban phenomenon of "city flow" could be understood as a distinct kind of an urban public.

In the 1983 film *Koyaanisqatsi*, Godfrey Reggio and Phillip Glass beautifully capture how people flow along the sidewalk and point to the possible performativity of periodic patterns in the city with Glass's minimalist music. Without doubt people use intentional actions to guide themselves around obstacles with focused engagements. However, I believe that entrained engagement also plays a part in the negotiation of cooperative motility. The thrust of walking functions as a movement quality that can foster choreographic groove. Based on similar periodic movement patterns side by side on the street, choreographic groove can facilitate one's own way of walking and also determine the quality of flow of that walk. The collective speed of walking in New York City, for example, could then be understood as a collective performance of reciprocal measuring of the qualities of walking, which in turn affects cooperative motility. Robert Levine found that there is a constant walking tempo that seems to be specific to each city (1997, 8). Entrainment could help explain that constant. The tension, bounce, or relaxedness of city life would not be a given of a particular city but rather the product of collective negotiation of its quality of moving. In the film and research of William H. Whyte, *The Social Life of Small Urban Spaces* (1980, 1988), one can see that the collective relaxation on city plazas is not negotiated by face-to-face units. If one wants to relax on a plaza, Whyte shows that one keeps one's distance from the others. I would speculate that behind the person or in the periphery of their visual field, synchronization processes would be at play. This means that we could understand public spaces (like, say, Times Square) as negotiated through sensations of proprioception and, indeed, choreographic groove. As entrainment functions through unfocused engagements, Simmel's detached urban cosmopolitanism with his idea of the "blasé" attitude in urban life (Simmel [1903] 1950) would derive not from too many stimuli but rather from rhythmic interaction. The existence of choreographic groove needs to be further researched in the city itself and can only be put forth here as an idea. However, its existence would change how we understand the potential of cooperative motility and the effect our behaviour has in places of assembly in the public realm.

DANCING URBAN PUBLICS

What I have tried to outline using the three examples of dance encounters is that with a diversified approach to perceiving dance one can reconfigure the constitution of dance performance in both theatres and public spaces. Each relation between audiences and performers – constituted by their physical positioning, kind of gaze, social addressing, and type of choreographic material – works towards different behaviour patterns and specific engagements. Virtuosic, out-of-the-ordinary movement patterns evoke an audience role with a single-focus attention that provoke a sensation of *anybodyness*, while interchanging dancing moves with pedestrian patterns bring about a divided attention, distributed away from a single-focus event towards all the bodies and actions in the situation, facilitated by civil inattention. The processing of periodic movement patterns through entrainment as a choreographic groove can function as a dance encounter and is not carried within the interactional territory of intimate face-to-face units. Each of the three modes of engagement draws differently on the principles of the urban public realm to address copresent others in a particular way thus producing a specific urban public. When dance as a performing art is situated in experimental spaces – whether in urban public spaces or theatres – it can function as a platform for testing behaviour patterns and as a practice of perception and engagement that can create new lines of inquiry into the sociality of urban public space. However, theatres as a test site always create a self-consciousness in viewers and participants. Audiences come into the art event and art context knowingly, and this self-awareness colours their behaviour. Dance in theatres is also more frequented by certain social groups and operates within a class structure. It cannot stand in for the diversity that is one of the defining features of the public realm. For that reason, it has been very productive and important for me to engage with setups like the *Champ de pixels*. In contrast, the theatre offers a safe space to try out other experiments in dance that would be refused in public space due to the principle of civility towards diversity: viewers would seem to ignore the experiments, rather than engage with them. The theatre offers a different experimental attitude and a willingness to stay for the duration necessary to overcome one's own habitus of viewing. The experience with the "Allemande" in *Danserye* shows that a certain length of time must be spent with the quality in order to establish its repetition and to enable the audience to alter their gaze. In public space, in a moment of boredom or confusion one would leave to continue on one's errands. To continue this dance-driven inquiry into the sociality of urban public space, a comparative approach involving an exchange and inclusion of different formats and contexts next to each other seems to be crucial and indeed would reflect the idea of the city as an agglomeration of different contexts coexisting next to and reciprocally informing each other.

Notes

1 Excerpts of the *installation chorégraphique participative* at *Champ de pixels* in Montreal can be viewed at https://www.youtube.com/watch?v=xBelZ_sIZJk. Accessed 29 May 2016.

2 A montage of excerpts for *Danserye* in Bern is available at https://vimeo.com/63808197. Accessed 29 May 2016.

3 With this argument I follow a line of thought put forth by Kai van Eikels (2013, 116) on participation in the performing arts, applying my research on groove to other audience/performer relations and their consequences.

4 Viewing example: https://vimeo.com/112579291. Password: allemande.

5 For further discussion of groove, *entrainment*, and how movement facilitates a positive emotional response to music, see Matthias (forthcoming).

6 Little research has been conducted about groove in dance. Jeff Pressing defines "groove" in African-American music as a "cognitive temporal phenomenon emerging from one or more carefully aligned concurrent

rhythmic patterns, characterized by [...] effectiveness in engaging
synchronizing body responses (e.g., dance, foot-tapping)" (2002, 288). While
understanding the term to be a fixed musical pattern, Tobias Widmaier
(2004) also connects groove to physical movements. He associates the term
with the pleasurable experience of the sexual act: "groove" has been used
in jazz music since the 1930s when it was a synonym for vagina in African-
American slang. The expression in jazz music "to get in the groove" had
the connotation of repeating, thrusting, and pulsing movements, which
where stimulated by the music and associated with movement sensations
during sex (Widmaier 2004, 2). For a discussion on groove in the context of
electronic dance music, see Butler (2006; 2012). Tim Olaveson and Melanie
Takahashi (2003) tried to prove in a collaborative study that the central
experience of going clubbing is the somatic sensation of "connectedness."
On "collective energy" see also Fikentscher (2000, 80). Over the next
three years, I will be conducting artistic research on this theme with the
performance series *groove space,* which began in Berlin and Zurich and
will continue to Freiburg (Germany), Jakarta, and Tokyo. This project is an
attempt to deepen my understanding of choreographic groove in the city
through different cultural contexts.

Robert Bean, Léola Le Blanc, Brian Lilley,
Barbara Lounder, and Mary Elizabeth Luka

4

—

NARRATIVES IN SPACE+TIME SOCIETY (NiS+TS): THE HIPPODROME PROJECT

We were so lucky –
Under a prairie-like sky
Two white Mercedes

Old men fly toy planes
Spy an illegal picnic
While orange blazer

Recites
Uncertainty

– Léola Le Blanc

Narratives in Space+Time Society (NiS+TS) is a locative media group based in Halifax that collaborates with artists, planners, urbanists, and members of the public in creative explorations of living networks and narratives created by walking, simultaneously mapping spatial and temporal connections between on-the-ground experiences, contemplative moments, curiosity, and discovery. NiS+TS created the *Hippodrome Project (Notes from the Desire Paths)*, a workshop for seventy-five people, at the defunct Montreal Hippodrome on 9 May 2013, during the international *Differential Mobilities* conference sponsored by the Pan-American Mobilities Network in collaboration with the European Cosmobilities Network.[1] These research networks investigate the movement of people, information, and objects of study. The 2013 conference focused on the dynamics of power implicit and explicit in the facilitation and deployment of such systemic movement, including access dependent on physical and other hierarchies and abilities. "Desire paths" are those unauthorized and unofficial walkways and trails that are created simply through processes of erosion as people walk where they want to (instead of where the sidewalk forces or permits them to). They are visible traces of the independent desire for movement, and relevant in any discussion of power and the facilitation of mobility. The Hippodrome project proved to be our initial foray into what has become a much longer and deeper process of research-creation and public art engagement incorporating practices of walking, historical storytelling, and dynamic presentations which grapple with present-day social issues.[2] At first drawing on the potential of Guy Debord's *dérive* (1958) to activate game theory in the context of Michel de Certeau's (1984) "practice of everyday life" through walking, the NiS+TS event at the Hippodrome entailed a rethinking of the relationship of urban narrative to public space in a research-creation context. Originally conceived as a small, optional workshop for up to fifteen people, after discussion with event organizers it grew to become the main evening event on the second day of the three-day conference.

The Montreal Hippodrome is a Foucauldian heterotopia: a liminal space of opportunities, histories, and disconnections sitting side by side (Foucault 1986). For more than one hundred years it was the Blue Bonnets Raceway, used for horse racing and betting (figure 4.1). Since 2009, the Hippodrome has accommodated rock concerts, dog walking, and off-site storage for city hospitals. A 43.5-hectare tract of "vacant" land on the edge of the urban core, it is slated to become a sustainable housing development, with 5,000 to 8,000 residential units planned (Bruemmer 2014; Rail 2012). Delving into the history of risky businesses on the site, including the spectacles of sulky racing and massive concerts, the site's pending redevelopment and its heterotopian nature, the NiS+TS event provided ten visceral, affective, and mediated experiences for participants. NiS+TS used a website, locative media app, live performances, great food, and free transportation to draw the *Differential Mobilities* participants to the site on 9 May. This "out of bounds" project used walking and other forms of self-propelled movement as heuristic methods for spatial investigations and interventions at the Hippodrome. Heuristics brings autobiography,

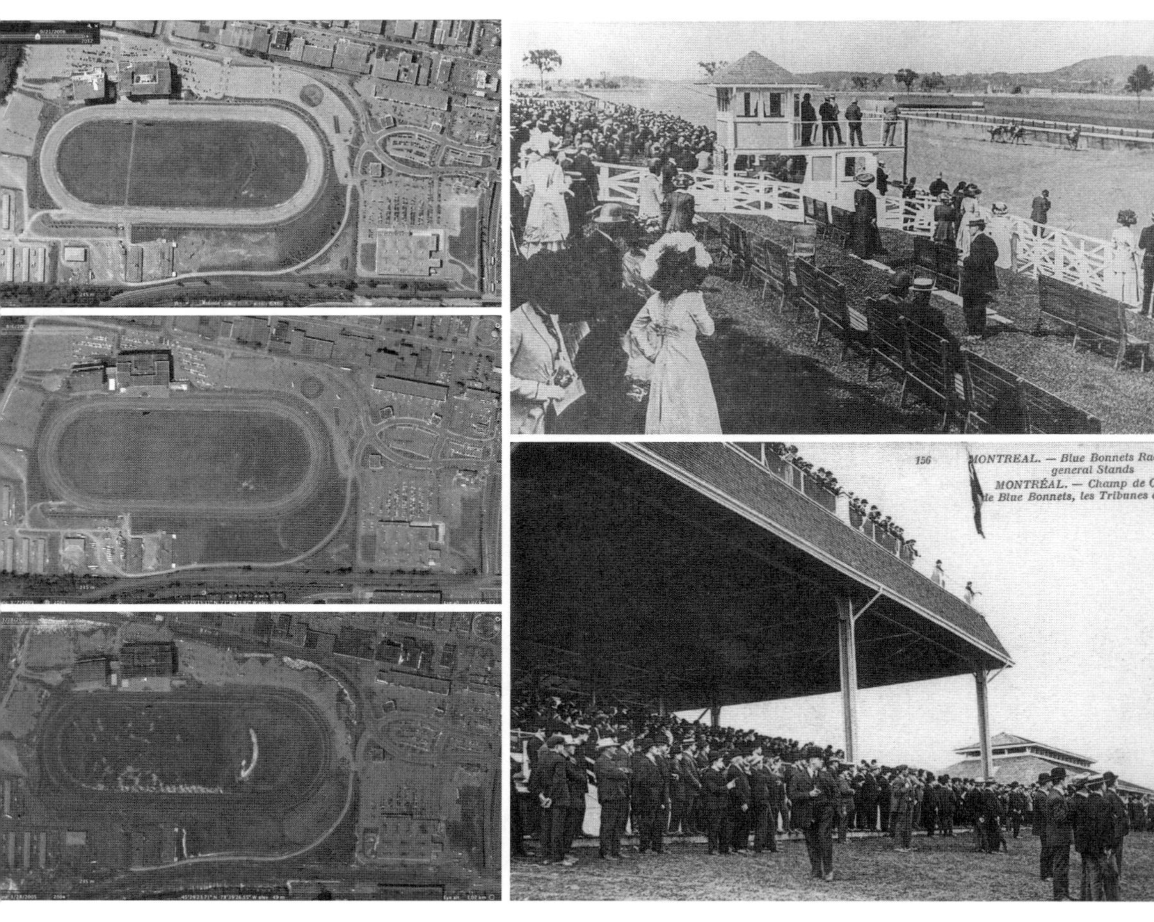

4.1 Exploring the site from a distance. Images were culled from left, Google Earth timeline, images Google, DigitalGlobe and right, local archives.

Above right, Blue Bonnets Race Track, Montreal, about 1910.
Print: Anonymous. McCord Museum.

Below right, General Stands, Blue Bonnets Racing Track, Montreal, about 1907.
Print: Neurdein Frères. McCord Museum.

sensory experience, intuition, social and political agendas, and common sense directly into research and can generate powerful methods in public processes such as envisioning and community consultation (Dunne 2001).

However, perhaps ironically, *Notes from the Desire Paths* began and ended remotely, across expanses of what is known as Hertzian space, which oscillates and resonates between people and their electronic devices, across networked electromagnetic fields, through time, utilizing varied communication approaches and forms of documentation. As Mark Shepard (2010, n.p.) notes:

> Today, as the data clouds of the twenty-first century descend on the streets, sidewalks, and squares of contemporary cities, we might ask: to what extent are these Hertzian weather systems becoming "as important, possibly more important" than built form in shaping our experience of the city? On any given day, we pass through transportation systems using magnetic stripe or Radio Frequency ID (RFID) tags to pay a fare; we coordinate meeting times and places through SMS text messaging on the run; we cluster in cafes and parks where WiFi is free; we move in and out of spaces blanketed by CCTV surveillance cameras; and we curse our wireless provider when its cell towers are not in reliable range of our place of residence. Hertzian space is all around us, coming in waves of various frequencies, lengths, and intervals, embedded in manifold ways within the course of our everyday lives.

The affordances of Hertzian technological devices in shaping today's social encounters seem to support optimistic interpretations of Henri Lefebvre's notion of the "moment [as] a fullness, a connection, a social connection of like-minded people" (Merrifield 2011, 479). In relation to Lefebvre's conceptualizing of rhythmanalysis as method (Ryan Moore 2013), Andy Merrifield analyzes such Lefebvrean moments as opportunities or expressions of the collision of world-historical time and the everyday time of lived experience. He reads a potential "politics of encounter" between people into these moments, allowing for citizen action, if citizens can only be mobilized (Merrifield 2011, 478). Similarly, by bringing people together in a specific place, NiS+TS intended for each person to engage with one another, with history, and with potential futures. Nathaniel Coleman (2013) employs an equally optimistic utopian approach that he also sees embedded in Lefebvre's work, particularly in relation to how citizens experience, understand, and influence their own urban environments. "Lefebvre's holistic critical method effectively reveals the interrelationship of social and architectural forms, including the economic and spatial conditions out of which they arise" (Coleman 2013, 351). From our perspective, then, the spatialized, historicized Hippodrome experience that we developed had the potential to generate an observable and idealized (or aspirational) form of civic engagement through a combination of Hertzian virtual experiences and Lefebvrean everyday encounters. This chapter probes the Hippodrome workshop as a momentary and mediated heterotopia and simultaneously as an affective and sensorial experience that was both physical and Hertzian.

SITE SELECTION AND RESEARCH

Research about potential sites for the NiS+TS event in Montreal was initiated remotely early in 2013 with the help of digital archives and mapping resources, as well as scouting probes by colleagues based in the city. Discussions at group meetings in Dartmouth, Nova Scotia elicited a few potential sites that would be substantial enough for at least a half-hour walk within easy reach of the conference location. The Hippodrome rapidly became our first choice because of its ambiguous status as a public site in transition, its large scale, and its rich history, as well as group members' access to knowledge about its history and use. Our Hertzian research included "viewing" the site through satellite photography (Google Earth maps) and reviewing related historical, digitized photographic images from the past one hundred years at the McCord Museum and the Archives nationales du Québec. We also studied the seemingly empty site virtually through an FTP server that held hundreds of images made for a contemporary urban planning research project at McGill University (Luka 2012; Geledi 2012). However, these Hertzian inspections were not quite enough for us to develop a clear understanding about where we were heading, so we asked a colleague, Tom Hall, to do a site visit in March 2013. He scouted the current conditions of the site and sent a few updated photos using his iPhone. These latter images of the Hippodrome site in winter (figure 4.2)

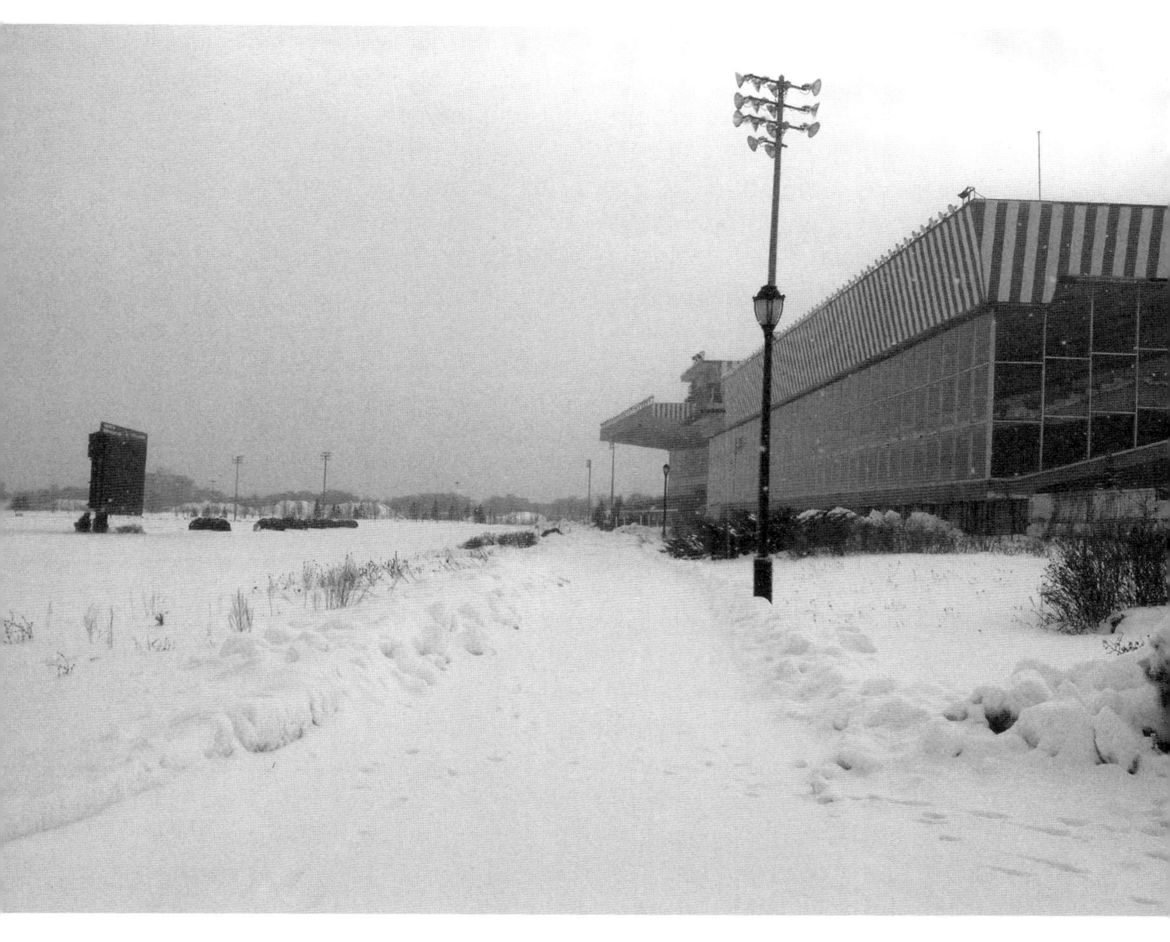

4.2 The Hippodrome site in winter, as seen by proxy.
       Photo: Tom Hall, 2013.

reflected meanings that seemed dormant and frozen. At that stage, it seemed likely that the Hippodrome must inevitably return to this state, as its more recent histories receded further into the past, and notwithstanding our anticipated event.

We worked with all of these collected images to plan the parameters and locations of our project: none of us actually saw the site until the day before the workshop. We came to think of these digital viewings as "proxy" image-based experiences, remote Hertzian representations of a place on which our sense of that place depended. Of course, all images are proxies in some way; ones that exist and circulate only as data are even more so, sometimes revealing and sometimes obscuring information. The word proxy also resonates with "proximity," as in nearby, close to, or in the neighbourhood of (but not the same as). The idea of proximity chimes with Lefebvre's argument that the simultaneity of the small screen "does not simply dissimulate what is dramatic and tragic; it also disguises time and obscures diachrony" (Lefebvre, Régulier, and Zayani 1999, 11). Our initial experience of the Hippodrome as several obscured digital spaces and times rather than a unified physical "site" was also reflected in its placement as an open-ended common space crowded by highways and neighbourhoods at all edges. It is a big, open repository of historical events in the middle of a crowded city, begging for reuse in some ways (for example, the planned redevelopment). In other ways, it asked to be left alone to develop organically as a recuperative heterotopia for city-dwellers. From a Lefebvrean perspective of rhythmanalysis as method, the heterotopic site holds the potential to evolve into an example of how to "critique the growth [of the] dominance of the linear over the cyclical [time]" (Ryan Moore, 2013, 73). Many in the city and beyond know about the Hippodrome and have never been to the site but have seen dozens of images of it, in use and in disuse. It was a risky place, abandoned at some level, yet actively used by dog-walkers, miniature airplane builders, and runners that we could not see until we arrived. Belying Marc Augé's (1995) argument that the rapid pace of life discourages people from claiming space in meaningful ways (collectively or individually), the varied evidence of our many concurrent Hertzian engagements with an unbounded urban wilderness at the Hippodrome was evident to us, even from a distance (figure 4.3). As a site from which many signs of history, narratives, identities, and social relations seemed to have been removed, it

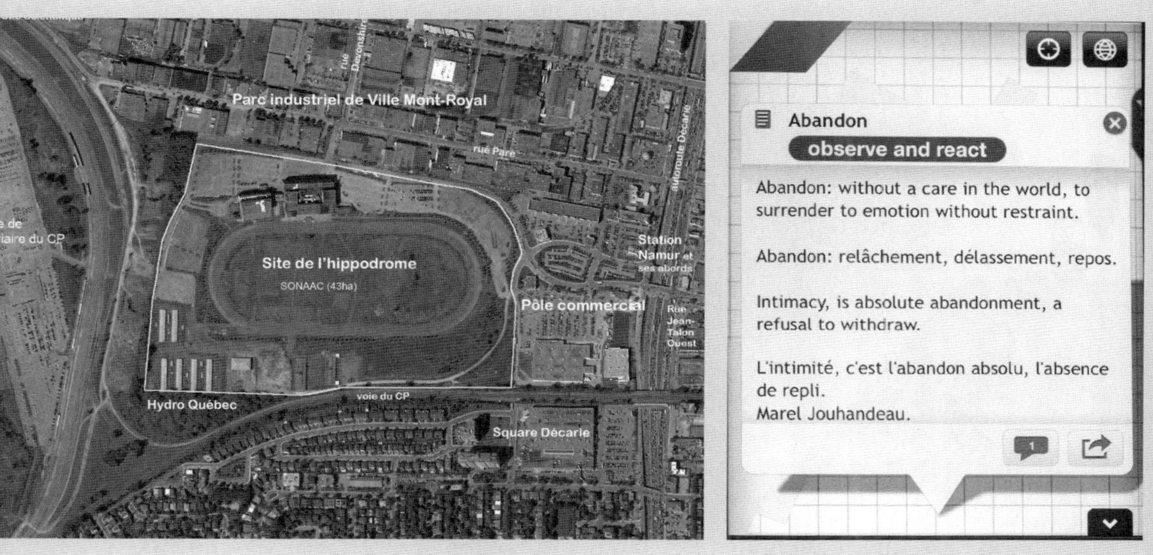

4.3 Hertzian spaces: A mediated experience of trespass and transgression prompted during the NiS+TS project at the personal level.

Left, a satellite image of the empty (abandoned) Hippodrome overlaid by proposed development information. Image: Google Earth, DigitalGlobe.

Right, screen grab of NiS+TS Pin Drop 1 activity on 7Scenes "on" the Hippodrome track. Image: NiS+TS.

had only partially transitioned from being an example of Augé's concept of a "place" of modernity to a "non-place" of supermodernity, a site where people don't belong.

RESEARCH-CREATION PRODUCTION

We decided that developing several digitally produced and "live" narratives for participants to encounter on the site would provide a rich exposure to the issues and themes associated with the Hippodrome, including the production and sustainability of energy and place, the relationship of desire to risk, the performance of history through smells, sounds, and touch, and the experience of trespass and transgression. Saskia Sassen (2006) refers to the importance of making interventions in public spaces through the use of digital devices, understanding that they will affect urban flows and mobilities. In all, ten narratives were developed for the site; all but one had a digital component. Two software packages were employed to help prepare, translate, and map the action digitally: a WIX website and the 7Scenes software, which linked prepared narratives to maps (figure 4.4) in a mobile device application. Data about how many people logged on and accessed the pin drop narratives was collected, including the mapping of paths used.[3] The 7Scenes manufacturers graciously sponsored the project by providing us with access to the professional version of the software to upload the digital components of the ten experiences without charge. However, for all of our careful preparation of the stories, we knew there would be nothing like being there. The conference event at the Hippodrome was promoted as a "tailgate party": an experience speaking to trespass, a slightly illegal incursion on a public space, and a readiness to run away should the situation require it. A tailgate party refers to serving food and drinks from the trunk of a car or back of a truck, in a parking lot, and is often associated with large sports events. The invitation read in part: "Come experience the installation and enjoy a 'tailgate party' and homemade picnic spread prepared by the Mobile Media Lab. Bring your umbrella. Bring your friends, family, comrades. Dogs welcome."

In the end, we had no formal permission to be there. Not that we hadn't done our due diligence. In the two months preceding the event, we made contact with a member of the committee responsible for advising

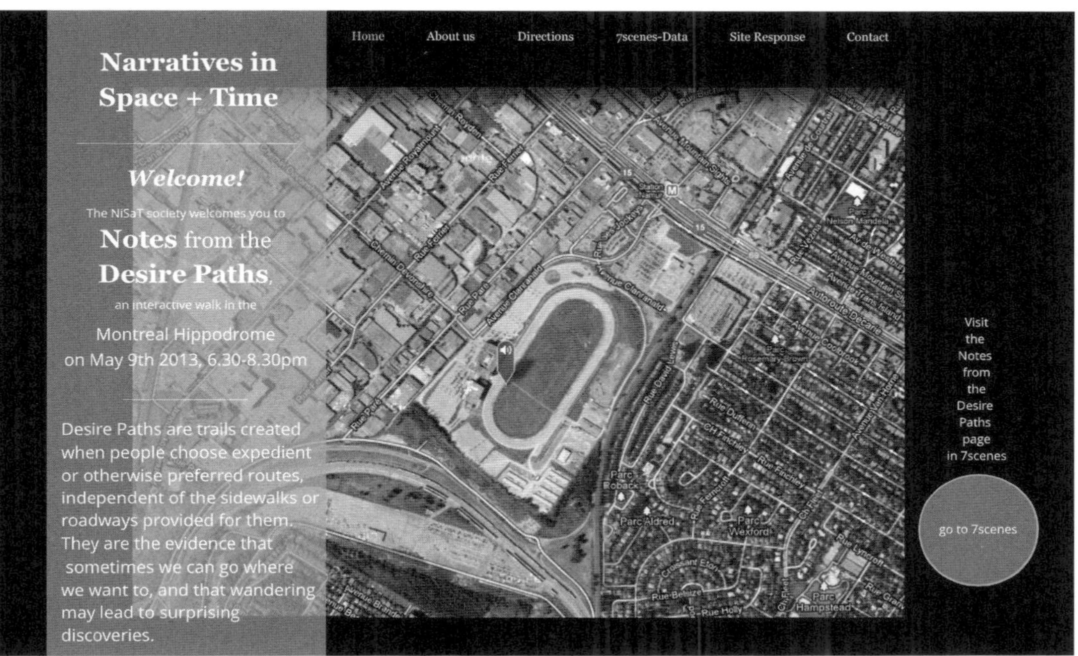

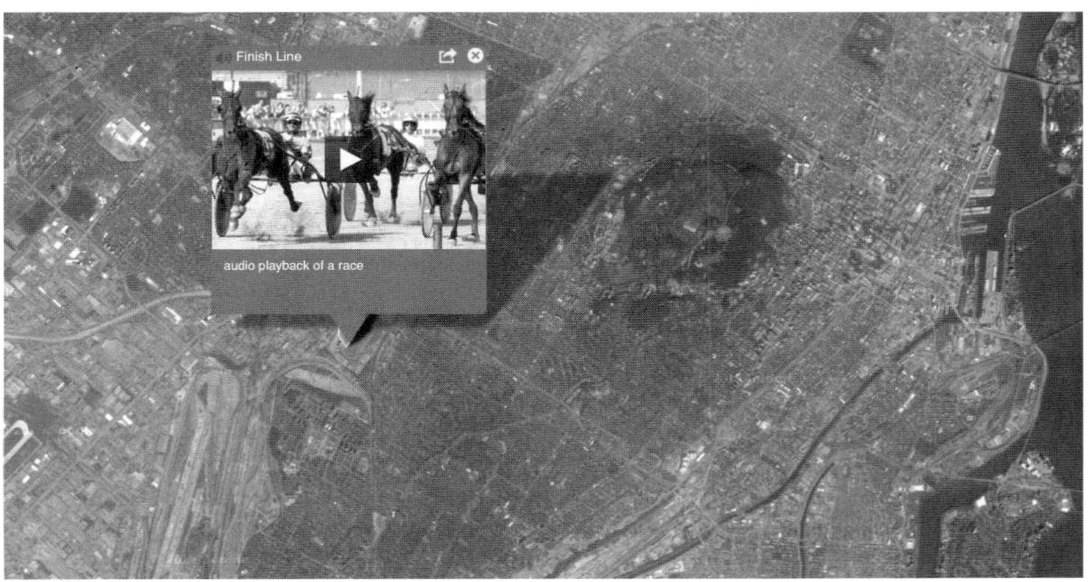

4.4 Above, project website and below, locational screen in 7Scenes software application for smart phones. Images: NiS+TS.

the City of Montreal on how to consult with the community about the Hippodrome redevelopment project and on the spectrum of redevelopment options. The contact had made informal enquiries, only to be judiciously ignored initially, then given delicately worded advice that it would be too complicated to secure formal permission for use of this public space. The promisingly transgressive nature of the experience added to the sense of risk already so evident in the history and thousands of existing images of the site. The project was characterized by such tantalizing uncertainties and possibilities.

The visual form of the map or atlas, whether as digital information or object, can function as a series of narrative threads, or a nonlinear polyvocal network, in artistic works. This is consistent with the embodied and narrative nature of research-creation work by artists and academics such as those documented by Karen O'Rourke. In her book *Walking and Mapping: Artists as Cartographers* (2013), O'Rourke describes various ways in which contemporary artists use the language of mapping, including tracking the movement of the body through space, crossing back and forth over political boundaries, and using technologies to create "emotional maps," among other new representations of place, self, and story.

THE EVENT

Setting down roots for a night proved to be magnificently workable. A delicious and gigantic picnic was provided by the conference organizing team under three pop-up tents and a dramatic sky threatening thunderstorms that never materialized. Accessible by transit, car, and on foot, the Hippodrome is located in the northwest quadrant of the city. A bus from the main conference site downtown was organized to ensure that everyone could reach the event. During the day leading up to the event, several participants attempted to download the free 7Scenes software to their mobile devices from the conference site at Concordia University. However, the firewall there prevented them from doing so. As a result, on the way to the site, we paused beside two local coffee shops with free Wi-Fi in order to help participants complete the process.

The site itself was remarkable for its constant tension between absence and presence. The abandoned space and our appropriation of it, temporarily, through the sharing of food, walking, conversation, and response to the physical space and to digitally-created experiences, created a new environment within which strangers to the city – scholarly, artistic, and activist visitors at the conference – could experience something other than a university classroom or a downtown restaurant. The track was regulation-sized and all-dirt. There were no washrooms, no sinks, and no sidewalks. Small animals had taken over the interiors of the abandoned buildings on the site. Since we hadn't known what condition the track itself would be in, we had planned a relatively short walking route for the ten prepared narratives and activities. Laying them out digitally from Halifax, by 14 April 2013, we had identified ten GPS spots on the track starting right in front of where the picnic site was planned (figure 4.5). We marked these spots digitally with "pin drops" on Google maps and on the project's 7Scenes application before coming to Montreal. Once we arrived on site on 9 May, we assembled our real-life pin drops (red balloons tied to short, lightweight posts attached to wooden bases) and installed them to correspond to the GPS locations reflected in the software used, adjusting them only slightly by connecting back by cellphone to the colleague who had stayed in Halifax.

The purpose of the installation was to engage viewers as on-the-spot and virtual participants in key past, present, and future narratives of the Hippodrome site. In other words, we sought to assert a Lefebvrean experience of the "right to the city" (Lefebvre et al 1999) and perhaps even to generate a "moment" that could activate an urban "politics of encounter" (Merrifield 2011). On site, participants could upload direct responses to 7Scenes at each of the ten pin drops (locative media in action) or opt for real-life discussions with NiS+TS group members and other participants. (Each pin drop experience is described in more detail below.) Some assumptions regarding the congruence of real-life and digital interfaces that we had made from afar did not play out in terms of reactions. Crucial among these was that several international participants did not have mobile phone roaming plans that would allow them to use the software on site. Instead of aggregating individual experiences through 7Scenes, the event facilitated subgroup, face-to-face experiences, often with one or two NiS+TS members as guides. In this way the (online and on-site) pin drop alignments functioned more as markers for a "test track." That is, pin drops indicated locations to test reactions along a particular path and

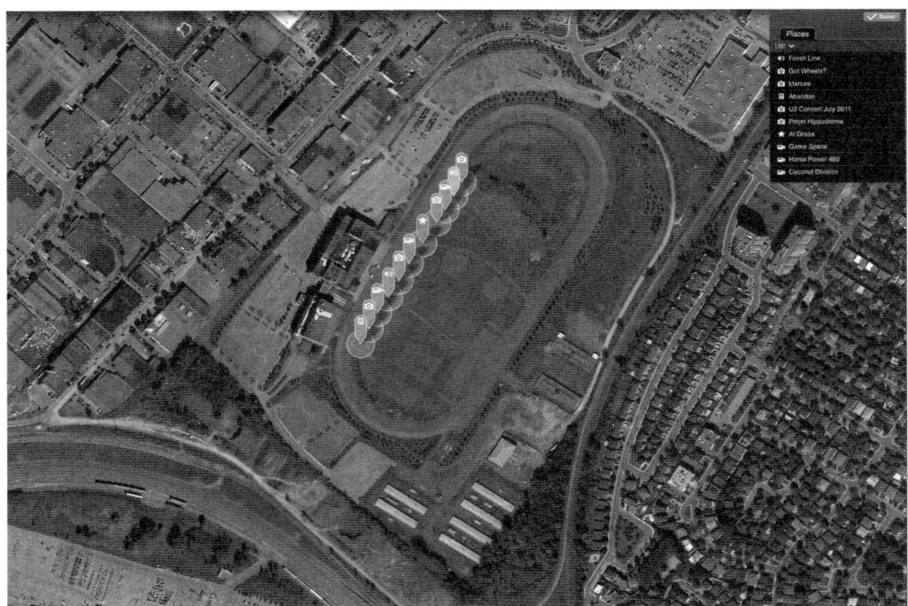

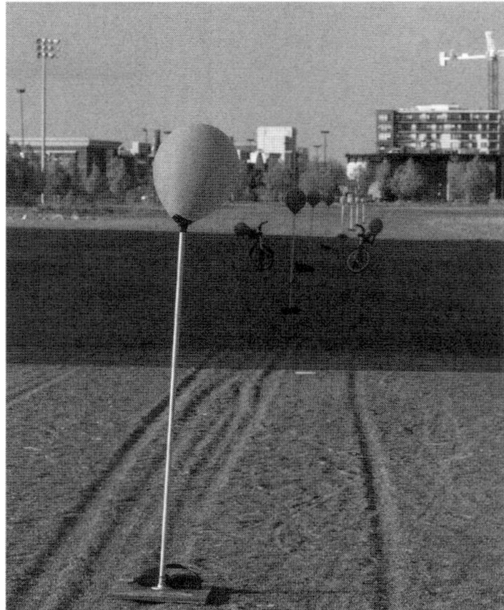

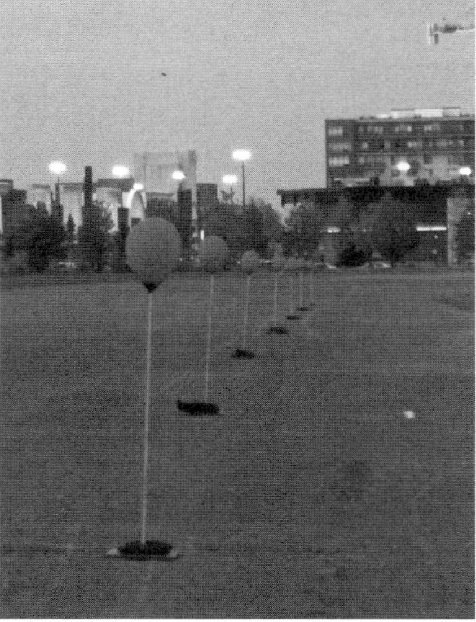

4.5 Above, pin drops laid out digitally beforehand on the 7Scenes software and then adjusted onsite, day and evening views, below left and below right. Images: NiS+TS.

simultaneously provided the opportunity for people to record their own cumulative "tracks" on the Hippodrome "race track," if we or they used the 7Scenes mapping function. These mobile exchanges involved thoughtful conversation, delicious food, and dramatic weather "on-the-move" on site, as well as providing evidence of the mobility of the experience through the recorded tracks, texts, photographs, and other traces. As the sun went down, the skies threatening spring thunder, lightning and rain resolved into brilliant pinks, purples, oranges, and yellows overlaid with growling greys, while murmurs of laughter and easy conversation permeated the site, interjected with critical comments and movements (figure 4.6). The pin drop locations themselves were successful as subgroup loci, ranging from a large group gathering for a poetry reading to a smaller group listening experience of a horse race broadcast to unscheduled races using the Bixi bikes rented for the event.[4] But they did not result in the prolific uploading of digital responses we had hoped to secure. In the end, the experience we had crafted more easily aligns with Debordian "situations [which] are much more spatial … and much more urban in orientation than the Lefebvrean moment" of engagement (Merrifield 2008, 182–3).

To help picture the event more clearly as a Debordian situational experiment, below we unpack key themes, narratives and activities that the participants experienced.

Pin Drop 1: Abandon. Bringing the theme of trespass to the surface, this first participatory locative activity invited participants to record an audio or visual response on the 7Scenes application, reacting to the term *abandon* (in French or English) while using their mobile device on this forsaken physical site. Transgressive possibilities were welcome.

Pin Drop 2: U2 Concert. Drawing on social critiques of entertainment and the spectacle, and concomitantly the racetrack's use as a venue for mass events, the 7Scenes pin drop commented on a seductive image from Irish rock band U2's massive 360° concert (from their "No Line on the Horizon" Tour) held in the then-about-to-be-abandoned Hippodrome space in July 2011. The original performance included views from space, connecting the band to Space Station imagery and live interviews with astronauts. U2 combines particular forms of musicality, masculinity, social activism, and egotism in its identity and brand within the global, transnational rock music world. Few of the NIS+TS participants responded to this simple image or to a similarly straightforward secondary virtual

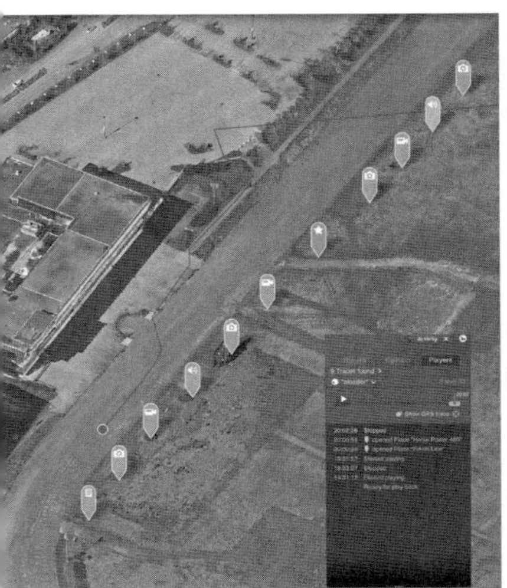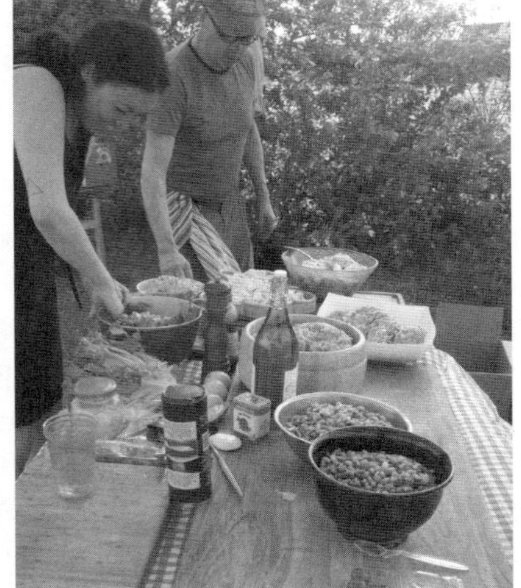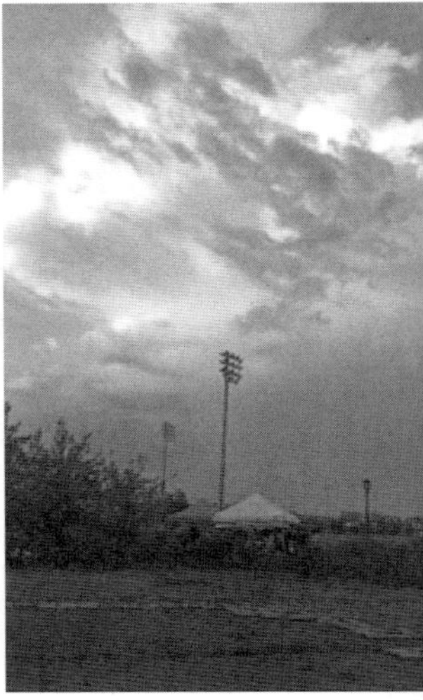

4.6 Left, tracking participant paths using the 7Scenes mobile app software, juxtaposed with middle, food preparation for the picnic, and right, the dramatic physical reality of the location and event. Images: NiS+TS image at Pin Drop 10, suggesting the importance of more active Hertzian audio/visual and live content.

Pin Drop 3: Horse Power 480. This activity consisted of a slide show of historical images edited together by NIS+TS to watch on a smart phone in 7Scenes. Familiar and unfamiliar images commented on one hundred-year-old concepts of horsepower and sustainable energy generation (figure 4.7) in order to provoke consideration of the site in terms of its engagement with humans, horses, and sustainability. Informational statements were incorporated, including, for example: "Watt: Human Power is roughly equal to 0.1 horsepower over a sustained period."

Pin Drop 4: Finish Line. This fast-paced audio playback of a radio broadcast of a 1922 "Race of Champions" horse race's final moments, hosted on the 7Scenes app and played back on the site through the app, was a huge hit with participants who felt it inserted them directly in the history and atmosphere of the site.[5]

Pin Drop 5: Got Wheels? One of the more popular participatory activities of the evening, this experience allowed attendees to race the entire track themselves using several rented Bixi bicycles brought in by NIS+TS (figure 4.8). After the cheers and thundering hooves of the previous pin drop, it was easy to imagine the crowds that had come to this site on countless occasions over the last one hundred years and the physical mastery required to excel in this space and at related sports events such as the Olympics and Paralympics. The digital component showed images and information about sulky racing at the Hippodrome, drawing attention to changing modes of risky transportation and gaming over the last century.

Pin Drop 6: Coconut Division. Drawing on sculpture, audio, video, and performance art, the digital component of this activity included an excerpt of the firmly tongue-in-cheek bureaucratic instructional video developed by the Monty Python creative team about how to use coconut halves to generate the sound of horses trotting. Accompanied on-site by physical coconut halves engraved with the Python instructions to bring the halves "together and apart," this was a favourite interactive piece, incorporating recent media history and sound. By virtue of its easy enjoyability, the interactions around this piece also addressed the venue as a locus for entertainment for many classes of people.

Pin Drop 7: At Grass. Sporting a lime green, orange, and white jacket by Lilly Pulitzer (a famous midcentury Palm Beach clothing designer),

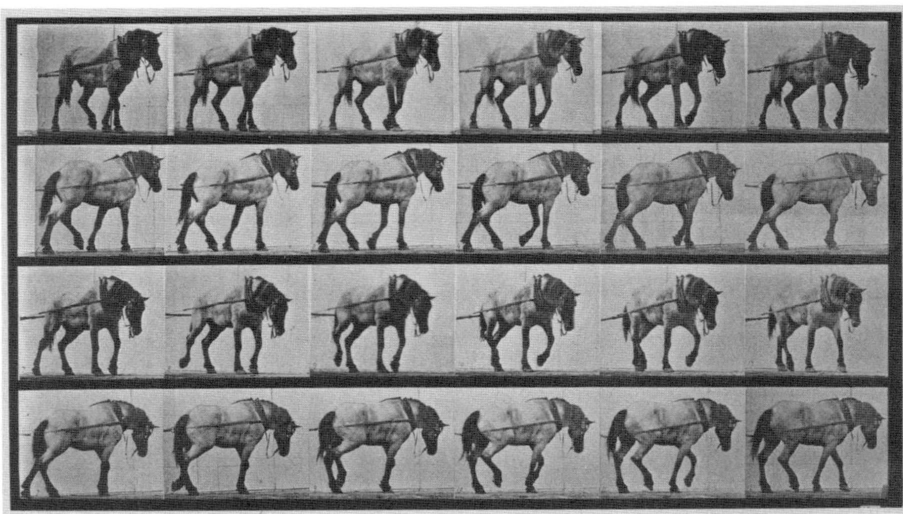

4.7 Horse power: the production and sustainability of energy related to place. Above, "Human power" slide and below, a still of Eadweard Muybridge's *"Hansel" hauling* photograph, both from NiS+TS slideshow prepared for 7Scenes mobile app software. Photo: National Gallery of Canada.

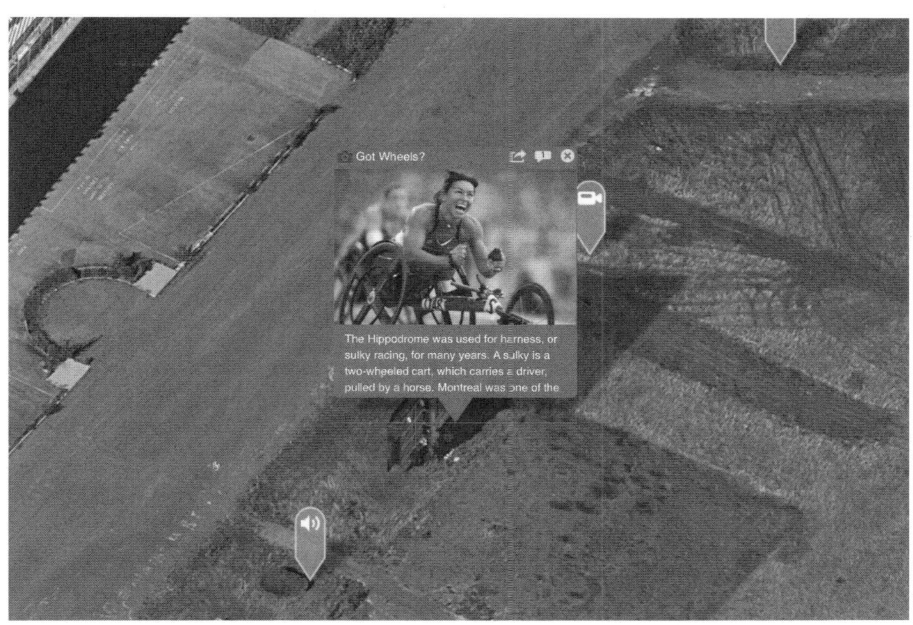

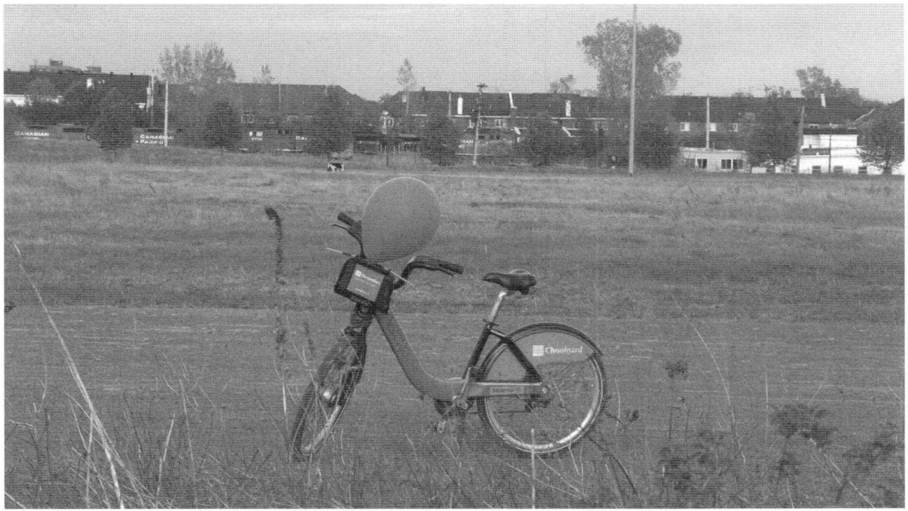

4.8 Got wheels? Above, screen grab from the 7Scenes mobile app showing detail from Pin Drop 5 and below, Bixi rental bicycle. Images: NiS+TS.

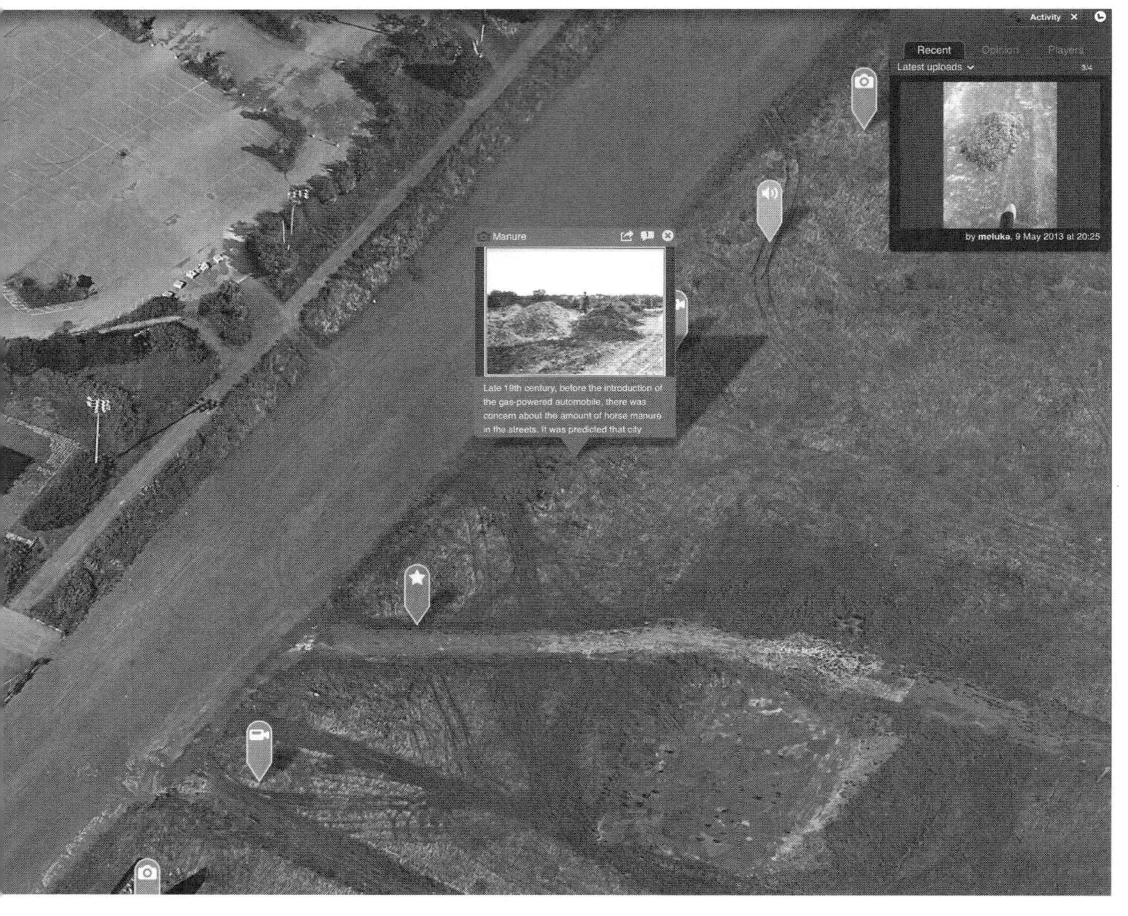

4.9 Experiencing the walk. Screen grabs from the 7Scenes mobile app, showing left, a narrative and feedback example uploaded to Pin Drop 8 and right, a video freeze frame on the 7Scenes app at Pin Drop 9. Images: NiS+TS.

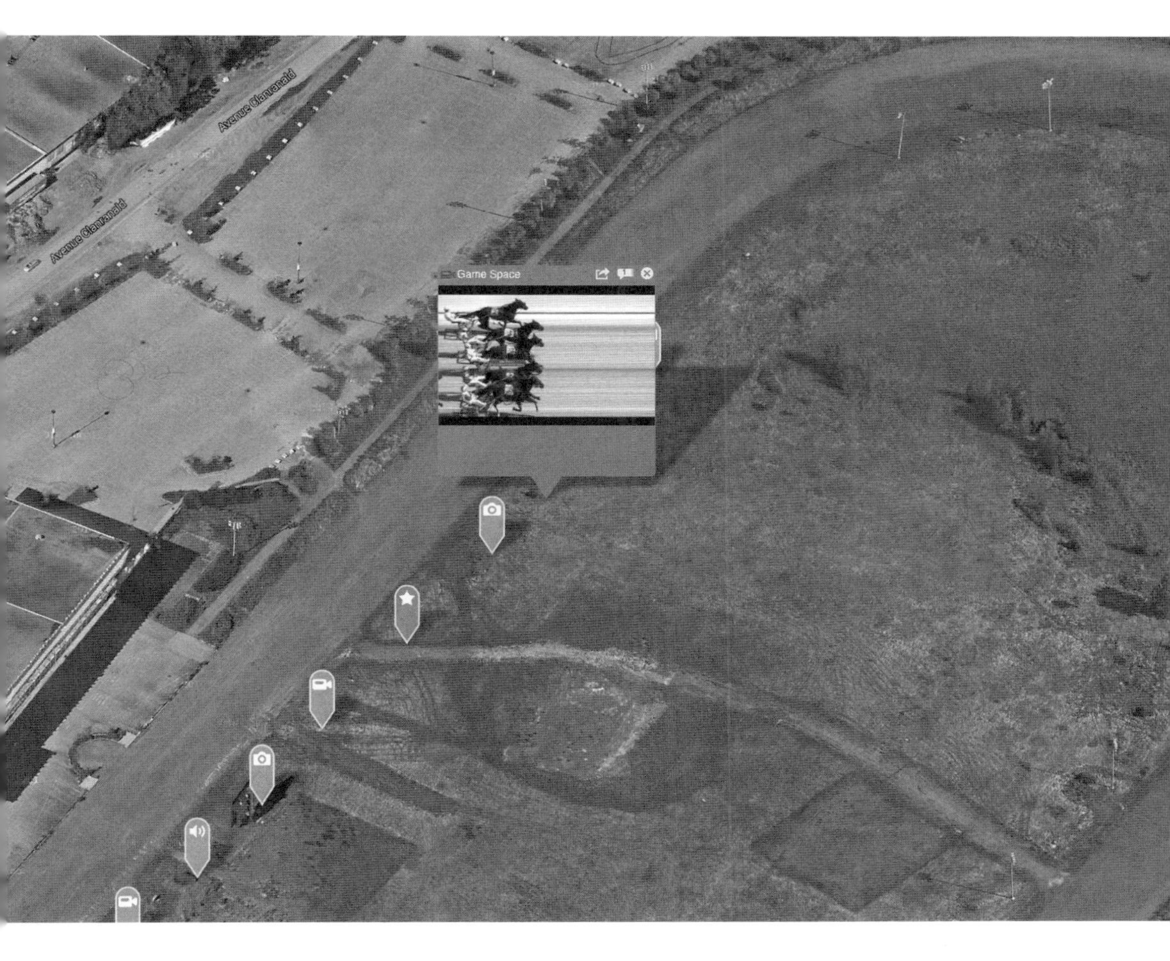

Avenue Clanranald
Avenue Clanranald
Game Space

perfectly in keeping with the history of the site, actor Brian Downey kicked off the formal participatory proceedings of the evening by delivering live readings of Philip Larkin's (1950) poem "At Grass" at this pin drop. The poem commemorates the accomplishments of horses and athletes at similar sites: some of the twentieth century's key entertainment – and gambling – locations. His interpretation of the poem, including his commentary about its meanings, prompted some participants to move with more confidence towards other pin drops and try out the activities, and prompted others to linger and chat on the track.

Pin Drop 8: Manure. A rather visceral on-site experience, the pile of fresh horse manure located at this pin drop brought attendees to a sight and smell experience that would have been common during most of the Blue Bonnets history (figure 4.9). It was augmented on 7Scenes with images of piles of manure and the statement: "In the late 19th century … there was concern about the amount of horse manure in the streets. It was predicted that the city streets would be 9 feet deep in manure by 1950!" Shifting the experience from visceral to conceptual and historical, this activity (among others) drew on the history of engaging public participants in mobile, multisensory and site-specific performance experiences, an approach pioneered by US artist Suzanne Lacy (1995) in her "New Genre Public Art" projects dating back to 1977 (see, for example, "In Mourning and In Rage," 1977).

Pin Drop 9: Game Space. A slide show of historical images and commentary pointed to the use of the space over the course of a century as a site of legal and illegal wagering. The phrases quoted in the slide show were meant to emphasize the site's relationship to risk-taking, behaviour modification, and game theory, and came from a variety of sources, including behaviour and instructions from the Situationist International (specifically, Ivan Chtcheglov). For example:

The changing of landscapes from one hour to the next will result in complete disorientation (Chtcheglov [1953]1982, 4);

Win * Place * Show (a commonplace term used in parimutuel betting, adopted in the early part of the twentieth century, e.g. Reiss 1991);

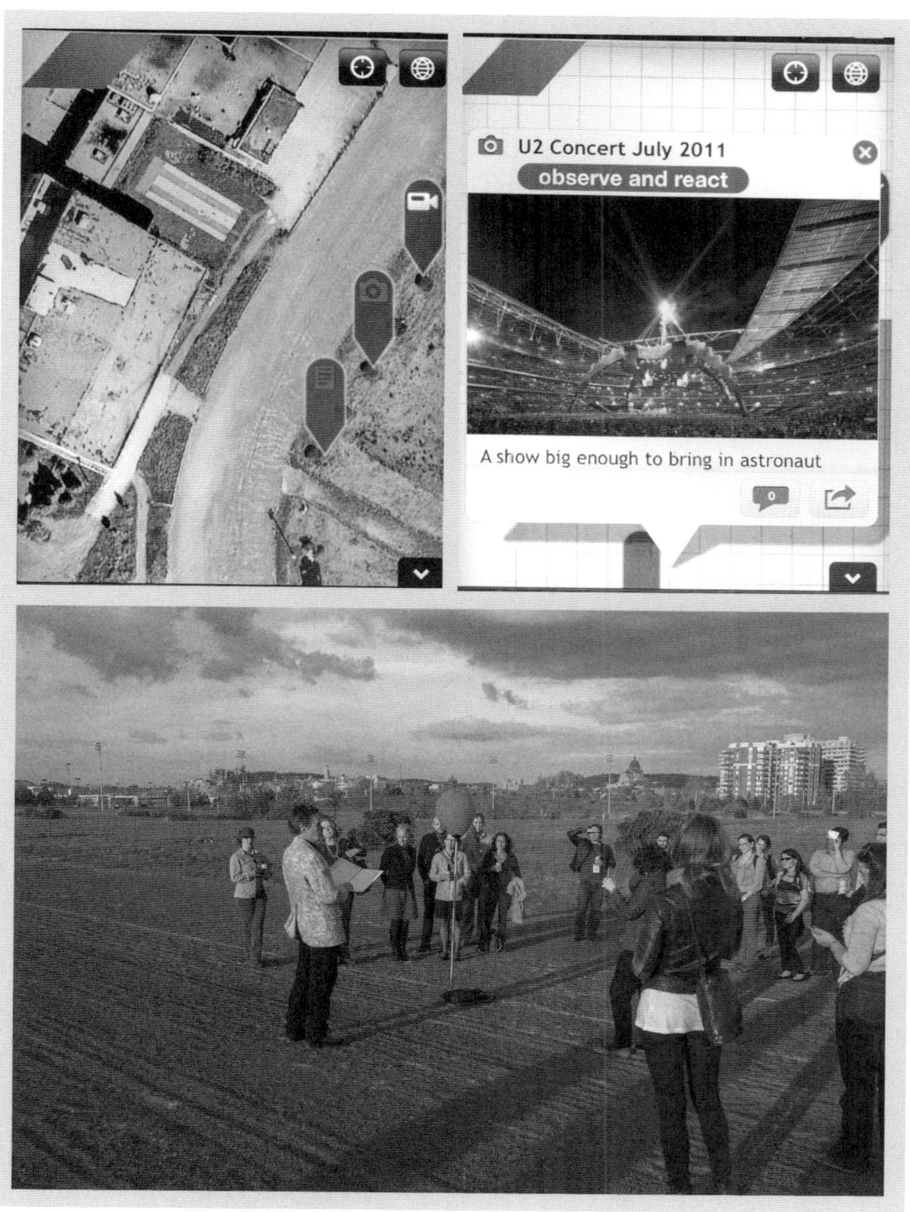

4.10 The performance of history and the history of performance: above left and above right, two screen grabs from the 7Scenes application and below, Brian Downey reciting Philip Larkin's poem "At Grass" at the 2013 NiS+TS event. Images: NiS+TS.

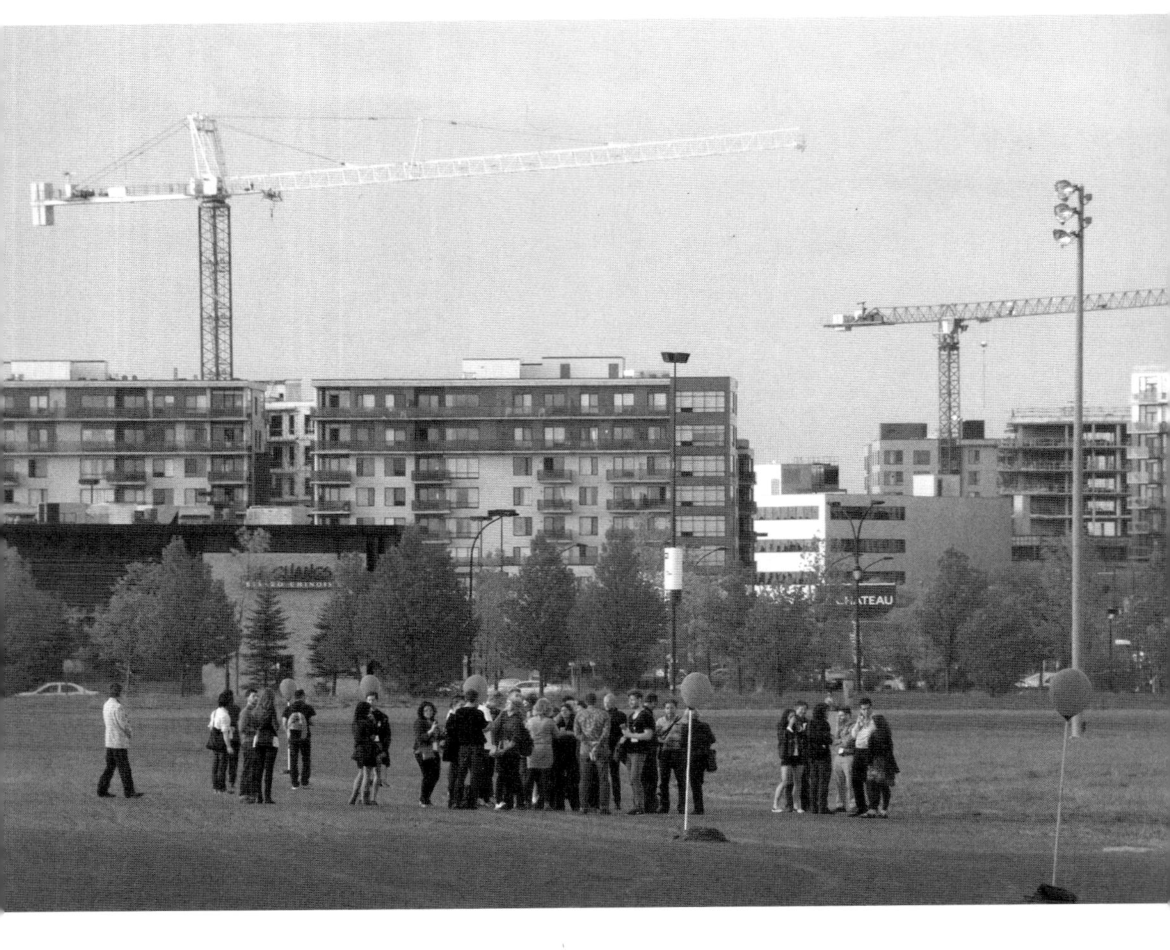

4.11 The future encroaches. Participants at 2013 NiS+TS Hippodrome event. Photo: NiS+TS.

Game theory is a tool used to analyze strategic behaviour by taking into account how participants expect others to behave (*Financial Dictionary* 2015);

Game theory is used to find the optimal outcome from a set of choices by analyzing the costs and benefits to each independent party as they compete with each other (*Financial Dictionary* 2015);

Payoff: In any game, payoffs are numbers which represent the motivations of players. Payoffs may represent profit, quantity, utility, or other continuous measures, or may simply rank the desirability of outcomes. In all cases, the payoffs must reflect the motivations of the particular player (Shor 2005);

Games are forbidden in the labyrinth (Chtcheglov [1953]1982, 3).

Pin Drop 10: 3Qs for future planning. One of the more didactic items in the sequence of ten, the digital component at this pin drop included an audio interview with an urban planner and scholar involved in the City of Montreal's advisory committee concerning the redevelopment of the site, including a request for participants to upload responses to three questions about the Hippodrome's future. A secondary virtual-only pin drop provided the web address for the city consultation associated with the redevelopment. Connecting the conference event to the imminent future of the Hippodrome, pin drop 10 invited participants from within and outside Montreal to make suggestions about how to rethink this in-between space, linking it to research on historically laden sites that hover precariously between past and future, or between urban wilderness and redevelopment (Gagnon 2006).

REFLECTIONS: A PROVISIONAL CONCLUSION

The momentous physical reality of the place in some ways transcended the narrative histories and our planned-for feedback loops that we had hoped would invoke de Certeau's practice of everyday living through walking,

Lefebvre's "moment," Merrifield's "politics of encounter," or Debord's situational *dérive*. Speculation about the heterotopic nature of the space through conversation was readily apparent though, perhaps because of the spontaneous casual groupings that ebbed and flowed, in combination with excellent food and dramatic weather (figure 4.10). The presence of the manure, like the coconut halves, and the ability of the participants to record responses at each pin drop, blurred audience and artist roles, as happens with some site-specific performance art strategies, such as de Certeau's "practice of everyday living" through walking and Debord's *dérive*, discussed earlier, as well as Mierle Laderman Ukeles's *The Social Mirror* (1983) and *Manifesto for Maintenance Art* (1969).

Finally, a number of participant remarks focused on the Hippodrome as a wilderness or nonspace, that is, as something extraordinary and outside normal time or categorization. Robin from Vancouver remarked that being there was like "being on the edge of urbanity." Kim expressed an aspect of the site as being "hidden" as it is so close to Montreal's core but so off the radar. A group of academics from Brazil particularly enjoyed the horse race radio recording at pin drop 4. Many participants from different academic domains and countries commented that certain artifacts from the past (empty stands and stalls, cheerful awnings, a tumble-down scoreboard, the track itself) lent an atmosphere of eerie nostalgia and risky business. Andrew was impressed with the sheer scale of the place, especially the sky, but thought that the "wide open qualities" would be difficult to maintain with the proposed high-density development (see, for example, Rail 2012). Whereas future development seeks to reflect the site's nostalgic character by using the horseracing track to shape edifice foundations, the tumbledown scale of the place during the event reveals urban and historical connections and possible futures equally as relevant.

In retrospect, the event functioned best as a mediated combination of experiential and digital worlds. Carefully planned, but not scripted, the event unfolded along trajectories that revealed both the genius and limitations of working on a compelling, richly historical site from a distance. Later, some participants and other users of the software reviewed the digital activities and stories we had uploaded to the 7Scenes application, to emulate the experience, even though each realized that the Hertzian could not stand in for the visceral. Others participated only as observers during the event (or only in the gustatory dimension), foregoing not only

the augmented experiences afforded by the app but also the opportunities
to ride Bixi bikes, bang coconut halves together, or go for walks around
the site. Multisensory, and/or mediated, the workshop was experienced
(and endures in both memory and archive) as an array of possibilities and
choices about whether and how to move, and alongside what narratives. In
the end, the space itself completed the project. The urban ruin embraced
its visitors as liminal space supercharged with history, narrative, sound,
and image; always open to new interpretations.

Notes

1   See http://www.mobilities.ca/differential-mobilities-conference-
    montreal-2013/. Accessed 30 May 2016. We would like to acknowledge
    the support of the organizers of the *Differential Mobilities: Movement
    and Mediation in Networked Societies* conference for providing food and
    transportation and generally making the Hippodrome workshop possible,
    and the sponsorship of 7Scenes, which enabled us to use the software
    application for the workshop.

2   For more information, see our website
    http://www.narrativesinspaceandtime.ca/. Accessed 30 May 2016.

3   See http://nisat5.wix.com/nisat-hippodrome; http://7scenes.com/
    scene/3760689/Notes-from-the-Desire-Path. Accessed 30 May 2016.

4   Bixi is the public bike-share system in Montreal. Similar systems are found
    in cities around the world.

5   Listen to the original audio on the 7Scenes event page and at
    http://youtu.be/ytG73haroEl. Accessed 30 May 2016.

Part Two

ALEXANDRINE BOUDREAULT-FOURNIER
AND MARTHA RADICE

: Making Art, Making the City

This section presents four chapters that show how public art is entangled with the processes, materialities, and politics of the production of urban space. They address the relations that emerge from artists and their artwork and the city itself: its infrastructure, streets, and buildings, among other things. Some chapters position the body of the artist or the researcher herself/himself as an amplifier of sensory experiences, as a mediator of urban sensations. Others connect the street to broader political intentions of economic and social planning. The chapters investigate how various forms of public art creation draw on or contribute to the material and symbolic creation of the city. In other words, they look at how art "makes the city" – or potentially unmakes it.

For anthropologist Tim Ingold (2013), "making" is always a creative act, which he understands as a process of "correspondence" between a maker and the materials, tools and environment she or he is working with. Correspondence involves a continuous, sensorial, and reciprocal engagement among all the things that are used for making. For example, just as the grain of the wood guides the path of the axe used to chop it, so any material will guide the tools and processes that alter it. Artists (and makers in general) bring materials into correspondence with each other; they transform them and give shape to them with their bodies (in walking, touching, drawing, sculpting, listening) and with the tools they

use (camera, GPS, sound recorder, clay, pencils). Their artworks
generate new relations between things and their environment,
and between the people who attend to them; the artworks are
also shaped by their context as well as these new relations. In this
sense, artists working in the urban public are in correspondence
with the city. Their artworks help weave at least a small patch
of the city's fabric and texture – and they too are altered by the
tools, materials, and acts of making.

For instance, Ellen Moffat and Kim Morgan treat systems of
intraurban mobility as a method of making art, using video,
audio, locative, and biometric data that they collect with custom-
made devices as they drive through Halifax and walk through
Paris, Regina, and Saskatoon. Moffat and Morgan approach the
city as a surface through which the body moves and makes its
way like a sewing thread. As a consequence, the body becomes
inscribed by the city; walking through its streets, climbing its
stairs, and hanging out in its malls affect the data collected by the
devices; the city leaves its traces on the body, altering its pulse,
giving it different rhythms. Moffat and Morgan's chapter brings to
mind rhythmanalysis, an approach developed by Henri Lefebvre
(Lefebvre et al. 1999, Lefebvre 2004) to record and investigate the
rhythms of daily life, including those of bodies in urban space.
Rhythmanalysis aims to expose the implicit structures that affect

how our bodies correspond with the urban environment. In collecting all of this data, Moffat and Morgan locate their bodies in the city and register the traces it leaves on them. The thread left by their journey weaves into the fabric of urban life; their bodies correspond with the city both directly and through the devices they used.

Similarly, Boudreault-Fournier and Wees experiment with recording visual and audio clips of back alleys, those almost secret passages that are not marked on many city maps. Corresponding with the alleys, they take a relational approach to the city and, subsequently, provide an alternative reading of these ubiquitous urban spaces, more sensorial and based on the experiences of the anthropologist-creators. Boudreault-Fournier and Wees explain that precisely because they are interstitial, often-neglected spaces, back alleys make excellent sites for creating new encounters with art. They suggest that anthropologists should reflect on the ethnographic fieldwork enterprise in considering how the visual arts, and especially research-creation approaches, can open up novel ways of experiencing the spaces they study. Indeed, the creativity of interstitial urban spaces seems to have captivated most of the authors in this section. Such spaces allow for the exploration of the public versus private divide (Moffat and Morgan; Boudreault-Fournier and Wees), and for new interpretations of how cities change and

how arts might be integrated in urban development and revitalization (Bird and Nagler; Bain and Rallis).

In their chapter, Lawrence Bird and Solomon Nagler discuss a
film installation produced in collaboration with their students in
Winnipeg and Halifax respectively. The students made films documenting interstitial and dysfunctional spaces in each city, which
were projected onto a three-screen structure in Grand Parade,
Halifax. The viewers' shadows blended and were superimposed
on the screens, adding to the poetry and symbolism of the cinematic representations. More importantly though, as they slipped
around and between the screens, the viewers helped close the
loop of this architecture of encounter. Written as a dialogue
between the two authors, the chapter conducts a fascinating
comparison between architecture and cinema, exploring how
the creative gestures and political contexts of each practice can
shape urban space. In creating a different way of watching film
(standing in a park and moving around and within a three-screen
structure), the authors propose a new architectural experience of
cinema and, consequently, a new configuration of cities merging
and emerging through the screens.

The installation also allows Bird and Nagler to discuss how cities
change and how interstitial and abandoned spaces become the
sites for new development. In this sense, the creation of new

architectures of encounter through making and projecting film or through recording and editing landscapes and soundscapes (Boudreault-Fournier and Wees) destabilizes established conventions and norms of architecture, functions, and aesthetics. It also creates a correspondence between a space, its audiovisual recording and its representation(s). In their conversation, Bird and Nagler also develop a critique of urban planning, explaining how artworks can be instrumentalized and spectacularized in economic development, leaving artists and arts marginalized. Yet, they also recognize the complexity of how art is integrated into new projects, suggesting that artworks might yet create unexpected moments of encounter.

Alison L. Bain and Nicole Rallis propose a similar argument to Bird and Nagler on this last point, although as geographers, they arrive at it from a different approach. Their chapter sheds light on the transformation of James Street North, located in downtown Hamilton, into a site of creative consumption. In a pattern typical of contemporary processes of gentrification, city-boosters have relied on the spectacularization of culture to promote the development of this street. Bain and Rallis's critical analysis of three public art installations encountered during the *Supercrawl*, an art event in the neighbourhood, shows how the artworks both question and reinforce the official policies promoted by the municipality. Through the festive art event, the street becomes its own work of art, which, despite everything, is still at the service of a city-boosting mentality.

This section engages with the textures and strictures of the city by considering how artworks and artists engage in the making and remaking of the city and in the creation of new sociospatial and sensorial experiences.

Alison L. Bain and Nicole Rallis

5

—

CRAWLING WITH ART: PUBLIC ART INSTALLATIONS ON JAMES STREET NORTH IN HAMILTON, ONTARIO

This chapter examines how a street in downtown Hamilton, Ontario has been curated as a public art performance and an arts destination. Amidst profound struggles with homelessness, poverty, and addiction in the inner city, an arts and culture scene flourishes along James Street North that reimagines both the street and the city as places of artistic production and consumption. Such reimagination of place is powerful for the ways in which it can seduce city leaders, attract artists, and lure reinvestment but, more importantly, also erase other street-based cultures and lived experiences. We argue that the instrumentalization and spectacularization of culture through arts festivals and public art as an economic development tool has profound political consequences for those whose representations, meanings, and experiences of place are legitimized and those who are further marginalized.

Discussion in this chapter begins by establishing a conceptual framework grounded in Guy Debord's theory of spectacle. We then locate Hamilton geographically and socially, before contextualizing how culture has been instrumentalized in the city's urban policy and planning scripts. The chapter moves on to examine how James Street North was transformed over the last decade into a place of leisured consumption for creative types. Central to this transformation are an ongoing monthly Art Crawl, a spin on the pub crawl tradition in which galleries stay open late and visitors walk between exhibition sites, and an annual Supercrawl arts festival. In documenting how a grassroots arts event has become an increasingly corporatized place-marketing exercise, this chapter reveals the centrality of public art installations to the narration and legitimation of Hamilton's postindustrial transformation. A critical analysis of three public art installations encountered on James Street North at the 2013 and 2014 Supercrawl events uncovers how these works of art interact with the street and question, as well as reinforce, creative city policy and planning discourses that rely heavily on urban spectacle as a place-marketing strategy. Analysis in this chapter is based upon participant observation at the 2013 and 2014 Supercrawls, thirty-six semistructured interviews with cultural workers in Hamilton conducted between August 2013 and August 2014, and research undertaken for the documentary film *This Is Hamilton... After the Steel Rush* (Rallis and Mashkoor 2012).

Guy Debord's theory of the spectacle, as detailed in his book *The Society of the Spectacle,* offers a valuable conceptual lens through which to examine Hamilton's Supercrawl arts festival and the strategic use of public art installations within it. Debord asserts that spectacle is the defining character of twentieth-century urban life. From his neo-Marxist vantage point, spectacle is the dominant mode of production in late capitalist society – it is "capital accumulated to the point where it becomes an image" and takes precedence over material objects (1994, 24). In capital's manifestation as representation, spectacle elevates sight – the most abstract and deceivable of the human senses – and "corresponds to the historical moment at which the commodity completes its colonization of social life," becoming "all that there is to see" (Debord 1994, 29). Illusion, then, "overtakes reality and images impose themselves as the tangible and are taken as the real: illusion is authenticated as more real than the real itself" (Thorns 2002, 145). Debord (1994) treats commodification as a by-product of a way of life wherein individuals consume a world made by others rather than producing their own world. Urban arts festivals, like Hamilton's Art Crawl and Supercrawl, are visual attractions. They exemplify commodified forms of leisure and entertainment – spectacle – deployed, Debord would argue, as part of capitalist institutional and technical governance apparatuses to pacify and depoliticize people. For city managers in many municipalities, urban festivals have become just another urban imagineering tool in the neoliberal place-promotion toolbox to create place distinctiveness and to disseminate positive images of place that are attractive to residents, visitors, and investors alike. Over the last three decades, the dramatic increase in the number of urban festivals in cities around the world can be attributed, Quinn (2005, 932) claims, to this drive by city managers to raise the international profile of their city and attract visitors through "hard branding" and an emphasis on "the spectacular as opposed to any real consideration of process." In what follows, an analysis of Hamilton's Supercrawl reveals how this arts festival has been produced as an economic and marketing generator for the city.

(RE)PLACING HAMILTON

The City of Hamilton is located in southwestern Ontario on Lake Ontario, about a forty-five-minute highway drive from Toronto and approximately sixty kilometres from the United States border. The city was founded in 1816. With its harbour, port facilities, and position on the Great Western railway line, Hamilton was once a major regional and national transportation hub. When competition from other railway lines threated the local economy, foundries that manufactured wheat threshing machines and cast-iron stoves helped to secure Hamilton's reputation as an industrializing city (Weaver 1982). In the early twentieth century, the consolidation of local steel mills by the Steel Company of Canada (Stelco) and Dominion Foundries and Steel (Dofasco) solidified steel and trade unionism as the city's primary products.

Over the intervening years, Hamilton has grown to become the ninth largest city in Canada and the third largest in Ontario, with a census metropolitan area population in 2011 of 721,053. Since its founding, Hamilton has reinvented itself, enduring cycles of financial and industrial growth and decline, at times rivalling Toronto for resources, status, and potential. With the monikers Steeltown and The Hammer, steel mills and other heavy manufacturing industries have played a central role in the city's development trajectory, looming large on the landscape, supporting working-class livelihoods, and crafting a reputation for Hamilton as a gritty, smog-filled steel town. Through the 1980s and 1990s, in the face of global economic restructuring and local deindustrialization, Hamilton grappled with factory downsizing and closures (Corman et al. 1993).

By 2010, only 20 per cent of the population was employed in manufacturing and 75 per cent in service industries, with retail and health and social services being the major sectors (Weaver 2010). Scarred by the steel industry and the steady loss of manufacturing jobs Hamilton contends with significant disparities in neighbourhood social capital (Kitchen et al. 2012; Wakefield et al. 2007).

Hamilton is a geographically and socially divided city. The Niagara escarpment slices through the city creating an upper "Mountain" and lower downtown, which, in conjunction with the harbour, has channelled urban development along an east-west axis. Class divisions play out in the residential landscape. Affluence concentrates in the south, west, and upper areas of the city, and poverty is found in the east, north, and lower areas of the city in proximity to industry and the downtown. In the postwar era, to address concerns with traffic congestion, a one-way street system was imposed on the lower city. Local journalists have documented how the resulting increased volume and speed of traffic has had dramatic adverse environmental, social, and economic impacts on the streetscape and quality of life of inner-city neighbourhoods, "inhibiting residents from developing connections with neighbours and feeling a sense of attachment to the community" (Wayland 2012). The construction and expansion of the highway system through the 1960s and 1970s further decentralized growth and investment away from the downtown core, exacerbating central city decline. As occurred in many cities across the country, in the face of dramatic suburbanization and urban decay, the public sector invested heavily in downtown redevelopment megaprojects that demolished heritage buildings, cleared a sizeable tract of land, and displaced significant numbers of businesses and residents. This 1970s vision of urban renewal included a "super block" with a shopping mall, theatre, civic art gallery, convention centre, arena, library, and farmer's market (White 2013). In the present day, these formal cultural institutions remain important community anchors, but a local arts scene that is increasingly confident and publicly boastful about its edginess and grittiness is thriving nearby in smaller, more independent venues.

Drawing on the work of Will Straw (2015), in this chapter we understand Hamilton's arts and culture scene in spatial terms as a workplace where materials and resources are transformed and where different values and sensibilities collide. Straw (2015, 478) asserts that "scenes perform the often invisible labour of pulling together cultural phenomena in ways which heighten their visibility and facilitate their circulation to other places. Scenes, in this respect are spaces of enlistment and convergence, which act[s] in a dynamic fashion upon creative labour to constantly reorder its locations and outcomes." It is important to appreciate, as Silver and Clark (2015) and Blum (2003; 2001) do, that scenes are characterized by their intensified theatricality, local authenticity, and by "their publicly observable clusters of urban sociability" (Straw 2015, 483) embedded in particular places and practices. "The scene is an occasion for seeing and being seen and so, for *doing* seeing and being scene" (Blum 2001, 14). In the case of Hamilton, the city's cultural life has a publicness – a quality of seeing and being seen – that is most visible downtown along James Street North.

"Art is the new steel" was a fundraising slogan used by Centre3, a printmaking artist-run centre in downtown Hamilton. This slogan has gathered significant traction within and beyond the city. Neo-bohemia and its associated entrepreneurial derivatives are being positioned to become the new industry in Hamilton as they have been in so many postindustrial cities in North America (Lloyd 2006). Creative class boosterism is hard at work in Hamilton, with economic development officers and journalists celebrating the "cultural migration" from the Greater Toronto Area in a bid to attract artistic denizens and cultural entrepreneurs (McBride 2012). The allure for artist transplants is the affordable stock of heritage houses, gallery, loft, and live/work space in industrial warehouses and heritage buildings, and the rapidly gentrifying art axis of galleries, cafés, and independent businesses, and a monthly "art crawl" along James Street North. This street offers a particularly poignant example of the incongruous tensions derived from old poverty and new arrivals, from realism and idealism, from decay and fresh paint, and from artists and entrepreneurs.

Canadian urban geographer David Ley (2003, 2535) has provocatively used Pierre Bourdieu's theorizations of cultural capital to explain some of the tensions between cultural and economic imaginaries of "artistic habitus":

The related but opposing tendencies of cultural and economic imaginaries re-appear; spaces colonised by commerce or the state are spaces refused by the artist. But as scholars know, this antipathy is not mutual; the surfeit of meaning in places frequented by artists becomes a valued resource for the entrepreneur.

Artist and cultural entrepreneurs carry different, and sometimes oppositional, forms of capital, despite their purported common membership in the privileged so-called creative class (Florida 2002). Such tensions between artistic practice and cultural entrepreneurship are evident on James Street North. On this downtown street, artists and developers reimagine, contest, and share ideas about the redevelopment and rebranding of the neighbourhood – ideas, this chapter shows, that are bolstered through performative spectacles like Art Crawl and Supercrawl.

TRANSFORMING STEEL INTO ART:
THE GROWTH MACHINE OF CULTURAL PRODUCTION

In an interview for the documentary, *This Is Hamilton... After the Steel Rush* (Rallis and Mashkoor 2012), former Hamilton East MP and MPP Sheila Copps discusses Hamilton's overall metamorphosis from a one-industry steel town into an arts and culture hub. Tracing a genealogy of sorts, Copps attributes the preliminary stages of Hamilton's postindustrial transition to the arrival of the McMaster medical school in the 1970s, sparking Hamilton's now dominant and growing health services industry. She also discusses in detail the emerging arts and culture scene. Copps vividly remembers how during her time as MP and MPP, in the early 2000s, other provincial cabinet members discussed and divided provincial monetary allocation in binary terms of "sewage versus culture": "The thing is we live in a city that is overshadowed by Toronto. At the meeting these members scoffed at the idea of a public art gallery in Hamilton, even after we had collected all this private funding. The cabinet members ... and this is at a provincial caucus meeting ... they turned to me and said, 'Well Sheila, you know there's no f-ing culture in Hamilton anyway.' How could you sign an agreement that says everything outside of Toronto is sewage and water, and Toronto has all the culture?"

This quotation from Copps highlights some of the political prejudices directed towards Hamilton and its perceived potential to become "cultural."

Her recollections offer important reminders about how grassroots citizen and private sector initiatives to develop an arts and culture scene in Hamilton along James Street North are conditioned by municipal and provincial political actors. In the context of ongoing processes of neoliberal globalization, it is also important to connect Hamilton's postindustrial transition within larger discourses of creative city policy and branding strategies that have been championed by Richard Floridaites from Amsterdam to Detroit. A brief examination of key Hamilton cultural policy documents reveals the multifarious nature of the emerging arts and culture scene, while also showing how creative city policy and planning discourses rely heavily on urban spectacle and consumption as place-making strategies.

The close relationship between economic development and cultural production in Hamilton emerged in official policy discourses between 1989 and 1997, when the Hamilton-Wentworth Regional Council created a primarily citizen-led task force to explore the concept of sustainable development through a review of all regional policy initiatives. Along with environmental, social, and economic pillars, a summary of the study concluded that culture should be listed as a key pillar of sustainable development. This finding was formalized in 2012, when Hamilton's general manager stated in a draft cultural plan that "culture is the fourth pillar of sustainable development and it is one tool we can use in building a vibrant, sustainable city that attracts and retains talent" (Appendix A to Report PED12117(a), 5). "[P]arallels between the current creative economy discourse and practice and the early ecological cities movement" have been noted by scholars of postindustrial cities (Breitbart 2013, 279). Ecology/sustainable development and culture/creativity are urban policy discourses being deployed by city boosters and place entrepreneurs as broadly politically palatable and accessible rebranding themes. Hamilton's emergent cultural policy framework echoes other ongoing trends of urban rebranding across small to medium sized cities in Ontario, such as the City of Kingston's ongoing sustainability project (http://sustainablekingston. ca/; Lewis and Donald 2010).

Hamilton's official narrative about creative branding was solidified in 2005 with the formation of the Hamilton Creative City Initiative, mandated to report on how to nurture cultural development in the city. The first phase of the report, released to the public in 2007, highlights the importance of fostering an emergent downtown arts and culture scene. A subsequent *Building a Creative Catalyst Feasibility Study* discursively frames Hamilton's music industry as ideally positioned "to be harnessed and catalyzed as a means to grow Hamilton's economy, re-activate the downtown area, improve the physical condition of the buildings and neighbourhood" (Norton and Shaker 2009, 2). Hamilton's most recent official cultural policy narrative comes from the cultural plan, *Transforming Hamilton through Culture* (2013), which emphasizes downtown renewal, neighbourhood revitalization, and fostering welcoming communities. Despite the attention given to Hamilton's downtown, only one direct mention is made in the plan of the growing arts and culture scene on James Street North with a quotation from a *Toronto Star* article: "The best evidence of Hamilton's growing artistic muscle is the year-round Art Crawl" (City of Hamilton 2013, 48). While the word "festival" is only mentioned a handful of times in this sixty-eight-page cultural policy document, "festivals and events" do get their own concept bubble in the culture mapping chart (25). Festivals are also listed as the second most popular cultural activity, after visiting natural heritage parks and forests and "91% of Hamiltonians [are said to] attend a local festival" (54).

Although arts festivals have perhaps not been fully realized in official municipal cultural policy narratives as a development tool (as denoted by the lack of specific mentioning of the Art Crawl, Supercrawl or James Street North in the 2013 cultural plan or the Creative City Initiative), the tensions surrounding the cultural capital of an emerging downtown arts scene and the gentrifying processes associated with it, highlight how creative city branding, tourism, and property value play into place-marketing strategies and spectacle via culture. It is also important to note the larger regional forces at play surrounding the growth and expansion of the Greater Toronto-Hamilton Area in relation to James Street North and the downtown core. Hamilton's affordable housing market, its close proximity to Toronto, and its expanding arts and culture scene have made it an attractive relocation destination for upwardly mobile families who can no longer afford to live in Toronto. The government of Ontario along with the transit coordination agency GO-Metrolinx have, as of 2014, drafted policy regarding the building of a James Street North Mobility Hub, which will intersect the CN main rail line with the future City of Hamilton rapid transit A-line. This new GO station/hub also includes the development of Pier 8, an upscale multiuse condominium and business real estate project, further emphasizing the consumptive nature of creative branding discourses along James Street North. Such branding strategies exclude voices and narratives of residents who do not adhere to the new upwardly mobile, artistic, entrepreneurial, creative class. Such exclusions in official and media narratives of James Street North matter because their representational effects can become material effects. When civic leaders ignore certain older social and cultural groups and organizations in favour of others in the framing of municipal policies, that inattention can shape the allocation of resources within the city. While James Street North has become the most hyped street in Hamilton over the last decade, it is valuable to recognize its long and diverse history.

JAMES STREET NORTH: A BRIEF HISTORY OF A STREET

James Street North is named after James Hughson, the son of one of Hamilton's founders. Geographically central, James Street North is an extension of the downtown core that runs north from King Street to Hamilton Harbour, dividing the city east and west, north and south. Historically, this street was the entry point for new citizens to the city, especially Jewish, Italian, and Portuguese immigrants. A strong Portuguese presence is still visible today on James Street North in the social clubs, street markets, restaurants, and churches. Connecting the port, and later the CN railway station, to the downtown, James Street North was not only an important transportation corridor in the nineteenth century but also a nexus of business, industry, government, and entertainment. The city's market and first Town Hall (1839) were built here along with establishments like the Lister Block (1852), Grafton's Department Store (1895), and the Arcade Store (1915) that was later bought by Eaton's and then Zellers. Organizations like the Mechanics Institutes (1853), the Royal Hotel (1857), the Federal Building (1856), and the McQuesten Iron Foundry (1835) located here in addition to the Grand Opera house and the Princess (later Tivoli) Theatre (Sage 2013). James Street North thrived for much of its early history, with a lively street life fostered by generations of independent business owners who ran hardware, grocery, and clothing stores well into the twentieth century.

By the 1970s and 1980s, forces of suburbanization and selective urban renewal combined with poverty and crime to leave the streetscape of James Street North pockmarked with boarded-up storefronts, abandoned buildings, and absentee landlords. Plans in the mid-1980s to designate James Street North a heritage conservation district failed to get municipal approval. While official heritage planning mechanisms did not kick-start renewal along James Street North, in 2002, in response to a recommendation made at a downtown revitalization charette organized by Architecture Hamilton several years earlier, the street was converted back from one-way to a two-way thoroughfare. While opponents to this conversion anticipated gridlock and property neglect, the street has instead experienced significant renewed investment in buildings and businesses and an increase in pedestrian traffic.

The revival and "stabilization" of James Street North over the last decade has been undertaken, in large part, by individual cultural workers who have made significant financial and sweat equity investments in property (gallery owner, interview, August 2013). The affordability of downtown real estate has allowed individuals to purchase and renovate entire buildings. Property investment by arts stakeholders has been accompanied by a sense of civic ownership of, and stake in, the street and the living culture being promoted and created here. The street is approached by many members of the arts community as a collective public art project made stable and sustainable through property ownership, networking, and collaboration.

An arts and culture scene has become spatially and psychologically embedded in this street, especially in the nine blocks that extend from King Street to Murray Street. There is a remarkable concentration of cultural capital here in the nineteenth-century brick buildings that are a mix of low-rent street-level retail, restaurants, and cafés with studios and apartments above. As Phanuel Antwi and Amber Dean (2010, 22) note in their study of art, gentrification, and cultures of surveillance in Hamilton:

There is a burgeoning arts "scene" on the main downtown thoroughfare of James Street North, where galleries have begun to outnumber the workingmen's watering holes and Portuguese or Italian grocers that once predominated in this working class, immigrant neighbourhood. One might hope that this would provide a venue for different imaginings of the city, different ways of picturing and thinking about the city that challenge conventional frameworks. No doubt some such re-imagining work is taking place. However, the most well-publicized and talked about representations of the city in spaces for art on James North have worked primarily to bolster conventional frameworks that give evidence of poverty and neglect as signs that the city is lacking spaces for "culture."

Small commercial and independent art galleries, three nonprofit artist-run centres, art studios, artists' collectives, performance venues, independent arts-based businesses, and creative business incubators exist in close proximity to one another interspersed with social service agencies and ethnic grocers. CBC Hamilton has set up its studio on James Street North beside a retail outlet for the Art Gallery of Hamilton and a couple of blocks up from Tourism Hamilton's Visitors Centre. A storefront museum, HIStory and HERitage, uses video displays to exhibit the social, cultural, and architectural history of Hamilton in conjunction with the "Hamilton Store" which sells all things Hamiltonian. In between are vintage clothing and antique stores, and a selectively curated art supply and gift store. Multiple condominium projects are in various stages of construction. There are no chain businesses on the street, and "the handmade, vintage, craft, and art aesthetic" that thrives here has been characterized as "industrially quaint" (Sage 2013, 194). The faded imprint of hand-painted advertisements on brick exteriors, the disused signs above new businesses, the original wood floors, the exposed brick interiors, and the painted tin ceilings all provide a certain character and presumed sense of authenticity. Such atmospheres have long attracted cultural workers to see the creative potential in socially and culturally diverse neighbourhoods that had long been abandoned by the white mainstream middle class (Zukin 2010).

In Hamilton, "the influx of artists is creating a whole new identity" for James Street North "as Hamilton's Arts District" and "arts zone" leading to "a phenomena [sic] that is being recognized across the country as an emerging model for successful urban renewal led by the creative class" (SOS: Soul of the Street 2011). Arts-led renewal on James Street North has received significant local, regional, and national media coverage, intensifying public debate about the future of the city. A recent art exhibition curated at the Workers Arts and Heritage Centre, entitled *Art as the New Steel? Changing and Challenging Perspectives on the James Street North Community* (2014) extended this discussion, exploring the politicized roles of art and artists in neighbourhood redevelopment. As the curators explain, "this exhibition seek[s] to respond to important questions regarding access, agency and change in our community but to also explore issues of migration and displacement as they relate to the historical and contemporaneous changes that have been, or continue to be, experienced by the diverse range of communities who claim James St North and its surrounding environs as their own" (Berinstein et al. 2014). As this quotation emphasizes, cultural workers are not the only community group with a spatial claim to James Street North. As interviews and participant observation confirmed, the street is inhabited by residents who variously identify as social justice activists, working-class people, immigrants, at-risk youth, sex workers, and people on low incomes. While James Street North is framed in the contemporary public and policy imaginations as a street where arts and culture are created, displayed, and consumed, it is important to remember that embedded in this street are the many textured and layered materialities of people and things that may have little, if any, relationship to the arts community (Sage 2013).

DESTINATION CULTURE: THE JAMES STREET NORTH ART CRAWL

The association of James Street North with the arts was reinforced nearly a decade ago with the initiation of the James Street North Art Crawl. This monthly event was started by a small group of gallery and business owners and artist-run centre directors trying to build an audience for the artwork they were exhibiting in the buildings they owned while simultaneously battling public misperceptions of the street as a rough and run-down place. On the second Friday of every month art galleries and independent businesses stay open late. By synchronizing art openings, artists and galleries were able to build a critical mass of viewers and to initiate a broader dialogue about art in Hamilton. Initially, it "was a showcase and a venue, and a party for the converted" (photographer, interview, October 2013) with artists and other workers in the arts scene breaking out of "a community of solitudes" (gallery owner, interview, September 2013) to patronize each other's galleries and barter art for art. In the intervening years, the Art Crawl has grown from fifty attendees to nearly 2,000. It has morphed into a festival of food and commerce. As one artist-run centre program coordinator laments, "if you want to come out and see art, especially if you're looking at it critically, the Art Crawl is not the night to come. It's too busy and too noisy" (interview, October 2013). He goes on to describe how the low-income Somali and Karen students for whom he runs arts programming do not frequent the Art Crawl: "the Art Crawl is this different cultural group. It's people in Hamilton from Strathcona and the West End. They come from Ancaster and Burlington for a night out of socializing and not to see anything specific."

Art Crawl has also become a contested event on social media platforms such as Twitter. In 2011, a group of community artists and arts enthusiasts formed the online monthly Twitter event, #Exchange1111. Initiated originally to discuss Art Crawl, the virtual discussion soon expanded to include topics related to artistic, creative, and cultural industries in greater Hamilton. In an interview for the documentary *This Is Hamilton* (Rallis and Mashkoor 2012), a downtown record store owner describes #Exchange1111:

> It became about how to be more inclusive in the community. We started talking about issues regarding different Hamilton demographics and we talked about different ways to get people involved … One idea was to try to have some kind of reoccurring event up on the mountain similar to Art Crawl, so we're trying to work on something that way … The thing is about this exchange and social media is that information is important too – there's no one newspaper or website that can list all the functions that are going on. How do we gather and disseminate information?

This social media platform afforded some community actors an opportunity to voice concerns and ideas surrounding public art, place making, and creative branding in Hamilton. The executive director of the Hamilton Arts Council, for example, tweeted "An art event can generate great enthusiasm and energy, but what comes after that? How do we continue that participation?" (11 July 2012). Other community members responded the same day by suggesting a need to focus on the "prosperity of youth"

(@DrDiscHamilton) and the provision of "multi-use space [that] would allow opportunity to diversify programming for youth" (@ciaramckeown). Still others suggested that the definition of arts is "too wide for the general public" (@interestica) and that "the dance community is definitely under-represented in the city. More space and more patrons needed" (@seagrams). Such dialogic moments, brief as they are, have emerged out of the strategic terrain of the Art Crawl. Public conversations about artistic possibilities have become increasingly common in Hamilton.

In 2007, the James Street Art Crawl received an award of merit as a "visionary project" from the City of Hamilton at the annual Urban Design and Architecture Awards. However, as the Art Crawl has gained mainstream popularity, much of its novelty has worn off for local cultural workers. As middle-class residents from Hamilton and the surrounding municipalities increasingly treat the Art Crawl as a safe and entertaining evening out downtown, perceptions of its critical artistic merit have declined. What started organically as a coordinated evening of art exhibition openings has been built up by the owner of a local record label and recording studio, Sonic Unyon, into an annual, publicly funded weekend festival of live music, performance, food, and art known as the Supercrawl.

SUPER SIZE ME: FROM ART CRAWL TO SUPERCRAWL

The first Supercrawl was hosted as an independent and self-funded event in September 2009. Since then, it has grown from a full-day event into a two-day programmed arts festival that attracts upwards of 80,000 people. This event is now supported by the City of Hamilton and receives more than $100,000 in city council funding to stage and police it. James Street North is closed to cars for the weekend, and the festival takes over the street, including the redeveloped superblock between King and York Streets in front of the mall, farmers' market, and the central public library. The festival organizers reinforce an atmosphere of civility and security by facilitating a very visible police presence. Police officers patrol James Street North and main intersections to foster the flow of traffic and people. The police presence is intended to deter opportunistic crime, to enact surveillance on marginalized social groups, and to displace potentially disruptive individuals from public space, while offering uniformed reassurance to middle class consumers (Cook and Whowell 2011). Such overt "proactive policing" has been an ongoing tension for some local residents who attend, but also occasionally protest, Supercrawl and Art Crawl (Bennett 2015). In 2013, the June Art Crawl was disrupted by a brief moment of counter-spectacle when a group of local activists held a police brutality awareness rally. With banners and chants, activists declared "NO POLICE. Killer Cops! Police State!" and "Who do you call when the police assault you?" For downtown business and property owners and visitors, the police presence at Supercrawl is intended to impart feelings of safety, control, and comfort while simultaneously enacting a form of impression management for the downtown core (Németh 2010). The yellow-jacketed teams of officers on foot and bicycles who are part of the recent Addressing Crime Trends in our Neighbourhoods (ACTION) program have become increasingly visible in the downtown with the support of the Downtown Hamilton Business Improvement Association, which represents 470 businesses and 175 property owners (Bennett 2015).

During Supercrawl, James Street North is divided into corporate-sponsored zones anchored by large elevated stages scheduled with live music performances: the Hamilton International Airport Stage; the Hamilton Community Foundation Stage; the TD/Arkells Stage; and the ArcelorMittal Dofasco Family Stage. A VIP beer garden and tourism zone is sponsored by the local regional tourism association in conjunction with the Royal Bank of Canada, and the catwalk in the fashion zone is sponsored by a local community college. The symbolic economy of prominently displayed sponsor names and logos is a reminder of the power of entrepreneurial capital to shape the form and character of urban public space (Zukin 1995). The different thematic zones are reminiscent of a theme park where modernist planning principles are applied to strictly separate and bound activities. The spatial boundaries of Supercrawl are carefully defined and colour coded into festival guide maps so as to limit encounters with social deprivation at the northernmost extension of James Street North and on eastern side streets. Supercrawl is geographically staged so as "to reassure cultural tourists of a safe encounter with the city" (Quinn 2005, 936).

The information and merchandise booths, combined with the prominently displayed promotional materials (like postcards, brochures, posters, and oversized performance schedules), stamp the street in the brilliant blue of the Supercrawl brand and give it visual coherence. This visual strategy works to build a total experience of James Street North as a cultural destination. Local businesses and arts organizations hawk their wares and use the event to profile their merchandise and activities, but the visual arts-based programming of the private galleries, artist studios, and artist-run centres is not officially profiled in the festival guide:

> The Supercrawl is run by cultural entrepreneurs in music and performing arts, so they have a bias there. But it's also not acknowledging what exists on the street already. Whether it's conscious or not, thinking about the little people on the street. We experience exclusion. You can't say they actively turn us down because it's more by omission. They've done it again this year. We had all kinds of activities happening this year, but we didn't get included in the promotional material and they're getting a lot of public money from the city to run this festival and they're not including what the artist-run centres are doing. It's a frustrating tension. We give the information of what we're doing and it's not there. (arts administrator, interview, November 2013)

This quotation emphasizes a sense of disconnection experienced at the Supercrawl between grassroots, community-based arts initiatives, which animate James Street North year round with their programming, and the branded spectacle and visual manipulation of the festival. Local Hamiltonians produce culture and are an established audience for culture, but their labour is often not meaningfully celebrated or showcased by the organizers of Supercrawl.

Central to the formal animation of the streetscape in each of the music zones are food trucks and retail stalls, as well as curated public art installations. Following a call for submissions and with funding from the Ontario Arts Council, local businesses and the city, eight site-specific works of public art were selected in 2013 and ten in 2014 to "inspire both local art lovers and those new to art." A festival guide and map profiles the performers and public art projects and locates their placement on the street under the heading "Art on James North." Thumbnail photographs, short paragraphs of description, a map symbol, and a number take the spectator to the corresponding street installations where festival plaques designate the installations as public art. The guide is an entry point to James Street North that constructs and stages a particular image of the city designed to comfortably align with a consumptive middle-class tourist experience. It structures that experience by reinforcing a divide between the spectacle and the spectator or consumer. The gaze of festivalgoers is strategically directed to where they can eat and drink, shop, hear music, and see art. In recent years, the festival has also become a place for attendees not only to consume culture but also to act as amateur ethnographers documenting the "realness" of Hamilton's downtown population. A CBC Hamilton reporter wrote an article entitled "Humans of Supercrawl," referencing the photo project "Humans of New York," which suggests that the art is not what makes the festival entertaining, rather, the main attraction is watching people watching each other (Rieti 2014).

The art that matters for Supercrawl organizers is the curated public "Art on James North" exhibition listed in the guide. The everyday artistic presence of arts organizations on James Street North is seldom acknowledged or mapped in the festival guide. Some local cultural producers who are rooted in place and who engage in participative, communal art practices feel sidelined by festival organizers. What, then, does the official public art at Supercrawl have to say about Hamilton and the change experienced on James Street North? In what follows, we undertake a critical analysis of three public art installations encountered on James Street North at the 2013 and 2014 Supercrawl events to reveal how these works of art interact with the street and work to question, as well as to reinforce, creative city policy and planning discourses. Our critique is neither intended as a dismissal of the possibilities and potentialities of civic spectacle nor as a denial of the critical art works embedded within the spectacle (Haiven 2012). Like Haiven we too identify "civic spectacle as a manifestation of systemic, cultural, and economic forces beyond the control of any individual" and contend that in all likelihood, the majority of the artists contributing to the spectacle "would decry neoliberalism, gentrification, and the instrumentalization of the arts," while their works of art can be interpreted as oscillating between contestation and ambivalence (14).

PUBLIC ART INSTALLATIONS ON JAMES STREET NORTH: PLAYING WITH PLACE

At the 2014 Supercrawl, in front of the main festival stage, local graphic artist, David Collier, drew a comic strip in ink and watercolour that he enlarged and reproduced on adhesive vinyl (figure 5.1). Entitled *Our Move to Hamilton: One Family's Story*, the comic is a reprint of his comics published in *The Hamilton Spectator* from 2002–14 and is based on his graphic novel *Hamilton Illustrated* (2012). It tells the personal story of how Collier came to live and work in Hamilton. As new young parents who had recently left Saskatoon, Collier and his wife borrowed an unused, family owned cottage in the Ottawa Valley while Collier looked for steady employment. When extended family members described them as "bottom-feeders," they felt pressure to find their own home, but as his wife questions in the third frame "Where are we going to go? You're a good artist, but you don't earn enough to support us anywhere."

Collier's story highlights the precariousness associated with artistic labour – the material and existential uncertainty and instability derived from flexible employment arrangements (Bain and McLean 2013). As an occupational group, artists usually have higher levels of education than the general work force, yet they also "show higher rates of self-employment, higher rates of unemployment, several forms of constrained underemployment, and are more often multiple job holders" (Menger 1999, 545). Many artists earn the majority of their income from employment in a secondary job (Bain 2005), but relative to other technical and professional workers of a similar age, education, and training, artists earn less on average and have greater income inequality and variability (Maranda 2009). As the "super core" of Richard Florida's rather "fuzzy" creative class concept (Markusen 2006), artists may not possess the same economic capital as their professional creative counterparts in law and medicine, but they are celebrated for their cultural capital and mobility. Creative city policy à la Richard Florida aspires to nurture and nourish this core creative class with attractive urban amenities and to harness and channel their talents (Peck 2005).

In a later frame in the comic strip, Collier describes how a friend called to tell his wife about a cheap apartment for rent down the street

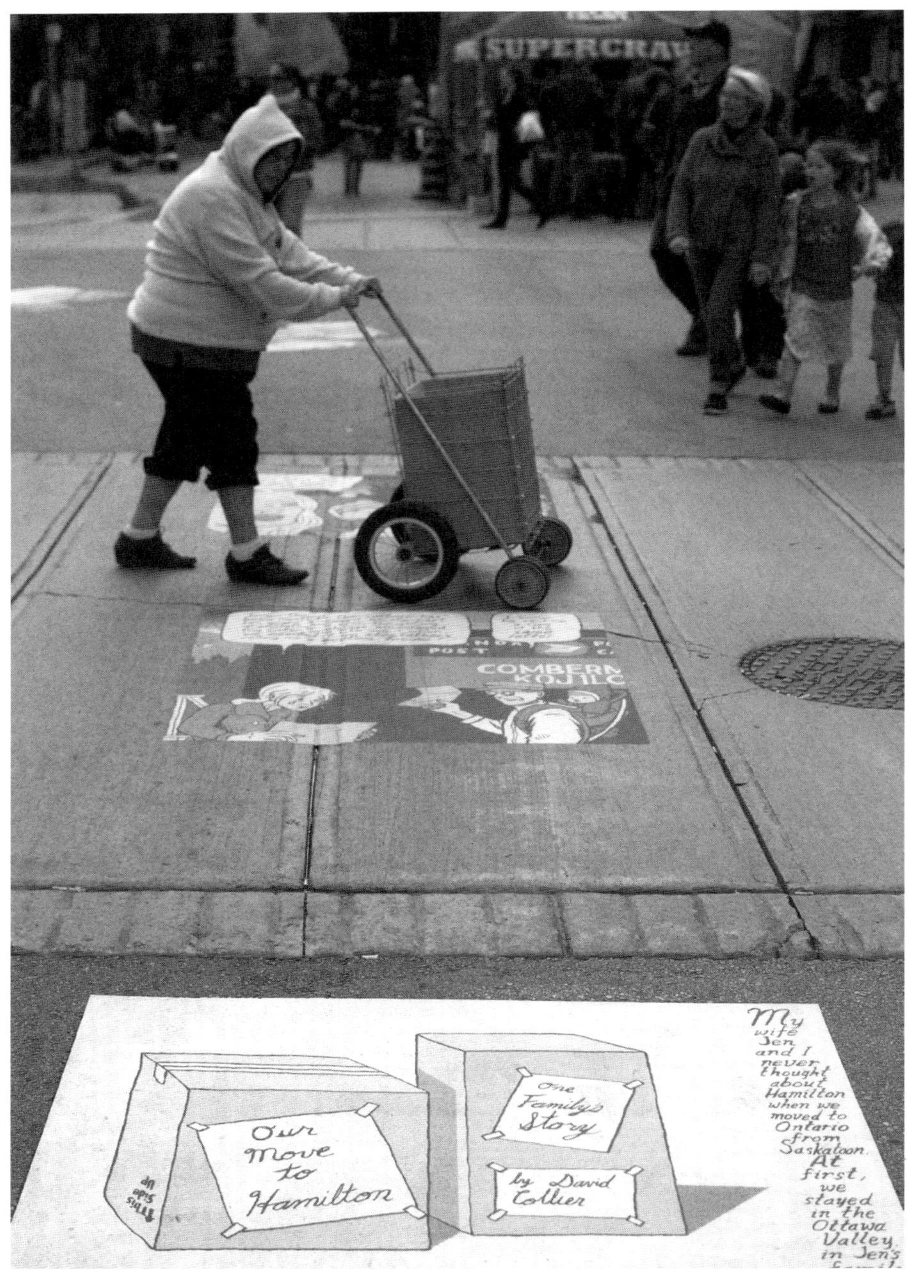

5.1 Opening frames from *Our Move to Hamilton: One Family's Story* by David Collier. Photo: Alison L. Bain, 2014.

from her in Hamilton. His reminiscences of Hamilton capture a sense of the city from an outsider vantage point, stigmatizing it as a gritty, working class, steel town. He describes travelling to the city on the GO bus from Toronto with a sketchbook in hand seeking "inspiring ambience." A younger Collier is represented looking onto an unpeopled, almost lunar, landscape dotted with the outlines of vacant properties. He walks towards an ominous, dirty, fenced in, industrial city that proudly flies the Canadian flag, with a speech bubble above his head that exclaims "sublime!" A tear in the vinyl rips the city in half, exposing the black asphalt of the city's infrastructural underbelly; we do not know whether this rip was deliberate or not. The rawness and grittiness of this place is celebrated as authentic and inspirational, exercising a magnetic pull on Collier. A tight shot in the next frame shows Collier and his wife in the front cab of a U-Haul truck driving down the highway. This image evokes the capital and human mobility flows associated with gentrification. The text reveals that Collier's wife's aunt, a Hamiltonian, has confirmed that the apartment and the city are liveable and provides a familial connection to place. As the Supercrawl public art project marker boldly proclaims to spectators, Collier has invested in a semidetached house in the North End and has become a citizen of Hamilton: "loud neighbours, drug use, and cop calls were part of the day-to-day, but Collier came to love the community."

Collier's story with its white, heteronormative familial intimacies and positive narrative of overcoming poverty to find a sense of belonging, ownership, and stability aligns with neoliberal municipal urban boosterism strategies. He celebrates the friendliness and support of the local community in welcoming his family into the neighbourhood, the affordability of local real estate, and the employment possibilities for creatives. The final frame of the comic strip reads: "Jen thinks the move has been good for our careers. Hamilton is close enough to Toronto for meetings with big time art directors once in a while, yet far enough away to keep measure of one's independence. Since moving here, the fear of not being able to afford city living has been somewhat assuaged."

Our Move to Hamilton is described in the festival guide as "a way-finding tool" for Supercrawl. In the comic's renavigation of civic space, it is also unintentionally a way-finding tool to the hegemonic place-making narrative of Hamilton through the reinforcement of a neoliberal creative city place-marketing script. In this particular narration, despite finding inspiration in working class cityscapes, cultural production on James Street North is largely represented as fostered by an upwardly mobile creative class, making their exodus from expensive big city living in Toronto and surrounding areas.

A block up the street an outdoor parking lot was transformed by the Quebec art collective BGL (Jasmin Bilodeau, Sébastien Giguère, and Nicolas Laverdière) with their public art installation *Carrousel* (2013). Originally designed for the large-scale all night art spectacle Nuit Blanche Calgary in 2012, BGL reassembled its carousel in downtown Hamilton. The carousel is built out of metal crowd control barriers and shopping carts. At Supercrawl, visitors of all ages queued politely in anticipation of a ride in the upturned, dangling, and spinning shopping carts (figure 5.2). The festival guide describes the installation as "combin[ing] the mundane and the fantastical – it evokes something child-like and magical while appearing as an absurd conglomeration of dull metal objects." Indeed the shopping carts, in their slow and gentle revolution, mesmerize and delight passersby offering a playful reminder of childhood trips to the fair. But those same metal objects also evoke a legacy in the built environment of temporarily restricting and controlling the movement of people in privatized public spaces.

If scaled up, the carousel could be interpreted as a miniature theme park. It is not a free-flowing space, but rather it is ordered and controlled to ensure efficiency of pedestrian and traffic movement, regulated access to the ride, and safety of users. It is a contrived experience of organized spontaneity that affords a brief escape from the mundane reproductive activities that structure everyday lives. The time spent in the queue for the few minutes of excitement on the ride attests to the element of control. Patrons are invited to briefly enter a different world of spinning shopping carts where daily conventions of pushing groceries or personal belongings and constraints of access to affordable fresh food are momentarily subverted. New sensations are experienced, sitting on the interior backside of a metal trolley, legs dangling over the edge of the push bar. The spinning circular motion can be dizzying and disorienting, but the radial pattern of movement out from the centre is also a predictable and familiar theme park design. This public art intervention indirectly raises important critical questions worthy of sustained public debate about the redevelopment trajectory of downtown Hamilton. Is James

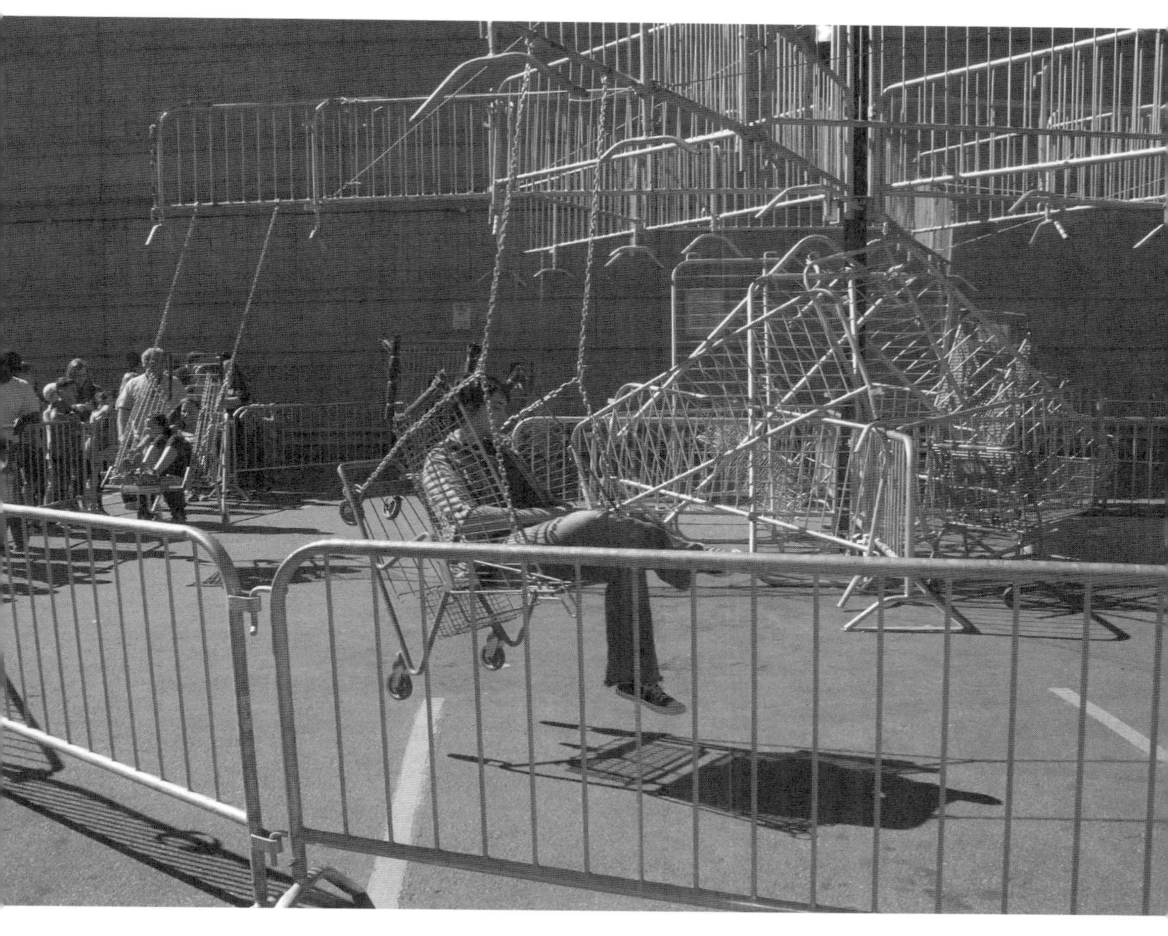

5.2 Supercrawl festival-goers taking a ride on *Carrousel* by BGL.
Photo: Alison L. Bain, 2013.

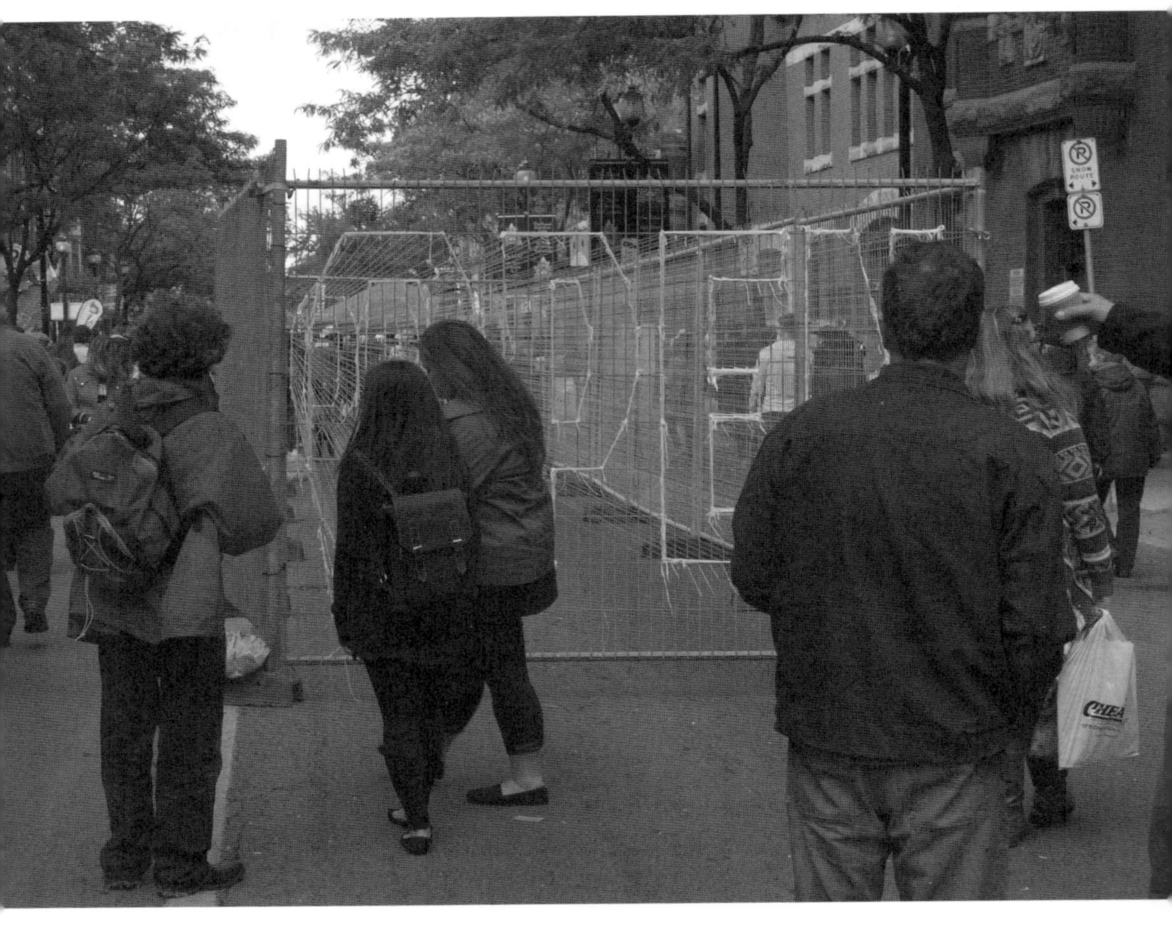

5.3 Rerouting pedestrian traffic around *Open* by Sean Martindale.
Photo: Alison L. Bain, 2014.

Street North little more than a theme park – a gentrifying playscape for the creative class?

Another couple of blocks up the street, across from two artist-run centres, at the 2014 Supercrawl was a cluster of three public art installations: *The Cocoon*, by Ariel Bader-Shami and Petra Matar, "an introspective refuge woven with naturally dyed fabrics that celebrates the beauty of change" while also creating "a calming place for transformation and growth"; *insecureTs*, by Andrew McPhail, a clothing rack hung with black t-shirts hand-stitched with silver sequined statements of insecurities (e.g., reject, misfit, dummy) that members of the public could borrow to wear at the festival; and *Open*, by Sean Martindale, a fenced enclosure delicately strung with the word "open" in yarn serving "as a warning of censorship and controlled definition." All three installations offer artful insights into how bodies and urban spaces are labelled, regulated, and changed. In their location and concentration, they also mark a stretch of James Street North that has a significant amount of grassroots arts infrastructure and investment. We have chosen, however, to focus on *Open* because of its sheer size and dramatic central location (figure 5.3).

Erected in the middle of James Street North, *Open* is a site-specific work of art that is anything but open. Resembling a fenced plot of land awaiting development, it is a rectangular enclosure erected out of industrial construction fencing, whose interior space is inaccessible and off limits. This same utilitarian fencing was used at the 2013 Supercrawl to barricade off James Street North to traffic and to demarcate the northern most end of the festival. It was also used at this same festival by artist Erika James in a site-specific piece entitled *Don't Fence Me In* (2013). Three wooden planks with white text, mounted on the metal barriers as a silhouette of agricultural fencing read, "When I was a child, fences were made for climbing. Now I know that fences are made to keep us divided." Further up the street Erika James offered festivalgoers another reminder in cursive white script about appropriate codes of conduct in public space: "Make sure you mind your own business, be polite, and reserve judgment until you leave the premises."

Like *Don't Fence Me In*, *Open* functions as a temporary barrier, occupying nearly a complete lane of traffic. An obstacle to the flow of pedestrians who have reclaimed the street from cars for Supercrawl, it confronts festivalgoers with a false message of openness and forces them to navigate around it. In its rigid materiality and placement on a rapidly gentrifying street, *Open* represents the closure and exclusion wrought by speculative real estate ventures that seek to redevelop land to its highest and best use. Discursively, however, the word "open," woven with string into the thin metal bars of the fence, is suggestive of imaginative and artistic possibilities. The technique used to write on the fence is reminiscent of knit graffiti or yarn bombing – an international guerrilla art movement whose practitioners seek to transform public space with "donated" works of art created out of yarn (Bain 2013).

Toronto-based interdisciplinary artist Sean Martindale explains in the program for Supercrawl that this public art installation "questions and engages with public spaces in new ways that consider our shared environments, how we use and navigate them, and the importance of civic awareness and engagement," at a "crucial moment of transformation in downtown Hamilton" (CBC 2014). Other artists in Hamilton have engaged with this theme of barriers that prevent public access to land. Back in 1990, the photographer Cees van Gemerden opened his show "No Trespassing" nearby at the artist-run centre, Hamilton Artists' Incorporated (www.ceesvangemerden.ca). The exhibition was first hung on the chain link fences along the harbour it documents. In a photo essay of seventy-eight images of Hamilton's industrial landscape, he explores the history of pollution, closure, remediation, and redevelopment of ten kilometres of the city's Lake Ontario shoreline, particularly the Lax Lands. In his own words: "When the city found out how polluted the area was, they put a double fence at the entrance. Hamiltonians, if you put up a fence, they climb over it and destroy it and open it up. It is one of the wonderful things that Hamiltonians do" (interview, June 2014). A selection of these images was exhibited recently at the Workers Art and Heritage Centre exhibition about urban renewal on James Street North, which concluded just before the start of the 2014 Supercrawl. This exhibition, like *Open*, questions access, agency, and change on James Street North.

Open references a "yet-to-be-determined future" for James Street North. Will this street become yet another example of what Sharon Zukin (1995, 28) describes as "pacification by cappuccino" and homogenization by the status symbols of the new urban middle class – "'opening' the place to forms of consumption by a larger population of visitors" (Vanolo 2013, 1796)? Or do other more socially inclusive imaginaries await?

THE FESTIVIZED SEIZURE OF JAMES STREET NORTH

In Hamilton, James Street North is a street that plays an important role in cultural production and, increasingly, in cultural consumption. Artistic labour and practice, in conjunction with cultural entrepreneurial reinvestment in the built fabric of James Street North, have transformed the street into its own work of art – but art in the service of a creative city toolkit that emphasizes growth-led logics and urban boosterism. The scholarly literature has shown that such neoliberal political visions are associated with "detrimental outcomes, including the gentrification of lower-cost neighbourhoods, zero-tolerance policing and the broader displacement of progressive and welfarist orientations in local politics and programmes" (Vanolo 2013, 1788).

This chapter has shown how the "festivize[d] seizure" of James Street North through the Art Crawl and Supercrawl has marketed the street as a place brand (Solnit 2000, 214). These two arts festivals have generated the consumptive spectacle, media coverage, and out-of-town visitors that city managers deploy in reimagineering strategies designed to ease the transition from an industrial to a postindustrial city. In so doing, however, they continue to reproduce inequalities between the rich and poor, between those with "high spending power who enjoy the new 'café cultures' which have emerged, often in gentrifying inner city areas, and the new urban poor, on the other, who are locked into marginal low-wage jobs or who survive on benefits and become short- or long-term clients of the 'food banks'" (Thorns 2002, 126).

In the wake of Art Crawl and Supercrawl, James Street North has become a heavily programmed and policed space with extensive rules and prescribed ways of being used. A shift has occurred on the street away from everyday services and businesses that cater to the reproductive needs of local residents, towards the provision of consumptive amenities that appeal to a mobile creative class. The public art installations curated for Supercrawl in 2013 and 2014 speak directly to this shift; they temporarily subvert and/or question social norms of public space usage while also ambivalently reinforcing neoliberal understandings of place as commodity.

Social theorists treat festivals as "liminal 'time out of time' spaces (Bakhtin 1984) replete with possibilities for challenging social conventions, social order, and authority, and inverting society's social norms" (Quinn 2005, 934). In their theoretical ideal, festivals, particularly street festivals, have the power to temporarily change the basic functions of a city and to open up spaces for new social interactions and understandings (Micallef 2009). That power is rooted in an understanding of the street as "democracy's greatest arena, the place where ordinary people can speak, unsegregated by walls, unmediated by those with more power" (Solnit 2000, 216). But the power to speak on the street, to meaningfully exchange words that push social boundaries and challenge the status quo, is increasingly muted. As Lefebvre wrote in his book *The Urban Revolution* (2003, 20–1), "[i]n the street, we merely brush shoulders with others, we don't interact with them"; the street has become "a display, a corridor flanked by stories of various kinds" where merchandise has become spectacle and has "transformed the individual into a spectacle for others." If the public spaces of streets are to be about more than movement, commerce, and entertainment, we need arts festivals, and the public art installations that may accompany them, to have the autonomy and latitude to provoke active and critical contemplation of urban space outside of the familiar logics and rhythms of consumption. We need public art that can not only connect with the everyday users of urban space but, more importantly, create new spaces for socialization across difference that expose the complexities and inadequacies of our existing understandings of urban space (Boivin 2009).

Lawrence Bird and Solomon Nagler

6

—

BRIEF ENCOUNTER

Brief Encounters was a film installation that took place in Grand Parade, a central public square in Halifax, Nova Scotia in October 2013, as part of an "artwalk" in the colloquium *Urban Encounters: Art and the Public*.[1] The projection was a collaboration between Solomon Nagler and Lawrence Bird. It originated in a group of videos produced by Bird's graduate architecture students at the University of Manitoba; these films documented dysfunctional spaces in Winnipeg, forgotten and disused spaces exhibiting social failure or physical degradation, and spun narratives around them. In response, NSCAD students in Nagler's film production class created 16 mm shorts on celluloid documenting similar spaces in Halifax. The two groups of films were projected at the centre of Grand Parade from the two sides of a multilayered screen designed and built by Winnipeg-based artists JNZNBRK. As the images from each set of films bled through the multiple layers of the screen, finally mingling with each other at the center, viewers – mainly film and art students – slipped between the screens. Complicated by the shadows and silhouettes of these moving bodies, the screen and the square became a space of encounter.

In an exchange that played out across several months while the two were busy with projects on opposite sides of the world, Nagler and Bird here discuss the parameters, execution, and reception of *Brief Encounters* and explore the ideas provoked by the project. Their dialogue is a counterpoint to images captured at the event, as well as stills from the original films.

The titles of both the film installation and this chapter refer to the 1945 film *Brief Encounter* (directed by David Lean). That film depicts two characters whose lives are briefly linked by a chance meeting. The phrase was also adopted as the subtitle of Ben Shapiro's 2012 film *Gregory Crewdson: Brief Encounter*, documenting that artist's use of urban space and implied cinematic scenarios to stage his photography. This project and this chapter involve a similar, shifting connection between multiple protagonists, embedded in an ambiguous urban space: part fiction, part real.

LAWRENCE BIRD: Sol, the two of us have approached *Brief Encounters* from opposite directions – you, a filmmaker interested in architecture and me, an architect interested in film (if either of us can be described so straight-forwardly). What was it that you were looking for from this mix? What do spatial disciplines offer the cinematic understanding of the city?

SOLOMON NAGLER: I've always felt that cinema is, in its essence, an archi-tectural gesture. Filmmakers sculpt *mise-en-scène* to provide a certain sense of space, similarly to architects who design buildings. Perspective ebbs and flows, you can lose yourself in the spectacle of the edifice or be-come trapped in a loop of double visions and self-referential mirrors. It is also architecture that enables us to experience the cinema effect, the "cinematographic cocoon" as Barthes (1986, 346) calls it, that seduces us, entraps us.

Don't you think there is something slightly perverse in the way that the theatre encourages us to contort our bodies into a too-small seat? Is this position a primordial gesture of reception and understanding? Or is it an artificial construct necessitated by the physiological fluxes of urban life? Isn't montage a form of *flânerie*, a wandering eye that compensates for the immobility inherent in cinematic reception? The cinema satiates the need for visceral intimacy and disembodied voyeurism ... an extension of anonymous city life in a black box. By quoting Alfred Hitchcock's curt assessment that "the movies are, first of all, armchairs with spectators inside," Paul Virilio (1998) emphasizes that as filmmakers, we are primarily engaged in acts of architecture.

I'm interested in film work that deconstructs this conservative architectural paradigm, through on-screen interventions, self-referential effects that turn the screen into a mirror, so that one becomes aware of watching a film and the mechanics of projection/reception. I guess this is why I am interested in collaborating with architects and why I have encouraged my students to think about narrative as the construction of space and cinema as an architectural convention created by and nurtured from the disappointments and shocks of everyday urban life.

LB: I wonder if those ideas can be mirrored, so you can look at architecture in turn as a cinematic gesture, where narrative finds a translation in space, in a spatial progression through a building or a city. You mention Barthes: didn't he also make the observation that the experience of narrative, when really writerly, requires diversions and ellipses on the part of the reader (1986, 29–32)? That's possible in reading but not in conventional cinema. In cinema, or at least mainstream cinema, you're swept along by the story – in fact that seems to be a corollary of the imprisoned and contorted body you mention. Only because we're pinned into a theatre seat can we be carried along by the narrative.

So perhaps architecture, with exceptions like jails and movie theatres, might be seen as a form of cinema, or visual narrative, where the body is not imprisoned. That's a little counterintuitive considering that built form is usually imagined as solid, in contrast to "fluid" film. There can be something emancipatory in our creation of narrative as we move through buildings if the architecture allows for diversions and escapes. In fact, at the art interventions that were part of Urban Encounters, this is very much the quality of a number of the installations – only to be discovered by accident, by turning the wrong way down an alley or through the crypt of a church.[2]

SN: With all these diversions, moments when we drift in and out of self-awareness, it is a meeting point between our two disciplines, isn't it? The twisted mysteries of the labyrinth, the agoraphobia and claustrophobia that architectural theorist Anthony Vidler (2002) claims became integrated into modern spatial design ... It is strange that we both consider losing ourselves in the city as nurturing a sort of "opening," an enlivened experience of place, a means of freeing our presence in the city, curing urban neurosis by letting go, drifting. Yet drifting off while watching a film ... A city without bodies, a cinema that encourages a pervasive Cartesian dualism

– perhaps this has caused the plague of omnoptic cruelty. I'm referring to Virilio's *Vision Machine,* where optics become active and interactive and watch us while we watch or record a hypermediated interactivity that "is to real space what radioactivity is to the atmosphere" (1998, 21). Can an ethical encounter only occur in open space, unhindered, unmediated? This is probably a question that can be answered by both filmmakers and architects in their varied practices.

LB: Considering that, how do we see our project *Brief Encounters,* which far from being a diversion was actually set up in the middle of a prominent public space? Grand Parade – the name says it all! So what was going on there? Were we just constructing another spectacle?

SN: Yes, Grand Parade. Historically a military parade ground, the space later became a parking lot for city bureaucrats, and apparently there was a big uproar from them when city planners proposed opening up the square again as a public space. I think proposing this as a projection space was an attempt to reconcile the contrasts that I see occurring when encountering art in public space; it anchors you in the moment, yet releases you from everydayness; it should surprise but also blend into the slathering of city spectacles. These unexpected circumstances of art in public space create ruptures in the city's fabric; they also offer people an opportunity to play, to step out of themselves. Placing the work in Grand Parade was both provocative and an invitation to soak up the poetics of experimental city symphonies, a primordial genre of filmmaking where the flows and rhythms of a city are assembled into a dynamic, radically subjective montage. Instead of projecting Walter Ruttman's *Berlin: Symphony of a Great City* (1927), I asked my students to create works for Halifax, *Symphony for a Forgotten City: Spaces Lost in Fog.* It was odd though, asking the artists who participated in the project to use forgotten, failed city spaces as their starting point for these works. Did anything surprise you about the projected works from either city?

LB: What surprised me was not so much the works themselves but their interaction with observers. The screen-makers and I anticipated the impact of the image, the effect of images bleeding in from two sides through a succession of screens. That was the intention, and it was all

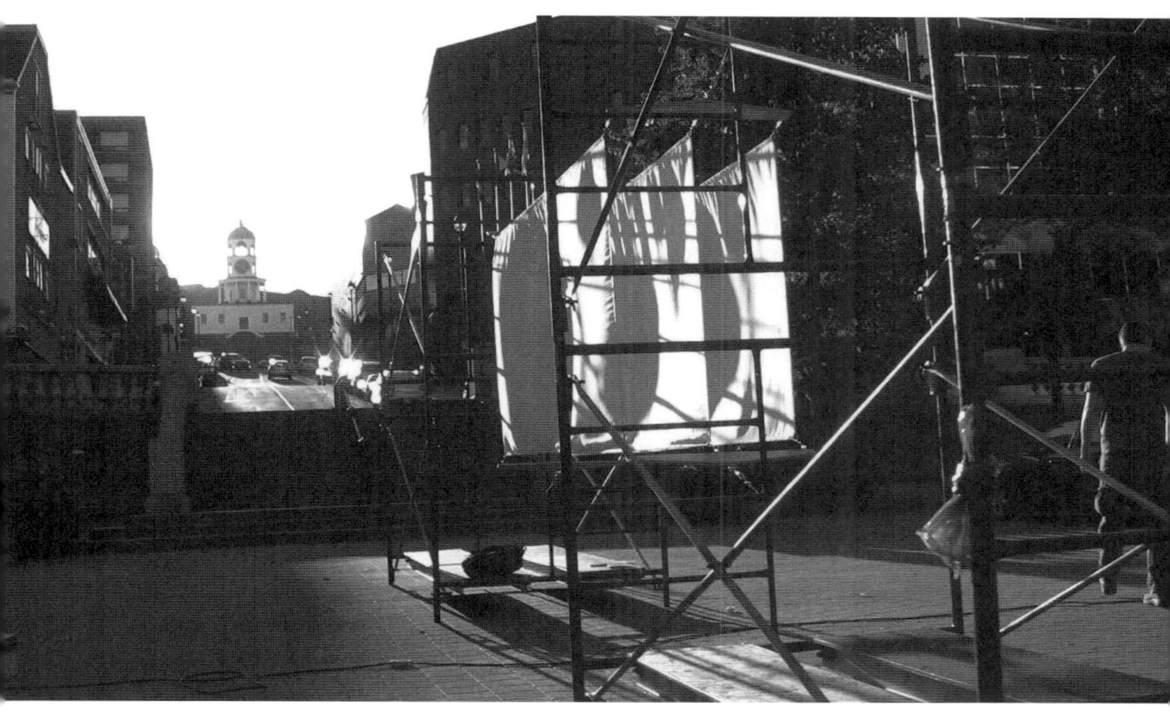

6.1 The screen made by JNZNBRK installed in the centre of Grand Parade, Halifax. Photo: Lawrence Bird, 2013.

about creating an encounter between the works. But the layering of screens, slightly set apart from one another, created architectural spaces between, constructed of fabric and cables. Our artwalk participants leapt straight into those spaces, with the films washing over them, and their shadows projected onto the adjacent screens, crossing between screens. So the walkers became new characters within the projected films – characters in two films at once. Perhaps this is what surprised me more than the content of the films themselves: how the films were remade in the place through the involvement of the observers. The Winnipeg films had been shot in urban sites that were disused or abandoned and were for the most part very personal takes on the displacement and alienation experienced in those places. A sweet irony that these failed spaces – which appear in both the Halifax and Winnipeg films – ended up bringing another urban space to life.

When I was working with the students in Winnipeg, their focus was really on the specific spaces and the narratives they imagined there. It was never part of our thinking at the time that these might be transported to another city entirely and impact an urban space there. It's interesting to me that these films about dysfunctional places in one city could end up breathing life into a space in another city. Architects are used to seeing the spaces they create coopted and appropriated, often in ways that were never intended. This was the first time I'd seen that in filmwork I was involved with. I guess that's more and more frequent in media today, with mash-up and meme phenomena.

During the event I couldn't help but recall the scenes from so many instances of cinema where films are projected into public space. Michel Gondry's quiet comedy *Be Kind Rewind* (2008), for example. It's about the shared concerns of media and cities. At the end of the film, the projection into the street of a locally made and completely fictional history takes back urban space that had been carved up by developers. It's a weak overthrow of capital, but it has an effect. Again public space becomes a space of play and a bit of madness that's essential to civic life. Something similar happens in the slightly schmaltzy *Cinema Paradiso* (Tornatore 1988), when a film is projected into a city square and becomes a spectacle with no admission charge for those who can't get into the theatre. Again we have urban spaces given back to the people – spaces that have been taken away from those who should have them by a right of possession that

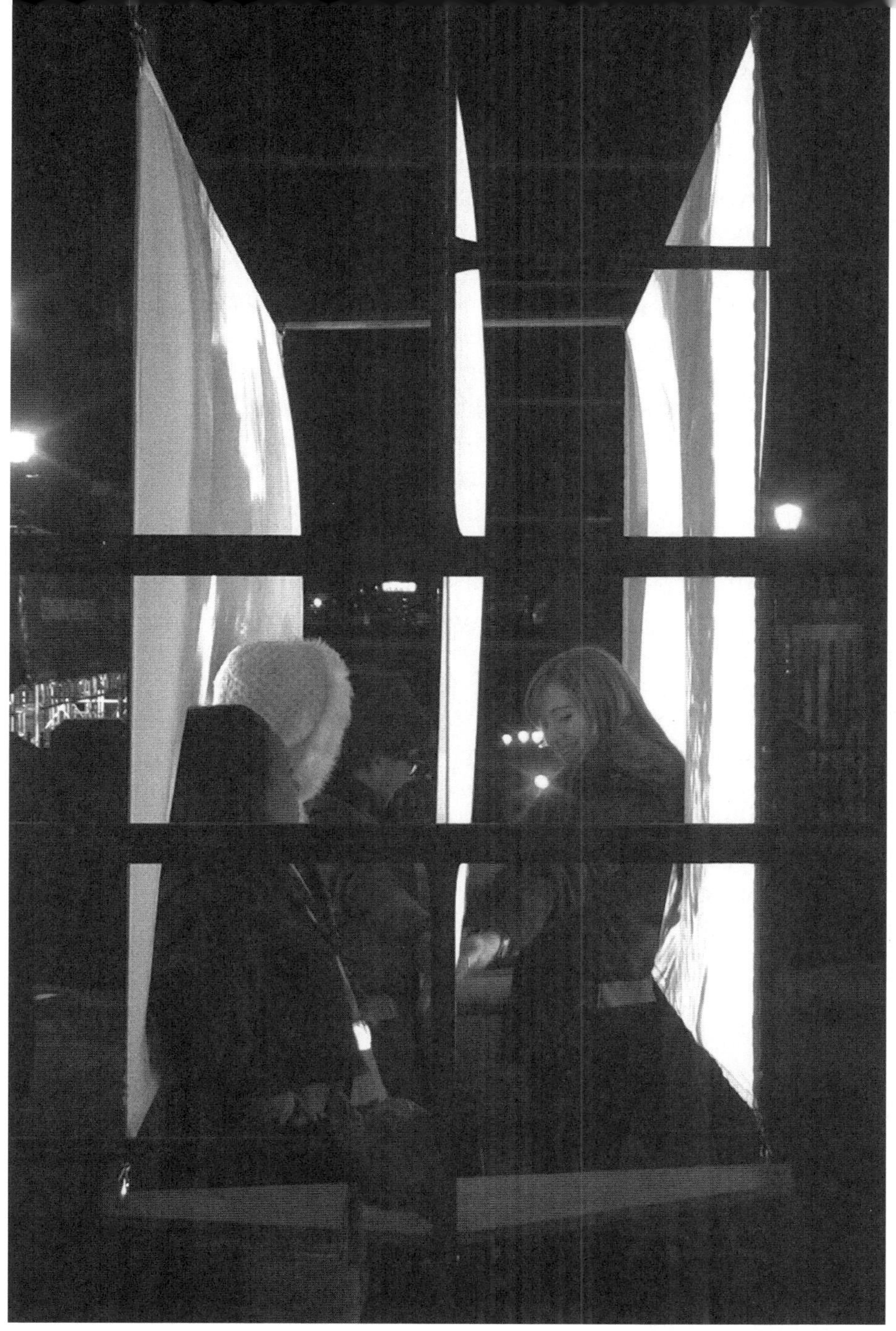

6.2 The space created by the triple screen was quickly occupied.
Photo: Lawrence Bird, 2013.

precedes ownership and should supersede it: another space taken over by cars, to come back to your history of Grande Parade! The idea of treating car-space as public space just seems to horrify some people. I suppose it's in some sense a response to that, that so many artists take over parking lots. A shared agenda of artists generally, and the planners who rescued Grand Parade specifically ... strange bedfellows? And both of them share a space with *Cinema Paradiso's* village madman who "owns" the square, and rushes around in frustration among the parked cars that have taken it over, crying "La piazza es mia!" It *should* be his!

I suppose there's a politics to all of this – poetry and politics occupying a shared space. A politics that works against omnoptics, if by that term we can mean the implacable swarm-like observation characteristic of social media today. As you say, a space that resists the omnoptic condition is a space of ethical encounter. Face-to-face at last without the intermediary distancing of devices ...

There was another encounter of course in *Brief Encounters* between forms of media. The Winnipeg films were all shot on video and the Halifax on 16 mm. I felt the distinction was clear in the images, but perhaps that's because I knew of the difference ahead of time. What some see as the transparency and hollowness of video versus the opacity of film ... Was that a factor for you in the way you read the projections?

sn: Proposing that my students use 16mm was a playful obstruction of a sorts, an engagement with a tactile process to complete their macabre city symphonies; finding points of interest in forgotten spaces, learning how to drift, creating psycho-geographical maps with hand-cut montages of work processed and painted by hand. We were hoping that the high-contrast nature of the film stock would offer great opportunities for indeterminate cross-dissolves, blending two film segments from different films, different cities, on different sides of the screen into one luminous projection.

The centre fabric was a remarkable meeting place for the two cities, and of course the spectators swimming in the interstitial spaces of the double projection screen was a pleasant surprise, as were the gaggle of drunk hockey fans who came pouring out of the arena down the street. Most of them were still in a full-on, half-cut battle-of-the-cities mode. When they heard about the Winnipeg/Halifax projection divide, the

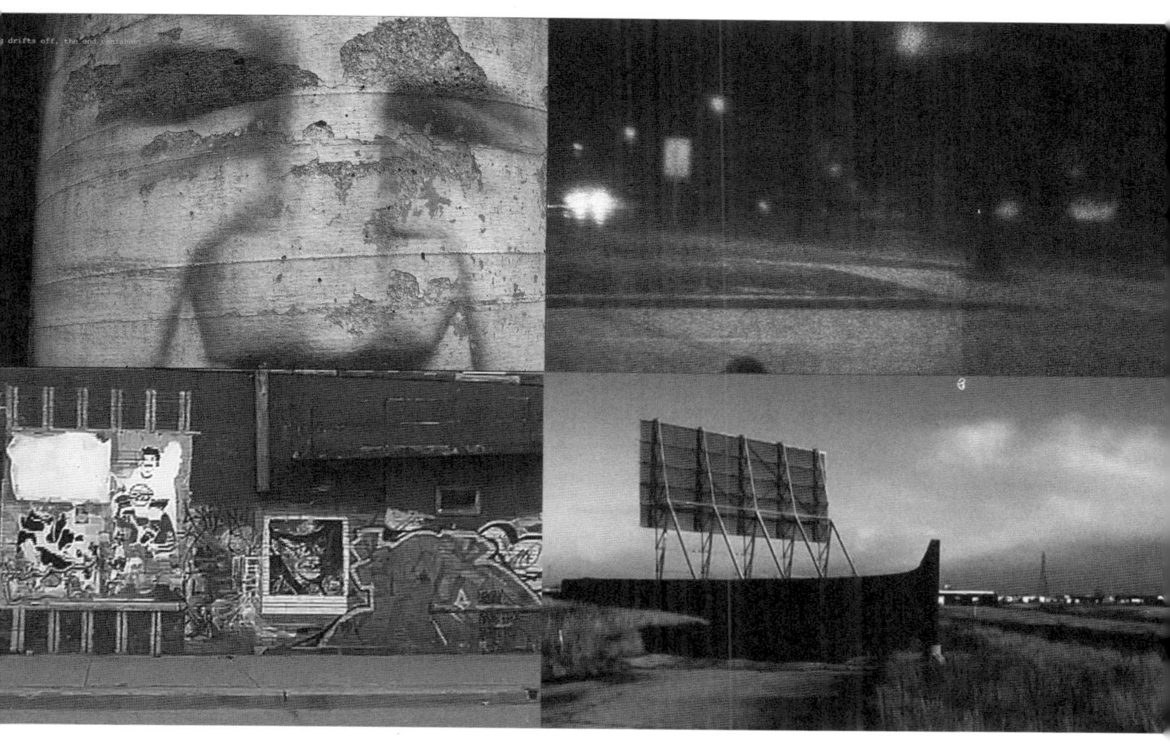

6.3 Stills from some of the projected films in *Brief Encounters* by, clockwise from top left, Anca Matyiku, Rhayne Vermette, Michael Maksymiuk, Zhi Yong Wang.

Halifax Moosehead fans stumbled over to work made by my students, cheering for the home team.

I assume that many of them would not normally enter into a gallery or theatre to see these types of experimental films, but the fact that it was projected in a public space made them feel braver. It was an opportunity to comment on and enjoy the work, without pretension or fear of entering into a formal screening space.

Speaking of hockey, on my frequent trips back to Winnipeg I notice that all those wonderful forgotten spaces in the downtown area have been or are now under threat of development. Sports teams and events like the Olympic Games, World cups, etc. have a way of pillaging the most wondrous, hidden spaces of our cities, transforming them for private/commercial interests. Halifax has the same potential threats, be it an arena proposal in the North End that will displace a tight-knit community or unruly developers who have an agenda of selling "cool downtown living" by creating those awful loft-style apartments. Our cities and urban life are under siege ... I blame Richard Florida (2004) and his ilk, who try to sell this absurd idea of a creative class, as if artists are an integral part of furthering the capitalist agenda of making our cities wealthier and "more vibrant." What does this even mean? Has all this current interest in city living and so-called investment in the creative class actually threatened the potential for cities to be more art friendly in a radical way?

LB: Urban development very often does erode the conditions that support artistic creation. Rents go up; that's key. The architects' offices gradually move in, a couple of steps ahead of the doctors and lawyers, and, dare I say, yoga studios and massage therapists. But I can tell you, speaking as someone who practices architecture as well as making efforts in film and visual art, it's complicated. Development always changes what's there. There's inevitably some kind of a loss as those beautifully neglected spaces are rendered "pretty," but there is potential to do critical work as an architect even in those conditions.

Winnipeg is struggling with this problem at the moment, as it goes through a small urban renaissance. A rather well-known local firm, 5468796 Architecture (they recently won the Prix de Rome and coordinated *Migrating Landscapes*, Canada's contribution to the Venice Biennale of Architecture in 2012; see 5468796 Architecture and Chon 2012) tackled the renovation of a neglected older building on Portage Avenue in the centre of downtown. It's known as the Avenue building, and among the gestures 5468796 chose to make toward the city was an array of balconies that stick far, far out over the sidewalk, all the way up the facade. Technically these infringe on the public realm, as they're in the air space over the public right of way. Developers love that because, if they can get away with it, this space costs them nothing! But that's only one side of it. One effect of the balconies is to project private lives out into the city as part of the scenography of urban life: you walk out onto your balcony, and you're in the public eye. In turn, the city becomes a part of each apartment, through the inhabitant's experience of dwelling for a while on the balcony, feeling the wind up there, hearing the traffic ... In fact, you could make the case that this perspective on the city just didn't exist until the architects built those balconies. Who looked along Portage Avenue from fifty feet in the air? It's kind of a crane shot – a very cinematic view. Anyway, these and a number of other designers are playing with the relationship between public and private space in a way that's at times quite provocative and also resonates with the blurring of public and private realms you see in contemporary media: a kind of expanded architecture. And perhaps this is another sense of the madman's phrase "*la piazza es mia*": what's public can be private, intimate, and vice versa. This kind of work <u>is</u> critical, I think, and often the freedom to do that work is only possible because it's happening in a part of the city that has been undervalued for a long time. So the architect (and often small-scale developer) is leveraging the same economic situation the artist is when she gets a cheap studio space. Given the right sensibility, their interventions in the city can augment what's there rather than displacing it.

At least, that's how I see it at the moment. I absolutely buy your critique of Richard Florida! The "creative class" – what a vague term, bundling up groups with completely different agendas. Perhaps we could appreciate his work better if it acknowledged the conflicts between these groups. I'm an optimist though, so I also kind of buy the idea that the contradictions in the development process can be productive. Maybe we're not all on the same team, but something exciting can come out of the conflict if we battle it out in urban space. Which perhaps is what your hockey fans intuited ... And this is another thing that is often forgotten about urban spaces in consensual models of urban life – cities have often been battlegrounds between social groups, and that's something acknowledged in the rituals and sports that took place on the game board of the city in the past. A few remaining urban rituals remind us of this, Siena's Palio for example, or battles between *mikoshi* in Japanese street festivals.[3] Before they were closed up in arenas, as plays and other urban spectacles were in theatres, sports were truly public, social, and political events. They mediated social conflicts. That's one of the functions of festivals and carnivals also, which are blurrings of sport and theatre – with architecture and often moving images thrown in for good measure. Conflict and difference were built into the rituals of the city, rather than being subsumed into the kind of bland spaces built by New Urbanism, lauded by Florida, and inhabited by gentrifiers.

SN: I sympathize and equally yearn for a "same team" scenario, but I can't shake this inherent sense of loss and mind-numbing apathy when we speak of the creative class. Can it include artists interested in creating radical, politically charged work? Surely urban development is conducive to socially conscious public practices to some extent, but so much public artwork has situated itself as banal ornamentation, completely ignoring the gloomy social inequalities so evident in today's cities. Our population is becoming more urban and consequently more indebted. Even though emerging technology has created innovative ways of nurturing social cohesion and connectedness, we are more isolated than ever. Twitter makes us thirsty, while Instagram amplifies the postmodern condition of infinite, incessant boredom.

I think this might explain my interest in creating celluloid public art installations, both in the Gallery at Artspace in Sydney and with the WNDX festival in Winnipeg (see Radice, Harvey, and Turner, this volume).[4] I also spent two months in 2014 travelling around New Zealand and Australia doing workshops like the one you and I did in Winnipeg, working with local artists to create celluloid works to install in public spaces. I reckon the resurgent interest in the material presence of analogue media has to do with it having the ability to stop. It ends, it starts, it exists definitely within a certain confine of space, and it will not stare back at you, tell on you, or reveal where you are: it plays no part in omnoptics. No one can use it against your will, it does not invade space, it actually works to define it.

I've become partial to Paul Virilio's technophobia. To return to his provocative comment that "Interactivity is to real space what radioactivity is to the atmosphere" (1998, 21), although celluloid was the first step in conquering and indexing real space, it has gaps: between the frames, an immovable void, a flicker into the virtual space of the mind where images blend together in a luminescent flux.

Although our installation in Artspace was in a gallery (free and open to the public), we incorporated, emphasized and reintroduce the "public" as a key element. Our past explorations in creating an "intervention of art in public space" were much more overt, in that we attempted to sculpt mobile cinema spaces in the city. The key in these instances was creating a darkened space in which we could present experimental celluloid works, *embedded in the urban environment*. In Sydney, we proposed an alternative intervention, one in which the public participated in the creation of the work in a formal exhibition space. As opposed to the other iterations of the Situated Cinema, the key was experimenting with architectural structures that create intimate, alternative cinema spaces while also constructing conduits (a translucent screen, three looping projectors) for using the flickering celluloid to sculpt the space in the gallery. In the back of the gallery, an 8mm projection space was set up for the purpose of screening amateur work – work otherwise relegated to basements and other storage spaces. The documentation was of family life, once simply inaccessible to a generalized public due to its "private" designation. The projection was a kind of reclamation, a valorization of a particular form of archive from which a growing number of people (the descendants of the amateurs) are alienated by virtue of the near perfect obsolescence of the required technology for viewing and, by extension, remembering. A call for entries was circulated, inviting people to submit 8mm films. A selection of these was looped daily for the duration of the installation. It was a reimagining of crowdsourcing, offering the public space of the gallery and our expertise in analogue technologies to seek collaborations with the public.

LB: So, crowdsourcing by analogue means. This brings me to another thought. Perhaps you're right that there's a basic contradiction between Florida's appropriation (and monetization) of urban creativity on the one hand and the radical creation you're talking about on the other. That radical understanding of art might always demand that the artist become a saboteur and the work a spanner thrown into the machinery to bring it to a grinding halt. In the same sense that celluloid has the ability to *stop* as

you put it. In defense of digital media though, can't something like this
be done from within video and the CPU (central processing unit, the part
of a computer that processes data)? Isn't this the point of glitch art, art
that explores the aesthetics of software errors, often as a critique of digital
technology?

SN: I recently curated a collection of glitch work for Galerie Sans Nom
(Moncton, New Brunswick). What interested me in this selection of work
was how they seemed to reject the outward, heuristic potential of digital
technologies. These artists turn these technologies inward, embracing esoteric abstraction and offering an alternative to the frequently empirical
functionality of emergent technologies. They create a boundless virtual
space that is reminiscent of the closed-eye vision and dialectical experience once nurtured by celluloid. They are wordless, textural works that escape the statistical intrusions of the Omnopticon and immerse the viewer
in ethereal shards of light that exemplify how experimental filmmakers are
approaching the digital turn.

LB: So there's a space in the digital for opacity and materiality. I found
the same thing when working on the installation *éCartographies* at RAW:
Gallery of Architecture and Design in Winnipeg. We constructed a map
of the city, a map woven from cables representing the major vectors of
urban infrastructure – highways, rail lines, bridges. The cables were anchored in the walls and columns of the gallery and then pulled taught by
counterweights assembled from found objects. We projected moving images over the whole assembly – videos shot in the various sites represented
by the map, all sites abandoned or broken in some way. I never anticipated
this, but as the video images were projected over quite some distance, their
composition from pixels became more apparent; so did the digital artifacts
emerging from various compression processes involved in the video editing and transcoding. As these fragments of image fell across materials that
were themselves broken, surfaces rough and weathered from exposure to
the elements, the damaged and torn qualities of both media and material
were amplified. So there was a simultaneous decomposition of image and
thing. That was the discovery, really: that the image breaks just as the city
does – and no less so for being a digital image.

For me this intertwining of image and materiality resonates with many urban practices – practices like parkour for example. *Traceurs* (parkour practitioners) inevitably end up online – there seems to be this desire to document what you've done and get it up on YouTube for others to see. It's visual and virtual, it's about the image. But there's no doubt that it's also profoundly about the material reality of the body, the risk or even the necessity that the body should break through its encounter with the city. There's a dual condition: our being is realized simultaneously through image and material. These practices are appropriated by film – even commercial film – and video games, where they're rendered in compelling, painful, eerie images that also seem to speak of that dual condition. Texture maps that break down – they're material and not. There's some animated film, mostly out of Asia, which achieves this.

I'm reminded of another installation that happened the same evening as ours. In *Habitués Conspicuously Emergent*, Bruce McClure used two projectors in a small alley at the foot of a church not far from Grand Parade, no film involved at all, only light projected across a rotating cloth, clearing the dust from the light, or scattering it with dust. The result was a 4:3 rectangle of light projected on the foundation of the building above, where – and I don't know if this was Bruce's intention – the light became, through association, another foundation stone for the building. Solid, massive, dirty light. This work, too, seemed to be about that dual material and imagic quality, a condition in which our urban and human existence is underpinned and undermined at one and the same time.

Andy Merrifield, a British academic who's developed some ideas from Henri Lefebvre, makes the case that "the urban" today is no longer bounded by the edge of the city, however the city is defined. The current urban condition is one in which we are both in place (rooted in a material, built environment) and circulating dematerialized in space (through mediated flows of information and capital). A result is a "shifting conjoining of people," a kaleidoscope of propinquity and simultaneity (Merrifield 2013, 8). This doesn't mean that we're disembodied; bodies still matter, just they are always somehow fluid or perhaps granular – in place but also always flowing elsewhere. A result is a politics of the encounter where collectivity is both situated and fragmented, both located and distributed. Here place and flow – like material and image – merge. Merrifield uses James Joyce's term *collideorscape* to describe this amalgam. I can't help but see something of this in the merging of bodies and light that happened in Grand Parade. The event paradoxically short-circuited geography – collapsing the space between two distant cities into a new city – while situating that short-circuit in a distinct *place.*

SN: Dissipation of the self, dissolution of the cinema spaces – philosophically the former causes me a great deal of anxiety: there is something very dangerous in eliminating all that divides us, be it cultural or aesthetic. Fluidity is not necessarily a means of uniting us; if anything, it can make us more susceptible to the metrics of consumer culture. I am, however, open to the possibilities of new forms of cinema emerging by tearing down the walls of an edifice that has become irretrievably conservative in the way work is created and projected.

LB: And likewise, new forms of architecture are enabling new forms of life parallel with these new formulations of media. What of the new people engaged in all of this? Any thoughts on the pedagogical dimension of what we've been doing? After all, students were integral to the project. They made the films that were projected into Grand Parade, and in fact the makers of the triple screen, JNZNBRK, are recent architectural graduates. Did any of this contribute to the learning and understanding relevant to their respective fields or to the development of theory? It would be interesting to speculate on where this project takes us in these terms.

SN: Absolutely. Throughout the term I was encouraging my students to think of their work architecturally, specifically, how a filmmaker sculpts space rather than tells stories in the cinema. It progressed from there and eventually led to the development of a new course at NSCAD called Sculpting Cinema; Intersections with Architecture. Many students who participated in the project at the Grand Parade went on to take this studio class, which explored how alternative experimental analogue processes (like the work screened on JNZNBRK's triple projection screen) and certain abstract narrative works can deconstruct the cinema from the inside out. We focused especially on studio work that rejects the notion of "losing oneself in the virtual space of the cinema." Rather, we explored experimental film and installation work that emphasized alternative forms of visuality that offer a more haptic and embodied experience of spectatorship.

Here I'm referencing Laura Marks (1998), who suggests that experimental film transforms the screen from a flat surface into a body that is encountered. In other words, the spectator is brought into the work not through immersion and transfixion but through an encounter more aligned with how one may encounter work in an art gallery or public projections such as our collaboration in Halifax. Such an encounter, Marks explains, requires that we approach the material with an embodied intelligence whereby the spectator is conscious of the apparatus of the cinema as a means and space for sculpting light. This awareness introduces an alternative duration (the here and the now) into the space of cinema, as the spectator – no longer immersed, no longer transfixed, no longer passive – comes to participate, to collaborate, in the making of meaning.

LB: So she connects the duration of the now to the embodied experience of space – that's a really interesting parallel. This notion matters for architecture too: we talk about a thick present, a temporality evoked (or invoked, presenced) by built space and its materiality. This idea is important to certain approaches to the history and theory of architecture, which is part of my background. And it leads us to a perspective that's particularly appreciative of the role film can play in architectural thinking and design. This helps us see architecture as fundamentally communicative: about language and poetics, rather than narrowly technical. It emphasizes the need to situate architectural creation in a social and cultural context, engaged with many other arts – particularly those associated, like film, with public ritual and spectacle. This understanding of architectural history – in Canada, its most prominent proponent is Alberto Pérez-Gómez (1994) – draws on historical precursors: individuals and moments in which architecture was particularly alive. So, for example, we might look back to Sebastiano Serlio (1475–1554) whose treatise on architecture drew explicitly on stage design and engaged implicitly with the social and political role of theatre (particularly satire) – that art form in which time and space are mutually embedded, as they once were in ritual (Serlio 1982). The architectural imagination has long been informed by a sense of space, especially public space, as theatrical and performative – playing out over time.

SN: Interesting that you bring up the idea of the social and political role of the theatre. It brings to mind Dan Graham's writing and experimental architectural proposals for a cinema that was never built, where he discusses the inherent narrative and hierarchy of the structure and design of cinema seating (1993). Modeled after the view planes and stage perspective of the theatre, the architectonics of perspective were designed and distributed according to social class. By replicating the social ranks of the outside world in the architecture of the theatre (and the cinema by association), the seating arrangements and perspectival design were arranged to reflect an orderly, coherent sense of political hierarchy. To counter this, Graham proposed a cinema project, *Cinema (1981)*, that deconstructs immersion in the projected image by utilizing two-way mirrors for its facade and screen. In his cinema proposal, when the cinema is dark, the viewers watch the film and the pedestrians outside. The screen, also a two way-mirror, hangs at eye level. During screenings, pedestrians would see both the projected image through the mirrored facade and the frontal gaze of the spectators when the light-cone bounces off the mirror-screen back into the theatre. When the house lights are up, the spectators become aware of their bodies, "the screen and sides of the theatre become literal mirrors (as opposed to the illusory 'mirror' of the film), reflecting real space and bodies and looks of the spectators" (Graham 1993, 168). Graham's architectural proposal would create oscillating perspectives: an anonymous surveillance of spaces outside the cinema with an awareness and self-monitoring of spectators' subjectivity, their presence in the cinema.

I always thought that Graham's opening of the cinema with a set of architectural proposals could be compared to the on-screen interventions of artisanal film artists. These artists sculpt within the cinema, rupturing notions of immersion and identification with alternative representational forms. I often discuss works such as this in my Sculpting Cinema course. It is a great way to introduce intersections between cinema and architecture.

LB: There's certainly a profound connection there and one that involves society and community, as Graham's project makes clear. There's an old story in architecture that underlines this point too. The earliest Roman writer on architecture, Marcus Vitruvius Pollio (c. 80–c. 15 BCE) writes of what he claims is the origin of architecture, in *The Ten Books on*

6.4 A collideorscape of images and bodies.
    Photo: Lawrence Bird, 2013.

Architecture, a far-ranging text touching on buildings, war machines, time pieces – a very open sense of "making" (Vitruvius 1960). According to Vitruvius, we humans formed our first community around a discovered fire, created not by us but by a storm in a forest. As we gathered in awe around the flames, we first began to speak – communicating and telling stories. Then we built architecture around this new community, around the fire and the shared words.

I've always found this narrative profoundly touching for two reasons. One is that it underlines how architecture arises from something that is not, in simple terms, architectural: it arises to shelter storytelling, community, and communication. Architecture serves the human world (and perhaps for this reason the world owes it a debt) but not in a merely utilitarian way – what use is a story? The second reason I love this particular tale is that, for me, a group of people standing around a fire, gazing into it, and telling stories seems proto-cinematic. We have all seen stories play out in the light of burning embers, dark hollows, and roses of flame succeeding each other in the flickering fire, and dramas cast onto surrounding walls or trees by a group huddled round the flames, each member becoming through their shadow this or that hero, this or that creature. That fundamental experience of light, storytelling, and place is perhaps the shared origin and the deepest commonality between film and architecture: an embryonic form of what George Toles (2001) refers to in another context (if I'm not misreading him) as "a house made of light."

Of course Vitruvius's treatise (like Serlio's) was explicitly pedagogical. It was meant to train us how to be good makers. It's significant that such narratives underline the bond between stories, society, scenography, and space. Perhaps that's another way to look at the reality lived by both the film and the architectural students as they danced, light and shadows flowing across their bodies, in the interstices of the screen at Grand Parade.

Notes

1   Lawrence Bird would like to thank the many graduate students at the University of Manitoba whose videos were included in *Brief Encounters* and acknowledge SSHRC and the Manitoba Arts Council for their support in the production and dissemination of the work. Solomon Nagler would like to thank the undergraduate film students and technicians at NSCAD University who assisted in the production of the 16mm films that were

included in *Brief Encounters*. Both authors thank JNZBRK for their work on the projection screen for the installation.

2   Christof Migone (author of chapter 9) exhibited a new iteration of his audio piece, *Crackers*, in St Paul's Church, Grand Parade. Bruce McClure showed his experimental cinema installation *Habitués Conspicuously Emergent* in an alley off Barrington Street, below ground level at Halifax city hall.

3   The horse race known as the Palio is organized, in part, as a competition between Siena's Contradas or urban districts. A *mikoshi* is a portable shrine associated, in many Japanese festivals, with a specific site in a community. These are usually carried by representatives of a local parish who compete with the bearers of *mikoshi* from other districts, for example by ramming into them.

4   More details on these installations can be found at http://www. cinemaofruins.com/situatedcinema.php. See the Situated Cinema at Arstpace, Sydney, Australia, at https://v meo.com/92179620 and at WNDX in Winnipeg at http://vimeo.com/52432509. Accessed 29 May 2016.

Ellen Moffat and Kim Morgan

7

—

BODY RHYTHMS IN URBAN SPACE: FIELD EVIDENCE

As artists, we focus on body rhythms in urban space, using wearable technology (ECG sensors, smart phones) that collect data to investigate the interstitial space between the private and the public in relation to art. Our primary question is how we as humans affect space and how space affects us. Our work brings together creative production, computer and engineering sciences, and social science as an interdisciplinary project. The context of our inquiry is *Tracing the City: Interventions of Art in Public Space,* a broader program of research-creation funded by the Social Sciences and Humanities Research Council of Canada.[1]

Our collaboration brings together our independent artistic practices and concerns. Kim Morgan (Halifax) is a sculpture/installation artist working in extended media. She explores cross-disciplinary collaborations through the research and creation of interactive public art projects that use public space as a laboratory. Within this framework, her work addresses the impact of technology on the human body, perceptions of time and space, and the shifting boundaries between the private and the public. Central to Ellen Moffat's (Saskatoon) practice are sound, space, language, and image, rooted in the vocabulary of sculpture – the body, space, and materiality. Her emphasis on sound and visuality proposes a poetic and conceptual inquiry into communication, social relations, and perception using high-low aesthetics and technology, experimentation, and proposition.

BODIES AND URBAN SPACE

The city is a complex space of human actions and relationships, constructed environments, and behaviours through which the individual body moves. A living entity, the city affects and is affected by that which moves through it or interacts with it. We used the city as a surface and interface for our physical performance as individuals. By tracking, recording, and locating the body within different urban sites, we explored how place(s) may affect, connect, or disconnect us, or how we may affect place(s).

The body is an active agent in the urban environment. Locative mobile technologies allow us to test the parameters of the physical, analogue world and our interactions with it. We track, record, and locate the body within different urban locations using wearable devices to capture biometric data and video. Thinking of the devices as an extension of the body, the city becomes a platform for the physical performance of the individual. We engage with the urban space through our actions using the devices to collect data. Both the city and the body are interfaces to be performed and performed on.

Our project explores the ways in which individual phenomenological and sensorial experiences of the city can be understood as simultaneously reflecting and constructing collective urban life. Our questions include (1) how the body's movement through urban space translates into affective experience, (2) whether and how that experience can be captured using digital technology, and (3) how data can then be expressed or represented as works of art that reflect the sensorial experience of the city.

LOCATIONS

We completed fieldwork in Paris (2012), Halifax (2013), Regina and Saskatoon (2014) using varying modes of movement and approaches. As artists, we live and work in different cities, but we both have personal and professional relationships to each place. Our choice of the specific locations reflects both chance and circumstance. Our response to each location reflected a unique approach for the situation.

In Paris, we were both tourists. Spontaneity, play, and situations shaped our experience and the field data using the *dérive* as a method.

We moved on foot through the city following pedestrian routes and routines as a means of navigating, knowing, and claiming space. We wore microcontrollers equipped with ECG sensors and smart phones to collect data of our body rhythms (pulse), as well as of sites, everyday (inter)actions, and chance events. Thinking of these devices as extensions of the body, our bodies were sometimes subjects, sometimes objects, and sometimes triggers. Locations of our walks ranged from cultural and tourist sites (Benjamin's Arcades), to arteries of trade and commuter flow (la Gare de Nord, La Defense, Lafayette), to commercial and organic markets (Galeries Lafayette, Forum des Halles, La Bastille). In these sites, we employed the Situationists' methods for "getting lost" and exploring a place on "intuition."

In Halifax, we travelled at night by car due to weather, safety, distances, and time of day. This provided a controlled and private space within a public environment. One artist was the passenger and one the driver. Our route was the main downtown drags of Quinpool Road, Spring Garden Road, Barrington Road, and the downtown container port. These locations are easily recognizable city sites. The video was shot through the car windows; the results were often blurred or reflective images. Being in a vehicle, our bodies were static; perhaps, as a consequence the resulting sound – the rhythm of our heartbeats – was less erratic than in Paris.

In Regina and Saskatoon, we were pedestrians, moving through locations that were familiar to us (we have each lived in both these cities). As another method of collecting data, we "conjoined" ourselves to become a codependent unit. As a result, we expanded both our line of vision and the data collected, creating a new perspective as eyes on the front and back of the head.

We moved through pedestrian, transportation, and shopping malls in the downtown core of both cities. In Regina, we focused on the Cornwall Centre and Scarth Street Mall – the central downtown core. In Saskatoon, the Bus Mall is located in the downtown core and is the city public transportation hub. This method of moving through urban space expands both our perspectives and challenges our independent performance as moving bodies.

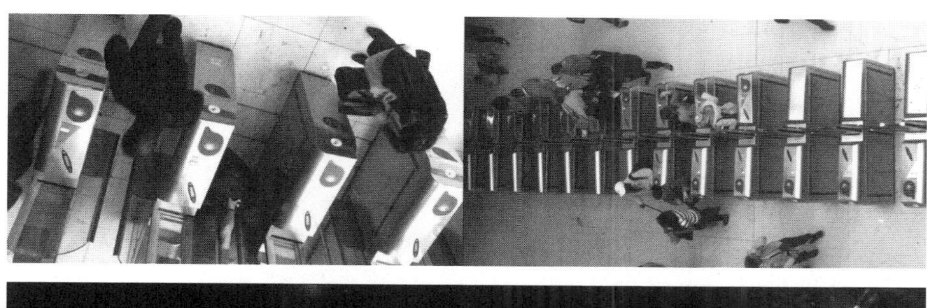

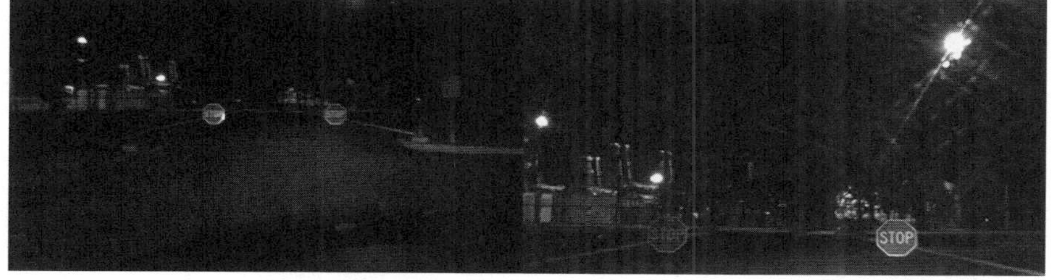

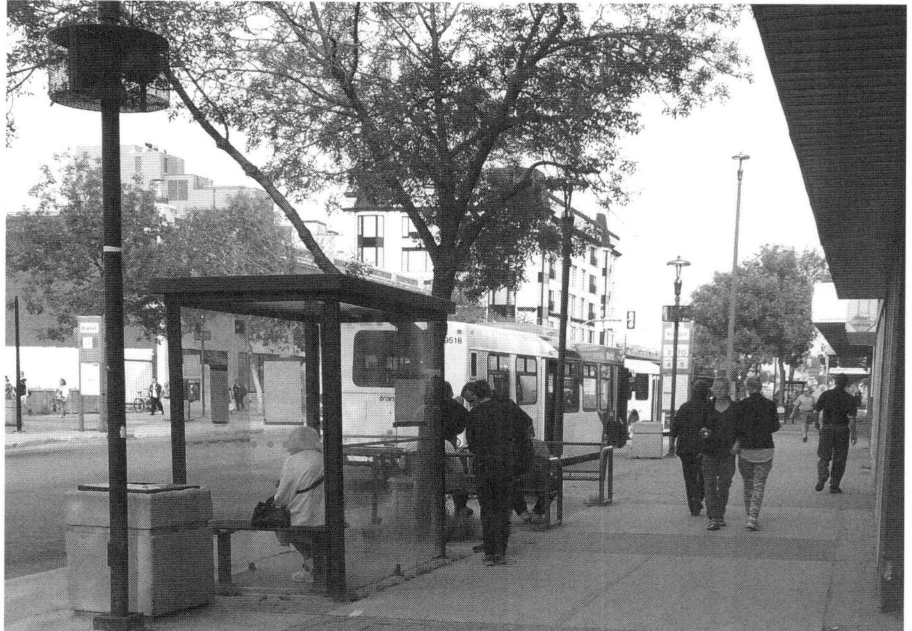

7.1 La Gare du Nord, Paris. Video still from *in pulse,* 2012: Ellen Moffat and Kim Morgan.

7.2 The Port, Halifax. Video still from *Cruising*, 2013: Ellen Moffat and Kim Morgan.

7.3 The artists on foot, walking backwards/forwards to make *Tracings*, Saskatoon. Photo: Martha Radice, 2014.

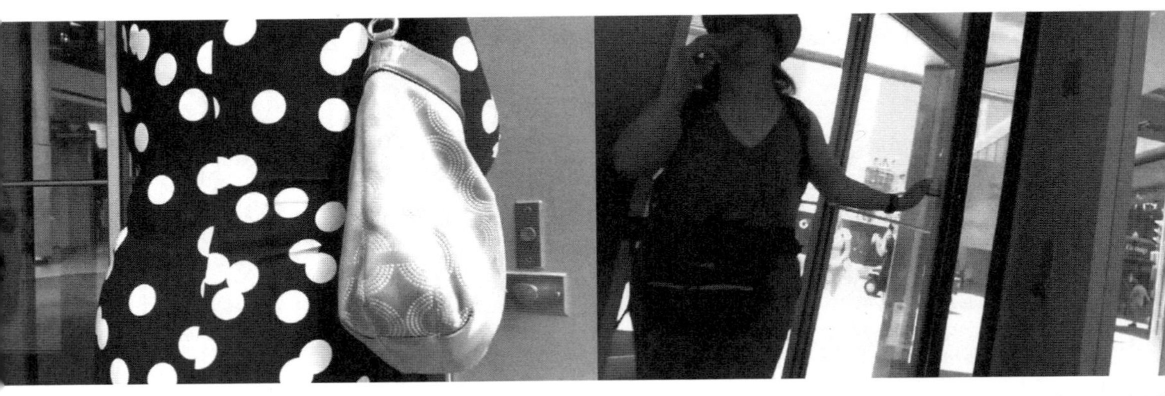

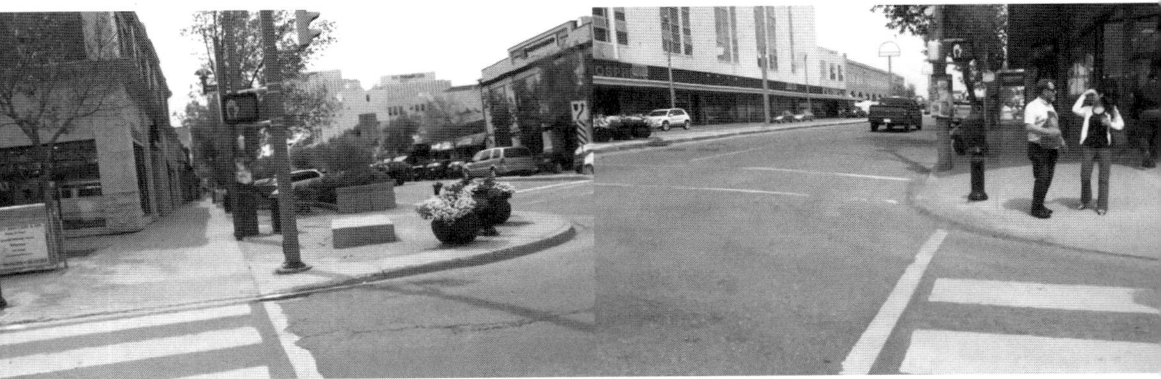

7.4 Cornwall Centre, Regina.
Video still from *Tracings*, 2014: Ellen Moffat and Kim Morgan.

7.5 Bus mall, Saskatoon.
Video still from *Tracings*, 2014: Ellen Moffat and Kim Morgan.

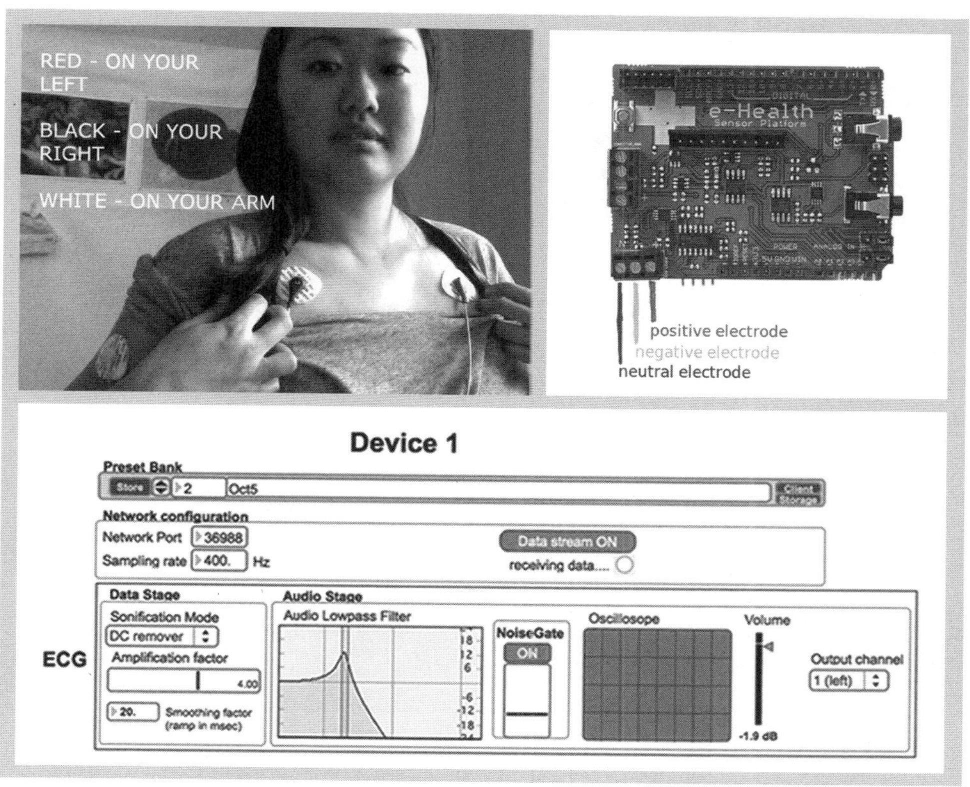

7.6 Above left, ECG sensors worn by Annie Onyi Cheung, research assistant, NSCAD University. Credit: Annie Onyi Cheung, 2014. Above right, e-Health Sensor Shield. Credit: Martin Peach, 2014. Below, screen grab of the software (Max/MSP) to convert data into audio. Credit: Ellen Moffat, 2014.

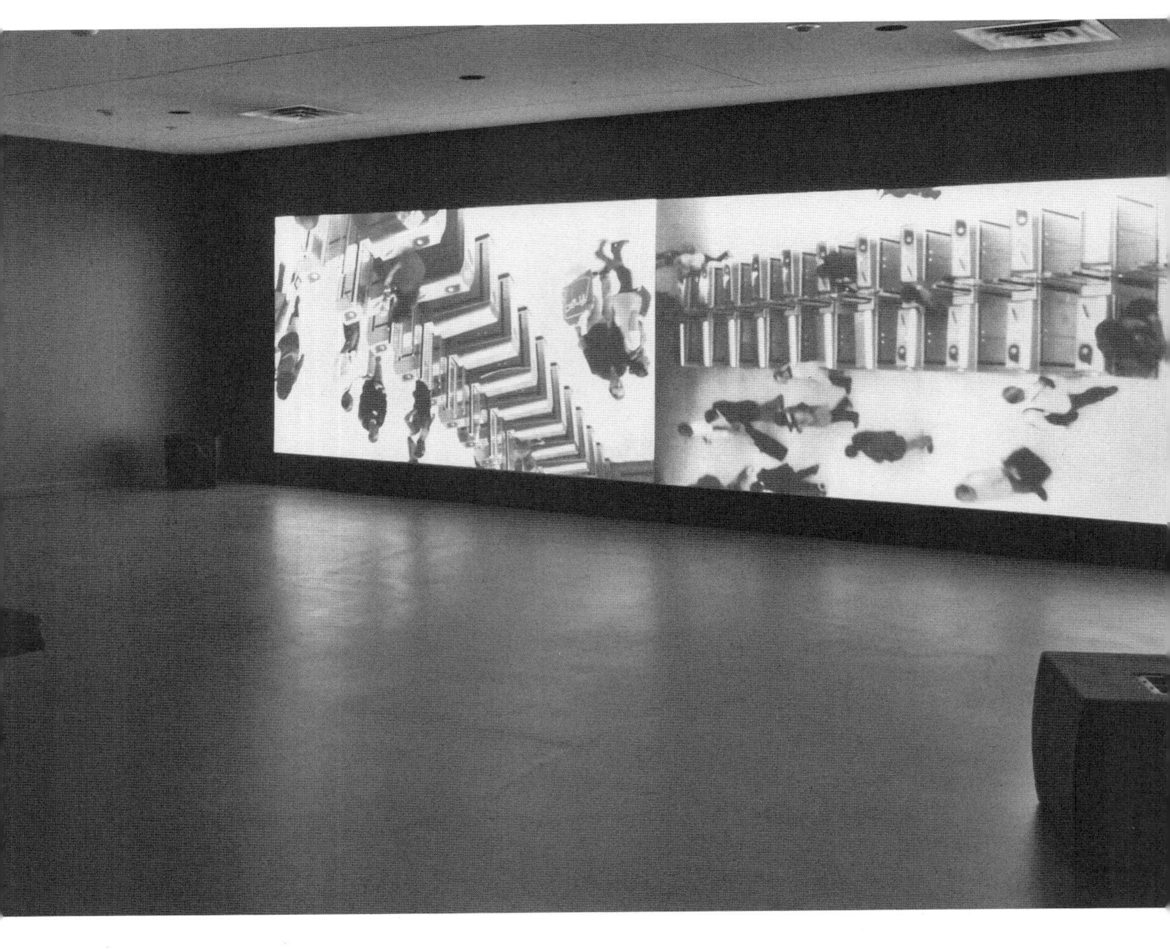

7.7 Ellen Moffat and Kim Morgan, *in pulse,* Dalhousie Art Gallery, Halifax, 2012. Photo: Steve Farmer.

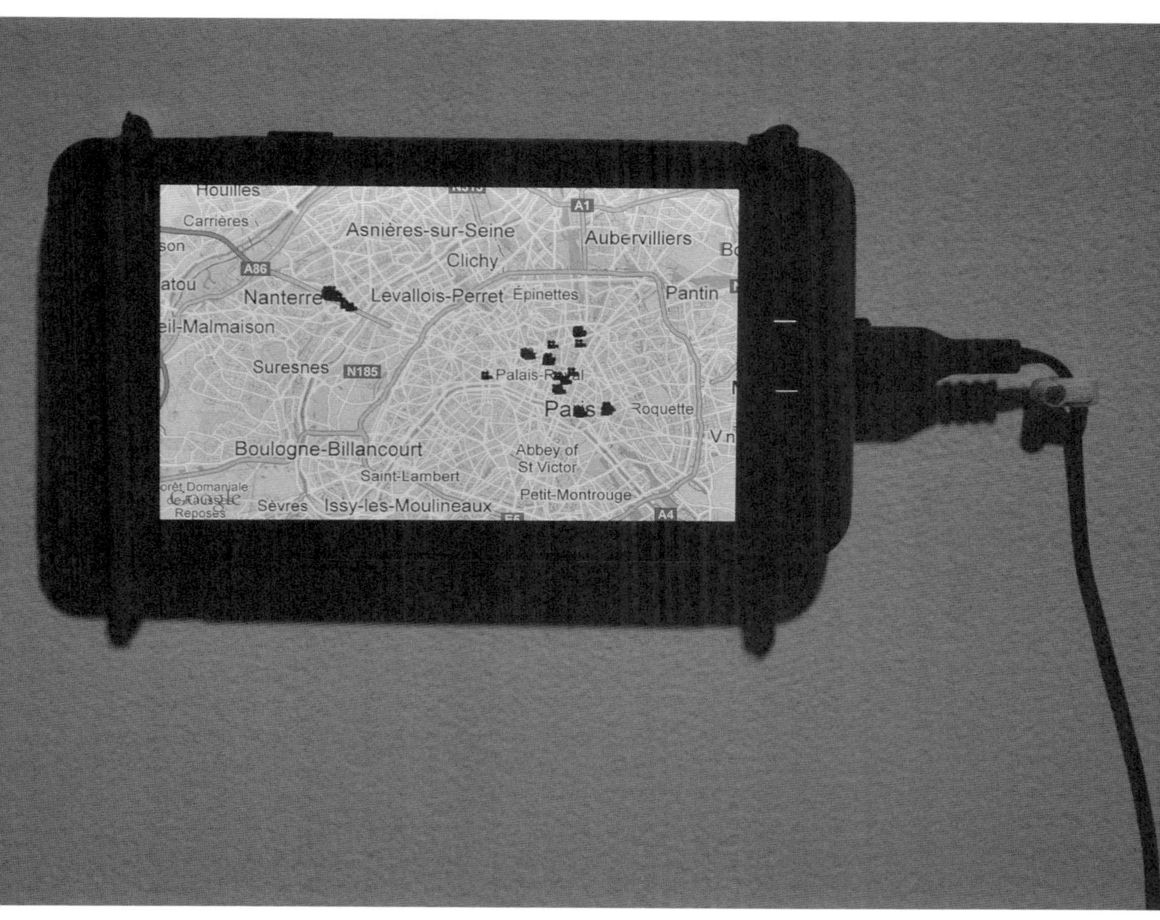

7.8 Ellen Moffat and Kim Morgan, *in pulse* (detail), smartphone with Google map, Dalhousie Art Gallery, Halifax, 2012. Photo: Steve Farmer.

TECHNOLOGY

We used technical devices to collect data: Arduino microcontrollers, e-Health shields with ECG sensors, smart phones with GPS and a custom-designed app. The ECG sensors attached directly to the body collected the pulse as data that was later converted into low frequency audio signals.

The devices are relatively compact and wearable. The sensors are connected to an Arduino board that is carried in a waist pouch. Once activated, the Arduino collects biometric data from the electrodes and sends the ECG data to a smartphone over WiFi. An application on the smartphone timestamps and geocodes the sensor data as it is received. The smartphone application also captures and synchronizes video to the ECG data. Both ECG data and video are used later as documentation of the fieldwork.

Specialists in computer science, physical computing, new media, and sound and electrical engineering developed the devices.[2] Several prototypes have been developed and tested, driven by user needs (mobility, ease of use) and technical requirements (streaming, conversion, programming, and geocoding).

Technological challenges inhibited our mobility literally and creatively. The devices were awkward to wear and much of our time and energy was directed toward troubleshooting the technology. Ironically, over the three years of project development, we have seen the proliferation of personal biometric data devices coming out of fitness and health research. While commercial devices are available, affordable, and user friendly, they still lack the ability to collect sufficiently high-quality data for the audio component in our art installations.

PRESENTATION

We have used the data in conferences, screenings, and art installations.[3] Our most developed artwork was *in pulse* (from the Paris fieldwork), an art installation exhibited in *Place Markers: Mapping Locations and Probing Boundaries* (2012), Dalhousie Art Gallery, Halifax, curated by Peter Dykhuis. *in pulse* consists of two large-scale video projections with two-channel sound presented as an immersive, embodied environment.

The installation reflects the six sites in Paris through synchronized video projections and spatialized sound as looping media. The sound is the differentiated rhythms of our hearts; the amplified signal used subwoofers to emphasize low frequency rhythms, making the sound more visceral. Audiences could view a Google map of locations and raw video footage, on a smartphone screen, mounted on the back wall of the gallery.

Our project reflects chance and circumstance. We feel the process was driven predominantly by challenges of technological development to the neglect of creative potential. What we imagined the technology to be capable of was not possible. We had to accept these limitations, adjust and modify the way we interacted with the city and with each other. Over the project, we shifted how we actually engaged in the urban space and with each other using disruption as a strategy rather than going with the flow. We progressed from being observers to creators of spectacle through collaborative actions. We continue to see potential with the devices for future fieldwork.

Notes

1   Additional funding for this project was provided by NSCAD University and the Saskatchewan Arts Board.

2   We would like to thank Dr Anh Dinh, Electrical and Computer Engineering, University of Saskatchewan; Dr Craig Gelowitz, Software Systems Engineering, University of Regina; Emmanuel Kuatsidzo, MACS, Computer Science, Dalhousie University, Halifax; Annie Onyi Cheung, MFA, Visual Arts, NSCAD University, Halifax; Martin Peach, Montreal; Lukas Pearse, Halifax; Dr Derek Reilly, Computer Science, Dalhousie University, Halifax; Lukas Steinman, Halifax.

3   This project has been presented at the conferences *Affective Cities, Scenes of Innovation II*, Toronto, 2014; *Urban Encounters: Art and the Public*, Halifax, 2013; *Poeticizing the Urban Apparatus: SCENES OF INNOVATION*, New York City, 2013; *Ambiances in action: 2nd International Congress on Ambiances*, Montreal, 2012.

Alexandrine Boudreault-Fournier and Nick Wees

8

—

CREATIVE ENGAGEMENT WITH INTERSTITIAL URBAN SPACES: THE CASE OF VANCOUVER'S BACK ALLEYS

Back alleys are often imagined as dark, mysterious, and dirty urban places where illicit and hidden activities take place. From an urban planning perspective, they are frequently unnamed, forgotten, left aside, and consequently under-utilized and under-appreciated (Cameron 2013). Yet, back alleys also escape the usual constraints that more firmly structure behaviours and uses of space in, for example, the street. Back alleys are urban interstitial spaces because of their "in-betweenness." Some might argue that in-between spaces afford individuals more freedom in their understandings and interactions in and with that space (Karrholm 2011). But what does that mean concretely and in relation to back alleys, and how can back alleys be approached as creative public spaces where artistic and research projects interweave?

During 2013 and 2014, we conducted a research project called "Vancouver's Back Alleys: Towards an Audiovisual and Creative Approach to Urban Spaces,"[1] which took a sensorial approach to the urban environment in looking at issues of creativity and bodily engagement in relation to back alleys. Our research fits with other sensorial approaches to anthropology, such as those developed by the Sensory Ethnography Lab at Harvard University and the Centre for Sensory Studies led by David Howes at Concordia University. For example, Howes and colleagues including Martha Radice (coeditor of this volume and coauthor of chapter 11) and Kim Morgan (coauthor of chapter 7) developed a Sensory City Workshop to accompany an exhibition at the Canadian Centre for Architecture, which invited participants to experience the city through guided tours attending to the senses of touch and taste (Howes et al. 2013).

In this chapter, we offer a processual approach to public urban art, proposing a slightly different focus from the other contributions to this volume. Taking as our starting point that research is a creative process (Sullivan 2010), we argue that anthropologists should be understood as creative agents or producer-researchers in addition to being participant observers (Boudreault-Fournier 2012, 2016). The Vancouver back alley research project allows us to explore how a specific public space, which is often seen as nonproductive from an urban planning perspective, can offer certain possibilities for chance encounters, for the unplanned (Morehouse 2004). This presents an inherent creative potential for innovative reappropriation of urban space, not only from the point of view of the artists but also, and more relevant to this chapter, from that of the researchers. We adopt a research-creation approach, common in the arts, and apply it to anthropology in order to investigate back alleys as spaces of creative engagement and to stimulate novel ways of researching, experiencing, sensing and understanding the creative potential of these interstitial urban spaces.

In order to do this, we produced, in collaboration with sound artists and musicians, audiovisual clips about the back alleys we visited. These clips allowed for an alternative interpretation of back alleys – more sensuous and intuitive – which highlights the creative dimensions and potentials of this urban space as well as the creativity of the social scientists themselves during the research process. The alleys shaped our fieldwork approach in modelling our relation with the space; our intention was to stimulate a dialogue in which our investigation was influenced by the space itself, generating an experience rather than a reading of back alleys. Following in the footsteps of a "detailed listening" approach (Vazquez 2013, 16), this chapter discusses an *experience with* rather than a *detached ethnographic account* of Vancouver's back alleys.

BACK ALLEYS: AN INTERSTITIAL URBAN SPACE WITH CREATIVE POTENTIAL

Although back alleys have often been considered incidental to the infrastructure and social functioning of the modern city, they are attracting increasing attention within urban studies as sites of interest in and of themselves. While claims that back alleys are historically and spatially universal (Martin 2002) may be contentious, it is clear that so-called "empty spaces," the places in-between inhabited space and physical structures, are an inherent feature of any built human environment (Smith 2008). In the contemporary city, in-between spaces can exist on a large scale, such as at the edges of, or in between, urban centres (Remy 1987), or at the micro-level, such as small patches of unmanaged urban wilderness (Jorgensen and Tylecote 2007). They may refer to domestic, neighbourhood, and urban spaces that are left "empty" on purpose (Smith 2008). More specifically, the term interstitial refers to a leftover space, what remains when the intended structures are built, sometimes "with no defined function, between stages of formal development" (Jonas and Rahmann 2012, 51) like vacant lots (Smith 2008) or informal storage spaces (Grossman 2010), sometimes with only one use, like bus stops (Karrholm 2011) or parking lots (Wees 2013). These are pockets of what from a narrow functionalist perspective may be seen as at best underutilized or at worst unproductive and wasted (Levesque 2002).

However, space is not an objective preexisting empty container in which individuals operate; rather, it is produced by human agents and is in turn productive in that it helps inform human relations and one's place in the world (Lefebvre 1991). As much as it is physically built, space is constructed through shared knowledge and sets of bodily practices (Berger and Luckmann 1966). Representations of space are intimately linked to the temporal and rhythmic features of society (Lefebvre 1991, 1999). They are constructed via existing social conventions and structures. If social space is not neutral and devoid of political content, neither is the physical infrastructure of the city (Winner 1980) and its empty spaces (Smith 2008). How and what we build both reproduces existing power relations and affects how individuals engage with space. How space is organized regulates, to a large degree, the movement of bodies; conversely, it is the movement of bodies in space that define that space (Edensor 2010). And while it is possible to approach this issue from a top-down theoretical perspective – analyzing the movement of bodies, the flow of traffic, as abstract patterns of civic life – for the individual inhabitants of the city, it is a lived experience, one that relies less on abstract strategies than on tactical maneuvers, on embodied ways of knowing and being (de Certeau 1984).

In *The Practice of Everyday Life*, Michel de Certeau, looking down from the top of the 110th floor of the World Trade Center, describes New York City as a "sea in the middle of the sea," and "[a] wave of verticals" (1984, 91). Referring to the urban scene below his gaze, he writes, "Its agitation is momentarily arrested by vision. The gigantic mass is immobilized before the eyes. It is transformed in a texturology in which extremes coincide – extremes of ambition and degradation, brutal oppositions of races and styles, contrasts between yesterday's buildings, already transformed into trash cans, and today's irruptions that block out its space" (91). From this perspective, everything is drawn in miniatures and mystical textures. This corresponds to an "erotics of knowledge," which refers to a pleasure that people seek in "seeing the whole" (92), of looking down on. This representation echoes maps and the small-scale models of cities, buildings and landscapes that are often exhibited in city halls, museums, or tourist sites. This top-down perspective generates a visual experiencing of the city, a "visual simulacrum" (92) in which one is somewhat detached from the swarming atmosphere of the city. The photographer Navid Baraty's photo series *New York City from the Top Down*, commissioned by New York's Metro Transit Authority (Arts for Transit program), provides a visual representation of this.[2]

In contrast to the "god's eye" perspective, there are the "ordinary practitioners of the city" who live "down below" and who walk in the city, those whom de Certeau calls the walkers. Experiencing the city as a walker provides another sense of the cityscape, one that depends less on vision and more on embodiment. The walkers rely on specific forms of operations, or ways of operating, to engage with *"another spatiality"* (1984, 93; italics in the original). For the inhabitants of the city, it is at the level of spatial tactics, of corporeal engagement with the immediate environment, that the construction of space is most apparent. De Certeau takes us away from the geographical, the cartographic, and the geometrical representations of the city and towards an embodied form of experience that calls for specific forms of operations – or tactics – of moving, walking, interacting, interweaving, and intertwining. In this chapter, we add the processes of recording and editing as meaningful forms of mediated embodied engagement with an urban space. This is because we consider back alleys as interstitial spaces that foment unexpected encounters and spontaneous creativity.

Back alleys provide an opening, a fissure in hegemonic space, for the marginal and marginalized. These spaces in the modern urban environment, while built with a function in mind (among other things, garbage removal, or access to properties) are perceived as less regulated and regulating than other urban spaces and thus allow inhabitants to conceptualize and use them on their own terms to a greater extent. But this is not to argue that back alleys are unstructured spaces. Urban interstices are "institutionally created and controlled," and consequently the activities that are carried out in such spaces are subject to certain forms of social control (Tonnelat 2008). Even though they are frequently neglected in relation to the centres (Madanipour 2004), they can become sites of conflict – over use, over ownership, over who defines them and what those definitions are. Precisely because they are contested sites, they have the potential to produce new conceptions of self and place (Kirby 1996). More so than the street and other formal(ized) public spaces, inhabitants of the city can actively claim interstitial spaces, such as back alleys, in creative and novel ways – a reterritorialization of social space (Deleuze and Guattari 1987) on the terms of everyday users instead of official planners. In the case of back alleys, this can be seen in everything from the graffiti artist who sees not a brick wall but a blank canvas (Brighenti 2010) to the homeless person who stakes out a living space or from the guerilla-gardener who creates productive spaces to the child who enters an imaginary world in the quasi-wilds of the back alley.

A rare ethnographic perspective on back alleys can be found in the work of Heide Imai, who has produced several accounts of the lived experience of Japanese back alley neighbourhoods, or *roji* (2008, 2010, 2013). Imai focuses on the everyday experiences of inhabitants and other users of the *roji*. Her approach includes walking through these traditional back alley neighbourhoods, detailing the sounds, sights, smells, textures, and even tastes (e.g. foods purchased from street vendors) that she encounters there. Her concern is with the ways in which everyday users understand these alleyways from a sensory perspective – not as an abstract space to be mapped and claimed from without but as a world of daily practices and meaning-production centred on the lived experiences of individual social agents. In this, her approach has much in common with that of de Certeau (1984). She argues that these back alleys, at the "intersection between public and private" (Imai 2013, 59), are less tightly planned and controlled by centralized urban interests, allowing for differing possible interpretations and potentials for social interaction. In her descriptions of the neighbourhoods she investigates, she emphasizes that such "interstitial spaces [...] become re-embodied places of resistance, retreat and compensation" (65). As she walks, she encounters the new, the unexpected, the unplanned, mirroring the *dérive* ("drift") of the Situationists (Debord 1958). Imai's (2008) accounts of the *roji* are situated both physically and temporally. For Imai, back alleys are interstitial spaces between the past and present, "characterized [by] hybrid daily practices" (2010, 811–12), spaces that inhabitants of the city use every day and therefore imbue with meaning.

Through Imai's work, it becomes clear that "tactical" responses (de Certeau 1984, 104) to the interstitial nature of the back alley are predicated as much on the intentions and experiences of the users as on the actual physical space of the alleyway. The experience of space is directly linked to the body of the individual – not simply as an abstract political and historical concept but as a sensory, lived body. The two – body and space – are inseparable, both produced and productive, and constitutive of each other (Simonsen 2005). Pathways pace the ways of carrying the body: all of these contribute to the structuring of space (Edensor 2010). Movement is structured by the existing features encountered by the body, but it is also a creative engagement – one in which the chance encounter, the unforeseen event, may be seized upon as the basis for further explorations (Debord 1958; Grossman 2010). When conducting fieldwork, we approached back alleys as offering great opportunities for creative engagement with urban space, for a reclaiming of space in both its physical and social aspects. Recording images and sounds became our tactical response to our engagement with this interstitial space.

THE VANCOUVER BACK ALLEYS PROJECT

Back alleys are part of Vancouver's urban landscape, but most are nameless and not visible on official city maps. The variety of alleys is striking as one walks in the different neighbourhoods. As a consequence, their uses and appearance vary dramatically from one area to the next (figure 8.1, figure 8.2).

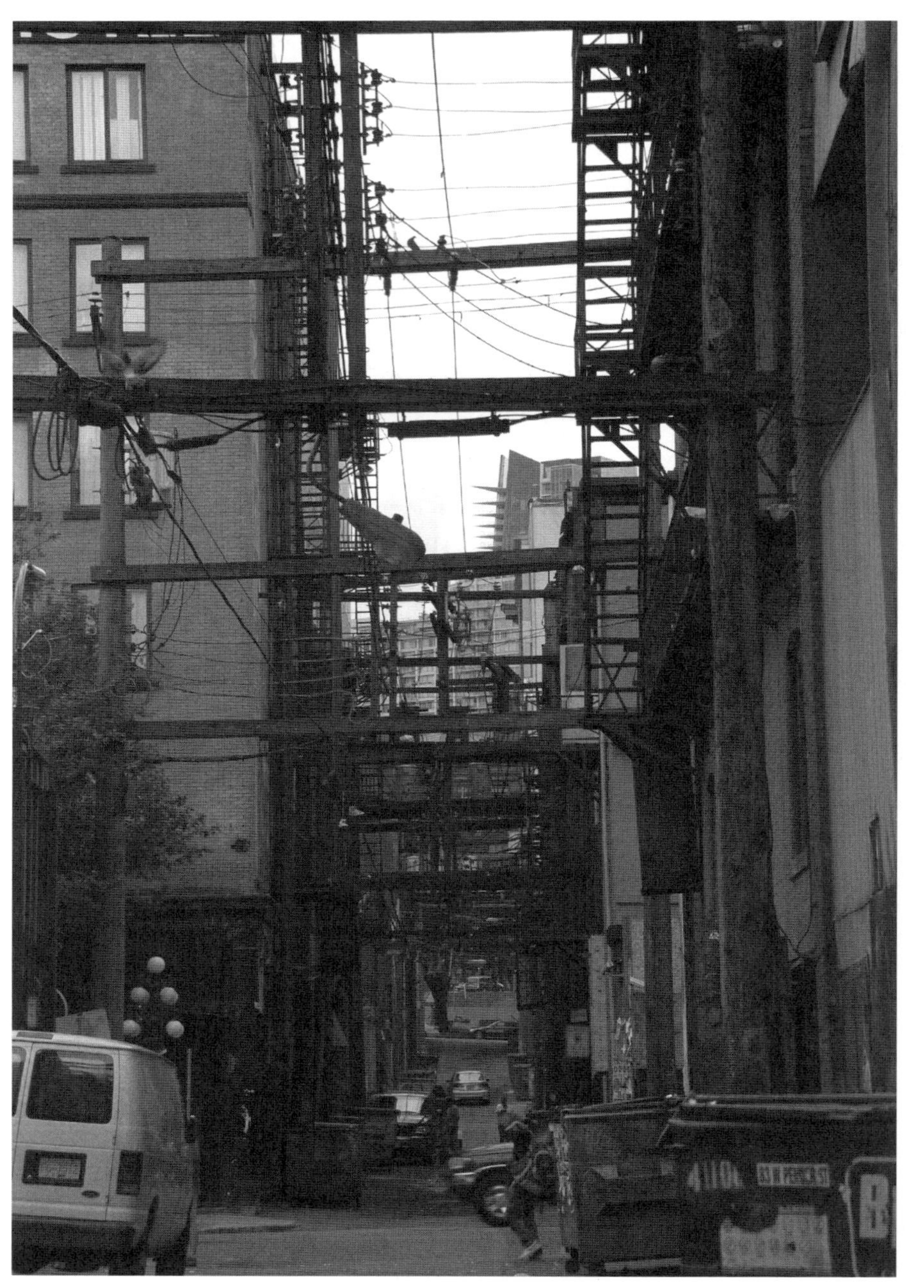

8.1 Back alley in Downtown Eastside Vancouver.
Photo: Alexandrine Boudreault-Fournier, 2013.

In trying to fulfill the challenge of becoming the greenest city in the world before 2020, the city council of Vancouver seems to be showing some interest in transforming back alleys into greener areas (Hutchinson 2013), yet this is a recent development. Sam Cameron, a member of the Liveable Laneways Vancouver association who wrote an insightful dissertation on the topic, observed that there is a "lack of perceivable evidence to suggest that either laneway activities – beyond conventional forms of functionality and utilitarianism – had occurred, or that facilitative policies had been endorsed and/or adhered to" (2013, 4). Despite this, Cameron mentions a few projects that have been approved by the city council, such as the Laneway Housing project (2009), a densification initiative that allows for the construction of laneway houses in single-family zones of the city. Other initiatives targeting economic development have contributed to the rehabilitation of back alleys (Cameron 2013). For instance, a program of revitalization approved by the city council in 2012 promises to improve Chinatown's laneways (Cameron 2012). Private interests plan to develop other laneways with art and retail (Chan 2013); many commentators also forecast the back alleys' appeal for tourists (Cameron 2013). Grassroots associations of citizens such as Liveable Laneways Vancouver and the More Fun Alley Association based in North Vancouver promote alternative uses of back alleys through concerts, arts, fairs, and other small-scale neighbourly initiatives.

At the end of the summer 2013, we acquired a sense of Vancouver's back alleys and some of the transformations they are going through by conducting sessions of observation and listening, data collection and audiovisual experiments in back alleys in four neighbourhoods: Gastown, Downtown Eastside, Grandview, and North Vancouver. We walked, stood, sat, listened, looked, often for long periods of time, and recorded sound and video clips. We talked with neighbours and flâneurs and felt the often-contrasting ambiences, essences, and acoustic landscapes of the back alleys of Vancouver. The project specifically engaged with two main questions: How are back alleys experienced from a visual and sonic perspective? What can sonic and visual composition teach us about the appropriation, interpretation, and use of back alleys by social actors?

In order to explore the first question, we not only listened and recorded sounds but also intervened and played with the acoustics of the back alleys. We were interested in developing a relational approach, an

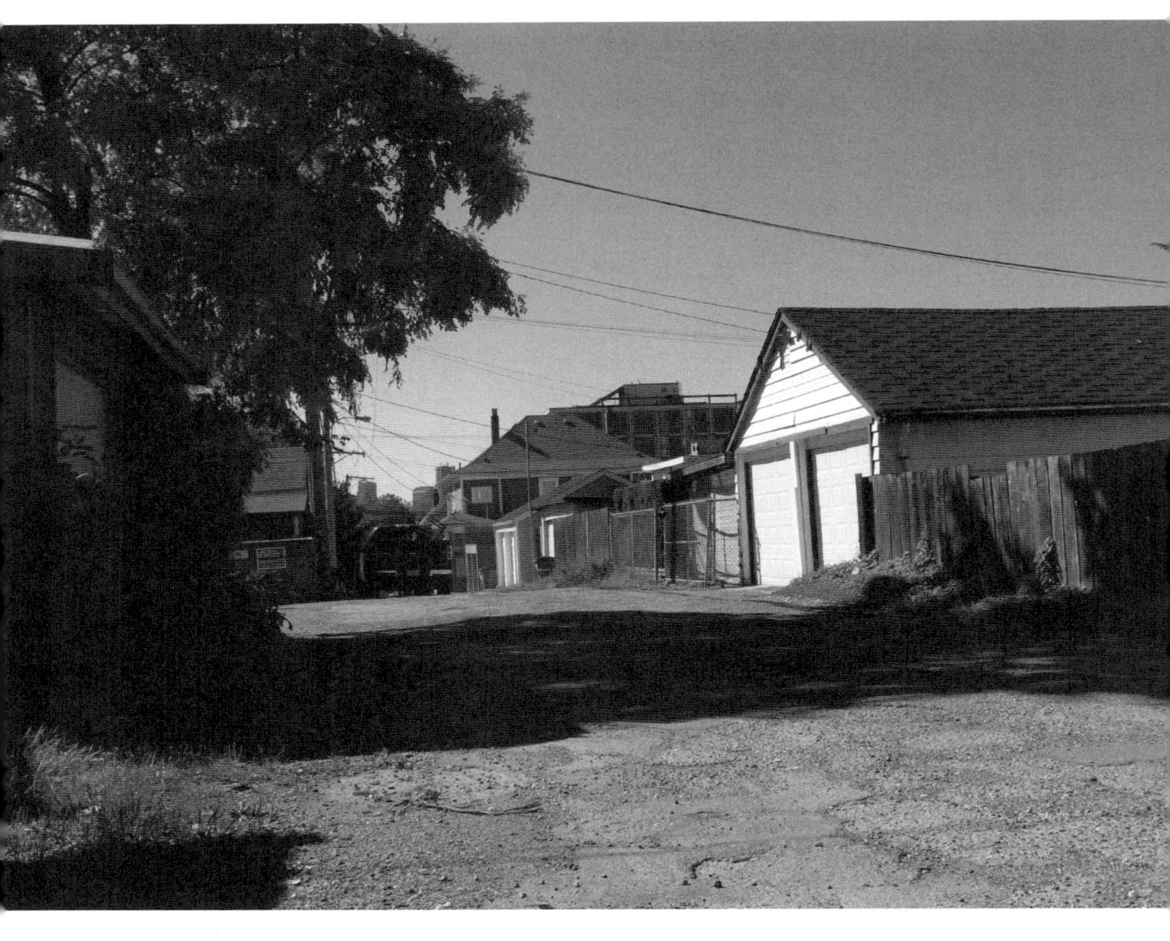

8.2 Back alley in Grandview-Woodland neighbourhood.
Photo: Alexandrine Boudreault-Fournier, 2013.

ethnography of the encounter (Boudreault-Fournier 2012) by provoking collaboration between different individuals in different places. Therefore, our approach can be located in conversation with new understandings of contemporary art, often referred to as "relational aesthetics," a term adopted by writer and curator Nicolas Bourriaud, which refers to artistic practices emerging in the 1990s "that take as a theoretical and practical starting point all human relations in their social context, rather than in a private and autonomous space" (1998, 117; our translation). Relational art offers both challenges and creative opportunities to the discipline of anthropology and can specifically be used as a tool to reflect on the concept of mediation and the nature of relations in ethnographic fieldwork (Boudreault-Fournier 2016). For instance, we organized a jam session with the saxophonist Noedy Hechavarria Duharte and experimented with the acoustics of the back alleys in Gastown. After collecting audio-visual data, we produced a short audio-video clip about this jam in the alley.[3] DJ Ali Dahesh, rapper and hip-hop producer from Vancouver, also spent a day with us in Gastown. Ali knows the streets and the back alleys of downtown Vancouver, but not just in the geographical sense. He knows the streets and the people who live in them; he feels the street is his home, a connection that strongly ties him to hip-hop culture. While we walked with him in Gastown and the Downtown Eastside, we met at least eight people who knew Ali and who were all very happy and excited to see him. One of them had just opened a legal marijuana dispensing business that was promoted with graffiti in the adjacent alleys. Ali introduced us to a young man whom he described as being the Eminem of Vancouver. Hanging out with Ali was in many ways reassuring, and there was a clear sense that he was opening paths, opening up the space of the back alleys in mediating encounters between people, the place, us, and our embodied experiences. Ali was a mediator; he was a transducer (Helmreich 2007) of experiences in the back alleys.

Ali walked, listened, and recorded sounds. He also produced sounds with bricks, glass, sticks, and keys that he brushed on the various textures of doors and walls. He rapped and improvised hip-hop beats. We asked Ali to record sounds in order to produce an original soundscape based on – but not limited to – the sounds we collected in situ. We told him that we would engage with his piece by producing a video clip inspired by his soundtrack and the places we visited. Ali edited some of the sound clips we had recorded, and, a few weeks after we met him in Vancouver, sent us an original composition titled *Alley Project*.[4] Ali's piece is definitely musical: it has a hip-hop rhythm, some rap, and samples of the saxophone player we recorded together. It is also full of sounds of broken glass, cars, and voices of people we met while walking in the alleys. For instance, Ali decided to use the clip of a man saying "God bless you!" recorded in an alley we visited. The track is made up of a complex sonic texture that mixes voices, drum and bass rhythms, and electronic sound samples. The content is urban and the sound texture almost dirty with an underground tone. Interestingly, Ali decided to include at the end of his track a sample of a discussion we had while recording broken glass that day, emphasizing the context in which this clip was made. Ali's track provides one sonic interpretation of back alleys. The listener is invited to imagine the place from the perspective of the one who produced the audio clip.

Sound compositions are more abstract products compared to standard audiovisual documentaries, yet they are better suited to highlighting "people's sensory experiences and mental worlds in more expressive and relational ways" (Eylul Iscen 2014, 127). Ali's track encourages us to think about back alleys by interweaving various components such as space, rhythm, and aesthetic, as well as the presence of people who inhabit and walk through the space.

Some back alleys we visited presented a microcosm of experiences, momentary visual and audio narratives. One such spontaneous encounter with a microenvironment occurred in Gastown. It was early afternoon when we entered the short alley that runs between Hastings and Cordova Streets, approximately a ten-minute walk from the famous Vancouver steam clock. This alley is only about forty-five metres long (compared to the more typical 200 metres or so of most of the alleys in the area) and seemed cleaner than some that we had visited further east, towards the Downtown Eastside. A few passersby walked through the alley while we stood there. We had not planned on staying long, but as we started to record what we saw and heard, we realized that, even there, there was a great deal of interest to us. We spent over an hour filming and recording sound, exploring the alley with our eyes and ears, but mediated by the technologies that we employed.

Pretty soon a couple of men in orange safety vests came into the alley pulling wheel-mounted garbage bins and emptied them into the dumpsters.

They were intrigued by what we were doing, and one commented, "You never know what you might find in the garbage bins." As they worked, two women on bicycles came through the alley; one of them stopped and took pictures of us with her phone as we recorded images and sound of what was around us.

A cook from a restaurant that opens onto the alley engaged us in conversation, telling us that she frequently sees tourists taking pictures in the alley. She was intrigued as to what others could find so interesting about a place that to her was simply a short-cut and an everyday place where people who work in adjoining businesses take cigarette breaks. She told us that people sometimes use one of the empty boxes stacked outside the restaurant's kitchen to make a seat – creating a personal space in the alley. To her, it was simply a functional space, with no particular aesthetic value. Only the week before, she said, a wedding party came into the alley to have their photos taken. She shook her head: "I don't know why anybody would want their wedding picture taken in an alley. I don't see what's so special here." At the same time, she acknowledged that Vancouver's back alleys are distinct from the ones in most other cities because of the imposing presence of poles, lines, and overhead electrical infrastructure.

Clearly, our presence and our somewhat unusual activities – recording the visual and sonic features of the alley – provoked other individuals to stop and consider the space of this short alley, the activities that can take place there, and what sorts of meanings these might have. The sonic and visual recording of this space, in addition to the discussion we had with the employee of the restaurant, positioned the back alley as a fundamentally social place where different actors interact in a public space temporarily made private or restricted in certain ways. The appropriation of the space could be observed in the transformation of the back alley into a momentarily semiprivate, retracted area where, for instance, boxes become chairs, or window frames, benches, and drain pipes become decorative structures for a wedding party. The sound and images we collected served as the material for producing a context-based video clip, which offers an interpretation of us experiencing this urban microcosm.

Nick also created a soundtrack based on original recordings from this laneway and sent his composition to Alexandrine. Inspired by a combination of what Nick produced and by her experience in the alley, Alexandrine edited a short video clip.[5] From the beginning of the soundtrack, one can hear the garbage lids closing repeatedly; these sounds introduce the listener to the infrastructure of the alley, the walls, the street, the poles, and the electric transformers. We can hear one of the workers who is emptying the garbage saying, "Looking for activity inside the bins or what?" The clip content suggests, among other things, the omnipresent olfactory dimension of the alleys when we walked through them. Describing his experience of walking in Vancouver's back alleys, Cameron (2013, 45) writes, "On more than one occasion, the rank smells were so overpowering and nauseating, that I had to retract myself from the laneway altogether, therefore, hindering any prolonged observation" – a sensation we also experienced. As the camera moves along the alley following the wall, one notices the wood box that serves as a seat for workers who take a break and a purple bow attached to a drainpipe, a remnant of a festive use of the alley.

Recording sound and moving images in the back alleys and producing original audiovisual clips, as part of our creative process, precipitated remarks, thoughts, observations, reflections, bodily experiences, and self-transformations that would not have emerged had we not adopted a research-creation approach. For instance, it is through the process of editing the sounds and the images that we fully realized the ubiquity of electric poles as well as the sound of electricity travelling through the cables. We included these characteristics of the back alley into the video clip. Like archaeologist Monica L. Smith, who explores empty urban spaces in the ancient city of Sisupalgarh in eastern India, we travelled through the back alleys recording "the sequence of events rather than a defined space that is always and only for a particular kind of activity" (2008, 219). Our video clip shows the evidence or traces of how space is made through a sequence of events (the workers emptying the bins, the back doors open, the seat for the workers to have a break, a cigarette butt, the bow left behind, etc.). Similar sequences characterize each alley we went into, each of them offering us its own stories.

Adopting this approach to explore back alleys involved the conscious experiencing and making of a place, mediated and even augmented by the recording devices and the production of the context-based video clips. We experienced the city with our bodies instead of just looking down (to refer to de Certeau's analogy). We gave serious consideration to the creative contribution of the anthropologist in the research enterprise along with the everyday life creativity of the ones who inhabit these spaces. As such, the creative act became a way of bridging different perspectives, backgrounds, and knowledge about an urban interstitial space.

ETHNOGRAPHY AND RESEARCH-CREATION

Anthropological fieldwork can and should be more than simply holding up a subject for examination as though we can approach something from the outside and understand it simply by describing it. Indeed, anthropologists should not just look downwards. The research-creation approach we aim to develop encourages anthropologists to engage with the spaces in which they conduct fieldwork through creation – in addition to, or instead of, the more common participant observation approach associated with the discipline. Research-creation requires an immersive strategy, one in which we place ourselves within the study and which provides the opportunity to expand beyond either just a simple cataloguing or a purely theoretical examination. Immersion implies adopting a local way of knowing and doing, exploring something from the inside out, acknowledging one's theoretical predispositions, and recognizing that theorization is largely improvisational and is informed by and develops alongside field research (Cerwonka and Malkki 2007).

Just as we consider back alleys to be interstitial urban spaces, so too our approach proposes an exploration of the interstices between disciplines. Research-creation, a methodology associated with artistic disciplines such as visual and media arts, theatre, dance, and music, as well as with architecture and design, is an inspiring avenue of exploration for anthropologists and other social scientists because of its potential to open novel ways of imagining the fieldwork enterprise. Research-creation proposes a rearrangement of disciplinary conventions and boundaries, beginning from the arts domains and potentially expanding to other disciplines. Authors – mainly artists and art critics – have demonstrated how the visual and media arts domains can benefit from the discipline of anthropology, mainly from ethnography, its main methodological approach (see for instance Foster 1995; Fortin 2009; Wynne 2010; Inagaki 2010). Anthropologists have also begun to encourage collaboration between artists and anthropologists, conducting research or developing conjoint artistic projects in order to explore how bridges between disciplines can be constructed (Schneider and Wright 2006, 2010, 2013).

It is only timidly, though, that some anthropologists have begun to write about how visual arts methodologies, such as research-creation and other arts-based approaches, can contribute novel ways of thinking and doing research within anthropology, a discipline that generally defends itself as belonging to the social sciences. George Marcus (2010), for instance, argues that some concepts associated with staging, design, and performance in the domains of film, theatre, and scenography can offer inspiration in redefining the *mise-en-scène* of anthropological fieldwork. It is in the interstice of the anthropological and the artistic gazes that we can experiment with a new configuration of fieldwork (Marcus 2010).

However, we argue that applying research-creation's methodology to anthropology goes further in encouraging not only collaboration between individuals coming from different disciplines but also experimentation with different approaches that are more conventionally associated with other disciplines. To put it simply, our intention is not to become artists but to engage with how artists conduct research in order to reflect on the potential of such a methodological approach to anthropology. This is especially relevant to the practices of the two authors of this article: Alexandrine is a visual anthropologist who engages with audio and visual texts in editing and creating original media productions, and Nick is an engaged anthropology student and artist who has been involved in recording and editing music and sound art for more than ten years. In other words, our practice as anthropologists and sound students (in Sterne's sense, 2012) motivated our approach as producer-researchers in relation to a specific urban site: back alleys.

If we look more closely at some of the characteristics that define research-creation, we can better identify how anthropologists can benefit from this methodological approach. Research-creation aims to understand artistic practice in relation to the artwork, taking into consideration both the process of creation and the finished artwork. It is a heuristic approach, based on phenomenology and on the conscious experiencing of the practice itself (Gosselin 2009, 29). More specifically, the artistic approach, understood as an oscillation between the conceptual and the sensory, theory and practice, and reason and dreams (Lancri in Gosselin 2009, 29) becomes the focus of the researcher-artist – the source from which experiences and thoughts emerge. This implies that the perspective and voice of the artist are acknowledged, emphasizing the reflexive nature of research-creation (30). Representation is another key component of research-creation (ibid.). Artists constantly reflect on how the work of art is elaborated to *represent* or to model a phenomenon or a complex thought.

One cannot help but recognize the similarities between research-creation and the ethnographic approach, specifically in relation to the crisis of representation in anthropology during and after the 1980s. James Clifford and George Marcus (1986) were among the first anthropologists to raise a series of criticisms of the discipline. These mainly targeted the ways in which anthropologists traditionally conducted fieldwork and wrote ethnographies. Some of the criticisms highlighted the importance of including various voices in ethnographic writing – so that the anthropologist's voice is not the only one to be considered – as well as the need to reflect on the anthropologist's own subjectivity and consequently the challenges that must be addressed to achieve intersubjectivity. Other criticisms encouraged the anthropologist to think in terms of incompleteness, nonlinearity, and partial truth.

These critiques further targeted issues of representation (who can represent whom?), the temporality of ethnographic accounts, which tended to position the other as not living in the same timeframe as the researcher (see Fabian 1983), and the perception that the communities where anthropologists conduct research are stable and bounded. These marked a shift in the "anthropological imagination" after which the world is no longer perceived as being complete and coherent but rather fragmented and ambiguous (MacDougall 2005, 244).

So what can research-creation add to ethnography? Reflecting on our own experience in the back alleys of Vancouver, we highlight three main contributions. Firstly, it allows for a serious reconsideration of the processes and practices of ethnographic fieldwork as it emphasizes – in the extreme – the creative nature of research. Secondly, it allows for a more fluid oscillation between reason and dream (or imagination), two poles that characterize the practice of art (Gosselin 2009). In anthropology, imagination became a key element of research, mainly after the publication of *Modernity at Large* (1996) by Arjun Appadurai who considers imagination to be part of the *deterritorialization* that accompanies processes of globalization, in that people around the world can now imagine living somewhere else.[6]

More recently, anthropologists began to apply the concept of imagination to discuss how researchers can propose novel ways of conceiving and conducting ethnography, using, for instance, autobiographical public performances (Culhane 2011) and theatre (Kazubowski-Houston 2010).[7]

Lastly, the adoption of a research-creation encourages the researcher to engage in a process of "place-making," instead of approaching a site as waiting to be discovered. Derek McCormack (2008, 5) uses the term "thinking-space" to refer to an encounter with a site during which the research material is cogenerated with the place. The site is then conceived, facilitated, and imagined as a space of experience and experiment "for thinking relations between bodies, concepts, and materials of various kinds" (7). Echoing de Certeau, McCormack provides examples of actions such as dancing, writing, drawing, diagramming, or enacting lines of walk as techniques to encourage researchers to develop "thinking-space" as a process.

We imagined and engaged with Vancouver's back alleys through the mediation of sound and visual recording devices *and* through the process of editing audiovisual clips. A reflexive approach to the process of producing (recording) and post-producing (editing) the audio-clips as forms of representation became our fieldwork enterprise. The mediation of a site through recording devices requires close observation, embodiment, and connection with a place. Like Sterne (2003), we argue against the idea that recording devices promote a disorienting effect on our senses, maintaining, along with Sarah Pink, that visual recordings can become "routes to multisensorial knowing" (Pink 2009, 99). Senses are interconnected, and there is a need to understand them in practice, which for us implied walking in and interacting with the back alleys via our bodies as well as through the mediation of recording devices.

Sarah Pink explains that place-making through the use of recording devices can be interpreted at three different levels. The first level refers to the anthropologist experiencing a place through her body and her senses, behind the recording device, at the moment of the creation of what David MacDougall (2005) calls "corporeal images." Therefore, "place is made through the coming together of social, material and sensorial encounters that constitute the research event" (Pink 2009, 101). At the second level, she argues that place is further remade through the use of the camera, when it is recorded according to certain criteria and parameters. The clip itself provides another interpretation of a space. And finally, place-making reaches a third level when an audience (which includes the ethnographer) watches and listens to the recordings and uses "their imaginations to create personal/cultural understandings of the representation" (ibid.).

Although Pink addresses visual recording devices (video), a similar argument could be applied to sound recording and editing. Soundscape refers to any acoustic field of study, to the events heard, and to our sonic environment, as well as to the act of composing original sonic arrangements based on sonic recordings of a place (Schafer 1977). One of its practitioners, composer and sound artist Hildergard Westerkamp (2002), writes that a fundamental feature of sound recording and composition is intensive listening, both directly with the ears and via the microphone. This process immerses both creator and listener fully in their environment, fostering an increased spatial awareness. Engaging with the sounds of a place and recording them is part of constructing the representation of a place; it is about making place. In soundscape composition, "knowledge of specific contexts shapes the composer's work and invokes the listener's knowledge of those contexts [...] at the intersections of the listener's associations, memories and imaginations related to that place" (Eylul Iscen 2014, 127). It is a more abstract representation of the "real," yet it has greater potential than written and strictly visual texts to rely on the listeners' memory, sensory experience, imagination, and mental worlds.

Taking this into account, one important aspect is missing from Pink's three-level model somewhere between the second and the third level: the manipulation of sound and image – in other words, the process of editing the recordings. The idea of "making place" does not only occur through the audiovisual recording of a place but also through the conscious transformation of the clips into a meaningful form of representation. Consequently, we would argue with Drever (2002) that the process of editing sounds and images into original compositions and clips corresponds to the practice of ethnography. This is because recording and creating soundscapes, and by extension video clips, can shape and transform our understandings and representations of an urban space (which corresponds to Pink's third level of interpretation). In other words, editing a soundscape and a video clip becomes a process through which the ethnographer is making sense of the data recorded through the production of a meaningful representation of a specific place.

We could compare the act of editing sounds and images to writing an ethnography; both are processes of synthesis and creation. The absence of this level of interpretation from Pink's model might signal a certain discomfort, still prevalent in anthropology, with the idea of making sense through the manipulation, transformation, and staging of data through an act of creation (e.g. editing). In borrowing from research-creation, anthropologists can explore the dimension of manipulation, often missing from anthropological accounts, in more transparent and productive ways. The Vancouver back alley project is one example of how research-creation can open new ways of engaging with urban spaces in anthropology.

FROM INTERSTITIAL URBAN SPACES TO ALTERNATIVE ETHNOGRAPHIC UNDERSTANDINGS

Ethnographic fieldwork, which is traditionally considered to be the foundation of social and cultural anthropology, refers to the process of data collection in an identified milieu during a certain period of time. Yet, the "field" should not be solely perceived as a place that awaits discovery by the researcher as if it were a container of thinking (McCormack 2008). Rather, we argue that fieldwork requires the creative and embodied engagement of the researchers with a site, people, objects, and landscapes, among other elements. A creative practice such as video and sound recording, editing, and composition is a highly productive supplement to traditional ethnographic methods because it encourages alternative understandings of the field site to emerge. The audiovisual clips produced from recordings collected in Vancouver's back alleys during the research project allow for another reading of back alleys which in many ways highlights the creative dimensions and potentials of this urban space, a dimension that has been left aside until recently by urban planners.

In terms of contributing to the critiques of anthropology raised in the 1980s, research-creation encourages anthropologists to address, among other things, aspects of polyphony/multivocality (how different voices are incorporated in one work), of (inter-)subjectivity (how the anthropologists are themselves included in the production), and of representation (how the anthropologists make sense of a place). More specifically, in this case, it encourages us to consider how video and sound recording, and editing allow for the conscious orchestration and composition of our relation with a place.

Producing and editing the audiovisual clips became part of place in the making. In other words, our approach further proposes to engage the senses in ways that allow a multilayered interpretation of a place-in-making. If the built environments of back alleys are as diverse as the neighbourhoods in which they are located, then our research-creation approach highlights the richness, diversity, and complexity of the social life of back alleys, interstitial urban spaces where the public encounters the private, the hidden encounters the open, and the mysterious encounters the playful.

Notes

1 The research was funded by an Internal Research Grant offered by the Faculty of Social Sciences at the University of Victoria (2013–14).

2 Navid Baraty's *New York City from the Top Down* photo series is available here: http://www.shft.com.php5-20.dfw1-1.websitetestlink.com/reading/ navid-baraty-new-york-city-from-the-top-down. Accessed 4 October 2016.

3 The video clip is available at: http://vimeo.com/73407966. Accessed 28 May 2016.

4 Ali released the music track in the album *Collaborations Path Vol. 2* on 30 November 2014. The piece (#9) can be heard here: https://alidahesh. bandcamp.com/album/collaborations-path-vol-2. Accessed 28 May 2016.

5 The video clip is available at: http://vimeo.com/78777150. Accessed 28 May 2016.

6 See also the research project "Subjectivity and the Cultural Imagination" in the Department of Anthropology at the University College of London, coordinated by Martin Holbraad: http://www.ucl.ac.uk/isci. Accessed 28 May 2016.

7 See the Centre for Imaginative Ethnography: http://imaginativeethnography.org/. Accessed 28 May 2016.

Part Three

ALEXANDRINE BOUDREAULT-FOURNIER
AND MARTHA RADICE

: Meeting Art in Public

This section deals with what happens when people encounter art in urban public space. It discusses artistic engagements with the city – urban places and urban people – that put new twists in the sociospatial dialectic, shifting between the gazes of the artist, the curator, and the visitor or passerby. Meeting art in public is about the various encounters that emerge when people witness artists' work in the city (or not), a theme that covers but is broader than the idea of reception.

Two chapters, by Christof Migone and Wes Johnston, discuss two series of off-site works curated in partnership with university art galleries in which the artists left the proverbial white cube in order to create work out in their respective urban/suburban environments. They variously collected obsolete artifacts at the curbside, turned up to cheer on workers in their workplaces, dropped onto doormats as a feature in the local newspaper, and swam around the contours of municipal lakes. Their artworks and performances underline the communicative act of art, not just its aesthetic character. In their chapter, Martha Radice, Brenden Harvey, and Shannon Turner adopt a methodology of "pop-up ethnography" to discuss what happened around the Situated Cinema, a transportable cinema structure that was exhibited at four sites during an experimental film festival in Winnipeg.

In these three chapters, the variable forms and intensity of engagement of the artist(s) with audience, visitors, and participants are key aspects in the analysis. Migone explains that the main goal of his *Door to Door* exhibition series, organized at the Blackwood Gallery in Mississauga (2011–13), was to stage one-to-one encounters and exchanges between the artists and the citizens of this suburban city. The artists involved in the series developed highly original ways of creating this engagement, triggering many different relations and connections. Migone describes the *Door to Door* event as "an exhibition home delivery service" in which the artists came to "knock at the doors" of the populace in order to create moments of encounter and exchange.

Creating moments of encounter through art brings to mind the work of Nicolas Bourriaud (1998) and the art movement he characterizes as "relational aesthetics," in which artists see their work as having precisely the goal of developing relationships, exchanges, moments of sharing. In the following chapters, many distinct kinds of relations are created through the performances and installations reported. Furthermore, the kinds of engagement that the audiences and the artists have are also multiple. The range of possibilities is striking. Yet, recent criticisms of Bourriaud's work (Bishop 2004; Kester 2004;

Stallabrass 2004) have pointed out that the famous curator had erroneously taken for granted that any type of relation created by a work of art would be genuine and democratic. Claire Bishop has suggested that antagonism would be another prism through which to investigate the relations created through art. Many other approaches besides antagonism could be explored.

A more productive way to look at art could be to consider the work of art as gift and artists as givers, borrowing from the work of the anthropologist Marcel Mauss (1925). This approach, recently expounded by Roger Sansi (2015; see also Bruce Barber 2013 on donative and littoral art), is intriguing because it places art in a type of relation long conceptualized by Mauss as consisting of three obligations: to give, to receive, and to reciprocate. The question is, however, whether the viewer/visitor is not obliged to return (or even acknowledge) the gift – and if so, how? Looking at art as a gift is both challenging and thrilling because it locates the artist's role in the centre of the social relations that build the city – instead of at the margins, as artists are often perceived in North America and Europe.

The Artifact Institute, for instance, a two-person artists' collective presented by Johnston, plays with these questions of artists' intentions in performing the acts of collecting and archiving different kinds of data. In their *Investigations*, the artists are positioned in an interstitial space between the public and private, and between science and arts. The Artifact Institute take surveys of the electronics that people throw away and, dressed as garbage workers and driving a cargo van, collect electronics refused for collection by the municipality. They also offer workshops to the public on how to fix electronics themselves. This initiative convincingly shows how the roles of artists change depending on what and whom they meet. Here, they offer a public service while also articulating a critique of how electronics are wasted and, by extension, how this affects the world in which we live. And they do so in a very humorous way (at least from our perspective!). This example evokes not only the complexity of the artist's engagement but also the different ways in which it is accepted or not by the public. And here we go back to the idea of the gift – is the population accepting the gift of art or are they ignoring the offering? For the ones who are accepting it, are they returning the gift? But also, and quite controversially, what does the artist expect? Is reciprocity a conscious expectation for all artists?

It is hard to answer these questions, given the myriad intentions and interpretations that have to be taken into account. This also explains why social scientists have taken so long to be interested – and still so timidly – in the theme of reception. When investigating reception from a qualitative perspective,

the multiplicity of responses collected is often destabilizing if
not impossible to analyse. Yet, this is not the case for Radice,
Harvey, and Turner who developed an original methodology
to understand how people interpreted the Situated Cinema
at its various sites (and we could note that all three chapters'
installations and performances happen in movement). Radice,
Harvey, and Turner went a step further than just interviewing
passersby by also interviewing the artists, which allowed them
to better grasp the intersection and clashes between intentions
and reception. This dialogical strategy emphasizes the many
different senses in which an art installation can be interpreted by
its publics. It also suggests that experiencing a work of art might
take time, it might necessitate reflection, and, above all, it might
be difficult to express through words.

But after all this is the essence of giving or receiving a gift, isn't it?
Sometimes we do it by obligation, other times as a surprise, or for
a special occasion. Receiving a gift can also be destabilizing if not
compromising. The idea of the gift does indeed stimulate new
ways of thinking about how art in urban space is given, and then
reciprocated or ignored, and how these offerings constitute new
relations, how they become part of the urban public.

Christof Migone

9

—

DOOR TO DOOR TO DOOR

Do not knock.

Door to Door was a series of six off-site events produced by the Blackwood Gallery that took place between 2011 and 2013.[1] Each of the six events paired two artists and lasted a week. One of my curatorial intents with *Door to Door* was to continue to forge links between the Blackwood Gallery, based on the University of Toronto Mississauga campus, and the surrounding communities in Mississauga. The initial goal was to reach every single resident of Mississauga, population 700,000 plus – referencing Lucy Lippard's famous curatorial projects, which took the population of the city they were held in for their title (Butler 2012). Needless to say, the goal was not reached but completion in that sense was not, in the end, the principal purpose, which was rather the staging of one-to-one encounters and exchanges. In other words, Adorno's (1974, 40) negative imperative in the epigraph is reversed with *Door to Door*.[2] The knock that fosters the meeting and dialogue is encouraged, prompted, and incited here. The knock in an urban context can be a fraught premise, especially when it is unexpected and unrecognizable. *Door to Door* contained such elements of unpredictability, given that the art exhibition was no longer staged within the confines of a gallery. Unframed as such, the twelve exhibited works discussed below are tasked with the precondition of having to answer questions such as, put colloquially, *what is this?* That being said, that task might not always be an obligation, and indeed it is in that tenuous territory of the unknowable that encounters can lead to outcomes that art within the white cube cannot attain. So we embarked on this figurative knocking through the streets of Mississauga by way of performance and kinetic installation, by mail, and through print, signage, balloons, and stickers. Each project set its own parameters and thereby each intervened on the urbanscape with a specific skew and its corollary consequences.

My curatorial premise was unabashedly utopic: it pledges forthrightly with the implicit article of faith that art can act as a force of engagement, a conversation trigger, a tool for creative reflection. In this case, there was no naive presumption that reception would always be positive or that we would be welcomed. The encounter is not fetishized here. *Door to Door* was preceded and inspired by two editions of *The Projects: Port Credit*, two off-site exhibitions which took place in. Port Credit, Mississauga in the summers of 2009 and 2010. The first occupied the former offices of an architectural firm, and the second was staged in a condo showroom still in use as a sales center during the exhibition. As the title suggests, *The Projects: Port Credit* placed an accent on the proposal or propositional stage of a work (*what might or could happen*). In other words, the focus was on change, plans for change. *Door to Door* shifted the question to one of exchange. In his classic ethnographic study, *The Gift*, Marcel Mauss (1990, 39) summarized the practice of gift exchange as one containing "three obligations: to give, to receive, to reciprocate." The set of rules in the case of *Door to Door* were less rigid and regulated. With this particular frame, the economy at play required no reciprocity or even reception. It was the gesture of giving that was exhibited; the rest was beyond our control. *Door to Door* brought the off-site, off-campus curatorial thrust set by the previous projects in Port Credit to its logical extreme: *if you cannot come to the gallery, the gallery will come to you.*

The suburban/industrial setting of Mississauga, the sixth-largest city in the country but nestled beside the largest, is critical to consider. As an illustration of the status of art and culture in the city, in my capacity as director/curator of the Blackwood Gallery at the time, here is my 2012 contribution to a report intended for a general public that Stuart Keeler, the then director of the Art Gallery of Mississauga, was assembling:

What is a public? Is it you? What is art? Is it a thing, an idea or an attitude? What is a gallery? Is it a space-time where critical exchange is fostered? Is it a context where your senses are engaged? Is it a frame where new forms and ideas are experienced? How often do you go to one of the two public galleries in Mississauga? Where is the Art Gallery of Mississauga? Where is the Blackwood Gallery? Where should they be? What should they be doing? Does Mississauga need art? What does art do? Is it like a film on walls? Is it like a book spaced into rooms? Is it like a song you walk through? If you think art looks like X, can it also be Y? Is art singular or plural? Who decides what art is? Who determines artistic quality? What are the criteria for determining the value of an artwork? What function does art play in your life? Should art entertain? Does art playfully alter your perceptions? Does art expand your horizons? What is the place of the imagination in your life? What would daily life be without moments of insight? Does culture affect you? Do you affect culture? Can art be confrontational? Can art be political? Can art impact on the social? Can art educate? Can art make you laugh? What if you don't get the joke? Should art be serious? Should art be taken seriously? What if you don't get the point? Is it ok not to understand? If you are puzzled by an artwork, do you ask for information or do you dismiss it? Can art awaken? Is art synonymous with beauty? Is the sublime paralyzing or generative? Can art explore the mundane? Can art be neighbourly and provocative at the same time? Is a gallery there for you? Or is it there for the art and the artist? Can it be there both for the art and for you? Is a space that provides free access to art important? If it is free, who funds it? Are you willing to support it? What is a space that poses questions? Are you in that space now?

The series of questions provides a context for *Door to Door*; a curatorial project that required extensive dialogue with the participating artists, given the above mix of idealisms, polemics, and provisos. Myriad questions arise as soon as the tangible aspects of realization of a project with such utopic premises are considered: if someone answers the door once knocked, is the art shown, heard, given, or performed? Or is the art to be left at the unknocked door? If so, how many objects at each door or how many objects in total? What if the gift is refused? These questions are largely alien in a traditional exhibition that is sited both architecturally and ideologically. The givens of an exhibition have vanished; this is outreach, literally, a *reaching out*. The choice of dispersal activity becomes integral to the artwork. Questions for the participating artists included the following: Delivery of the art by car, on foot, by mail? How are the addresses selected? Is it a day-long dérive or a week of 6:00 a.m. wake up calls? Is an object given or just shown? Is it in an upscale neighbourhood or at a strip mall? Is it everyone whose last name starts with P or every blue door? Are you presenting yourself as a Jehovah's Witness, an encyclopedia peddler, or, blatantly and transparently, a contemporary artist? Or is the doorbell rung and you promptly run? A multitude of ethical and legal issues emerge from this process of questioning. They are acknowledged not as hindrances but as key encapsulations of the societal conditions which regulate exchange. The aim is not to endanger but to astonish, albeit principally in an intimate and furtive manner. As each project became concrete, divergences from the curatorial premise I outlined were inevitable, even welcomed. The proposition was not intended prescriptively, but as a point of departure, as a generative trigger.

DOOR TO DOOR 1

There|Here by Germaine Koh and Gordon Hicks was a fitting inaugural work for the series, consisting of a pair of doors in two different buildings connected through the internet so that when someone opens one door the other door follows the same action – a ghosting produced by a hybrid electromechanical controller device. Doors leading to nowhere, doors that can be bypassed, unnecessary doors – in through the out door. No longer entry or exit points but pointless passages where the threshold becomes the momentary staging where real and virtual forces meet. In this iteration of the piece, the two doors were not within eyesight of each other, which heightened the inscrutability of their presence. Furthermore, they were domestic doors within makeshift frames situated in an institutional context (a university campus) – they thus stood out as anomalous entities. They functioned as triggers for bemusement and as such foretold how each of the other works in the series would devise their own terms of engagement. Doors can be markers for an ethics predicated by access, that is, on the condition that they are or can be opened: "openness does not require

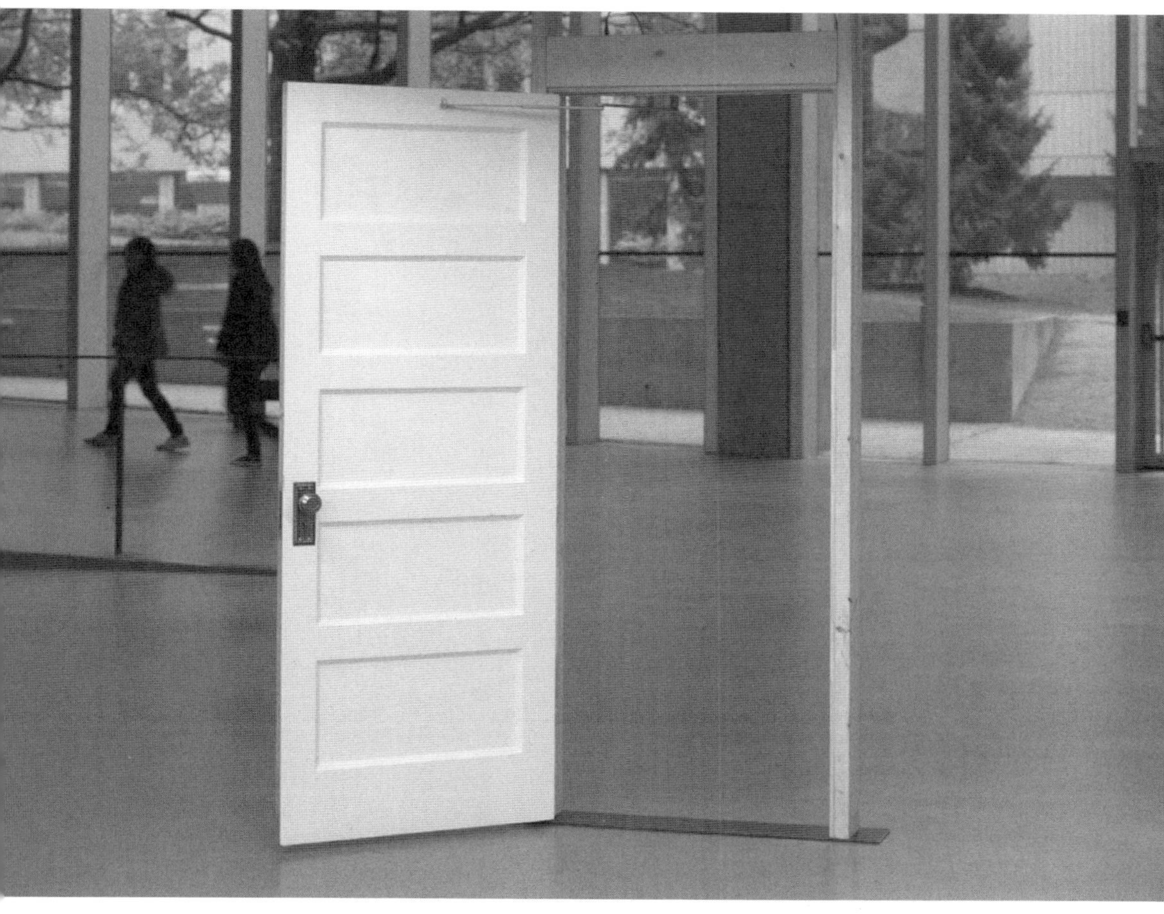

9.1 Gordon Hicks and Germaine Koh, *There|Here*, 2011.
      Photo: Gordon Hicks.

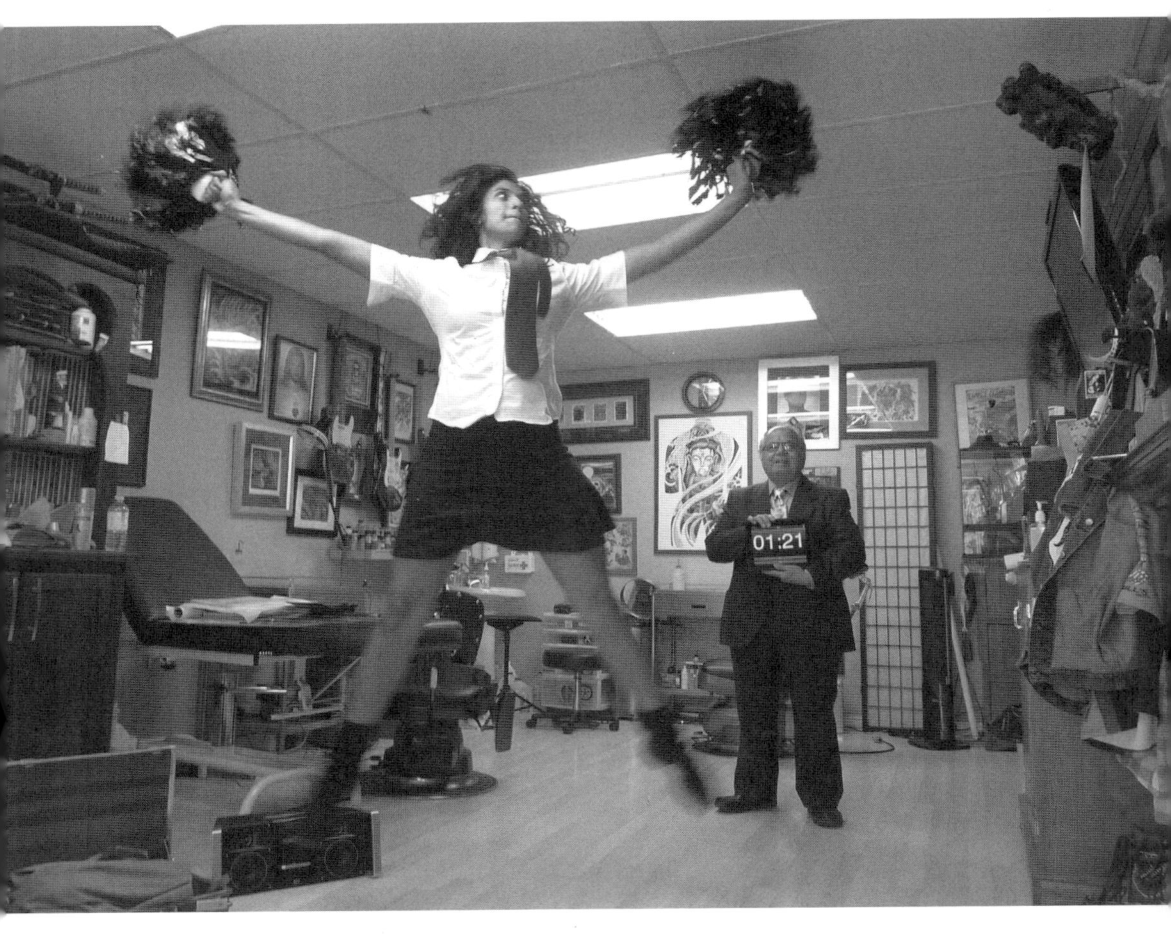

9.2 Camilla Singh, *Encouragement*, 2011.
    Photo: Walter Willems.

that one leaves the door open, but that one is always willing to open the door" (David Wood quoted in Hannula 2006, 52). These paired doors put that *will* into question; they playfully tested the fortitude of that openness – even while subscribing to the *will of the open,* which Reza Negarestani formulates as a key characteristic of responsible artistic engagement in contradistinction to the myopic *will of regions* (2011, 106). They tethered a conditional to the question of openness through the activation of a device that negotiated the uncanny presence of absence.

The tenuousness of a public is already put in play in *There|Here*; in Camilla Singh's simultaneous *Encouragement* performance, the "dissociative factor" is further investigated (Gaitán 2013, 36). Juan A. Gaitán identifies the capacity of an exhibition to be "non-integrated with the public sphere" (36) when it contains a certain criticality and "a logic of fragmentation" (38). Singh presents herself as a cheerleader performing a routine to a hip hop tune on a jukebox, with the intention of providing encouragement to people at their place of work. Cheerleaders, predictably, spell things out; they lead the cheer; they are unambiguously on message. Singh's exuberant miming undermines the attendant expectation for communication and thwarts the delivery. In other words, the encounter operates at a different register; there is subterfuge in the façade of the taciturn yet friendly performer. Singh's two-and-a-half-minute performances were sometimes prearranged, other times impromptu; her imposed pause after this time was up temporarily inserted a self-reflexive commentary on labour. Disguised as frivolous exertion and punctuated by the handing out of cards stamped with "thanks for the work you do" upon completion, Singh's close to two dozen performances (in a fire station, an auto body shop, an architect's office, a school, a health food store, an ice cream shop, a farmer's market, a florist, a butcher, a police station, a library, a beer store, and a barbershop amongst others) mixed earnest acknowledgment with an implicit critique of wage labour. The wordless cheer for the mute worker, mixing both employer and employee (and customers in some cases) as audience, ambiguously makes its point. As her routine is counted down by her assistant (the recently deceased José Talavera, the long-time front desk attendant at the Museum of Contemporary Canadian Art where Singh was assistant director/curator 2002–09), the utility of work, its purpose and value, its equity and precarity are beyond words – the body's rote moves (of goods, of services) are where a wage labour economy operates most insidiously.

DOOR TO DOOR 2

As the title implies, discussion is at the center of Alexander Irving's *Symposia*. A series of eleven aluminum 10-by-3-inch plaques with quotations by varied figures such as Einstein, Sontag, and Malcolm X, are placed in various public locations. The content matched the location; for example, "Conflict cannot survive without your participation" (Wayne Dyer) was installed at a paintball place; "It's never too late to be who you might have been" (George Eliot) in a library; "Time is not a line but a series of now points" (Taisen Deshimaru) in the hall of a students' residence; "If opportunity doesn't knock, build a door" (Milton Berle) on the door to the Blackwood Gallery director's office. The sources are not stated on the plaques; as such, the quotes peer through the utilitarianism and even mundaneness of typical signage and offer entry into a pensive train of thought or perhaps a pondering that will only be recognized as such after the fact – a thought-time-bomb if you will. That being said, the incongruence of the invitation's mode of delivery also lends itself to dismissal or misrecognition; its lack of immediate functionality makes it easy to give it no more than a glance. In other words, the message is blunt, while the method of messaging is subtle (though both can easily be blurred with each other). In a remarkable essay inspired by Henri Lefebvre's celebrated *Critique of Everyday Life*, Maurice Blanchot's "Everyday Speech" interprets the everyday as a dual and contradictory notion where only a "slight displacement of emphasis permits passage from one to the other" (1987, 13–14). So, we move from the everyday's seemingly engulfing alienation to its capacity to be "continually, though in the mode of discontinuity, in relation with the indeterminate totality of human possibilities" (19). Given that Irving's selection of clichéd pearls of wisdom (which is itself a cliché) are devoid of context, they work as floaters on the morass of signs that populate our everyday; they are raw matter that could readily recombine into the means to *escape the everyday* that is their setting (and "the everyday escapes" is a recurring turn of phrase in Blanchot's essay). An added element is the permanence of the material: the metal invokes a sense of the official, of

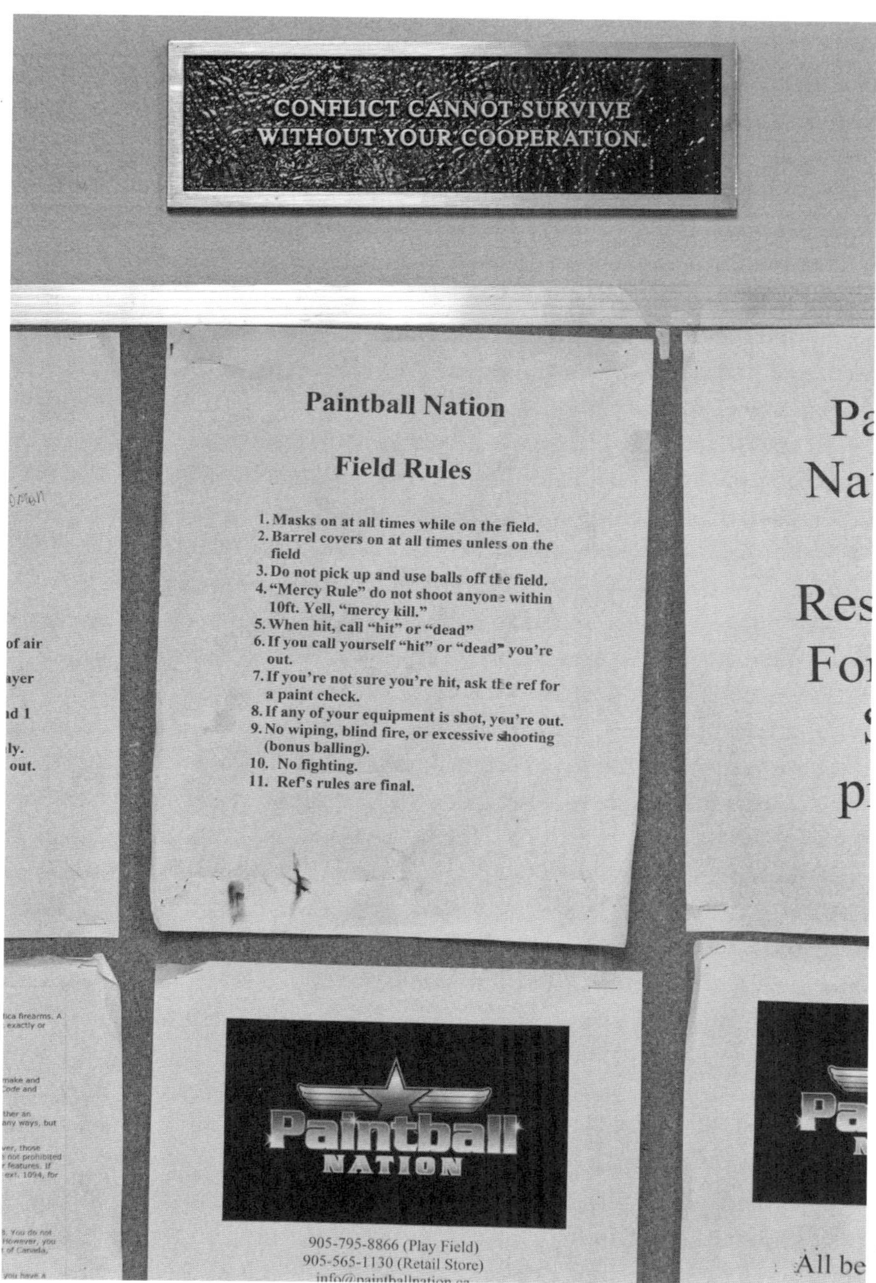

9.3 Alexander Irving, *Symposia*, 2011.
     Photo: Toni Hafkenscheid.

commemoration, of standstill; given their modest size they function as lowercase monuments (in fact, several years after the project's official run, a lot of them remain in place). As such, they persist as conditions of possibility, triggers awaiting activation, golems.

With *Double-Sided Page for the Mississauga News,* Micah Lexier enacted a similar insertion into everyday speech. A two-sided page of cryptic marks in the *Mississauga News* of 30 September 2011 composes an intelligible self-explanatory text only when the page is held to the light and the printed ciphers of both sides align, revealing the following:

> THESE MARKS ARE MICAH LEXIER'S CONTRIBUTION TO DOOR TO DOOR, AN EXHIBITION OF OFF-SITE ARTWORKS ORGANIZED BY THE BLACKWOOD GALLERY. A PART OF EACH LETTER OF THIS TEXT HAS BEEN PRINTED ON EACH SIDE OF THIS PAGE OF THE MISSISSAUGA NEWS. IF THE PRINTER DID A GOOD JOB OF ALIGNING THE TWO SIDES, THEN YOU SHOULD HAVE NO PROBLEM READING THIS; IF THE TWO SIDES ARE NOT IN ALIGNMENT, THEN THIS WILL JUST BE A JUMBLE OF MARKS.

There is a return reference to labour here and a certain cheeky redundancy in the concluding remark. Referencing the mechanics of the printing process and the skill required to perform the task speaks to the ethos of the conceptual artist aware of the frequent necessity of collaboration at the realization stage. In other words, the work is a test of technical ability first but also of the willingness on the part of the suburban reader to explore. Here the depth of the page opens and activates the pseudo palimpsestic possibilities offered by newsprint. This is Duchamp's infrathin instantiated – a condition particularized by subtle shifts, be they of planes or perceptions (Dworkin 2013, 17–18). Lexier's words are matter-of-fact and laconic: context and content provided in bits. They are as thin as the page in one sense, but they are also revelatory of more than their legibility. Akin to Irving's word-golems, the glyphs illuminate another lesson regarding the possibilities inherent in language. Apropos, returning to Blanchot's essay, which articulates the stakes of communication through unabated uncommunicative action: "What is essential is not that one particular person speak and another hear, but that, with no one in particular speaking and no one in particular listening, there should nonetheless be speech, and a

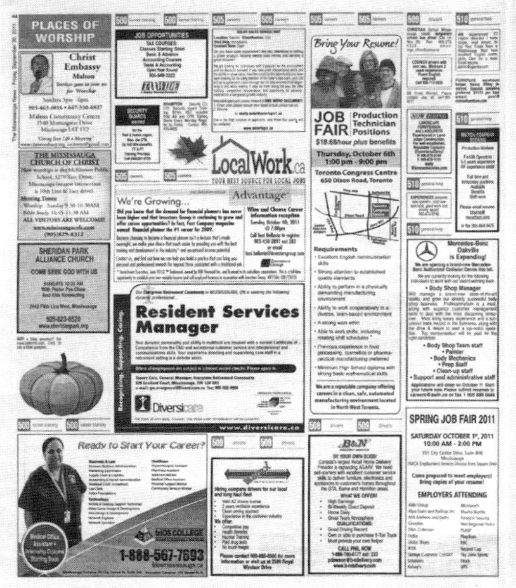

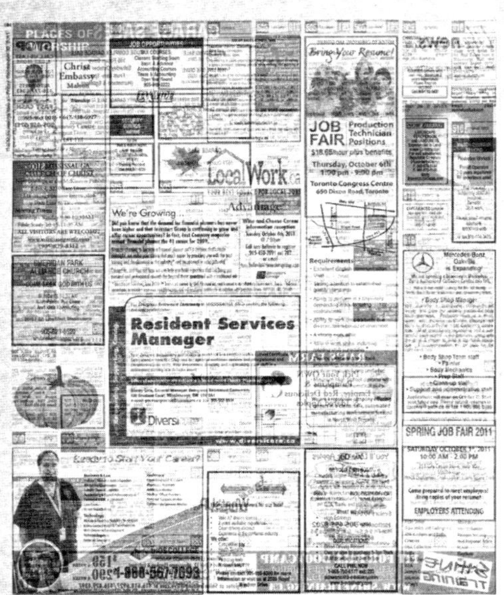

9.4 Micah Lexier, *Double-Sided Page for the Mississauga News*, 2011.
Photo: Toni Hafkenscheid.

kind of undefined promise to communicate, guaranteed by the incessant coming and going of solitary words" (1987, 14).

The triweekly paper has a significant circulation of 440,000 per week (this number comes into play later) and is run by a conglomerate of regional publications throughout Ontario. The editors deemed it essential to contextualize the presence of the quasihieroglyphs by including a front-page teaser (titled "What is it?") and a supporting article including an interview with the artist. The didactic intrusion was not unwelcome on our part; it certainly was an improvement from the initial calls to the editor, which resulted in categorically unreceptive responses from the managing editor. Evidently, the purpose of the gesture was not readily apparent – the basis of the reluctance hinged on this question. Mary Jane Jacob (1999, 103) summarized the typical issues facing public art as falling under three headings: "the categorisation dilemma, the collaborative crisis, and the analysis of effectiveness." All three had to be contended with to various degrees throughout the series. Here, the first two were intertwined. It is impossible to determine whether we finally convinced the paper by succeeding to define the project's merit to their satisfaction or by managing to raise the needed funds to purchase the space (to their credit, at a discount).

DOOR TO DOOR 3

Correspondence serves up mementos of moments, some mundane, others momentous, some discarded, others cherished. The heyday of mail art has largely waned alongside the fate of the postal system. Yet the strategies used by the former by means of the latter can still be effective. John Marriott's *Experience Attractor* and Karen Kraven's *Apartment Hunting* deftly engaged in multistep processes of exchange crisscrossing Mississauga through the post. Marriott's piece consisted of a piece of driftwood, knotted and gnarly, torn and truncated, sent unboxed through the mail to persons who re-sponded to an enigmatic flyer depicting the driftwood overlaid with the text, "This is an experience" and tagged with "Interested?" and an email ad-dress. The interested parties would then receive the unwieldy object and be instructed to mail it to the next respondent – receiver becomes sender. The resolutely nonrectangular object sat on doorsteps or mailboxes, painted

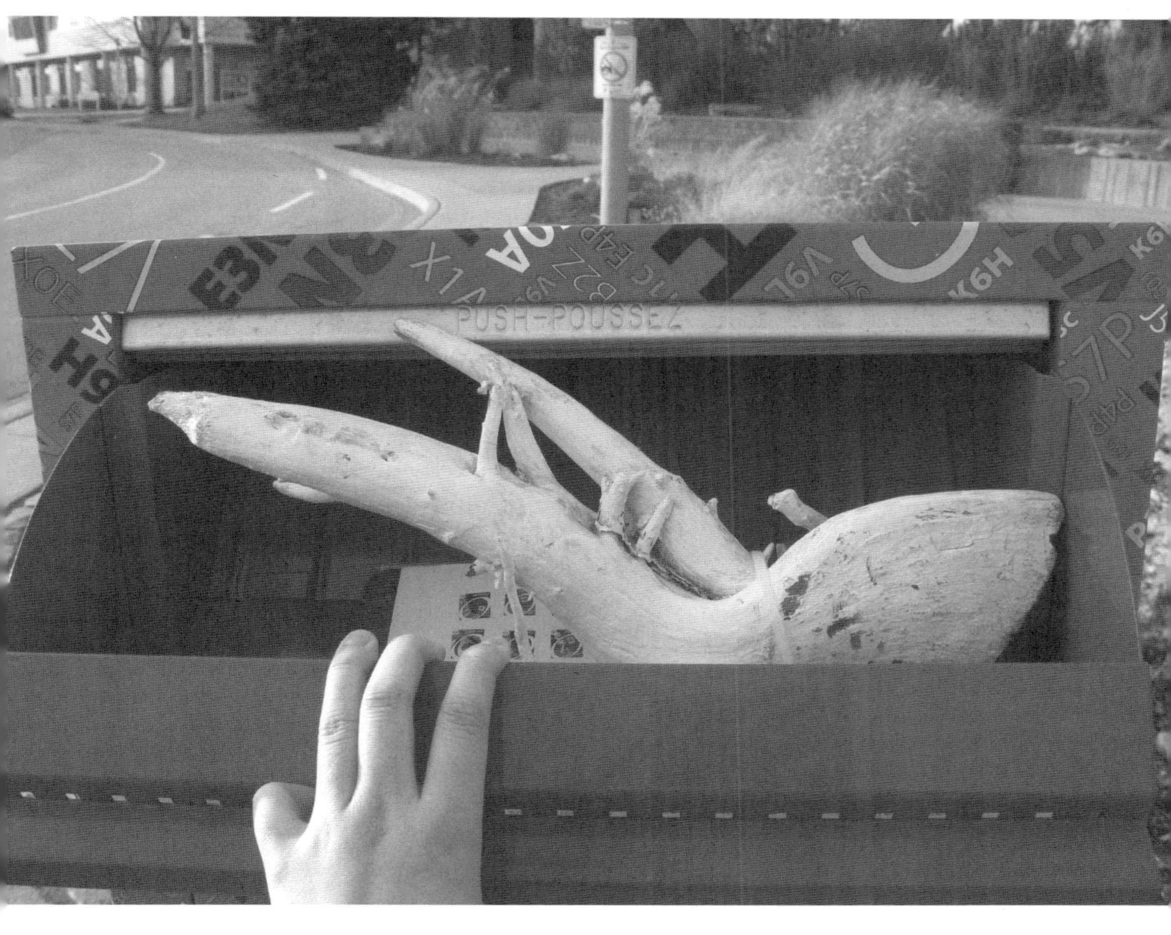

9.5 John Marriott, *Experience Attractor*, 2011.
Photo: John Marriott.

in white gesso but undeniably raw in form; its ill-fitting shape matched Marriott's purposefully convoluted drifting procedure. The piece of driftwood from Lake Ontario performed a dérive in a way Debord would never have predicted. The driftwood obligated a negotiation, both in terms of the aforementioned mailing procedure and, once the object has reached its new home, with the object itself. It cannot be opened and filed, it flaunts its foreignness – although its attached postage proves it has been sanctioned and accounted for. Herein lies both the attraction and the experience – an uncanny underlies the exchange. After all, the object remains recognizable, it is the mode of transportation that triggers a double take – a simultaneous "need for classification and fear from it" (Maurice Bouvet quoted in Kristeva 1991, 188). There is a playful subversion in Marriott's drift, of both the standard dissemination strategies for art and the strictures of the postal system.[3] But there are innumerable ramifications that further enrich the project: for instance, the dead hunk of tree inserted into a live circulation amongst flattened paper, the trust between the artist and the participants, the open yet stealthy propagation, the mute foreign guest commandeering a means of conveying information, the use of it as a device to draw dignitaries – we tried to get the mayor of Mississauga to agree to be the final recipient, to no avail.

Marriott and Kraven share not only the postal service as dispersal conduit but also its anonymous and surreptitious capacities. However, Kraven's project involved inadvertent participants, each receiving unsolicited drawings by the artist. The difference in tactic is significant and places the artist's gesture on potentially questionable ethical ground. First, let's recount the process: Kraven hunted for online postings of apartment rentals in Mississauga that included images and full addresses. She then redrew the pictures in an abstracted way and sent them to the occupant. Kraven (2011) calls the drawings "aspirational sketches." This generated the following two emails:

RECIPIENT A:
– Hi Karen, I currently live at xxx and I got mail from you
that was addressed to current tenant, I just want to know what
this paper thing that kinda looks like a window is because it's a
little creepy.

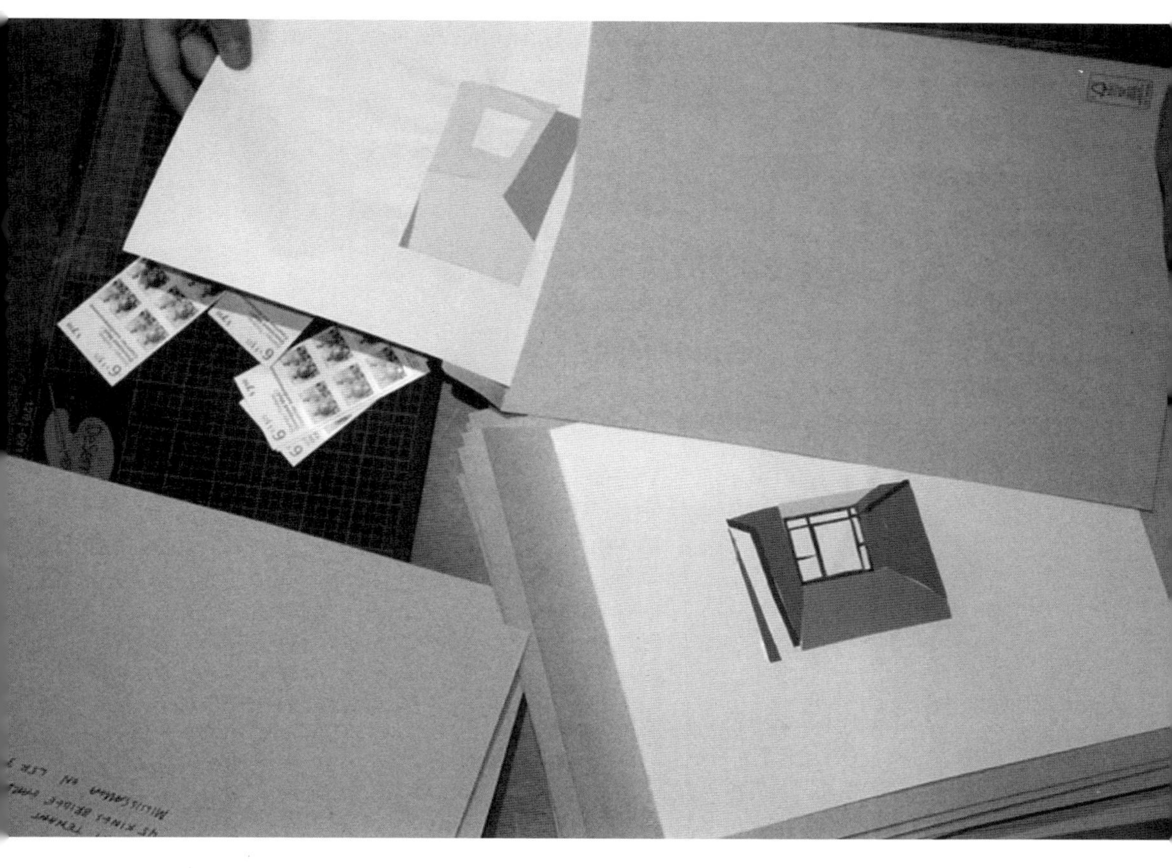

9.6 Karen Kraven, *Apartment Hunting*, 2011.
Photo: Dean Baldwin.

– Hi Sara, [...] I found an image of your apartment on craigslist this year. The drawing is an abstracted version of that photo. I apologize if it is creepy.
– I'm just glad you're not some creepy stalker trying to kill me lol.

RECIPIENT B:
– Hi Karen, [...] I received an envelope from you and am concerned as I am not sure who you are or how you know what the layout of my condo looks like. There was no note or explanation of what or why you are sending a replication of my home. I hope you can understand why this would be unsettling and provide an explanation.
– Hi Cheryl, [...] I found an image of your apartment on craigslist this year. The ad included an address. The drawing is an abstracted version of that photo. I apologize if it is creepy.
– That's awesome! I would have appreciated that info included within the envelope so I could have bypassed the mini-panic attack following the opening of the package... lol... but with that information to go behind it, I think that's amazing. I actually just moved in recently and am in the process of decorating and adding touches... I have a great thick black empty frame I think I will put your picture in and hang on the wall :). Thank you for the background information and your artwork.

The unsettlement articulated by both recipients is temporary, and one could posit that the positive end result needed to pass through a disturbance, an unmooring of normality. Wonderment becomes possible only once the art category is ascribed. The momentary void that precedes it flirts with danger (however unintended). One could even dub the artist as having performed a *passionate utterance* for, as Stanley Cavell asserts, it is "an invitation to improvisation in the disorders of desire" in a context where there is an "absence of convention" (2005, 233, 232). The fact that the gesture is mute amplifies its ability not just to blur but to dumbfound. The comprehensible desire to comprehend is stalled. In the timespan of the delay the seemingly innocuous gesture transgresses the threshold and enters private space. Could Mary Jane Jacob's aforementioned three headings apply to public art that transforms itself into private art? Does the

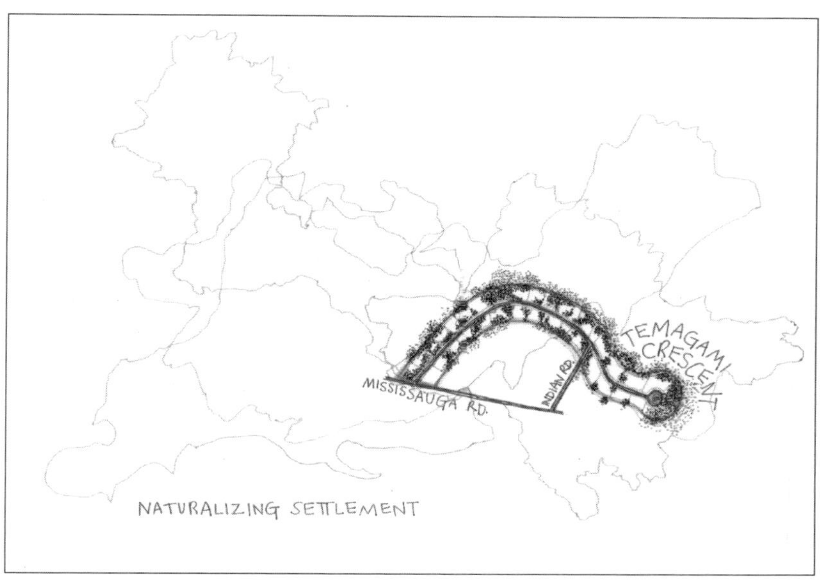

9.7 Gina Badger, *Temagami Crescent*, 2012.
Photo: Gina Badger.

transgression manifest precisely in the sudden presence of the public in the private realm? A momentary confluence of *host, hostility, hostage, hospitality* delivers the undercurrent here (Derrida 2000).

DOOR TO DOOR 4

Both projects of the fourth edition adopted tactics similar to those of the third. Consequently, they raised comparable issues. Gina Badger's project might have a mellifluous sounding title, *Temagami Crescent*, named after a street in Mississauga, but she reveals it to be a name for a place that is literally out of place; it "maps one Indigenous reality – in this case, Temagami First Nation on Bear Island, Ontario – onto another – Mississauga First Nation" (Badger 2012a; Badger 2012b). The nomenclature of displacement manifests displacement of peoples. Temagami Crescent is a small street; it crosses only three other streets – Mississauga Road, Nocturne Crescent, and Indian Road. The intersections further load the manipulative interpretation of heritage onto civic infrastructure. Badger utilizes the instance of this disjunctive metonymy to delve into other connected layers of vexed history. She produced five postcards that each track a different facet of that history: incarceration, watershed, flora and fauna, First Nations communities, and, fittingly, etymology. These are maps of contexts, maps of crisis, maps of critique. One kind per day was sent to each of the thirty-one addresses on the titled street. Only one response was received by the artist or the gallery, so reception at the immediate level from the target audience was minimal, but the nature of this project and many of the projects here is that the role of diffusion is taken up mainly by documentation (in other words, they have an afterlife existence). The projects do not depend solely on a primary audience; in fact, the residents of Temagami Crescent are more akin to unwitting foils or happenstance recipients. However contentious the statement might be, they became participants whether or not they recognized themselves as such.

The usurping aegis of "capital" founds the settler city; that city is "dissolved in the fluid called money" (Robertson 2006, 1) which operates with "mathematical ferocity" (Berardi 2012, 17), and the fact that Temagami Crescent is adjacent to the Credit River adds yet another apt conjunction. No other consideration or criteria can be mapped onto the official city plans

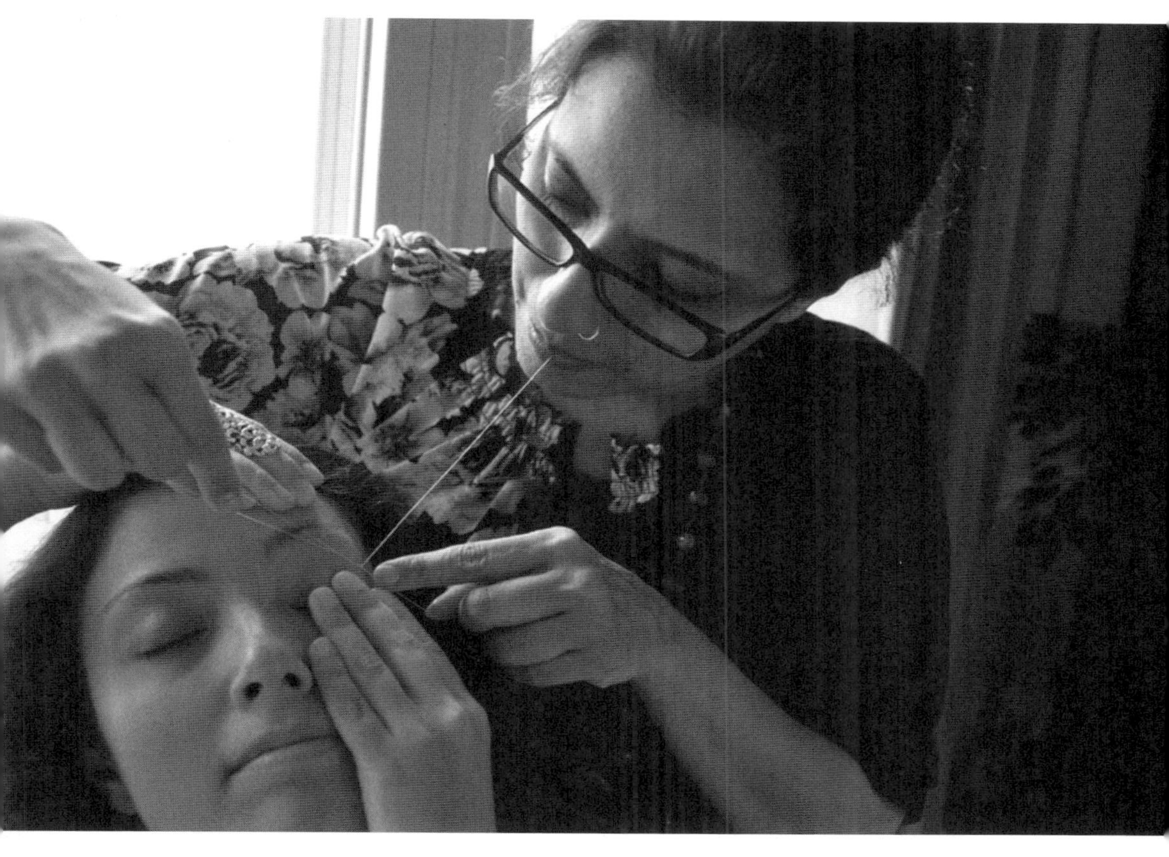

9.8 Tazeen Qayyum, *Threading Encounters*, 2012.
     Photo: Faisal Anwar.

– at least, not without significant difficulty if deemed devoid of economic value. In contrast, Badger presents her meticulously researched findings in hand-drawn postcard-sized maps; a certain lowercase ethos is evident. They constitute "an act that has a certain impossibility inscribed onto it, a certain productive failure … an act as an act within the contemporary field of art, but not an act as a work of art" (Hannula 2006, 11). The paired project, Tazeen Qayyum's *Threading Encounters*, shares Badger's somewhat furtive tactics or at least the particularity that it took place in a private setting. Both were works for the home: Badger's, a work for specific addresses and Qayyum's, a work to be carried out in the homes of willing participants. Their status as art cannot be disambiguated, but it should be clear by now that this demarcation is of little import to their value as engagement practices. In the case of this series, we could further specify them to be *engagement practices using furtive strategies to devise situations that address the urbanscape.* Qayyum's title doubles the focus on this dimension; additionally, the verb form of *thread* activates the premise. Through flyers and word of mouth, Qayyum sought women willing to have their eyebrows threaded by the artist. This South Asian practice of epilation partly serves as a pretext for the artist to enter the participant's home and attempt to "get to know each other" as she plainly puts it (Qayyum 2012). But it also serves a purpose because her amateurish skills (by her own admittance) in the ancient cosmetic method ensure that the encounter is not one predicated merely on services rendered but more one conducive to an informal exchange. The two work in tandem. The threading action is intimate, it requires a choreographic entwine. *Threading Encounters* foregoes definitive dictates or sweeping pronouncements in favour of one to one meetings fostering community in combat against the isolation and alienation so common in suburbia. However small the gesture may be, its ability to offer commentary and critique to these broader issues does not diminish.

DOOR TO DOOR 5

Adam David Brown takes Dorothy's familiar five words in *The Wizard of Oz*, "There's no place like home," and has them printed singly on balloons that are given to patrons of the Living Arts Centre as they head home after a sold-out improv comedy performance. For Brown the piece is partly an

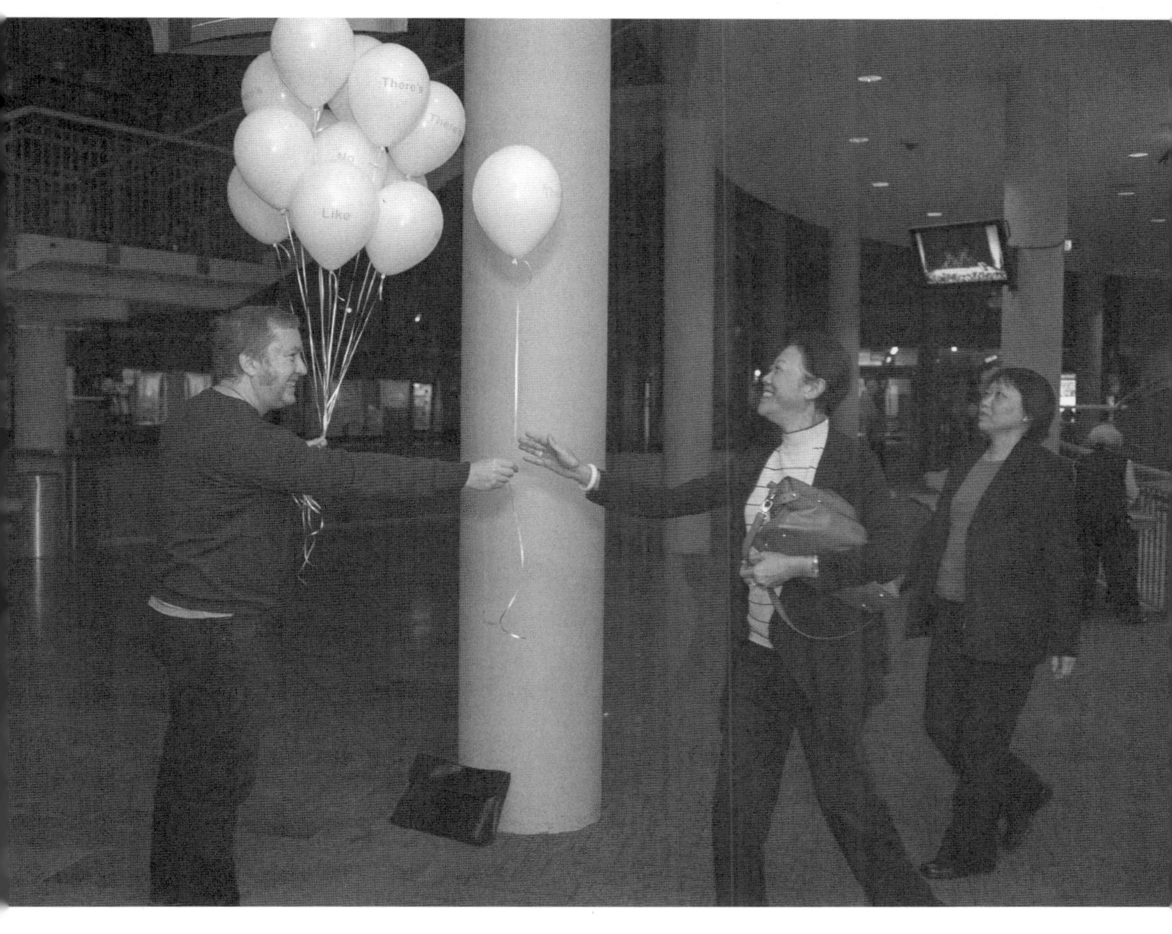

9.9 Adam David Brown, *There's No Place Like Home*, 2012.
Photo: Jenna Edwards.

autobiographical one: he was born in Mississauga but never lived there. His birthplace amounts to not much more than a name in his personal narrative. Statistically, his trajectory runs counter to the one for a large segment of the population of Mississauga, who live in the place they were not born in. Home is a fraught notion; it moves irrepressibly along lines of affect, hence it is mined by trite consumerism and mass marketing schemes. The parsed phrase There's/No/Place/Like/Home provides the opportunity to rejig the hackneyed saying depending on the bouquet of balloons one receives. If one receives less than the five that make the phrase, it is incomplete, aborted (admittedly, the arrangement and angles of view contribute as well to the possible variants). A lesser count might produce a simpler sentiment – There's/Home – or a nonsensical one – No/There's/Like – or a poetic one – Like/Home/No/Place. The attention paid to the phrase is warranted for it is ingrained with paradox; it is "a refusal that is an affirmation" (Blanchot 1995, 201). The semantic turns of phrase offer a multivalent approach to the tension between home and place. Reflecting on the events in Paris in May of 1968, Blanchot spoke of the profusion of posters, bulletins, and tracts that accompanied the event as "street words, infinite words" that "appear and disappear. They do not say everything, on the contrary they ruin everything, they are outside everything. They act and reflect fragmentarily. They leave no trace: they are a trait with no trace. [They] pass with the passer-by who passes them on, loses them or forgets them" (201). Brown's phrase performs a disappearing act – the words escape out of the Living Arts Centre, vulnerable to puncture or the inevitable deflation; sooner or later, they pass on.

Nancy Nowacek's project, like Brown's, attends to origins. But in her case, she is *Not From Here* – the project title forthrightly presents the roles of tourist, stranger, visitor, foreigner, outsider, newcomer, alien that she embodies in this work. The plethora of synonyms imparts the inflections each term conveys. The project is similarly layered despite the ostensibly straightforward quest the artist embarks on. Her trek began at Square One, the largest shopping mall in Ontario, adjacent to the Living Arts Centre, and her goal was to acquire all the goods listed as part of the original land purchase of Mississauga in 1788: cloth, blankets, laced hats, ribbon, brass kettles, mirrors, tobacco, fish hooks, ammunition, tools, gallons of rum (Stamp 1991). The reductive equation of land to property and the divergent mindsets implied between its ownership versus its stewardship

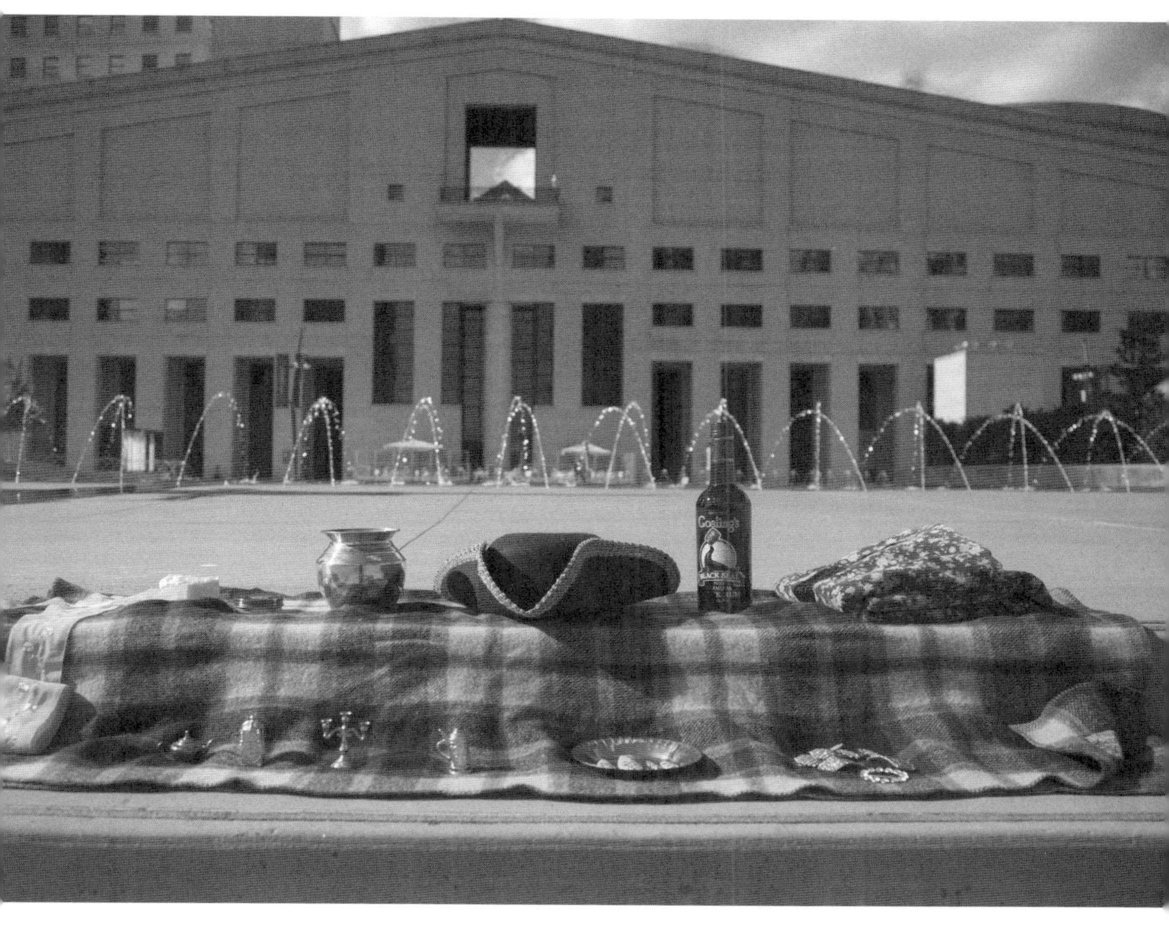

9.10 Nancy Nowacek, *Not From Here*, 2012. Photo: Jenna Edwards.

(or curatorship) persist as foundational issues we must face. Nowacek responds by walking. A walk with a purpose: the searching and gathering of the meagre substitutes for land mentioned above. One version of the transaction maintained that the area covered by the purchase could be determined by how "far back from the lake a man could walk, or go on foot in a day" (Stamp 1991). Over two days, Nowacek walked 18.7 miles (30 km). Mississauga's car-centered sprawl renders pedestrians to be anomalies; their scarce presence jars with the main mode of experiencing the Mississauga-scape. They slow it down; they serve as instant illustrations of the accelerated yet normalized motorized viewpoint. Nowacek is running errands: as a stranger in a strange land, she obtains destinations by asking those few she encounters for suggestions and directions. They direct her to the places that can furnish her the goods she needs; the research is not online but on the sidewalk. The piece culminates with Nowacek laying the objects down on the front steps of City Hall, which sits across the street from Square One, so it is a return of sorts. But in more ways than merely geographical, it is also a poignant reminder of ingrained conditions and a potent rejoinder on how these conditions lead to development running amok with tangible consequences on the everyday. Beleaguered by the lack of street life, as a postmortem, she drafted an open letter to Mississauga's city councillors and mayor advocating for a "pedestrian future for Mississauga" (Nowacek 2012). Her report card reads as a dire assessment of the present flâneur-phobic situation. To the city's credit, it should be noted that some recent efforts have somewhat abated the situation, especially through a progressive municipal public art program focused largely on the downtown Mississauga core (though parking lots still largely dominate the area). Also, it is worth noting that Port Credit and, the aptly named, Streetsville are areas of Mississauga which serve as notable exceptions to the car-cardinal rule.

DOOR TO DOOR 6

Sandy Plotnikoff meandered across Mississauga like Nowacek but with a more random approach. His *Clips Mix* was not quite aimless but focused on seizing opportunities based on finding surfaces on which to place, plant, position vinyl stickers. These are stickers of bread clips; the representations

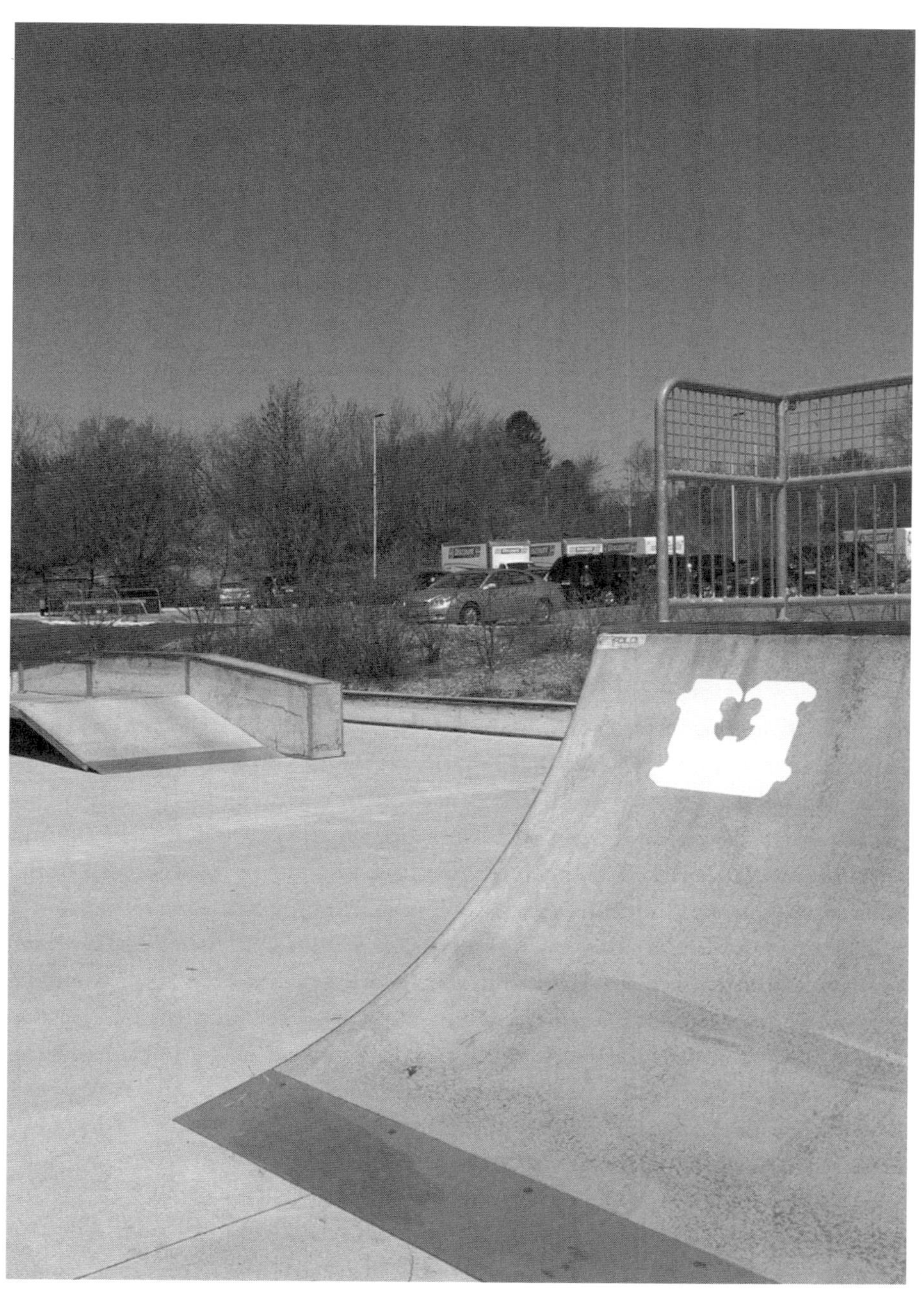

9 .11 Sandy Plotnikoff, *Clips Mix*, 2013. Photo: Sandy Plotnikoff.

range from those that are accurate and 1:1 to ones that are morphed, mirrored, doubled, distended, extended. Even when recognizable, their presence perplexes; why would a ubiquitous utilitarian oft-overlooked object be subject to such iconography and dispersal? One could cheekily reply that the answer is embedded in the question. After all, to pay attention to the heretofore ignored by shifting its context, morphing its form, or otherwise modifying it is a common tactic of the contemporary artist. *Clips Mix* is rooted in this methodology, but let's also consider some of its specificities. As a tool for preservation, it has a sly take on heritage, a heritage of the mundane and minute and, lest we forget, the manufactured; as detached attachment to a commodity, it is a product-less placement of itself; as repeated action onto locations which are themselves nondescript, it manifests what Debord and Wolman dubbed *ultradétournement* – a detourned action emphasizing subtlety and functioning in the everyday (quoted in Knabb 1995, 13); as refraction engine, its momentary mirage-like inducement of daily habits with daily staples; as mix, its improvisatory microurbanic plotting reflects Sanford Kwinter's concept of a new urbanism ("it does not plan, it does not precisely or inflexibly impose"; it is "a moving urbanism, a pastoral urbanism of inflection," quoted in Brown 2006, 134); as unsanctioned operation, it makes a meek yet effective inscription onto the "space already occupied by the enemy" (Kotányi and Vaneigem quoted in Knabb 1995, 67). Informing each entry of this nonexhaustive list is the unreadibility of each clip, in the sense outlined by Henri Lefebvre (1991, 143), making a distinction between produced space and read space. The clips *produce* an ambiguous void, a blank surface with a surfeit of possible reads emerging from their flattened plane but in stark opposition to a space of "transparency and readibility that is designed to conceal" the machinations and biases of centralized power (147). Their appearance marks an *opening outwards* (147), and their morphology evinces a reference that functions as trace, but they otherwise resist ready signification.

Signage could not be more unequivocal than three identical neon signs with the uppercase word GALLERY emblazoned on them. Nathalie Quagliotto's *Gallery Intervention* stages the word's bluntness, its status quo, its constancy – appropriately it stays constantly lit. With this piece we return to safe ground; after all, the sociocultural function is embedded in the piece itself; it announces its context; it might even bring along its

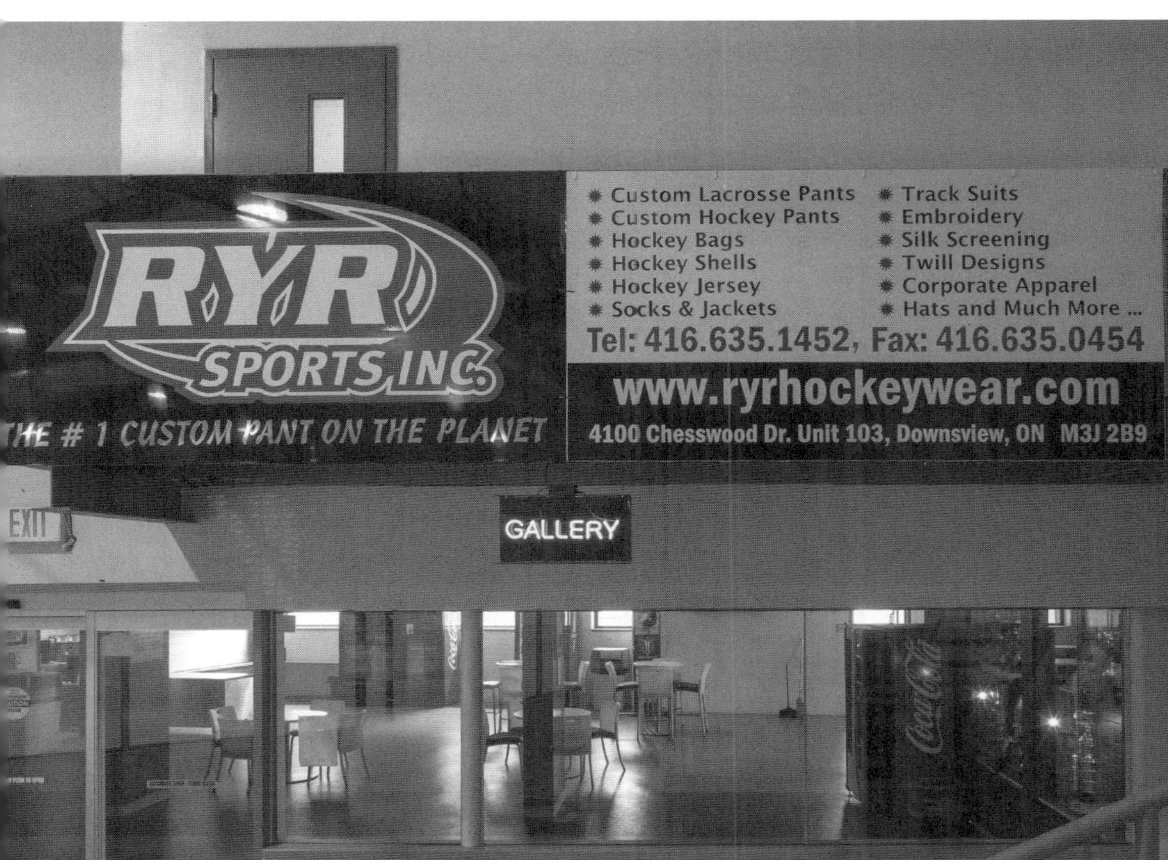

9.12 Nathalie Quagliotto, *Gallery Intervention*, 2013. Photo: Toni Hafkenscheid.

readymade white cube. Of course none of this quite fits. All signs point to deception. The setting of a hockey arena is where the disjunction occurs, not once but thrice. With each sign there is an amplification of the gesture. Additionally, their relative proximity to each other results in viewpoints where the redundancy is contained within one frame. The signs are modest in size and ordinary in their font type; however, in color they are not neutral, since they don the artist's signature yellow, resulting in a senescent look, as if waning. There is a quaintness in their overall appearance. They announce, but they do not deliver. They are stranded signifiers stuck demonstrating language's iterability – a basic tenet of language on display in public space, enabling scrutiny of the naming and signing conventions in their vicinity. But again, deception is the modus operandi; indeed, at the same time as they are framed they act as framers. They operate as conceptual converter machines – whatever surrounds them becomes artspace. For the week they were installed, the hockey arena in the community centre (Streetsville Arena/Vic Johnston Community Centre) doubled as an art gallery. At any other time, whenever they are plugged in, another place converts or, rather, acquires an additional capacity – a pop-up anywhere anytime gallery.

The artist attributes a proselytizing role to them or at least an awareness quotient wherein "the public who possibly have little experience with art would be pushed to think about what an artwork, an exhibition, and a gallery could be" (Quagliotto 2013). The sentiment is both laudable and laughable (as in playful, unassuming, open). We thereby return to the question posed in several previous instances, the one regarding effectiveness. In Quagliotto's case the query is ontological: what *could they be*, these markers of art? Posing such a question in a hockey arena is pertinent to *Door to Door*; it is precisely the sort of a speculative inquiry that needs to be undertaken. This is not to decry the merit of the white cube to house such investigations or to dismiss its ability to foster these debates. But expansion, however opaque or oblique, of the mode of address and its emplacement is critical. That being said, upon reflection, my qualifier just now regarding opacity should be amended: these types of moves *must* be furtive in order to remain nimble. To overtly obstruct, to usurp, to impose can often cause conflict and controversy which may also evacuate the power of play and paradox that artwork such as *Gallery Intervention* proposes and therefore may hinder its lasting impact.

Door to Door heeded part of Brian O'Doherty's call in the very last sentence of his "The Gallery as a Gesture" essay, which reads, "Or the gallery itself could be removed and relocated to another place" (1999, 107). Here the gesture goes further: it is no longer just off-site but both pluri- and para-site. Or, it could be said that it invokes the gallery site every time the artist shows up at the door and knocks or rings the bell. It is a curatorial premise that is simultaneously curious and quaint, even neighbourly. *Door to Door* was an exhibition home delivery service, a cumulation of instant sites, an exhibit of moments. The gallery was dislocated through a spatial and temporal splintering process. It was here *and* there, *and* there, *and* also there, *and* … Mapping projects by artists abound. As well, the street is often sought as a venue because it is perceived as a context where the public is at its most random and least contrived. *Door to Door* belongs to both of these lineages but investigated the threshold where public space meets private domicile. The audience was no longer the passerby but the resident, the occupant, the one who answers the door. The audience was both narrow and wide, individualized and massive, invisible and incalculable. In fact, when submitting the grant report for this project to the Ontario Arts Council, I entered "incalculable" in the place on the form that asked for the audience number. The grant officer emailed back saying that it was all well and good but an actual number was needed in order to satisfy the demands of her superiors. So I submitted the circulation number listed by the Mississauga News: 440,000 (this implies an audience size that in normal circumstances our small gallery on a suburban campus would take years to reach). The revision was accepted without further need for clarification.

Door to Door: an exhibition that knocks on your door and delivers itself. The question is, will you sign for it?

Notes

1 The *Door to Door* series was made possible thanks to funding by the Canada Council for the Arts and the Ontario Arts Council as well as numerous local partners. The series could not have happened without the participating artists and without the help of the staff at the Blackwood Gallery.

2 Adorno (1974), 40 (entry 19). The entry is titled "Do not knock" and proceeds as follows (emphasis added):

Do not knock. – Technology is making gestures precise and
brutal, and with them men. It expels from movements all
hesitation, deliberation, civility. It subjects them to the
implacable, as it were, ahistorical demands of objects. [...] *Not
least to blame for the withering of experience is the fact that things,
under the law of pure functionality, assume a form that limits
contact with them to mere operation, and tolerates no surplus,
either in freedom of conduct or in autonomy of things, which would
survive as the core of experience, because it is not consumed by the
moment of action.*

3 On the latter point, other such jinxes are tracked in the most entertaining
book by John Tingey (2010).

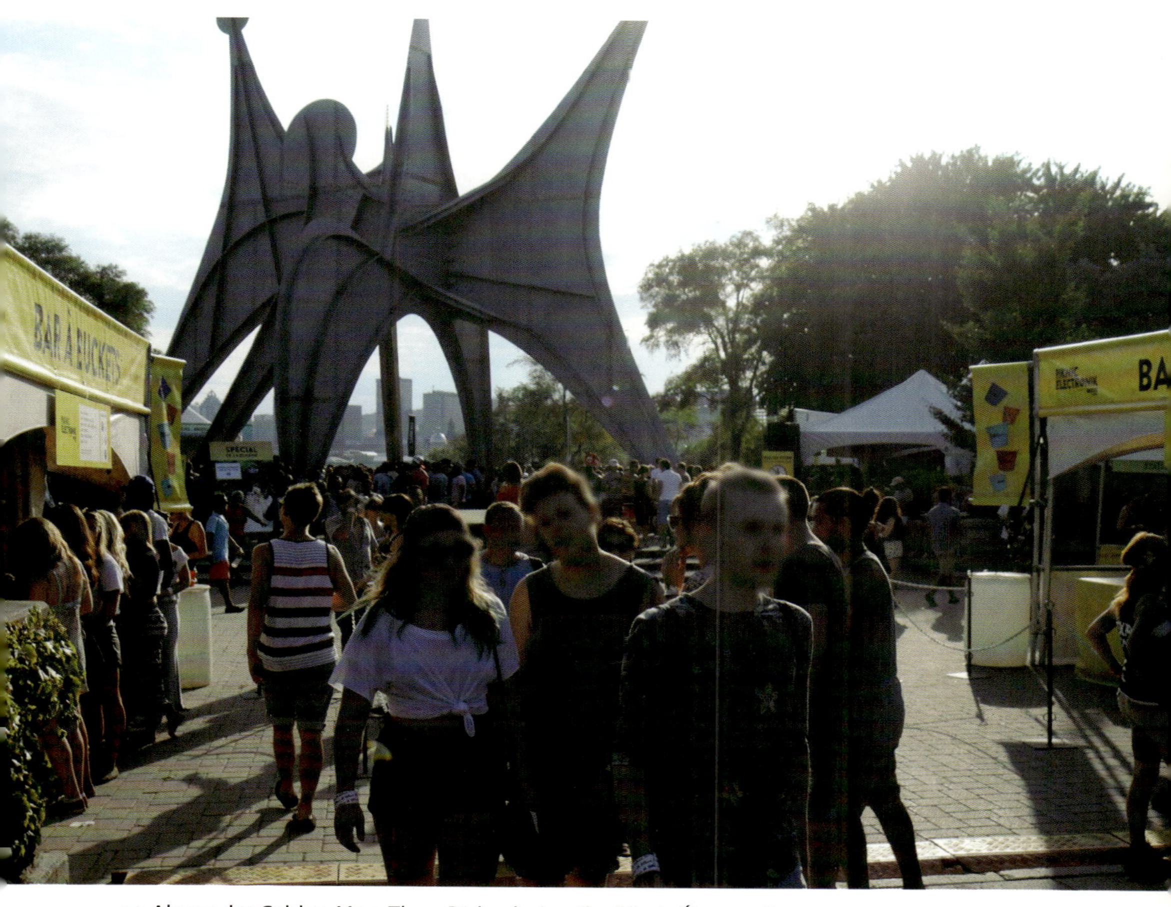

1.2 Alexander Calder, *Man, Three Disks*, during the Piknic Électronik

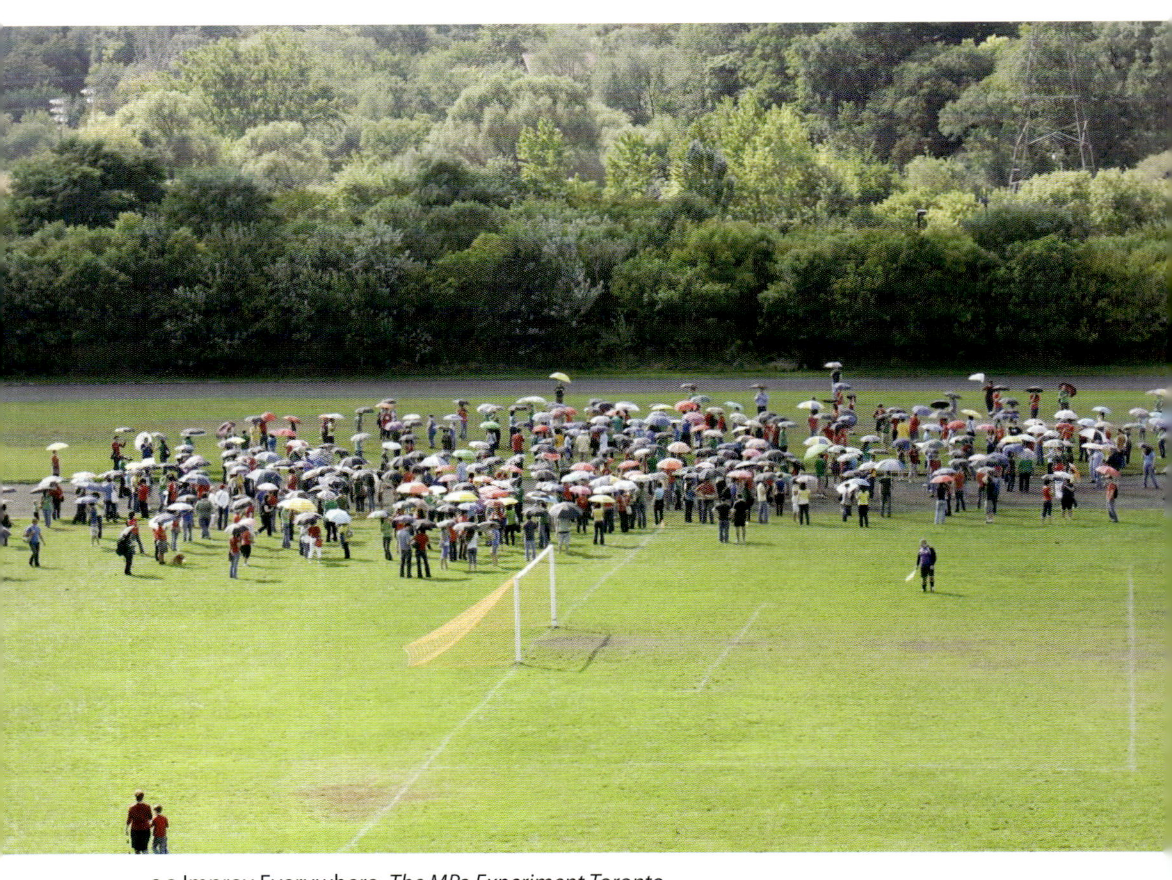

2.3 Improv Everywhere, *The MP3 Experiment Toronto*

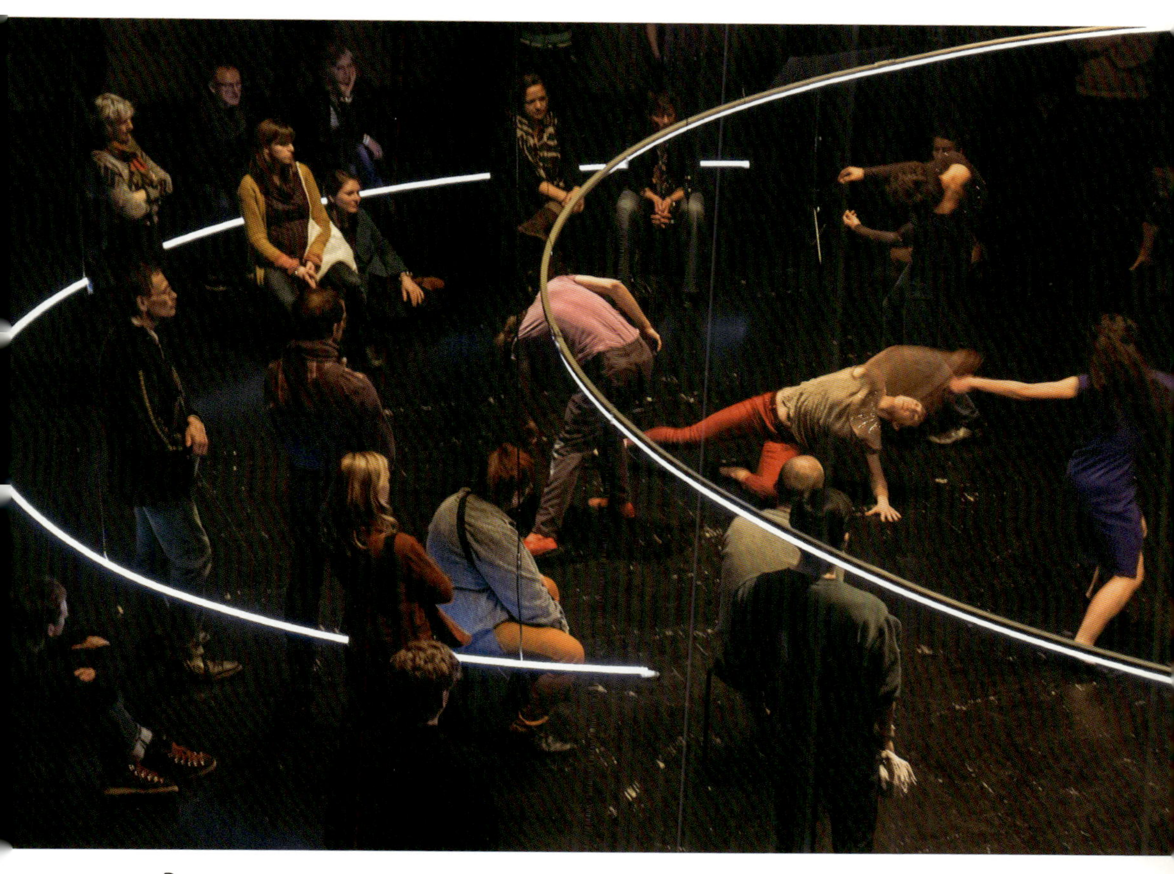

3.1 *Danserye*

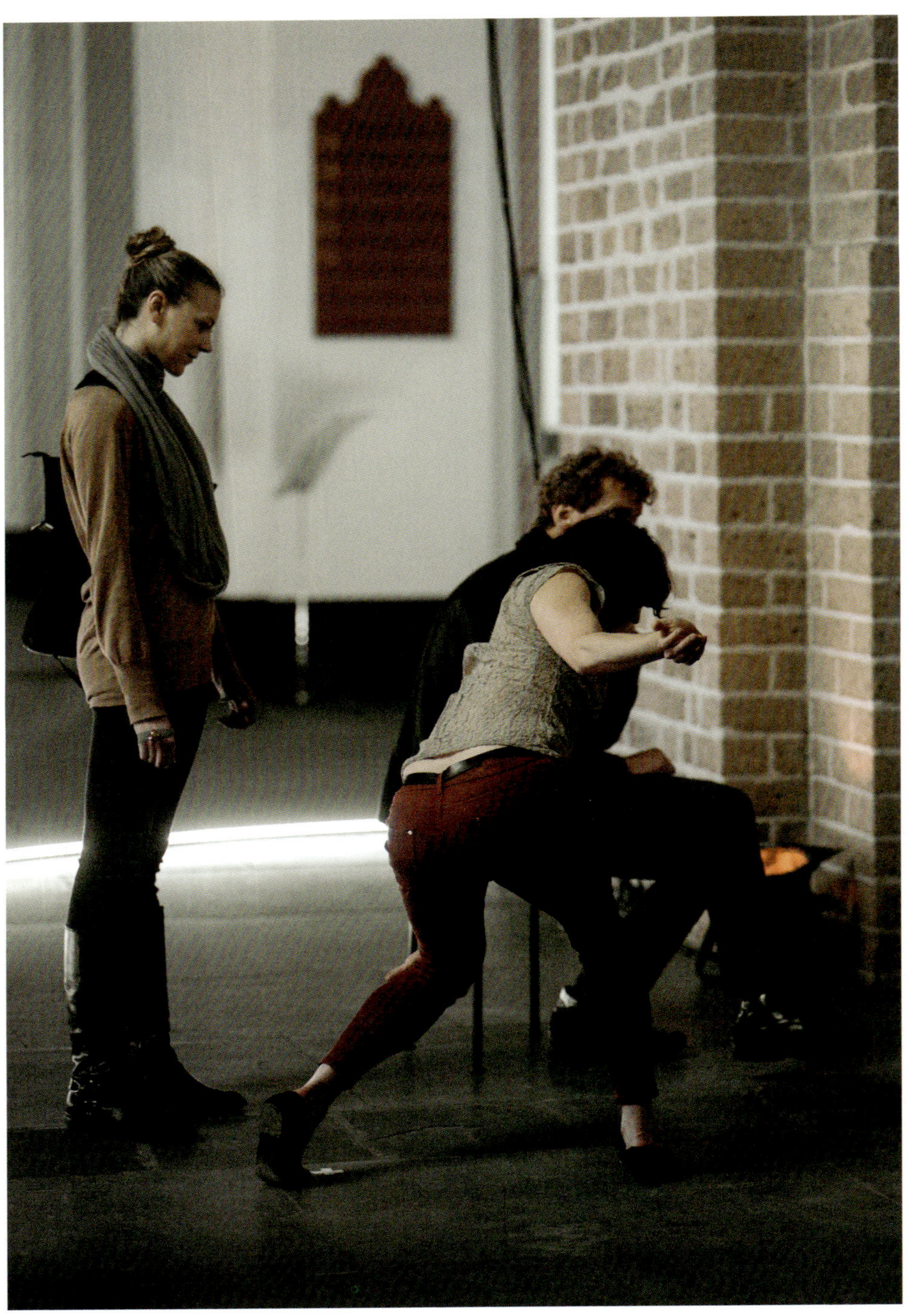

3.3 *Danserye*

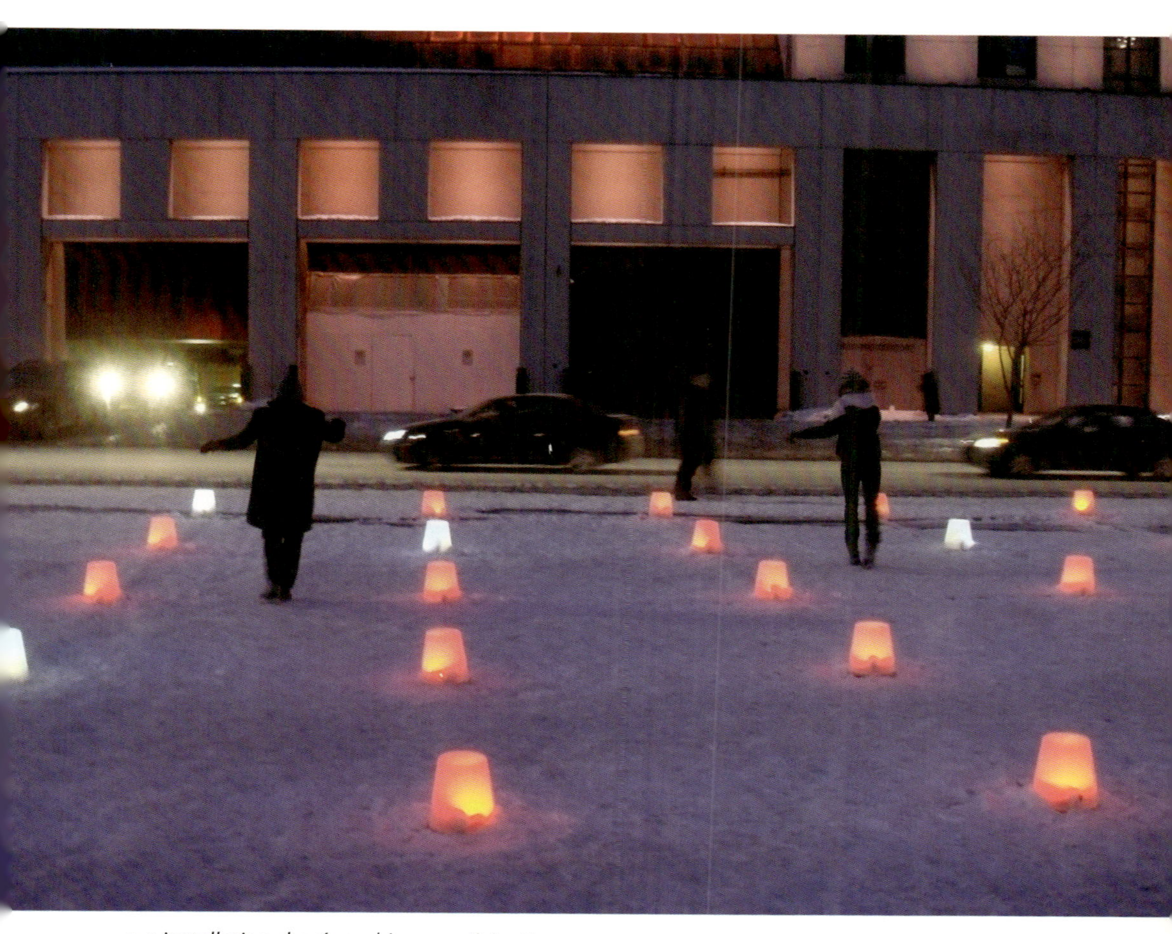

3.4 *installation chorégraphique participative*

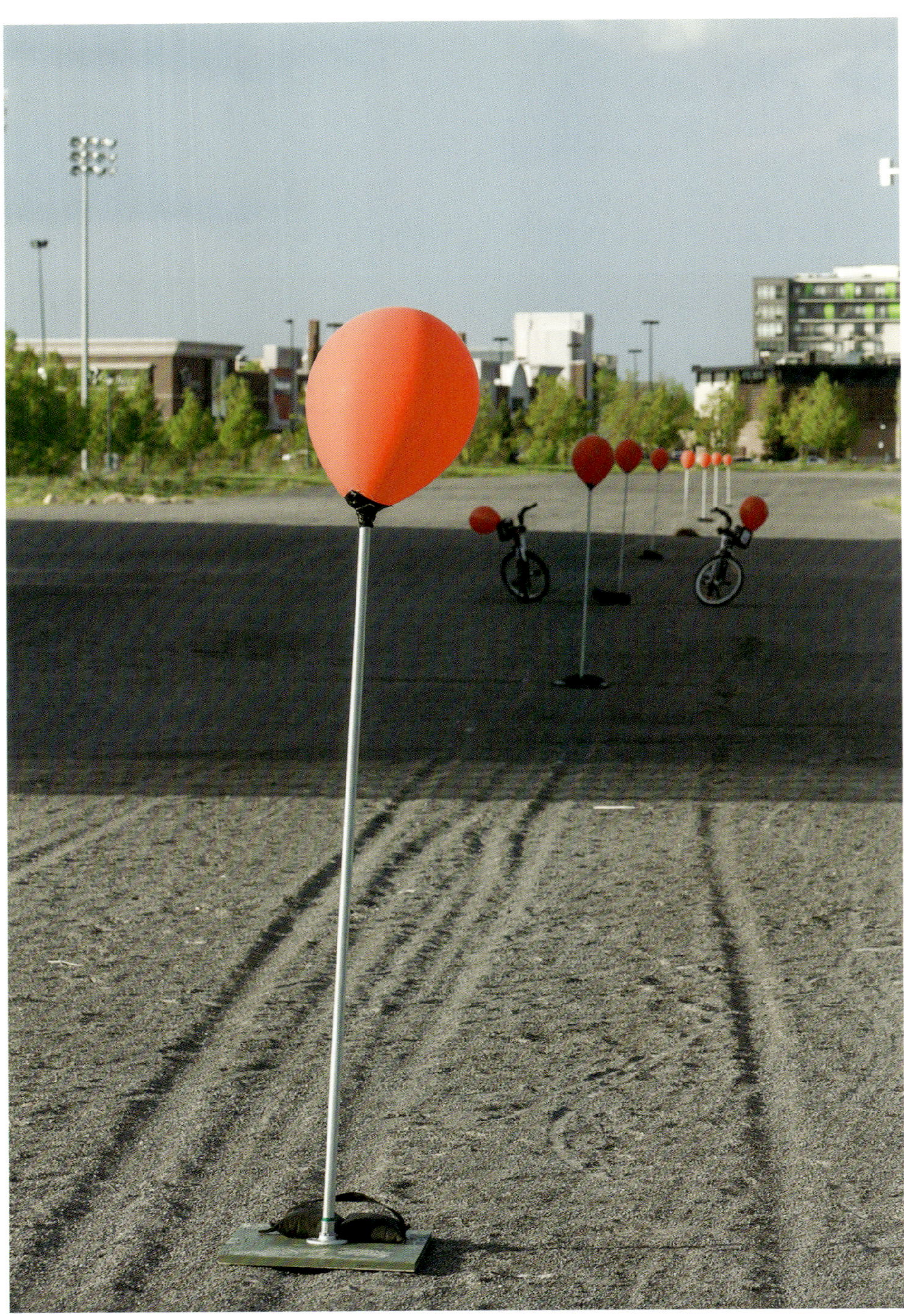

4.5 (detail), pin drop at the Hippodrome, NiS+TS

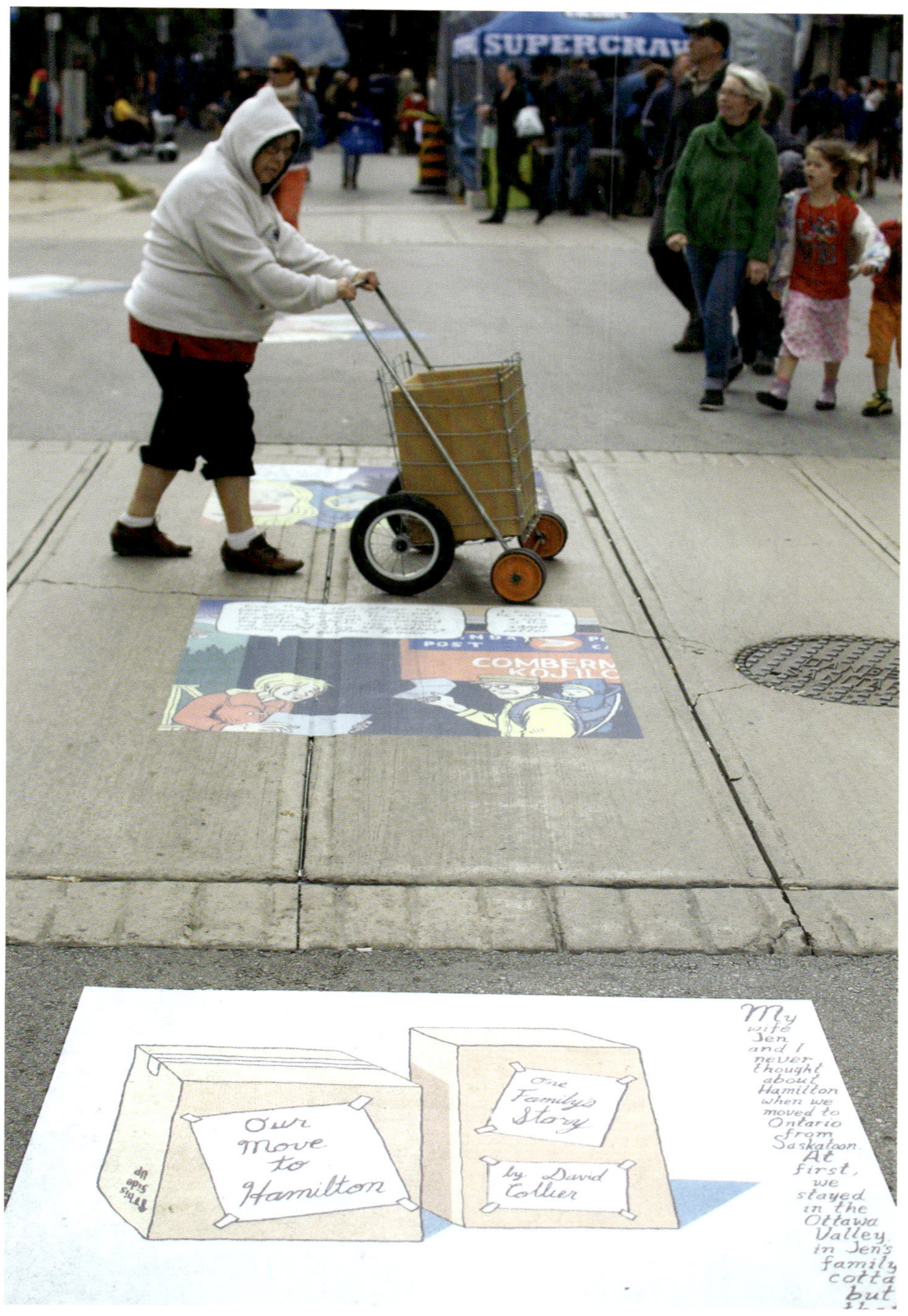

5.1 David Collier, *Our Move to Hamilton: One Family's Story*

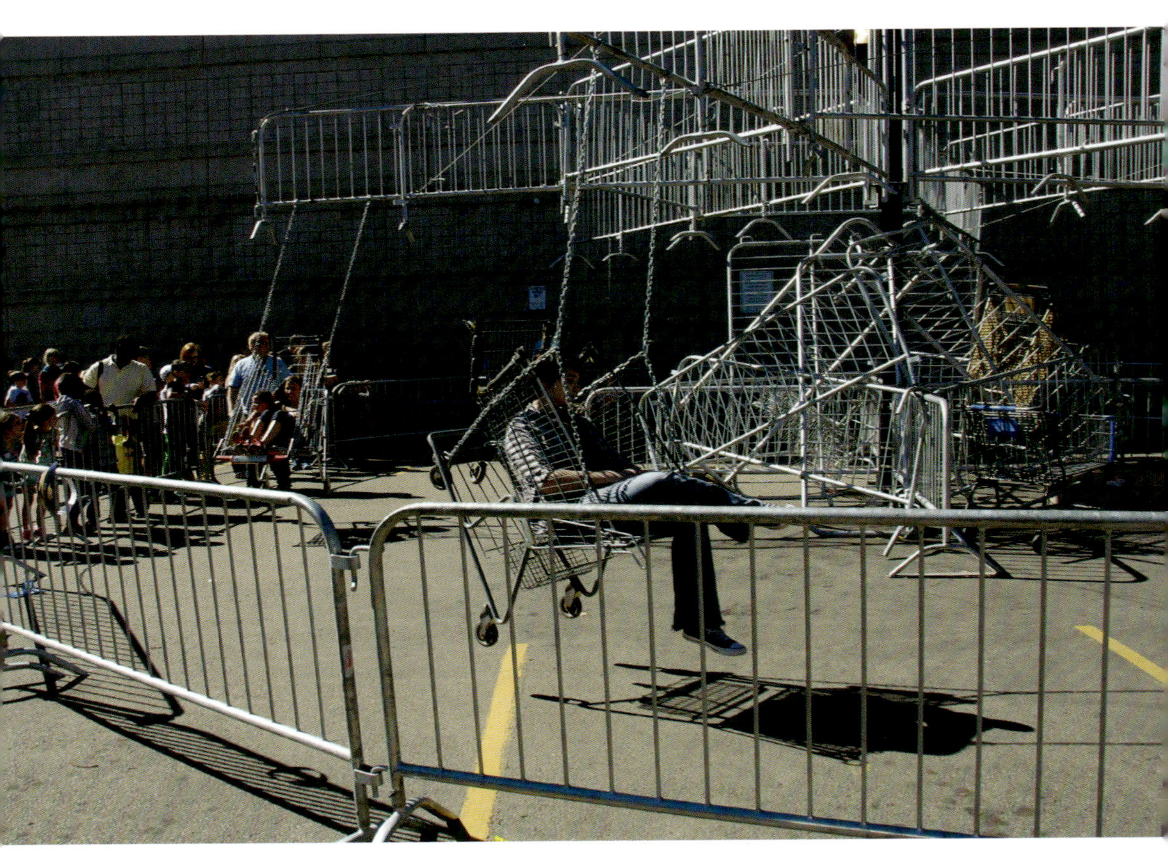

5.2 BGL, *Carrousel*

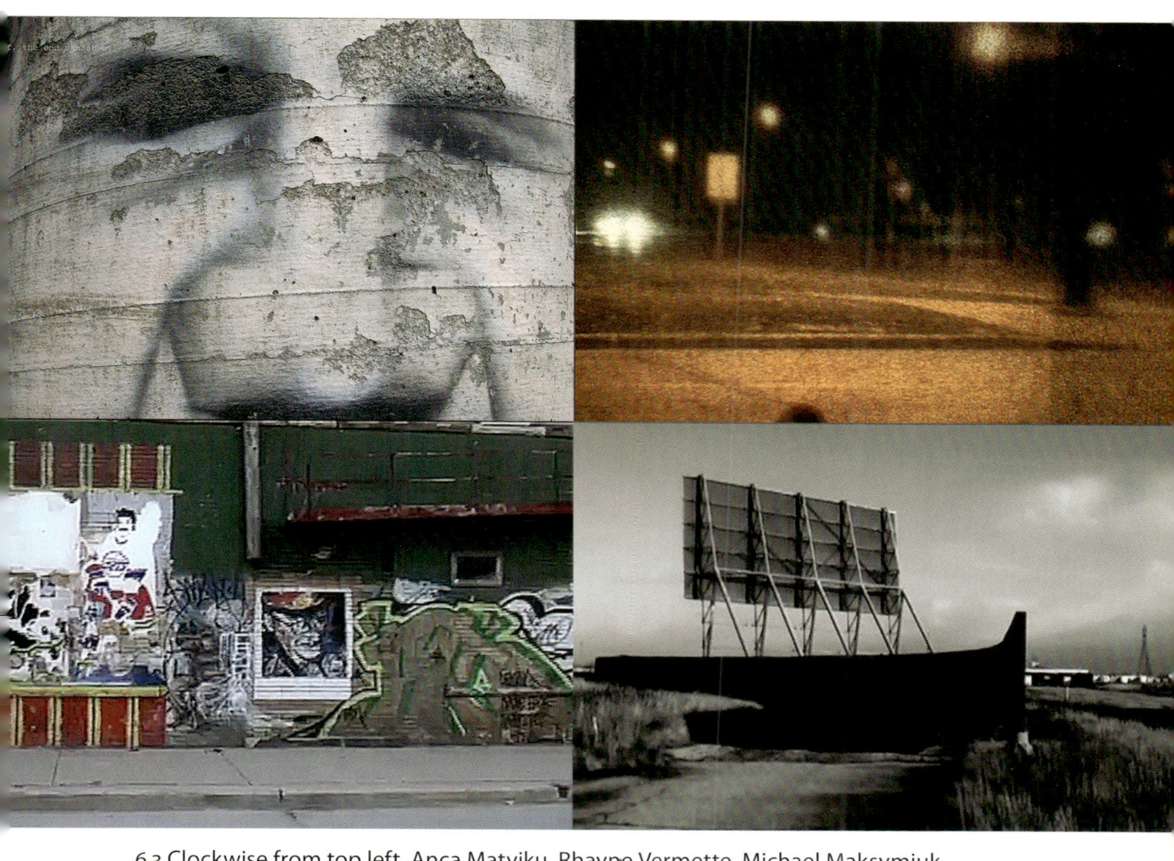

6.3 Clockwise from top left, Anca Matyiku, Rhayne Vermette, Michael Maksymiuk, Zhi Yong Wang, *Brief Encounters*

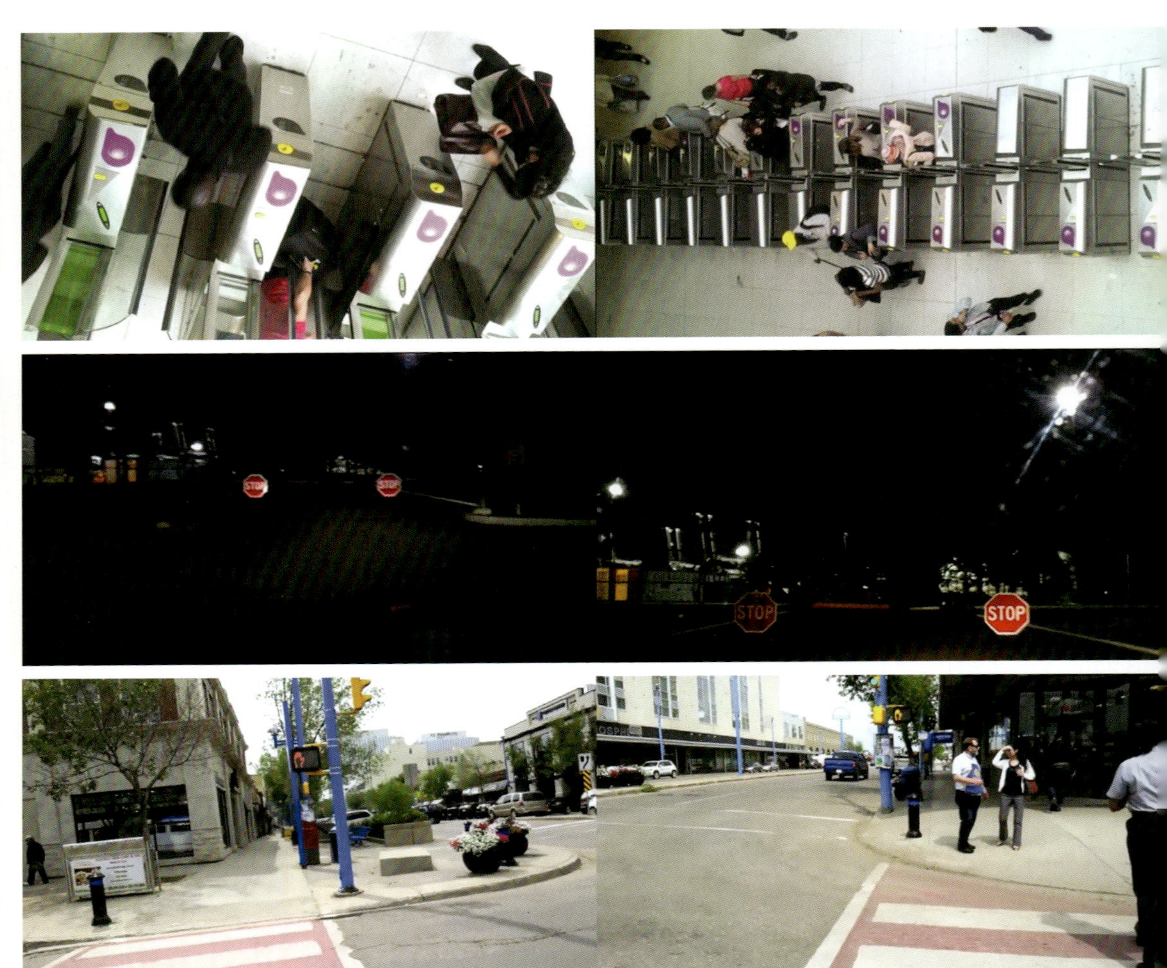

7.1, 7.2, and 7.5 Ellen Moffat and Kim Morgan, *in pulse*, *Cruising*, and *Tracings*

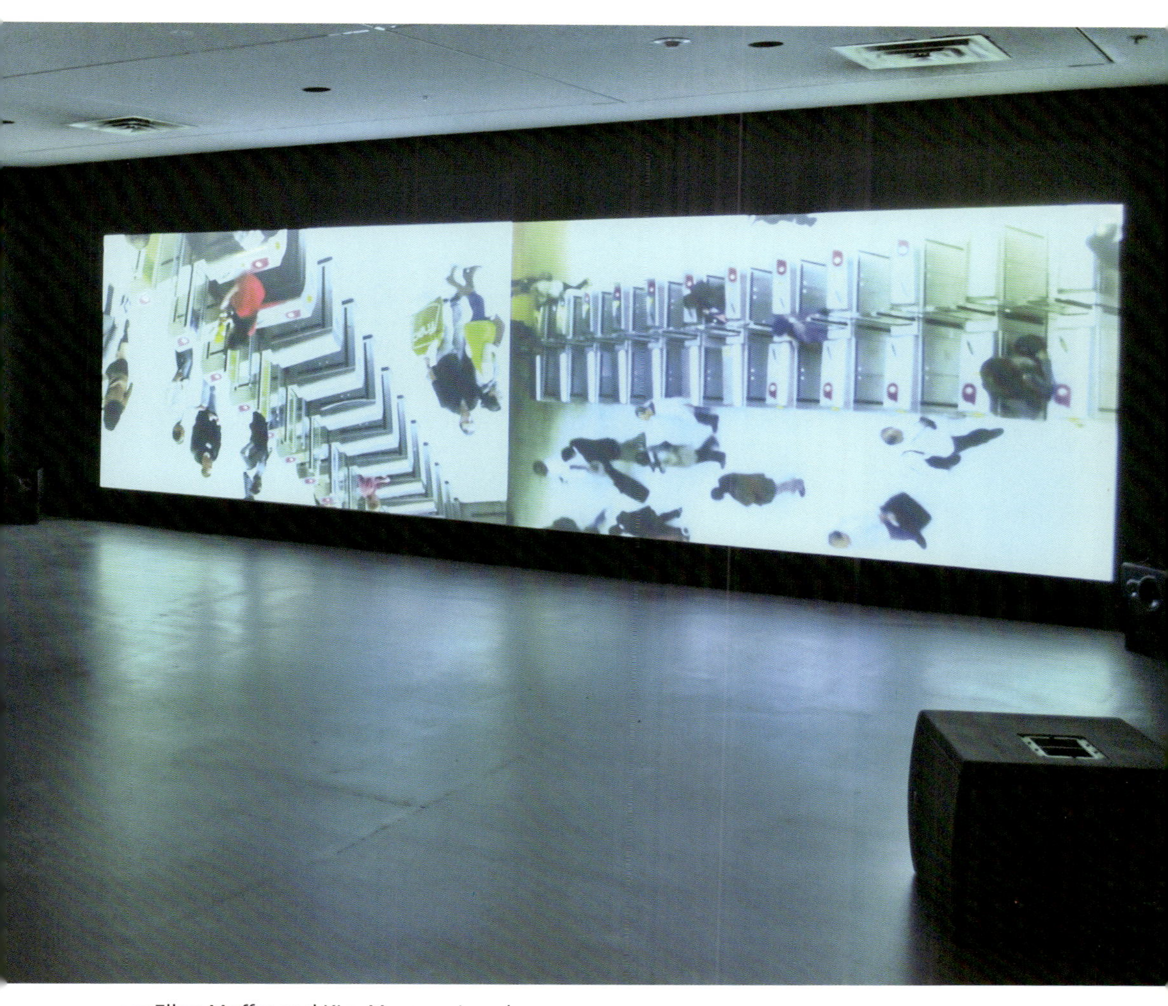

7.7 Ellen Moffat and Kim Morgan, *in pulse*

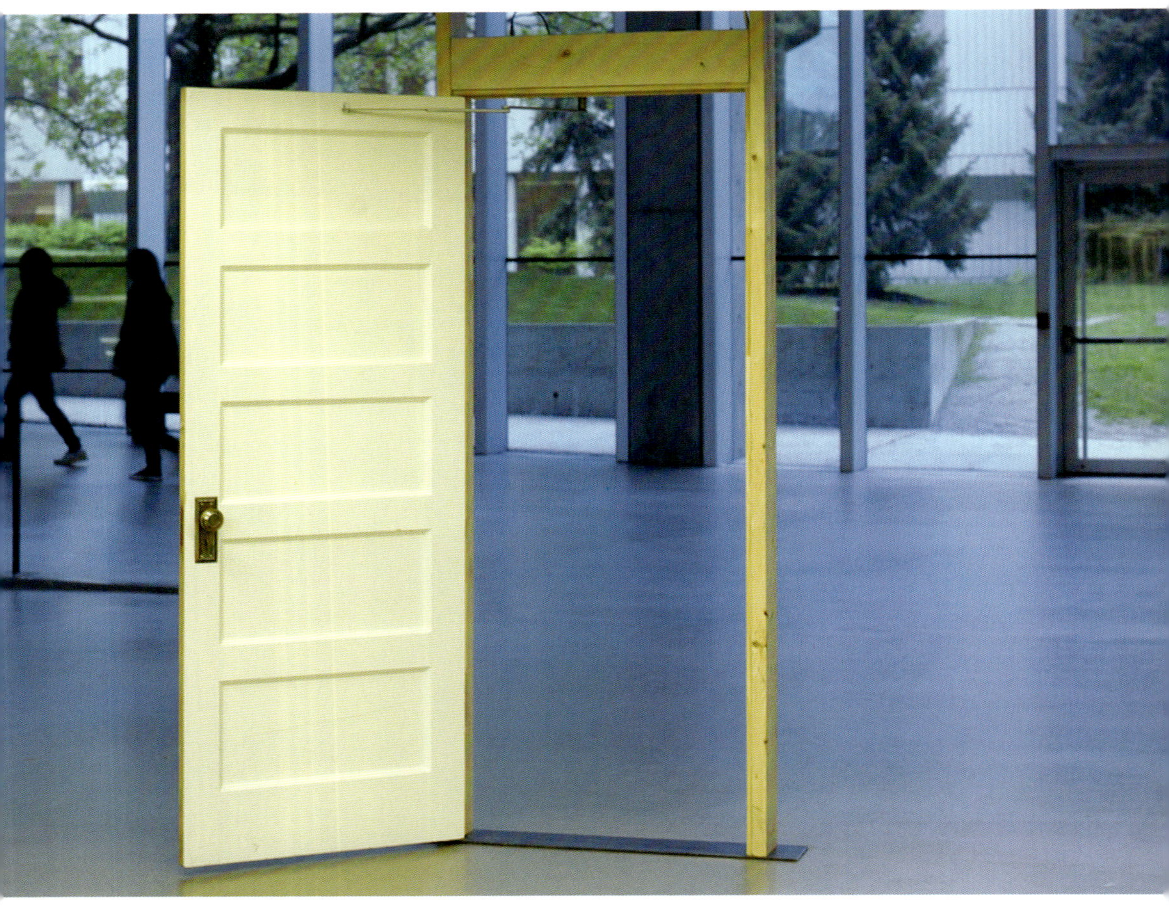

9.1 Gordon Hicks and Germaine Koh, *There|Here*

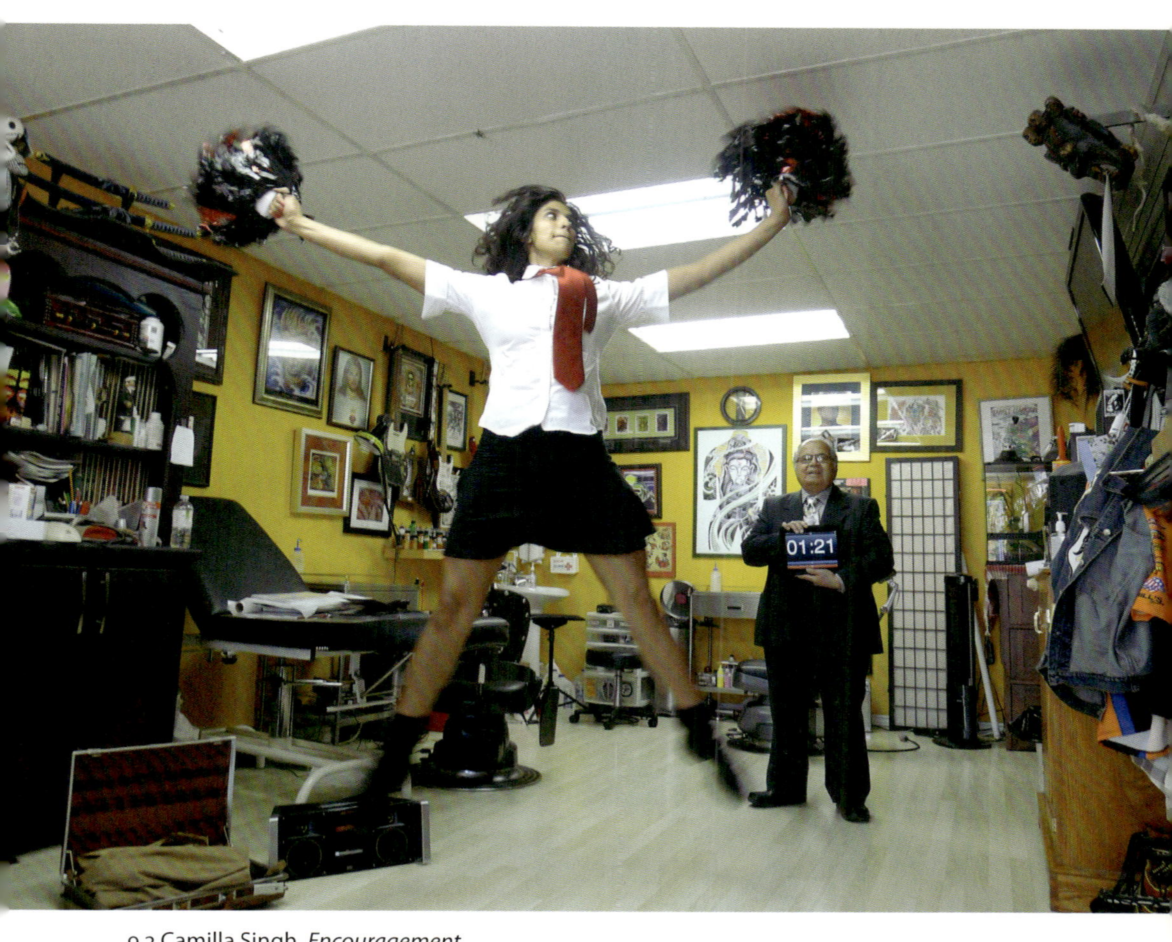

9.2 Camilla Singh, *Encouragement*

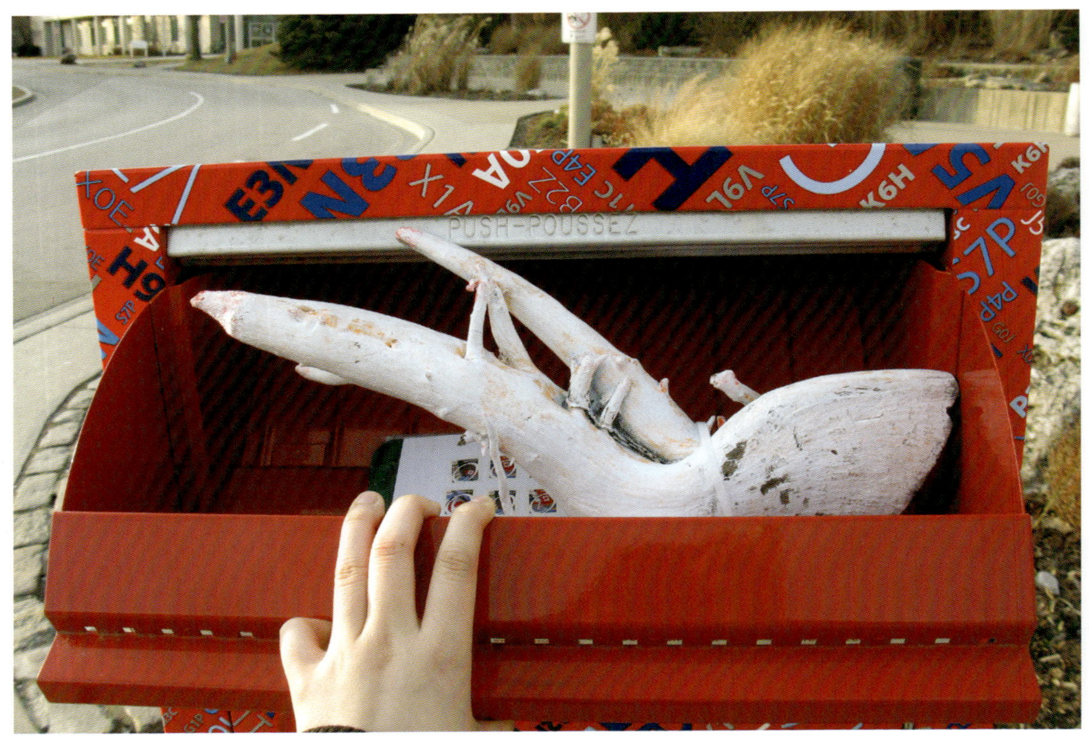

9.5 John Marriott, *Experience Attractor*

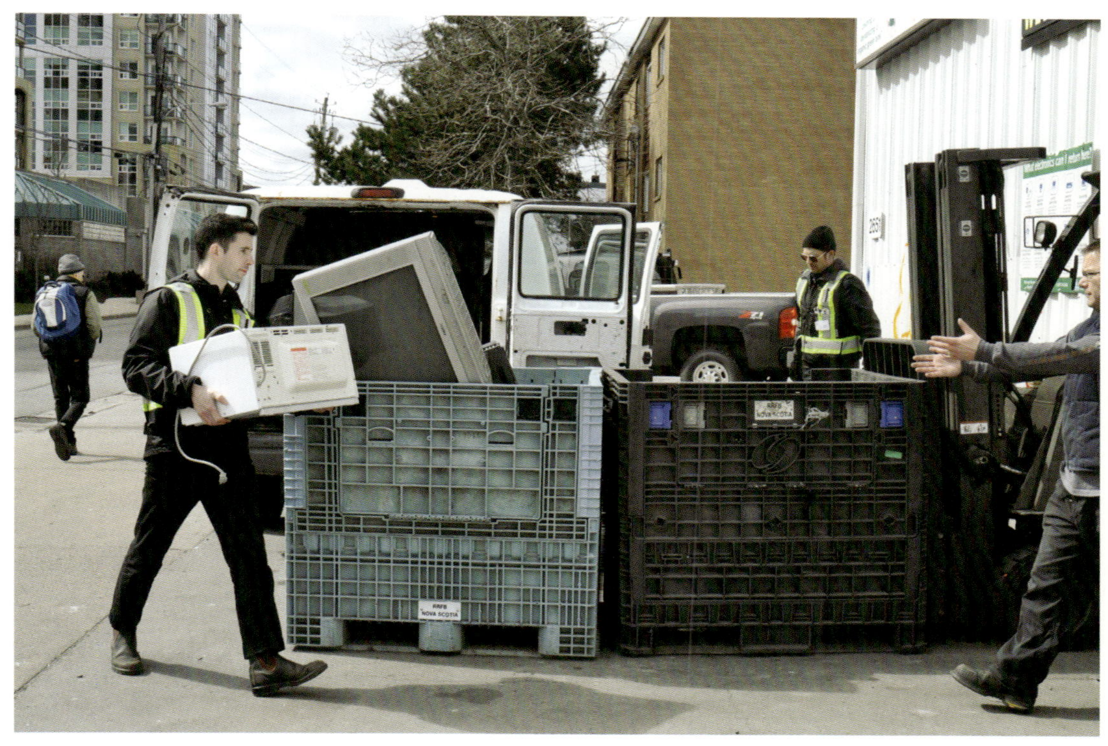

10.2 Artifact Institute

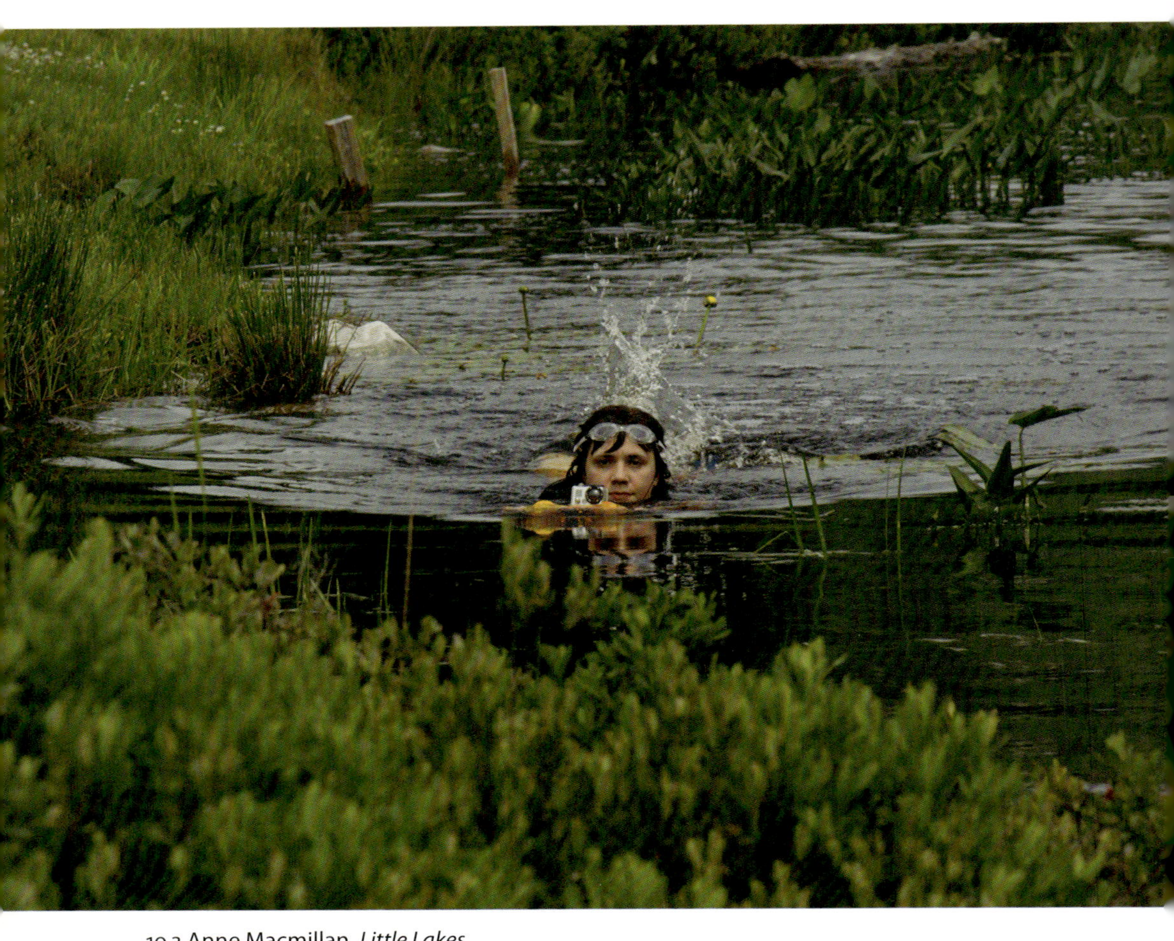

10.3 Anne Macmillan, *Little Lakes*

Wes Johnston

10

—

TECHNOLOGICAL REGIONALISMS: THE FIELDWORK RESIDENCY PROJECT

The Fieldwork Residency Project (FRP) was conceived as a platform for artist projects that adopt or appropriate research methodologies that are generally associated with the natural or social sciences. The framework supported artists in their research while minimizing the pressure of producing work for an exhibition, with a de-emphasis on the aesthetic spectacle of the artists engaged in (performing) their fieldwork. Rather, the residency provided space for artists to engage in depth with their chosen subjects and, especially, to consider the communicative strategies around their work. The first iteration in 2013 began with three projects conducted within the regional municipal boundaries of Halifax, Nova Scotia: Artifact Institute's *Investigation 2: Electronic Equipment Not Accepted for Curbside Garbage Collection by the Halifax Regional Municipality*, a study of a municipality's means of disposing of electronic waste – a forensic audit of sorts of consumer technology; Kelly Jaclynn Andres's *Propopropopo*, a site analysis of a community garden in the city centre and the needs and wants of its users; and finally Anne Macmillan's *Little Lakes*, a survey of a series of lakes within the municipal boundaries, which traced their edges by swimming the perimeter and tracking the routes with GPS.

The program provided its residents with project equipment, be it transportation, tools, workspace, or other resources necessary to perform their work. The activity of each project included research and reconnaissance in the field, most of which took place on public land but occasionally encroached on private property. Data and materials gleaned from these excursions were then processed by the artists both during and following the residency. Within the duration of each of the projects, a program of events such as workshops, outings, roundtables, and presentations made general information about the projects available to the public.

My role in the project as director/coordinator was to liaise with the artists in terms of the residency, its parameters and mandate and to assist them with any technical needs including project equipment. I also managed the public relations for the residency with assistance from the Dalhousie Art Gallery. As curator of the project, I was interested in providing artists with a framework for presenting research and experimentation in progress in completely self-directed projects.

Two organizations that were highly influential in establishing this framework were the Center for Land Use Interpretation (CLUI) in Culver City, Los Angeles, California, and Dare-Dare in Montreal, Quebec. Both centres support primary research from the sociospatial perspective as well as inventive forms of presentation and dissemination of this research. CLUI does not self-identify as an arts organization but nevertheless operates a residency program in Wendover, Utah, that is open to artists and nonartists alike and frequently collaborates with artists and arts scholars. For instance, it has an ongoing relationship with the Land Arts of the American West program at the University of New Mexico. CLUI produces guided tours and exhibits (as opposed to artist exhibitions), and with its mandate "[dedicated to] the increase and diffusion of knowledge about how the nation's lands are apportioned, utilized and perceived" (2015), much of its research and programming culminates in newsletters, publications, and searchable databases.

Making the case for CLUI's relevance to the art world, Michael Ned Holte (2006) attributes CLUI as pertaining to "small 'c' conceptual art" (as opposed to big "C" conceptual art that is primarily textual – Sol Lewitt, Lawrence Wiener, Robert Barry among others) but also connects it to projects by American land artists of the southwest, especially Robert Smithson. He writes, "the Center in a sense has recognized and adopted Smithson's dual persona of siteseer/tour guide. Adapted, this persona is no longer folded into the notion of the 'artist', but rather finds anonymity in the non-hierarchical structure of the 'organisation', the 'agency': the Center. Like Smithson, who once expressed his interest in the 'politics of the Triassic Period', the Center has a political outlook that is seemingly one of wilful neutrality" (Holte 2006). In so many words, Holte manages to peg Smithson's approach of artist-cum-researcher/ethnographer/ anthropologist as adapted to CLUI's organization. But Smithson's work is situated squarely in the art establishment, and Holte goes on to say that while celebrated by the large art institutions, CLUI is careful not to allow its activities to be construed as performance.

In contrast, Dare-Dare is primarily dedicated to artist projects as performative interventions in the urban landscape with an emphasis on direct public engagement. While it is classified as an artist-run centre (ARC), its unique position in Canada is exemplified by its long-term program *Dis/location, projet d'articulation urbaine,* initiated by Jean-Pierre Caissie in 2002, when Dare-Dare moved from a gallery space to a mobile site/ office trailer and, through negotiations with the municipality, was given permission to occupy public lands for variable durations of two to three years. However, since its inception in 1985 it had already been dissociated from the "white cube" type gallery and had always had an interdisciplinary mandate. Through successive administrators, its opportunistic attitude toward real estate and impermanence has landed it in a variety of rental spaces.[1] Dare-Dare programs work around the various communities that intersect its office's location – open calls were publicized for artists to intervene in the landscape and explore performative and experimental modes of presentation, with a strong emphasis on interaction, intervention, and impermanence. According to their mission, the artist-run centre "is a flexible, open space devoted to research, experimentation, risk and critical inquiry. The artist-run centre manifests a sustained interest in exploration and in the diversity in the modes of presentation" (Dare-Dare 2015). Embracing a certain volatility – the expression *dare-dare* more or less translates to "posthaste" or possibly the English expression, rooted in Cantonese, "chop-chop" – and catering to emerging artist's practices, the artist-run centre has on occasion found itself being reprimanded by the municipality from which it receives both financial and in-kind support. For the itinerant programming of *Dis/location,* the centre has been set up in sites that have been regarded as problematic from the perspective of municipal governance – sites known for drug dealing, prostitution, violence, or vandalism (Caissie 2008). What is interesting in Dare-Dare's model is their occupation of a liminal space, not only geographically but conceptually, in that they grant agency to artists to claim public space as a site for improvisation, performance, and nonnormative behaviour. This may not be unique among artist-run centres, but it is notable that the organization's mandate includes the word "risk," while the primary sources of funding – three levels of government, though their various art granting agencies – are bureaucracies whose functions ostensibly include the elimination of risk, especially concerning liability in public space. Dare-Dare is unique in that it inserts its programming exactly in the interstices, the ambiguous space between public and private, and the ambiguous territory around the laws that govern public space.

On the one hand, Center for Land Use Interpretation's apparent "neutrality" or self-characterization as collector/cataloguer of landscape phenomena invokes the figure of the ethnographer/anthropologist/ geologist. On the other hand, Dare-Dare's model invokes the artist as *agent provocateur* to incite, perform, and possibly collide with the environment and its inhabitants. The Fieldwork Residency Project attempted to create a platform for these two modalities to overlap, to consider the "fieldworkers'" capacity to become entangled in a dialogical relationship with their objects of study. It also aimed to open up a liminal space between professions in which participants, whether self-identifying as artists or not, would be at liberty to perform research, surveys, data collection, or process-based work without the pressure of conforming to scientific standards and without relegating the work only to aesthetic criteria of evaluation.

URBAN OR RURAL? THE FIELDWORK RESIDENCY PROJECT IN THE CONTEXT OF HALIFAX REGIONAL MUNICIPALITY

The FRP received municipal and provincial arts funding – the former through the Halifax Regional Municipality (HRM) Open Projects grant and the latter through Arts Nova Scotia – which was supplemented by in-kind contributions from Dalhousie Art Gallery, as affiliated programming. One of the conditions of the HRM Open Projects funding was that the FRP be administered and presented within the municipality's boundary. This pre- sented an interesting constraint for the project. As a regional municipality,

Halifax spans 5,490 km^2 but only 262 km^2 of this is considered properly urban, the difference in density being seventy-one people per km^2 overall versus 1,077 in the urban centre. Halifax exemplifies the trend towards amalgamation into sprawling, centralized municipalities and the dissolution of smaller nodes of municipal governance. Henri Lefebvre ponders this phenomenon as an immanent condition of Western industrialized societies: "Will the urban fabric, with its greater or lesser meshes, catch in its nets all the territory of industrialized countries?" (Lefevbre 1996, 120). In 1996, HRM emerged from the amalgamation of the City of Halifax, City of Dartmouth, Town of Bedford, and County of Halifax. As such, HRM finds itself presiding not only over urban and suburban developments but completely rural areas which encompass game sanctuaries, provincial parks, military bases, fishing villages, and so on. Arguably one of the largest attractions of the region, even for urbanites, is the proximity to water – Haligonians enjoy quick access to vast distances of publicly accessible shoreline as well as hundreds of lakes. Like this "city," the three projects covered the gamut of spaces from urban to rural. Andres's project *Propopropopo* was sited at the Common Roots Urban Farm, an urban portal to rural agrarian practice. Artifact Institute's roving project covered approximately 1,389 km of urban and suburban streets ranging in a 4 km radius from the city centre to Cole Harbour, Bedford, and Beechville/Timberlea. Anne Macmillan's project explored the most remote and rural areas of HRM, further than 100 km from Halifax's urban core in at least one instance, requiring her to leave the county and reenter it by another access road to reach the targeted lake.

For the purposes of this essay, I will discuss Anne Macmillan's project, *Little Lakes* and Artifact Institute's project, *Investigation 2: Electronic Equipment Not Accepted for Curbside Garbage Collection by the Halifax Regional Municipality,* as these two best articulate the terrain sought out by the FRP, namely the context for artists conducting fieldwork outside of a rigorous scientific framework and beyond their perception by various publics in the field as either artists or researchers. Furthermore, they provided examples of navigating urban, suburban and rural space with a particular orientation towards technology: in one case the retrieval of consumer technological "waste," and in another the exploration of the inherent limitations of GPS technology as a means of representing spatial experience.

Artifact Institute was formed in 2007 by Tim Dallett and Adam Kelly to "study and intervene in the processes by which artifacts undergo changes in use, value and meaning" (Artifact Institute 2015). Artifact Institute's activities encompass a range of presentation and dissemination strategies that stem from primary research in the form of surveys, audits, or investigations. Their formal projects fall under the categories of study, service, or, in this case, investigation. The precursor to this project was *Investigation 1: Electronic Equipment Discarded by Arts and Cultural Organizations in the Halifax Regional Municipality* (2009–14), in which Artifact Institute conducted a systematic study of electronic equipment discarded by arts and cultural organizations in HRM. Extending the survey of obsolesced electronic equipment in HRM, *Investigation 2* shifted Artifact Institute's focus to the larger or at least more ecologically concerning issue of consumer electronics and their impacts on the environment and waste management systems in the region. While *Investigation 1* involved a prolonged and thorough assessment of each artifact's use value, cultural significance, functionality, and so on, *Investigation 2* prioritized the study of the artifact's flow within a larger system, at a stage where the artifact is a priori deemed obsolete by being put to curb and is considered instead for its raw materiality. Artifact Institute's intervention is sited in the precise space and moment where the artifact's perceived use value shifts from asset to liability, hazard, burden, and finally to its economic value as raw material.

In 2008, HRM legislated a landfill ban on electronic waste and implemented a program of diversion through the formation an "industry-led group," Atlantic Canada Electronics Stewardship (ACES). The program is funded through fees applied to consumers at point-of-purchase, which go toward the operation of drop-off sorting facilities that process the electronics to be recycled into new manufacturing streams. As the subtitle of *Investigation 2* circumscribes, the Artifact Institute personnel, Tim Dallett and Adam Kelly, conducted a survey which included the documentation and collection of electronic waste (e-waste) rejected for pickup by HRM's waste collection. In this self-appointed task, Artifact Institute's activity consisted of shadowing the routes of HRM's waste collection vehicles, documenting artifacts that appeared to be rejected from regular pickup, and diverting the artifacts to an ACES depot.

The rounds were made in a cargo van that was provided to them as project equipment through the FRP. They conducted their activity in the evenings; this would condition the interpretation of their actions as well as the results of artifact collection in several ways. In terms of artifact collection, it may have allowed that the artifacts left behind were quite intentionally abandoned, having been put to curb for collection that morning; the owner/tenant/superintendent responsible for the artifact in question may have had the opportunity to consider the rejection sticker, assuming there was ample time between morning pickups and Artifact Institute's evening rounds. In the course of their rounds, Artifact Institute scanned the side of the road for discarded electronics and, if any were spotted, would pull over to document the artifact(s). This involved photographing the artifact *in situ*, as well as taking down general information on the artifact such as the date and time of recovery, approximate civic address, make and model of the product, and the condition in which it was found if relevant (figure 10.1). These reports accumulated in a binder that was made available to the public over the course of the project.

Once the artifacts were documented, they accumulated in the van until the end of each week when they were taken to an ACES recycling depot. The project ran for four weeks, during which Artifact Institute covered 1,389 km of roads within HRM and collected 152 artifacts. Artifact Institute hosted several public events in association with the project. This included a home electronics/appliance repair workshop as well as several information sessions held at various locations and a roundtable on electronic waste involving several community organizations with diverse perspectives on the issues raised by their project.

Information sessions were held first at the Seaport Farmer's Market, the Saturday Market at Alderney Landing, at Dalhousie Art Gallery – coinciding with a roundtable discussion – and at the Ecology Action Centre. In a separate electronics repair workshop, Artifact Institute provided a general framework for repairing electronic devices. Workshop participants brought their own malfunctioning devices and guidance was provided on how to approach their repair. These activities reflect Artifact Institute's imperatives for advocacy and education under an activist framework. In the same spirit, a more comprehensive and targeted roundtable discussion

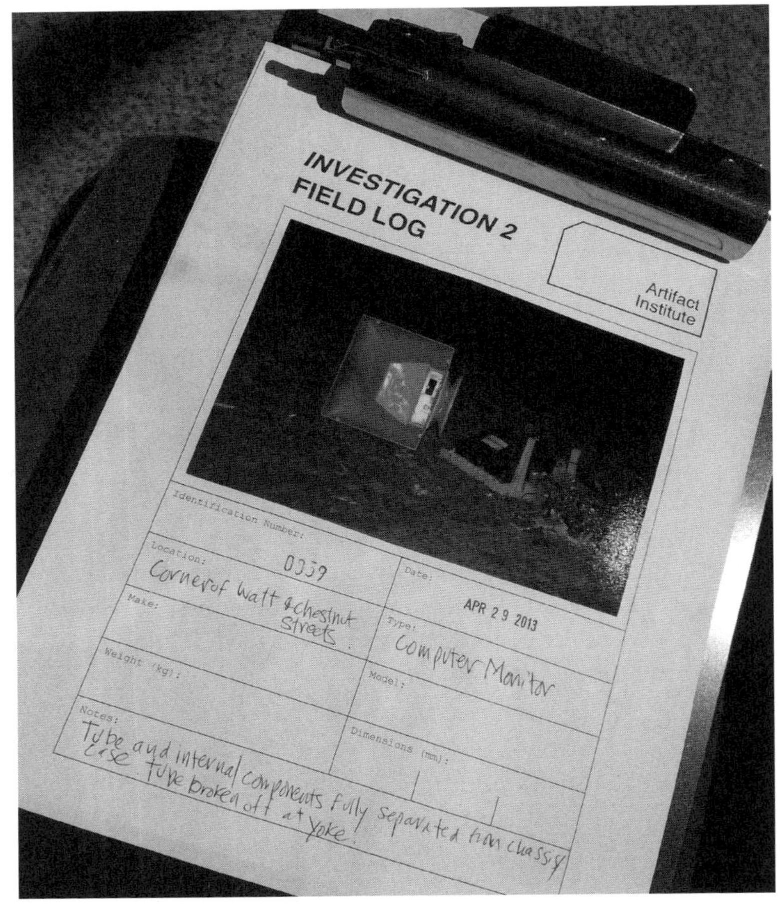

10.1 Example of an Artifact Institute investigation log entry.
Photo: Natalie Boterman, 2013.

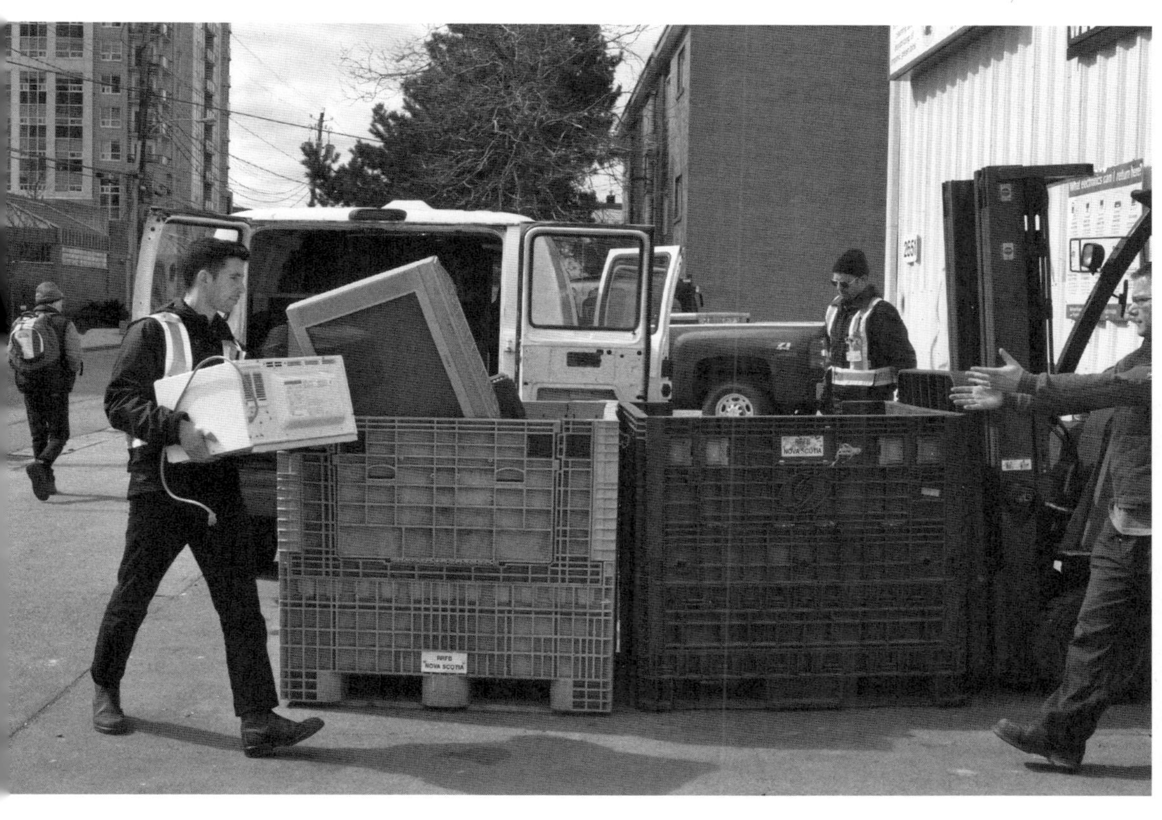

10.2 Artifact Institute at Clifton Recycling Centre, Halifax. Left, Adam Kelly, centre, Tim Dallett, and right, Centre manager. Photo: Natalie Boterman, 2013.

brought together people from a variety of fields to discuss the larger context surrounding *Investigation 2*. Representatives from Halifax-based artist-run centres and local practicing artists, Dalhousie University's College of Sustainability (an academic program) and Office of Sustainability (a service unit), HRM's Solid Waste Management and Resources Department, CKDU-FM (Dalhousie's Campus Community Radio Station), and the Ecology Action Centre were in attendance for a lengthy, open-ended discussion about planned obsolescence, material sciences, ecological issues, the history of technology, and the ways in which HRM deals with its waste.

In addition to these events where Artifact Institute engaged in direct dialogue about their project with a variety of professionals, the primary public component to their project would be the sustained fieldwork in public space, that of HRM's roadways and sidewalks, over the course of four weeks. A handful of mostly passive encounters took place with the municipality's citizens in the liminal space between private property and the curb. Residents and tenants often construed Artifact Institute's identity as that of a municipal bylaw officer, which would occasionally lead to defensiveness on the part of tenants and property owners. In such cases, Artifact Institute would explain that they had no intention of ticketing the individual in question but were just performing a survey. This typically resolved any tension created by their presence, accompanied by relief for the tenant or property owner when the artifacts were actually removed. Another common interpretation was that Artifact Institute was scavenging in the manner of bottle collectors or scrap metal collectors. While the former impression of Artifact Institute as bylaw officers or public servants would perhaps have been more prevalent if their work was conducted in daylight hours, the latter impression was reinforced by their nocturnal shift work and the fact that the cargo van that served as project equipment would not likely pass the health and safety standards for equipment of an agent of the municipality. There were at least two more or less innocuous run-ins with police officers, which might be characterized as stops for "nonnormative" navigation of public roadways.

The sites of Artifact Institute's activities – sidewalks and lawns, roadways, recycling depots, and residential private parking lots – comprise a convoluted tangle of private and public ownership. In particular, the space between the sidewalk and the road, alternately called a boulevard, hellstrip, verge, or parkway, depending on what part of the world you're in, features prominently in the documentation of artifacts and was also the site around which Dallett and Kelly would field questions from suspicious residents. The murky legal status of sidewalks has been the focus of much research in social science and legal studies. As Blomley (2005) points out, this space in particular typically falls under municipal ownership with certain caveats of maintenance to be fulfilled by the abutting property owner. The pact between private citizenry and public offices represented by this strip of land is an apt metaphor for Artifact Institute's tactical positioning within the field of technological practice, as it represents the space in which the responsibility for the technological artifact's disposal is being passed off and is sometimes contested. Among other things, this small strip of grass represents one part of the journey of the technological artifact from its starting point in the globalized manufacturing sector and the localized context for consumption and disposal. As was discovered through these casual encounters, there were a wide variety of reasons for having put dead technology (by far the most common artifacts were CRT television sets) to curb. Most commonly perhaps, as Laurie Lewis of HRM Waste Resource Management admitted during the roundtable discussion at Dalhousie Art Gallery (11 May 2013), people were unaware of the laws regarding electronic waste, despite the city's information campaign to educate citizens on what to do with their unwanted electronics.

"Technology-practice" is a central concept for understanding Artifact Institute's objectives. Arnold Pacey expands the definition of this concept by fleshing out the cultural and organizational aspects of technology-practice, beyond its more limited technical dimensions (Pacey, 1991). Artifact Institute's practice might be best understood as a panoply of conscientious activities aimed at synthesizing a dialogue between these categories. With *Investigation 2*, Artifact Institute's realms of activity drew connections between disparate but interconnected social and cultural circles, from the network of "gleaners" who harvest copper wire from CRTs for cash, to municipal sanitation workers, to bureaucrats administering official programs, to academics and cultural organizations who take interest in these matters from an completely different perspective.

But from my own perspective, having worked in such proximity to Artifact Institute during *Investigation 2*, an important feature of the work, which may be only partially evident in the logs, data sets, transcripts, and documentation, is the experiential dimension of discovering and processing an artifact.

> Theories of material culture show us the role of circulation and use in the creation and destruction of value; they illuminate the human and social contexts of objects in motion. But what happens when objects stop moving, when they get stuck on the verge abandoned or when they turn into urban debris? … If we noticed waste as things, what sort of new material relations and practices might this trigger? (Hawkins, 2006, 75).

As Gay Hawkins (2006, 74) puts it, it is this "encounter with the anterior physicality of the world, with the sensuous presence that exceeds materialization and utilization of objects" that shifts our apprehension of a waste object towards its *thingness*. She continues, "This approach shifts the focus from material culture's anthropological inflections to phenomenology and philosophy" (ibid.). The encounter with a television set whose chassis has been stripped away and yoke snapped off in order for a scavenger to harvest the copper wire coil for exchange says much about subsistence cultures on the edges of manufacturing and waste streams, but it also bears stunning evidence of the corporeality of the *things* resultant from these processes.

ANNE MACMILLAN – *LITTLE LAKES*

Anne Macmillan's *Little Lakes* consisted in her visiting the twenty lakes of the same name within the boundaries of HRM. Equipped with a waterproof GPS device designed primarily for professional and competitive long distance swimmers to chart their performance, Macmillan swam what she determined to be the swimmable perimeter of each lake (figure 10.3). This entirely subjective zone (subjective in regards to Macmillan's depth of stroke, threshold for collisions with objects, and stomach for brackish vegetation) could vary anywhere from one to five metres from the lake's edge, a space wrought with many obstacles, hazards, and unpleasantness such as large rocks, reeds, fallen trees, leeches, and sludge. In determining the swimmable edge, Macmillan produced outlines governed by bodily limitations, which can be compared to the respective coordinates produced by satellites (figure 10.4).

This project of Macmillan's comes out of a larger body of work through which she has investigated the phenomenon of *edges*. A recent project involved taking three-dimensional scans of rocks and creating faceted boxes for them; another involved tracing the contours of near-earth asteroids. In tracing the edge of lakes, Macmillan discovered a convergence of two homonymous but otherwise apparently unrelated fields – limnology, the study of freshwater lakes, and the more obscure and esoteric field of liminology, the study of border phenomena – the former being an expansive subcategory of environmental science, and the latter being an emergent topic in philosophical discourse. In the wake of press releases surrounding Macmillan's ongoing activities around *Little Lakes*, the artist found herself being approached by several freshwater lake researchers, many of whom expressed interest in further collaborations with Macmillan or, more specifically, asked if she would be interested in collecting data samples using their equipment in addition to her own, to which she obliged.

However, it was toponymy, the study of place names, that determined the course and shape of Macmillan's research. She took interest in the repeated use of "generic place names," focusing on lakes in Nova Scotia titled with descriptors such as Black, Crooked, Long, Rocky, or Sandy. In singling out "Little" lakes and deciding upon a perimeter swim, Macmillan created a scenario where one consistent element, the lake name, is measured against another element, the trace – one textual, the other iconographic. The outlines derived from the GPS trace of the swims reveal idiosyncrasies in both Macmillan's physical limitations and the limits of the technology. The geographical "snail trails" that Macmillan produces reinforce our ultimate subjection to an expansive geography; although there is a virtuosity and indeed incredible stamina required to systematically approach and "conquer" the perimeter, there is a humbling effect when the data is presented alongside the omniscient Google satellite view.

One of the central characteristics of Macmillan's larger body of work is that of limitations expressed through focus, attention, and resolution (representation). In assigning chance (using toponymy) to the selection of lakes, Macmillan draws a contract and resolves to dedicate her attention to

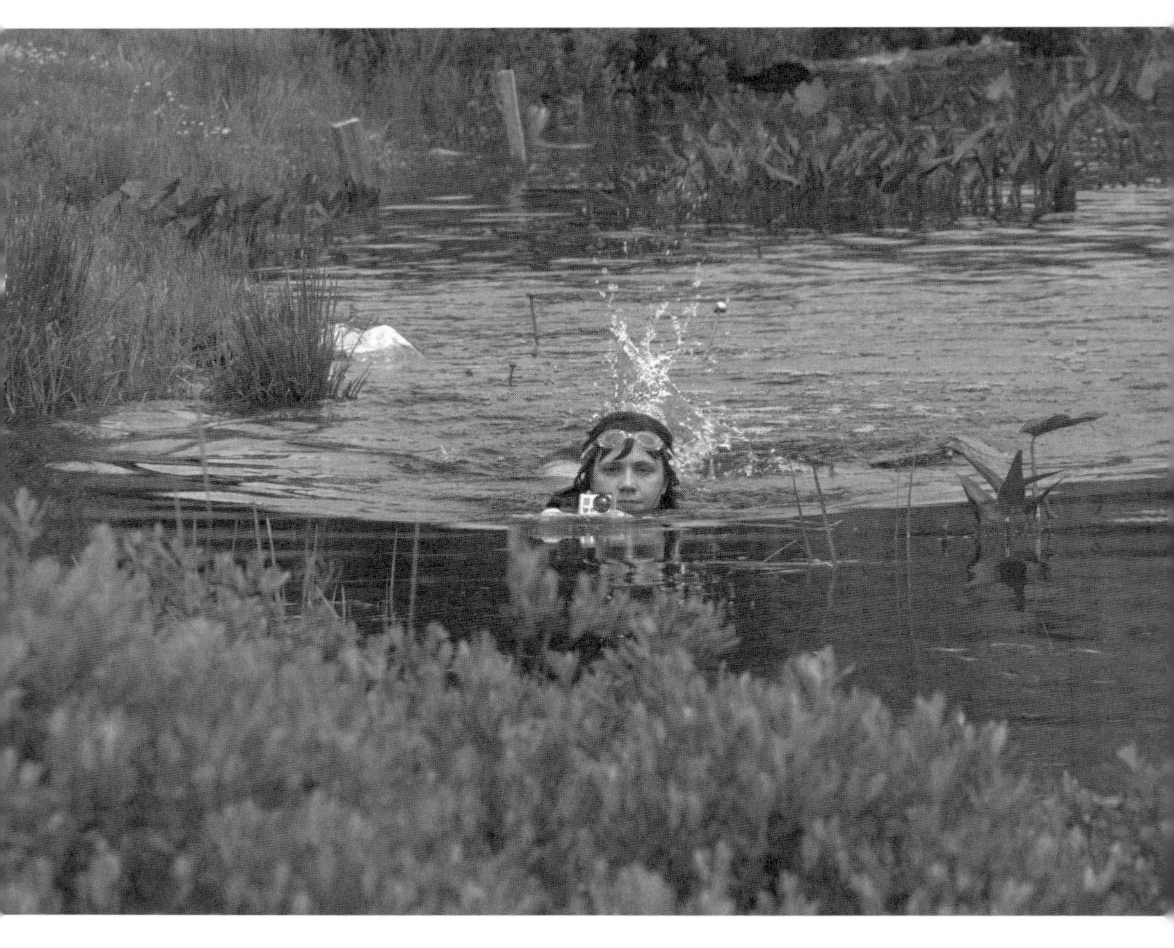

10.3 Anne Macmillan, *Little Lakes* swimming. Photo: Katie McKay, 2013.

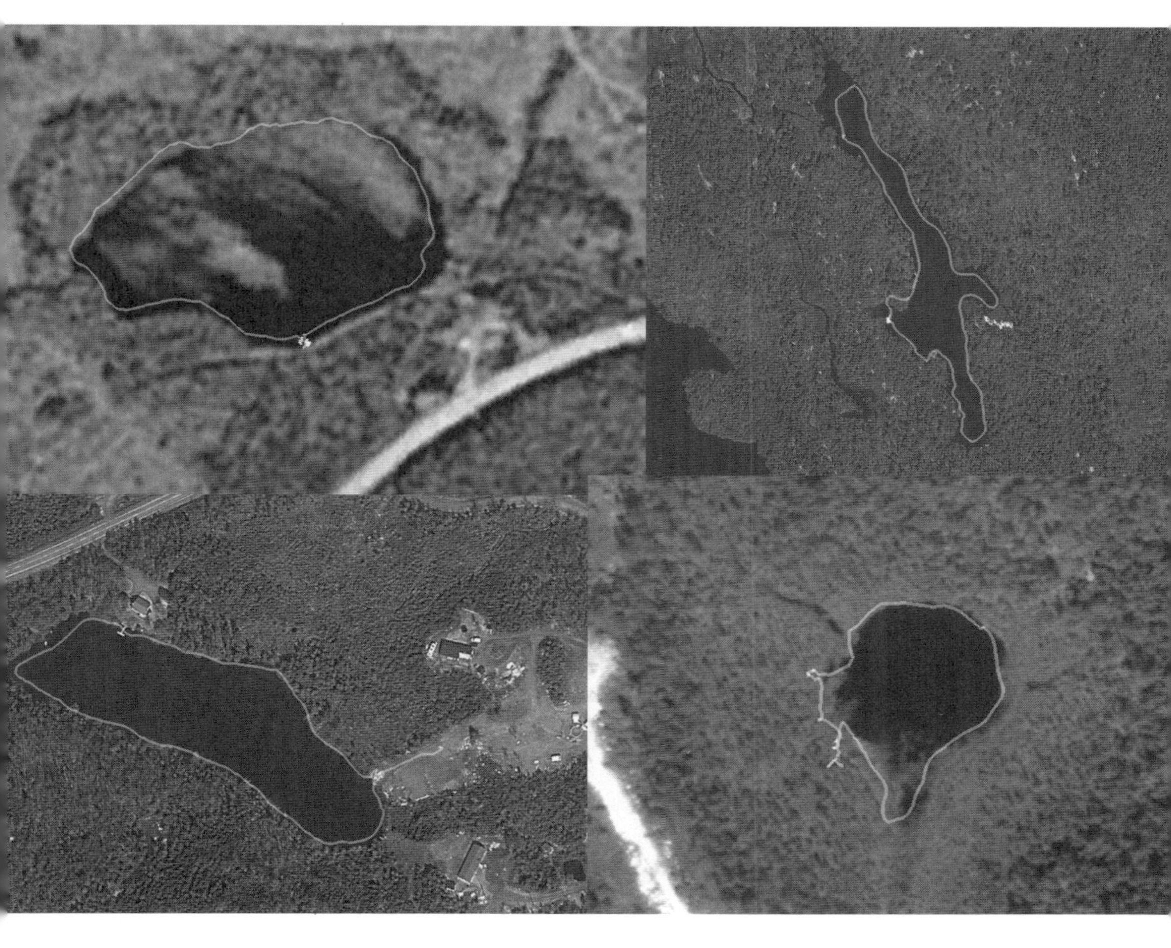

10.4 Traces of lakes, clockwise from top left: 44.9106381, -62.5549552, 44.755278, -63.440556, 44.668333, -63.936111, 44.775, -63.046389. Credit: Anne Macmillan, 2013.

the attenuation of a set number of traces. There is a gestural economy to the labour of swimming the lakes, and the result of this is the resolution of the work. Resolution in this case carries a double meaning: that of completion of a task but also of representation or (re)production of a drawing. As the resolution of the drawing is expressed in GPS units (minutes, seconds), there is an implied experience embedded in the trace that overflows this limitation. An analogy might be that its abstraction is similar to that of a recording committed to a magnetic cassette tape and that only in retracing the steps (in this case strokes) of the path is the full recovery and "fidelity" of the experience retrieved.

Macmillan's excursions were mostly discreet in terms of interactions with the general public. Any encounters were incidental – a typical encounter being a brief conversation with someone whose property was adjacent to one of the lakes. Through press releases, the project drew a considerable amount of attention from local media. While the tenor of much of this coverage was focused on the novelty of "swimming-as-drawing," it became apparent that Macmillan had touched on something: namely that lakes and by extension water are accessible and universal topics, which feature prominently in the public's imagination and in forming collective identity. It may also be that as rural and in some cases suburban locations, nearby residents would feel a degree of stewardship for *their* Little Lake or a certain pride or proprietary attitude regarding these bodies of water. There is of course the notion that water as our collective life-source is a much-needed yet much-disputed resource, which features prominently in public discourse and always will. While genuinely excited about the novelty of the Macmillan's methodology, the media coverage of the project tended to romanticize the prospect of "getting to" visit lakes as a matter of process, but Macmillan was careful to emphasize that her project wasn't merely a means to visit lakes, although the experience was nevertheless indispensible to the work.

TECHNOLOGICAL REGIONALISMS

Both Macmillan's and Artifact Institute's projects raise questions around the neutrality (or, alternatively, inherent bias) of technology in its various consumeristic uses in a global and regional context. Geographically speaking, their projects also trace a profile of an expanded municipality through navigating its networks of public roadways, sidewalks, and lakes, raising issues of access and ownership of these mutual assets. While many of the questions that emerged around these issues came directly from the firsthand experience of the artists working in the field, and are relayed through anecdotes or conversations about the work, the residues of these experiences are indexical traces in the datasets of the respective projects.

The connection wasn't so explicit when I initially considered inviting Artifact Institute to propose a project, but in an exit interview I conducted with Dallett and Kelly at the culmination of *Investigation 2* on 12 May 2015, they articulated several ways in which CLUI informed their larger collaborative project, Artifact Institute. Dallett suggests that CLUI's "one monolithic over-arching project and methodology" was influential when conceiving of Artifact Institute's own methodologies and identity; Kelly emphasizes their link to activist organizations, which may be a key distinction from CLUI's ostensibly "neutral" framework. Dallett also distinguishes between CLUI's framework for exploring the sociocultural aspects of the built environment whereas Artifact Institute's locus of activity surrounds the technological object, the artifact, whose site is nevertheless situated in the sociospatial. Dallett and Kelly both agree that whether Artifact Institute is framed or considered as an art project is superfluous to their objectives (considering the terminology/jargon that might be applied: relational aesthetics, sculpture in the expanded field, social practice, etc.). However, they readily acknowledge that it is arts funding that is most salient to the hybrid identity of Artifact Institute, hence their chiefly conducting the work and presenting it in a visual art context.

Among the presentations of Artifact Institute's findings to the public, the roundtable discussion held with key individuals with specific perspectives on the issues brought direct attention to the overall arc of their research within *Investigation 2* and their goals as an Institute. While initially proposed as *Service 2* in 2012, distinct from a survey, this would have emphasized the collection and diversion of materials rather than the analysis. Dallett and Kelly decided that this was not only neither feasible nor sustainable – for a personnel of two to service the entirety of HRM – but also beside the point since, from their perspective, the work they were doing ought to be funded and integrated into the municipality's waste management, as opposed to a supplementary service made temporarily available through an arts grant far from adequate for the level of intervention required. This irony, of Artifact Institute's receipt of a municipal arts grant providing the groundwork to come full circle into criticism of other municipal departments such as the ACES depots and HRM's waste management and resources, is reminiscent of artist Hans Haacke's (1975) *Systems* works in which he exposed the corporate interests and patronage of the galleries where he exhibited. While Artifact Institute bore no outward antagonism towards these agencies, one can wonder how the latter were perceived in their self-assigned audit of municipal waste management's shortcomings. In our exit interview, for example, Dallett recounted that he had experienced hostility when attempting to invite an ACES representative to the roundtable discussion.

In carrying out each swim for *Little Lakes,* Macmillan encountered a variety of situations regarding private property and the accessibility of the lakes. More often than not the path of least resistance to accessing a lake involved crossing private property, as many of the lakes were in relatively rural settings with few access points, surrounded by undeveloped crown or municipal land. In cases where there was no abutting property, Macmillan was often required to trailblaze in order to reach the lake. It is worth noting that a common use for the technology that Macmillan used, namely the handheld (in this case, swimming goggle mounted) GPS device, is "geocaching," a game often played out in rural areas as a means of experiencing natural landscapes. More specifically, the device that Macmillan used was designed for swimmers and runners as it records both the duration of the journey and the speed at various stages using an accelerometer. In this regard, Macmillan followed the prescribed logic of the technological tool that she utilized. As Russell Woodruff puts it, "we get artifacts to perform their functions only by following the rules built into the material forms of the artifacts" (1997, 125).

An association that necessarily emerges when framed in an art context is that Macmillan's project can be interpreted as an extension of traditional (painterly) representations of landscape. It's interesting that, whether intentional or not, Macmillan's work resembles a form of reconnaissance using GPS, a technology of military pedigree, and that landscape painting has its own historic associations with militaristic aims.

Insofar as Macmillan's task of tracing lakes carries a degree of discipline and self-determination (the parameters are not unlike some canonical text-based conceptual art works, such as Sol Lewitt's drawing instructions), the work has an effect similar to CLUI's in its idiosyncratic amassing of geographic knowledge. Her process, integrated into the user-feedback interface that such technology enables, is a clear example of the *navigational* rather than a *mimetic* practice of cartography (November, Camacho-Hübner, and Latour 2009). While many measurements and points of data collection, and representations of these, underlie both types, mimetic cartography obscures these processes with the flat image – the map – that "resembles" the territory. Navigational cartography, in contrast, is constantly recalculating the relationships between data points. The iterative aspect of Macmillan's labour in registering the occurrence of "reefs" (risk), that is, the cascade of pings to GPS satellites that track her progress, plots a series of signposts that correspond with a database, producing what could be considered a navigational aid. The resultant information is often quite at odds with the base map – the iconographic virtual image, via Google.

In its publicness, Macmillan's project tended to elicit responses from people on an emotional register – a fixation on the lakes as a common resource, a site of leisure, or a material resource to be protected, venerated, and the like. The act – the performative aspect – of producing each drawing invariably resulted in encounters with the sociospatial aspects of the landscape, and I would argue this partly comes about by Macmillan's continuously stepping in and out of public and private domains. Much like claiming space on a sidewalk or other intermediary public space, Macmillan's siting of her work in this liminal area draws parallels to Dare-Dare's own preoccupations with site and transgressions between public and private space.

Macmillan's project also directs our attention to a third space where public and private access is contested, the space occupied by the GPS satellites that are collaborators in this work. The data provided by these instruments, largely through massive public subsidization of space programs, have entered a new age of proprietary access, to which we have all become accustomed with Google maps and the like. Moreover, the existence of these technologies of measurement provide an Archimedean point, as it were, as elaborated in Hannah Arendt's essay "The Conquest of Space and Stature of Man," in which she reflects on the advent of nuclear physics and the global race for the conquest of space. Arendt warns of the imminent destruction of the human race if our ultimately reductive and dispassionate pursuit of pure scientific knowledge is not considered and illuminated from a humanist, anthropocentric point of view (Arendt 1963). More than fifty years later, with much to account for in terms of instrumentalized astrophysics, Macmillan's actions appear as a humble answer to this call, where the artist tests her own physical form against the formidable abstractions produced by these impressive instruments. While Macmillan's and Artifact Institute's projects may be perceived as transgressions, it strikes me that neither of them would attribute any kind of heroism to their deliberate actions; the determinacy of their movements through social space was simply acting out the motions of their self-assigned tasks. In both cases, their inquiries into social space are corollary to the ebb and flow of technological artifacts; rather than bending the technology to their own ends, they appear to be bending toward the technology: listening, following and recording the motions both implied in and inherent to the objects themselves.

Notes

1   Dare-Dare's *Dis/location 1* (2004–06) was sited in Square Viger, *Dis/location 2* (2006–08) was at the "Parc sans nom," Mile End, *Dis/location 3,4,* and *5* have all taken place since 2008 at the Saint-Laurent metro station, in the heart of the notorious red-light district. *Dis/location 6* started in May 2015 at Atwater Market.

Martha Radice, Brenden Harvey, and Shannon Turner

11
—

POP-UP ETHNOGRAPHY AT THE SITUATED CINEMA: CONFRONTING ART WITH SOCIAL SCIENCE AT THE WINNIPEG FESTIVAL OF MOVING IMAGE

In spite of the claims made by urban policymakers about the power of public art to enliven and uplift the public spaces of cities, and the analyses offered by scholars in the art world about how public art relates to broader urban historical, political, and cultural dynamics, remarkably little research explores what effect public artworks actually have on their urban social and spatial settings once they are installed. While controversial pieces such as Richard Serra's ill-fated *Tilted Arc* have attracted a great deal of critical analysis (see, for instance, Horowitz 1996, Kwon 2002), there are few more general studies of how the putative audiences of public artworks receive them (Hall 2007). Only a handful of scholars – such as Nathalie Heinich (1996, 1997), Joanne Sharp (2007), Martin Zebracki (2012, 2013), and Laurent Vernet (2015 and this volume) – have investigated in a more systematic way what public artworks do to and for their publics. It is in the spirit of contributing to this body of research that we discuss, in this chapter, what happened when members of the public encountered the Situated Cinema, a temporary, mobile artistic intervention that appeared during the WNDX Festival of Moving Image in Winnipeg, Manitoba, in September 2012.

We came to this empirical research project as three urban anthropologists versed in the study of public space and therefore most interested in the effects of the artwork on the people and places where it appeared. But we soon realized that there were other encounters at stake in this creative urban intervention. One was between artistic practices: the Situated Cinema was itself a hybrid project, grafting together experimental film, architecture, and industrial design. Another was between disciplinary perspectives: as our fieldwork unfolded, we were compelled to integrate into our analysis considerations of the potential differences between artistic and social-scientific approaches to artistic interventions in public space. Drawing on the semiserendipitous methods of what we call "pop-up ethnography," in this chapter we critically examine the contrasts in perspectives of each group of social actors involved in the Situated Cinema project: its designers, curator and filmmakers, members of the public, and us, the urban anthropologists. First, though, we describe the Cinema in more detail.

THE SITUATED CINEMA

The Situated Cinema was a "demountable micro-cinema," a semimobile structure designed and custom made by three architect-designers – Tom Evans, Craig Rodmore, and Will Vachon – for WNDX, Winnipeg's Festival of Moving Image, a small but critically important annual festival of experimental film and expanded cinema. Basically a large matte black box made of cleverly interlocking wooden panels, the Situated Cinema took two hours to build from its flat-packed state and about an hour to take down (figure 11.1).[1] It housed a 16mm film projector modified with a "looper" to show a continuous loop of five two-minute experimental films commissioned by the coordinating curator, Solomon Nagler (also a filmmaker, and coauthor of chapter 6). Members of the public (or, as we call them here, viewer-participants) entered the Cinema, navigated tight corridors designed to reduce ambient light and had to step through the projector's beam of light to reach an inclined tabletop-sized screen onto which the films were projected from underneath. A system of mirrors enlarged and reoriented the image so that it reached a sufficient size for projection within this "micro-cinema" (figure 11.2). The films, made by five filmmakers, were conceived as homages to the cinematic genre of the city symphony. Dating back to the silent film era of the 1920s, the city symphony is "a poetic, experimental documentary that presents a portrait of daily life within a city while attempting to capture something of the city's spirit" (Barrett 2014), loosely echoing a

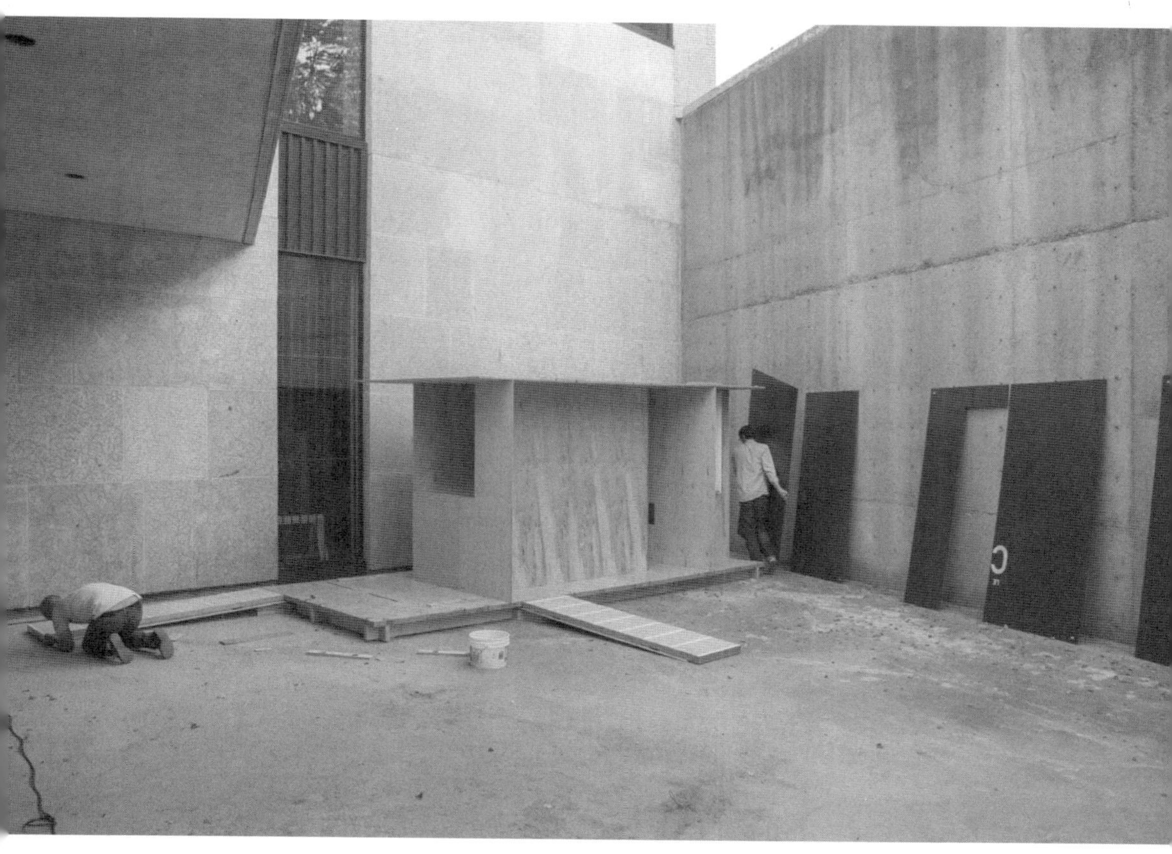

11.1 The Situated Cinema under construction at the Winnipeg Art Gallery
with the sloping screen visible in the nook at the left of the structure.
With architect-designers Tom Evans (left) and Craig Rodmore (right).
Photo: William Eakin, 2012.

musical symphony in its structure or motifs. Classics include *Berlin: Symphony of a Great City* (Ruttmann 1927) and *Man with a Movie Camera* (Vertov 1929), filmed in Soviet cities Odessa, Kiev, Kharkiv, and Moscow. The contemporary two-minute city symphonies (or city songs, perhaps) shown at the Situated Cinema each focused on the Canadian city that the filmmaker lived in: Alexandre Larose filmed Montreal; Alex MacKenzie, Vancouver; Caroline Monnet, Ottawa/Gatineau; Heidi Phillips, Winnipeg; and Izabella Pruska-Oldenhof, Toronto.[2] Another allusion to early cinema was the single subtle sign on the structure, a lightbox stencilled with a quote from the Lumière brothers: "Le cinéma est une invention sans avenir" (Cinema is an invention with no future).

In its city of exhibition, the Situated Cinema moved to a different public space each day for the four days of WNDX. The program for the event described it as "[a]n alternative cinema-going experience in which the interior of the movie theatre interacts with the city outside [...]. Through the mobility and permeability of the venue and the mingling of silent films and shifting contextual soundscapes, the project embraces the interactions and juxtapositions of the city and asks viewer-participants and five commissioned filmmakers to do the same" (WNDX 2012, 4). The Situated Cinema thus retained the essential elements of a traditional cinema – "a projector, film running through a projector, a screen, an audience, a darkness," as Rodmore put it during an artists' talk at WNDX – but reconfigured them in several ways. It was mobile, not stationary; it had doorways, not doors, so was open to its environment; the films ran continuously rather than at set times; one watched them standing up and looking down rather than sitting down and looking up. One of the artistic aims of the project was to disrupt the idea of the cinema as a secluded, protected, anonymous space in which the viewers forget their bodies and their surroundings and are transported to other worlds (Barthes 1986, 345–49; Nagler 2010). Instead, it would demand engagement with the sites in which it was situated. One of the aims of this chapter is to investigate how that engagement played out.

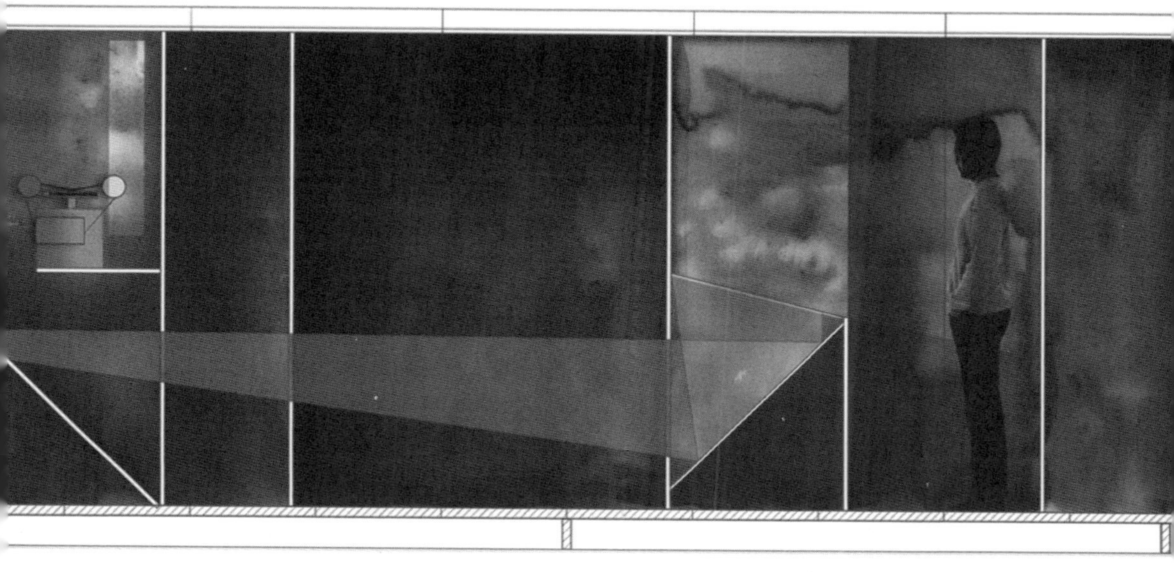

11.2 Architectural drawing of the Situated Cinema showing the projection system.
Credit: Will Vachon, 2012.

A POP-UP ETHNOGRAPHY

Both the Situated Cinema itself and our ethnographic study of it form part of *Tracing the City: Interventions of Art in Public Space*, an interdisciplinary research-creation project funded by Canada's Social Science and Humanities Research Council, which combined art (mainly site-specific installations and cinema) and social science (mainly urban anthropology) to investigate how art can intervene in the urban public and vice versa.[3] Although the first author of this chapter, Martha Radice, and the curator of the Situated Cinema, Solomon Nagler, were two of the project's coinvestigators (the third was Kim Morgan, coauthor of chapter 7), it should be noted that the three authors of this chapter were not involved at all in the design, construction, or curation of this particular creative intervention. We joined the venture well after its inception. That being the case, the inquiry that we present here is not a research-creation project, in the terms elaborated by Boudreault-Fournier and Wees (this volume) or in the ways practiced by the Narratives in Space+Time Society (Bean et al., this volume). Nor does it really constitute visual anthropology, which seeks to understand particular social or cultural groups by analyzing their visual forms or producing new ones (such as ethnographic films). Rather, it is an "etic" or outsider's approach to art: we were observing, not creating. Our goal was to analyze the interactions with the urban public – understood as both the people and places of the city – that the Situated Cinema aimed to stimulate. To do this, we conducted fieldwork for almost all of the short period that it was in installation.

At the outset, our main objective was to investigate viewer-participants' experiences of the Situated Cinema by observing how people approached and interacted with the structure and by inviting people to participate in short semistructured interviews outside the Cinema after they had been through it. Our set of questions covered how, why, and with whom they had come to the Cinema, how they thought the Cinema fit into the surroundings, what their experiences of the physical structure and their responses to the films were, how they would describe the experience to friends, and how they would characterize the Cinema in just one word. We also asked for some demographic information (but no names). Interviews lasted ten minutes on average; all were audio-recorded unless the interviewee preferred not or the environment was too noisy, in which case they were written up immediately. In all, we interviewed about fifty viewer-participants in about thirty interviews (several having experienced the Cinema in pairs or small groups). Due partly to technical hitches (as we shall see), we were also able to seize opportunities to observe and interview three of the featured filmmakers, the architect-designers, and the coordinating curator. Our observations of these "creators" of the piece were jotted down on the fly and later written up as field notes, as were some of our impromptu interviews; other interviews were audio-recorded and later transcribed. We also attended and recorded an artists' talk on expanded cinema that was part of the WNDX program, moderated by curator Solomon Nagler and featuring designer Craig Rodmore and filmmaker Alex MacKenzie (among others). In addition, we draw on printed and online documentation of the project, such as its catalogue (Rodmore 2013) and descriptions on the artists' websites, plus follow-up email exchanges with some of the creators. In this way, our ethnography "popped up" in an analogous fashion to its object of study.[4]

Of course, our "pop-up ethnography" was not exactly ethnography in the traditional anthropological sense. "Ethnography" is the term anthropologists use to encompass the various methods they employ during immersive fieldwork, typically lasting many months or years, with a particular social group or milieu; it also refers to the books that result from these investigations. Participant observation, the method in which the observer (the anthropologist) tries to learn to participate in this group or milieu in the manner of one of its members, writing up and reflecting on her efforts as she goes, is the cornerstone of the ethnographic approach. However, anthropologists – and other social scientists, although anthropologists' disciplinary identity is arguably uniquely bound up with ethnography – can also dip into a capacious and adaptable toolkit of other methods, including nonparticipant or environmental observation and interviews (which we used), focus groups, household surveys, kinship charts, discussions of vignettes, photography, video- or audio-recording, photovoice, sketches, mental maps, actual maps, sorting exercises, and more. Besides its potential multiplicity of methods, we would argue that ethnography has three distinctive features: long duration, flexibility, and reflexivity.

What we undertook at WNDX was clearly not long in duration. Unlike, for instance, Kate Crehan's (2011) study of a community arts organization, our "ethnography" spanned days, not decades, because it had to match the duration of the Situated Cinema's situations. That said, the context of our longer-term collaboration with Nagler, coupled with the ease of communication that email brings, allowed us to continue to refine our understanding – especially of the creators' intentions – well after WNDX ended. This chimes with many anthropologists' experiences: even if "the field" is halfway round the world, new communications technologies mean one never quite leaves it behind in the same way as one did a few decades ago (Simpson 2009). Other anthropologists have developed "rapid ethnographic assessment procedures (REAP)" or "rapid appraisals" in order to systematically yet quickly gather enough material from participants to form a good qualitative understanding of specific sociocultural contexts, especially those undergoing significant change. Originally formalized in the fields of public health and epidemiology and rural and agricultural development, REAP have been used in urban studies to look at people's use of public parks (Taplin, Scheld, and Low 2002) and the impact of 9/11 on a Manhattan neighbourhood (Low, Taplin, and Lamb 2005). In large part by relying on teamwork, as we did, ethnographic field methods can thus be adapted for settings (including art installations or festivals) with limited time frames.

While rapid or "pop-up" ethnographic methods may lack time, they retain flexibility. REAP expressly incorporate a systems (or holistic) approach to the setting, triangulation of material gathered by different methods, and iterativity – allowing the direction of research to be reoriented by the material gathered (Beebe 1995). Indeed, a distinctive feature of all ethnography, fast or slow, is that it integrates unexpected opportunities for gathering material. Our pop-up ethnography certainly did this: having set out to focus on viewer-participants' experiences, we realized once in the field that the filmmakers would be at WNDX, would come to see the Situated Cinema, and might therefore be available for interview too. Lastly, and closely related to iterativity, ethnography is underpinned by reflexivity, which means taking into account – and including in the analysis – how the researchers, by their actions and their characteristics, affect the setting being studied and the directions that the research takes. During this fieldwork, our awareness of our role on site was heightened. Since we were a constant presence at the Situated Cinema, we became in some sense a feature of the installation ourselves, a point to which we shall return.

In what follows, we discuss four themes that our pop-up ethnography revealed, relating to 1) the contrasts between each site; 2) the experiences of viewer-participants; 3) the ways the material constraints of the Situated Cinema shaped the films and their projection; and 4) the divergent aims, methods and expectations of artists and social scientists vis-à-vis art in urban public settings.

THE SITUATED CINEMA SITES: ACCIDENT, ACCESS AND AESTHETICS

While we, the anthropologists, popped up next to the Situated Cinema, the tiny structure itself popped up next to larger prominent buildings of Winnipeg in the manner of "pet architecture," a term coined by Japanese architecture studio Atelier Bow-Wow to describe the cheaply built yet cheerful and appealing little structures that appear in the interstices of the normal-sized buildings of Tokyo. Architect Yoshiharu Tsukamoto explains, "if decent buildings standing in decent spaces are to be considered 'human beings', small buildings standing with all their might in odd spaces would seem to be like pets in urban spaces, due to the sense of distance from human beings and the sense of presence in scenery" (2003, 249). Over the course of four days, the Situated Cinema was erected in four locations in central Winnipeg: by the RAW Gallery of Architecture and Design; at the Forks, a popular recreational site; on the University of Winnipeg campus; and at the Winnipeg Art Gallery, during Nuit Blanche, a city-wide nightlong arts festival. The exact location of the Situated Cinema at each site was the product of negotiation between the architect-designers of the Situated Cinema, who didn't know the city well, and the festival organizers and local site managers, who hadn't seen the Situated Cinema; in their final decision, they all had to take into consideration both the technical and the aesthetic properties of the sites.

Each choice of site significantly affected viewer-participants' access to the Situated Cinema, in terms of both physical accessibility – whether or not it was easy to see, pass close by, or enter the Cinema – and symbolic or social accessibility, that is, whether or not it seemed to be open to them as actors positioned in certain social categories or roles. As Henri Lefebvre (1991), Michel de Certeau ([1980] 1990) and anthropologists who study place and space (Low and Smith 2006; Low 2000; Feld and

Basso 1996; Rodman 1992; Rotenberg and McDonough 1993) make clear, spaces are never neutral but are produced through existing social relations such that they have different cultural meanings, values, and barriers or benefits of entry for people of different social classes, age groups, genders, or racialized groups, and in different kin or occupational or other roles. Art is not experienced from a neutral position either: sociologist Pierre Bourdieu established some fifty years ago that attendance, appreciation, and enjoyment of art galleries and museums were unevenly distributed across the social classes, due largely to education, with higher classes cultivating a taste for high culture (Bourdieu, Darbel, and Schnapper 1969). While the contours of Bourdieu's thesis have evolved, the insight still holds: not only the physical configuration of an artistic intervention in public space but also its less visible social parameters will affect people's experience of it.

The first installation of the Situated Cinema was on a Wednesday evening in a small parking lot opposite the RAW Gallery on McDermot Avenue, where the opening night celebration of WNDX was being held. The small size of the parking lot and its proximity to the sidewalk meant that here the Situated Cinema was physically accessible to all. However, its association with the WNDX opening night party probably made it seem less accessible to mere passersby who were not part of the festival scene – although some may have been drawn to the short presentation given by the curator and filmmakers out on the sidewalk. This is the one location that we were not able to observe ourselves, due to travel constraints, but based on the designers' reports and our subsequent observations, we surmise that while the Situated Cinema here received a fair number of visitors, most of them would have been aficionados of WNDX rather than members of the public at large.[5] We return to this distinction between types of audiences below.

On Thursday, from midmorning to late evening, the Situated Cinema was set up at the Forks, an attractive site with plenty of green and public space near downtown Winnipeg, where the Red River and Assiniboine River meet. The confluence of the rivers, with their walking and biking trails, a marketplace area, and other cultural and historic features make it a popular destination for both Winnipeggers and visitors. Because of this, the Situated Cinema was well exposed in a high traffic area, making it accessible to a wide variety of viewer-participants. While many people sought out the Situated Cinema intentionally, having heard about it through WNDX promotions or through friends, in this particular location, viewer-participants just as often (or perhaps more often) discovered it by chance as they strolled or biked through the area or dined at nearby restaurants. Couples and larger groups of family or friends were observed enjoying leisure time here, taking in the sights or passing through to other destinations in the city. More to the point, not only was the Situated Cinema highly visible and physically accessible here, it also fit in well with the environment, as one cultural or recreational attraction among many at the Forks. This meant that it was symbolically accessible, too: passersby were more willing to incorporate it into their activities as they moved through the space. As one interviewee said, "that's exactly what would be at the Forks [...] It's kind of like an artsy place that's an artsy thing." However, this "fit" was not necessarily desirable for the designers, who were pleased that (for various reasons) the Cinema had been reallocated from one spot of the Forks where there were other kiosk-type buildings to its eventual space, where it stood out as a more distinctive feature. They did not want the Situated Cinema to become part of the "tchotchke-y" architectural language of the "tourist trap."

On Friday, the Situated Cinema was set up downtown on the University of Winnipeg campus on Portage Avenue, one of the city's main arteries. It was erected on a large lawn often used as a sports field in front of Wesley Hall, next to a well-travelled walkway through the campus (figure 11.3). Large groups of people, presumably mostly students, were observed in the area, playing Frisbee or lounging on the grass, with many others passing by on the pathways and sidewalks. While there was a great deal of bustle nearby, the Situated Cinema was obscured from view from the campus walkway by a bed of thick shrubs and ornamental grasses, while on the street side, a low wall separated it from the city sidewalk, which created a physical if not visual barrier. The Situated Cinema was accessible via the lawn, but – as we could tell by the lack of "desire lines" (Bean et al., this volume) – the lawn was not a regular pathway through the campus, so people did not pass by that way. The university's site managers had originally proposed that the Cinema be built right next to the campus walkway, but that would have meant removing some bike racks, which the designers did not want to do. A second proposed site had no access to a power supply due to building work, so the installation ended up on the grass. In any case, to some degree, the designers preferred the idea that people should have to go out of their way to "discover" their creation. Thus, although Situated Cinema was at the University of Winnipeg during a gloriously sunny afternoon enjoyed by throngs of passersby, it saw the fewest visitors in this location, and the majority of viewer-participants we interviewed here were WNDX festival aficionados who had sought it out on purpose.

On Saturday night, the Situated Cinema was constructed outside the Winnipeg Art Gallery (WAG), at the bottom of a concrete ramp at the rear of the building that had once been used for offloading busloads of visiting schoolchildren. Huge numbers of people gathered at the WAG and on the streets nearby for the festivities of Nuit Blanche. Initially, the Situated Cinema did not seem very accessible here either: the ramp was long and went below street level, and there was no sign to advertise it. However, a popular local coffee shop had also set up a stall at this bottom entrance of the WAG, and, although that too was unsignposted, people knew the café was somewhere nearby. The allure of a hot cappuccino was enough to tempt many visitors down the ramp, where they accidentally discovered the Cinema. The symbolic accessibility here was high, in that many of the viewer-participants, as intentional patrons of the Nuit Blanche festival, were looking for this sort of artistic experience. They were more ready and willing to enter the Cinema here than elsewhere, trusting that it was there for them and would offer something to them. However, while the festival drew many visitors to the WAG, it also appeared to limit the amount of time viewer-participants were willing to devote to the Situated Cinema before rushing off to the next spectacle in an art-as-consumption scenario (see Haiven 2012; Bain and Rallis, this volume). Arguably, the Situated Cinema was most aesthetically dramatic in the WAG location, where its sleek minimalist design nestled comfortably beneath the hard lines and stark concrete of the building's modernist architecture (see figure 11.2 and the film cited in note 1), and its illuminated sign made a warm glow at the end of the dimly lit ramp.

In sum, each of the Situated Cinema's sites had different implications for the way that people engaged with this cinematic intervention in urban space. It was an obvious, anomalous structure at each site, yet its subtle signage and narrow doorways made it not immediately legible to passersby – what Loubier would call a "furtive" work, "brushing up against one's

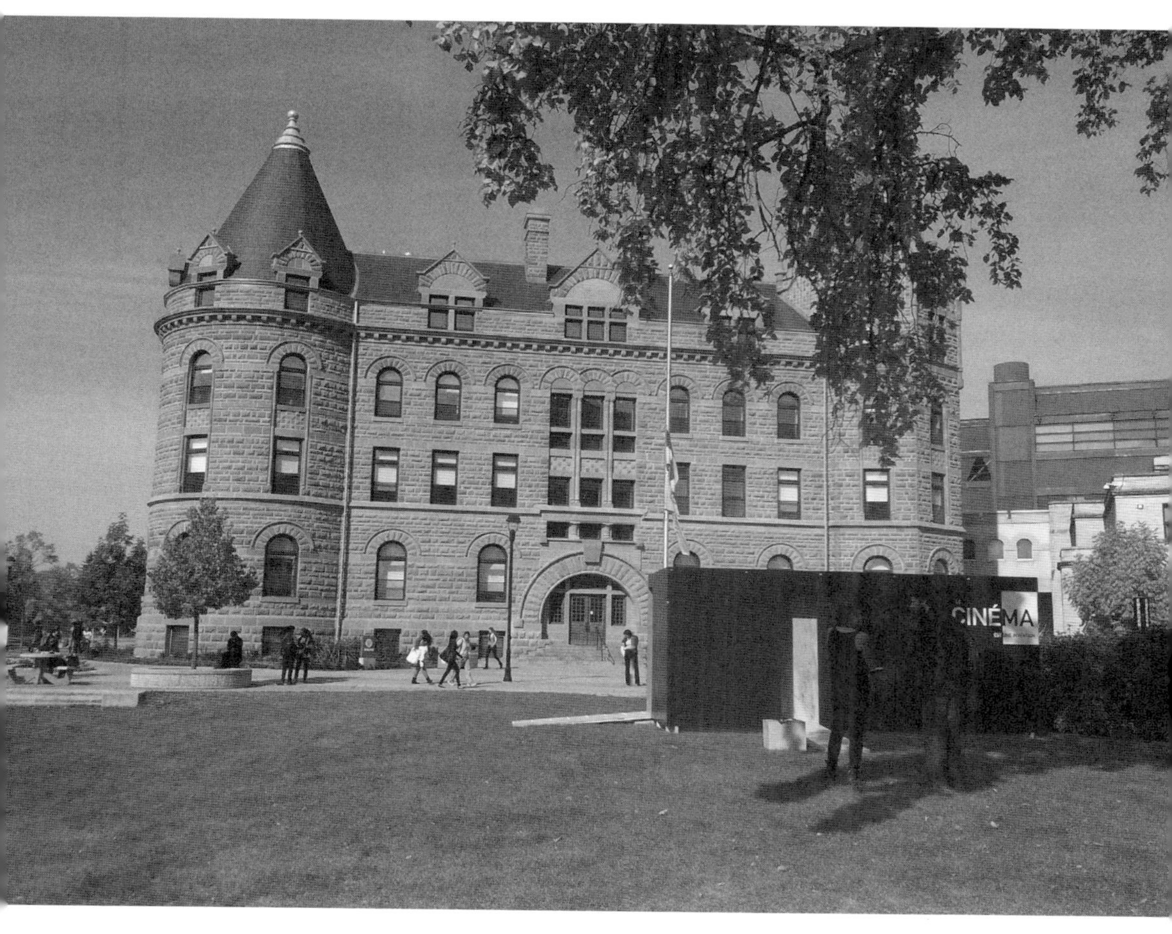

11.3 The Situated Cinema at the University of Winnipeg, in front of the Collegiate School, with Shannon Turner conducting an exit interview. The busy walkway is on the other side of the bushes to the right. Photo: Martha Radice, 2012.

attention, while still blending into the city's background; troubling, but barely," an infiltration rather than an imposition (2001, 24, our translation). As one viewer-participant put it, "it definitely does intervene, but in a way it does it in a very introverted way." At the University of Winnipeg and the WAG the Situated Cinema was off the beaten track, while at the Forks it was more visible, but its purpose was not evident at any site, even if it was an experience more readily assimilated into Nuit Blanche and the Forks. This ambiguity was to some degree accidental, determined by technicalities (how level the ground was, whether the van transporting the Cinema could pull up close by), but perhaps in larger part deliberate. While on the one hand, the Cinema's creators sought out aesthetically dramatic locations, where it would articulate an intriguing kind of architectural conversation with the surrounding structures (and, not coincidentally, afford a vantage point to get good documentation of the project), on the other hand, they did not want to draw too much attention to it or impose it on people by plonking it down in the middle of their pathways. They did not want to make a gaudy spectacle of their intervention into urban public space. As one of the designers put it, "If we'd wanted a bouncy castle, we would have [given people] a bouncy castle."[6] Rather, they preferred to "reward [the] curiosity" of those who took the time – or courage – to approach the Cinema. We now turn to the experiences of those who did so.

UNPACKING THE BIG BLACK BOX: THE SITUATED CINEMA'S PUBLICS

As noted above, some people deliberately sought out the Situated Cinema, while others simply happened upon it during the course of their everyday activities or their nocturnal sightseeing at Nuit Blanche. After analyzing our interviews, we found we had heard from roughly equal numbers of these two types of visitors, each of whom engaged with the Cinema in somewhat but not entirely different ways. The viewer-participants who sought out the Situated Cinema deliberately, having heard about it on the radio or through WNDX advertising, had generally studied or worked in creative fields such as fine art or art history, design, architecture, or film-making. Some were filmmakers with a film in the festival or friends of a filmmaker involved in the project. What became clear was that most of these intentional visitors were "experts": because of their training or practice, they were both literate in art and likely to seek out new experiences of art. This meant that they were more likely to critically engage with the content of the somewhat esoteric experimental films on show, and they could also make reference to the projection systems or the materiality of the films or the architectural references and design details of the structure. For example, one filmmaker (not one whose film was showing in the Cinema) noted that with the potential for light leakage the films needed to tread a fine line between detail and high-contrast images. While all interviewees, "expert" or not, talked more readily about the material structure of the Cinema than the films on show, the "expert" viewer-participants were most able to "read" and reference the films themselves.

That said, the accidental visitors or "lay" viewer-participants, as we call them, found their own ways to interpret the qualities and content of the films, mainly because cinema is such a popular mass medium of entertainment. When asked what memories or associations the films evoked, a considerable number of people referred to the golden age of cinema. For some, this association was derived purely from the black-and-white or desaturated film and the grainy, scratched, or blurry effects utilized by the filmmakers, while for others the use of found footage or stills of old postcards and photographs or the iconic imagery of their focal cities made the films reminiscent of vintage tourism reels. The familiar landmarks and urban landscapes allowed people to derive a basic understanding of the films as "city symphonies," at least once the term was suggested to them in one of our interview questions (which asked, "The films were meant to be a kind of 'city symphony.' How does that label fit the films, in your view?"). One man said he saw "streets weaving and overlapping each other, like a tapestry," but most people interviewed did not elaborate on the urban aspect of the films. This suggests that the "city symphony" genre was not that recognizable outside a certain circle of cinephiles or simply that other elements of the Situated Cinema were of greater interest to the majority of viewer-participants.

The nostalgic theme brought up other aspects of the heyday of cinema. One woman was reminded of the time when people "went to the corner to their local theatre to see the news" together, in contrast to the private experience of media today. For others, it was the unexpected discovery and private experience of the project that spoke to a sense of cinematic history. One couple interviewed called the Situated Cinema "a magical secret show that you just happen to stumble upon" and said it reminded them of a kinetoscope, an early device for viewing motion pictures that was often part of travelling shows and penny arcades, which permitted one viewer at a time to peer through a peephole on the top of the box. Other people similarly referenced funfair or carnival features; the mysterious, intimidating black box with its narrow entryways reminded many of the "haunted house." One woman remarked, "you don't know if the floor is going to drop out," and another said, "my first thought around the corner was like, I wonder who is in there, and what I'm going to find?" Many people found the tight corridors and limited space at the screen physically and socially awkward; the intimacy made it difficult to share the space with strangers. Given that the people we interviewed had obviously braved the unknown to go through the Cinema, it was striking how often they emphasized this sense of trepidation in narrating their experience. However, it seemed to be worth it; one viewer-participant felt that the films were like "a prize at the end of the maze." Interestingly, this echoed the designers' desire to reward curiosity, rather than imposing the Situated Cinema on all passersby in a busy place.

Indeed, many of the accidental viewer-participants appreciated the unexpectedness of their encounter with the Situated Cinema. They were enthusiastic about the idea of stumbling upon art or cinema in unusual places or unpredictable times in the city. One person called the Cinema "a cute little adventure" and thought that installations of this type might draw people back into the downtown spaces that had been abandoned for the safety and convenience of the suburbs. Similarly, another suggested that these sorts of installations make art more accessible to a wider variety of people, exposing them to new ideas and making them feel more "connected." Despite any initial discomfort and occasional criticisms of the Situated Cinema, most people we interviewed were very receptive to the idea of similar installations popping up in the fabric of their city, offering them the opportunity to experience something novel during their everyday urban itinerary. As one man remarked, "I think it's good to come to expect these kind of things out of the city, you know? Maybe it could become more common. It's like, 'oh, there's another box'." We suspect, though, that if this desire for more of the unexpected were met, the effect would paradoxically be undermined and the sense of surprise and serendipity extinguished.

The "box" itself, which exposed both the film projector from the outside through a window and the mechanism of projection on the inside, as people had to step through the projected beam of light when walking through the corridors towards the screen, seemed to be the most intriguing dimension of the Situated Cinema project. One man said that it was like being encased in a huge film projector – echoing what one of the architect-designers told us: "the user moves through the Cinema in the same way that the film moves through the projector – passing through the path of light just as the film does." Whether "lay" or "expert," and whether or not they were familiar with experimental film or city symphonies, viewer-participants discussed the structure of the Cinema more easily than its content. The box of the structure therefore gave people a way into interpreting the Situated Cinema. This concern with materiality leads us to a discussion of the filmmakers' engagements with the project.

THE FILMMAKERS: MATERIAL INSPIRATION … AND CONSTRAINTS

Like most artists, the experimental filmmakers who were invited to make work for the Situated Cinema are very preoccupied with the materials and the technology available to them, and the physical limitations of the Situated Cinema, as well as the curatorial focus on city symphonies, were a source of inspiration as they made their films. As he explained in an interview with us in Winnipeg and notes sent by email afterwards, Alexandre Larose gave himself certain constraints in creating his film, *Belvédère,* which would resonate with the design of the Cinema. Knowing that the films would be showing in a loop, he wanted his film itself to be like a loop, so he made it by making multiple exposures on the same reel of film of the same scene. He also chose his vantage point – looking towards the city centre from the Kondiaronk Belvedere on the top of the Mont-Royal, Montreal – to reflect the unusual positioning of the screen in the Situated Cinema: whereas in most cinemas one looks up, or across, to see the screen, here one looked down. So he looked down on an iconic view of the city, zooming into it from above. Knowing that the looper would "age" his film by adding its own scratches to it, Larose kept the film to a vertical pan so that the scratches would complement the content. Lastly, the effects of his film were made entirely through in-camera work, with no postproduction processing or montage, echoing the near-obsolete technology of analogue cinema – now an invention, as the sign said, with no future.

Izabella Pruska-Oldenhof also referenced the history of cinema in her film, *This Town of Toronto Is the Best Place I Ever Ran Into*, but in a completely different way. She combined archival footage and imagery with recent video shot with an iPhone through a magnifying glass, which "permitted what was behind me and in front of me and above to be all kind of melded together," distorting the overly-pristine quality of digital video in a satisfying way. Pruska-Oldenhof's film thus required a great deal of montage and postprocessing before it was transferred to the 16mm medium for projection in the Situated Cinema. With this busy, digital-analogue mash-up, the filmmaker aimed to convey the experience of what it feels like to be jostled around in a city; more formally, she furthered the city symphony genre by adopting the musical metaphor of polyphony in the film's visual composition.

Whereas Larose and Pruska-Oldenhof both drew on embodied urban experience in their films (the vantage point of the Mont-Royal, the rhythm and bustle of downtown Toronto), Alex MacKenzie's take on Vancouver, *Portal*, provided a more explicit social and political commentary, "shooting with [...] a 'dark lens'" and playing up the tension between nature and urbanism. MacKenzie said he felt like a good fit for the Situated Cinema because he deals very much with the materiality of film and projection in his creative practice, working with outmoded technologies and even making hand-cranked projectors from old spare parts. He filmed *Portal* on the first 16mm cine-camera ever produced, a hand-cranked Cine-Kodak Model A (from ca. 1923); the film itself echoes early cinema in its use of "vignettes," shots that are bright and clear in the centre and fade off at the edges. He found that the "hand-built mini-cinema," with its clever exposure of the mechanism of projection, echoed his artistic aims: "they've come up with [...] architecturally a really interesting shape that does something very similar to what I'm talking about, which is to demand a recognition of the formation of the image, and how it comes to be." The Situated Cinema brought to MacKenzie's mind another mobile black box: Edison's "Black Maria" film studio, built in 1892–93, which had a retractable roof and could be oriented to the sun to get the best light in the age before the invention of strong electric lights. Again, the form of the Situated Cinema recalled the conditions of production, as well as consumption, of celluloid film.

Our interviews with filmmakers had not initially been part of our research design, which focused on the experience of members of the public. However, several of the filmmakers were attending WNDX and therefore came to see the Situated Cinema in action, and Larose provided a great deal of technical assistance with the projector. What in fact gave us the opportunity to interview the filmmakers were the various technical hitches that the Cinema encountered. These included the long delay in setting up the Cinema at the University of Winnipeg (because the field was needed for a sports class first) and several delays caused because the loop of films broke. The projector in the Situated Cinema was left to run unstaffed in a little box, visible from the outside through plexiglass but not easily accessible. This meant that it could get overheated and also that focus could not be easily adjusted once the film was running. The technology of the looper that fed the films round and round (instead of going from reel to reel) scratched and put strain on the loop of celluloid. Scratches, soft focus, and light leakage thus made their way into the projections, rendering the experimental content even more abstract than it was already to viewer-participants and giving the filmmakers unexpected aesthetic effects to think about. Perhaps more problematically, time and budget constraints meant that the loop of films was not a reprint on projection-quality film stock but rather was a splice of the five films together on five different kinds of film stock ("That's a lot of splice time," as one filmmaker said). This led to the film breaking several times over the course of three days, so some viewer-participants who entered the Cinema saw only the projection of flickering broken film, and several times the Situated Cinema was shut down for an hour or more while the film and projector were repaired. This reduced the potential for discovery of the Cinema and its content by members of the public. (It also meant that only Pruska-Oldenhof's film, which was physically the most robust, was actually shown at the WAG during Nuit Blanche.)

On the one hand, these can be seen as disappointing and frustrating technical problems; on the other, they can be embraced as part of the continued interaction of materials, another layer in the technological assemblages of analogue filmmaking and cinema. Mainstream media culture demands that films be represented by means of seamless, flawless copies of the original, but glitches can be culturally generative, too. Anthropologists Brian Larkin (2004) and Lotte Hoek (2010) have studied, respectively, the reproduction of pirate videos in Nigeria and spliced films in Bangladesh; both attend to "the small, ubiquitous experience of breakdown as a condition of technological existence" (Larkin 2004, 304). Hitches and patches reflect and give rise to particular meanings in their cultural contexts so that, for instance, the fuzzing and fading of the pirate videos stands in for the political marginality and infrastructural inadequacy of Nigeria, and the films spliced to insert cut-pieces (censored scenes) or cover over burn-outs tantalize and torment audiences in an exuberant, unpredictable collective experience of reception in Bangladesh. In other words, breakdowns can be understood not as failures but as enrichments of the material – not only to those media artists who have embraced the new genre of "glitch art" but also, potentially, to audiences. In these ways, the intentional and unintentional material constraints of the installation both inspired and confounded the filmmakers, shaping the city-symphony films not only as they were created but also as they were projected and received. This leads us to a last potential interaction between components of the Situated Cinema and to the question of how our ethnographic project shaped this artistic urban intervention.

ARTISTS AND SOCIAL SCIENTISTS: A CURIOUS ENCOUNTER

Our pop-up ethnography was not a full collaboration between artists and social scientists in the manner of many that Schneider and Wright (2010, 2013) and Dear et al. (2011) present. We were not doing any kind of pop-up "ethnographic conceptualism" (Ssorin-Chaikov 2013), a melding of art and anthropology, which consists in conducting ethnography by means of conceptual art or making conceptual art by means of ethnography. Our collaboration with artists was partial. We had the consent of the creators to conduct fieldwork during the exhibition of the Situated Cinema but just as we did not shape the design of the Cinema, they did not shape the design of our research. What we did have was a rare opportunity to analyze a temporary art installation not only through the *a priori* intentions of its creators and the a *posteriori* interpretations of its critics and documenters but at the very moment of its exhibition to the public. Precisely because the Situated Cinema was mobile, requiring a great deal of labour from its architect-designers (to set it up and take it down) and its curator (to fix the fragile projector), and was also temporary, available for a limited time only as part of a four-day festival that most of its filmmakers attended, we were able to probe the creators' perspectives *in situ*. This is different from other empirical research on how members of the public interact with public art, which usually focuses on permanent artworks where the artists are not in attendance (e.g. Zebracki 2013; Vernet 2015 and this volume). Moreover, because we were communicating with the artists, we became much more conscious of how, as social scientists, our own approach and role at the installation differed from theirs. Our experiences investigating the Situated Cinema threw into stark relief the ways that the expectations, goals, and methods that artists and social scientists have vis-à-vis urban public art can diverge.

As observers who were most interested in viewer-participants' experiences (at least at first), we arrived in Winnipeg assuming that the "best" location for the Situated Cinema would be one that attracted the most people, and we admit that we were disappointed at the low numbers of visitors. However, it became apparent that once technical requirements were met, aesthetic dimensions played a more important part than mere traffic flows in siting the Cinema. One layer of the aesthetics was how the structure looked in relation to its architectural surroundings (the pet's owners, to recall Tsukamoto 2003). Another layer was the artists' rejection of the spatial language of the urban spectacle, and their consequent refusal to impose the Situated Cinema on busy public paths and places. Nagler, the curator, came to interpret the installation as a performative gesture, which would have been equally or even more beautiful if it had been executed in an empty prairie field where nobody saw it at all. Curiously, having set out to reconfigure the traditional cinema, the project ended up reproducing its interiority: as one of the filmmakers noted, "by hiding the [Situated Cinema] or putting it in not readily or easily accessible locations, it gives back this kind of isolated/personal/immersive experience which the actual cinema theatre can provide." However, this is the kind of reference that might have been lost on the public at large. The Situated Cinema, as a temporary intervention, effectively acknowledged the processes of the social production of space (Lefebvre 1991; Low 2000) in that it subverted the cinema as a hermetic structure and instead made it engage with the city. But – even though it was not site-specific in the strict sense of being explicitly created for and determined by its sites (Kwon 2002, 11) – it intervened more deliberately in the spatial, material, and aesthetic dynamics of the sites than in their social uses and relations.

What this highlights is that art in public space is not always art for the public, in the stronger sense of public art outlined by Phillips ([1989] 2004) and Massey and Rose as inviting "negotiation among diverse social identities" (2003, 19). For some artists – though by no means all – the engagement of audiences or publics with an artwork may not be as important as the act of creation itself. This can be difficult for some social scientists (especially those interested in the public's reception or experience of art) and members of the public to accept. We may want to believe that artworks are created in order to engage audiences in some kind of dialogue with their artists, and indeed, some artists would live up to that expectation. But understandably, the dialogue that is most important to many artists is going on elsewhere, with fellow practitioners and other colleagues in the art world (Crehan 2011, 29–31), not with the public at large nor with those social scientists who are so interested in the public. Different disciplinary training and mechanisms of recognition thus produce different goals for a semicollaborative project such as ours. There is a tension between the overarching objectives of art and anthropology, which Grimshaw, Owen, and Ravetz found in their interdisciplinary collaborations: "The artist's practice or art-work remained a fundamental premise of contemporary art, despite its growing interest in social worlds. This premise mediated other important relationships such as those between artist and audience. In anthropology, however, the crucial element was not individual practice but the social world studied. Without it, anthropology had little meaning" (2010, 156). We would suggest that although the Situated Cinema was intended for public space, the most important interlocutors for its creators were cinema aficionados at WNDX and, by extension, contemporary media art, architecture, and design world insiders. What our ethnographic approach was able to contribute to the conversation, though, was the degree to which "lay" viewer-participants, drawing on their own variable cultural repertoires, also picked up on the cinematic references in their immediate understanding of the intervention.

Our pop-up ethnography had its limitations. For instance, we are missing an analysis of the genesis of the Situated Cinema and WNDX in relation to arts and culture policy and the broader urban political economy in Winnipeg, as Bain and Rallis (this volume) achieve in relation to the art crawls and Supercrawl in Hamilton. Another point is that our continuous presence at the Situated Cinema undoubtedly affected the way that members of the public approached it. During periods with very low numbers of visitors, we perhaps had that air of market researchers or charity-donation-seekers just waiting for their next prey, which may have put people off. In addition, our methods – like all methods – are only partially adequate for understanding their object of study. The technique of exit interviews records immediate reactions, whereas art often lingers in the mind as something that resonates and is mulled over for a long time following one's first encounter with it. Our pop-up ethnography popped up to capture experiences *in situ* but could not record the traces that the Situated Cinema left behind. More to the point, the very fact of being asked to reflect immediately on an artwork shapes one's longer-term experience of it. Our interviews with viewer-participants did not simply record but generated reactions to the Cinema, a fact that a few interviewees explicitly commented on. The observer's paradox was clearly in operation here, as the urban anthropologists became as much a part of the artistic intervention as the films and the Cinema structure were. Social researchers can never extricate themselves completely from the social settings they study. Rather than trying to do so, we have found that thinking about our own implication in the Situated Cinema helped us think through how artists' and anthropologists' principles, purposes, and practices diverge – perhaps the better to reconverge. More fundamentally, this has made us reflect – inconclusively – on what and who art in urban public spaces is for.

The Situated Cinema was the site of many kinds of urban encounters: between passersby and an unexpected art installation, between the structure and four public spaces, between the designers and the site managers, between the filmmakers and the constraints of their brief and their materials, between the WNDX festivalgoers and a rich knot of cinematic references, between the Nuit Blanche crowds and an intimidating yet playful big black box, and between art and anthropology. Exploring some of the dimensions of these encounters opens up productive lines of inquiry into the sociality, spatiality, and artfulness of cities.

Notes

1 The Situated Cinema was funded principally by a grant made to WNDX from the Canada Council for the Arts with lesser financial or in-kind support from other federal and provincial government agencies, cultural organizations, and universities including the *Tracing the City* project (note 3). A stop-motion video of how the Situated Cinema was assembled (at the Winnipeg Art Gallery) and demounted (at the University of Winnipeg) can be viewed at http://vimeo.com/52432509. Accessed 18 May 2016.

2 The films were *Belvédère* (Alexandre Larose, Montreal), *Portal* (Alex MacKenzie, Vancouver), *Gephyrophobia* (Caroline Monnet, Ottawa/Gatineau; http://vimeo.com/39421642), *Between* (Heidi Phillips, Winnipeg; http://vimeo.com/52698828), and *This Town of Toronto Is the Best Place I Ever Ran Into* (Izabella Pruska-Oldenhof, Toronto; http://vimeo.com/77234210). Films accessed 18 May 2016.

3 *Tracing the City: Interventions of Art in Public Space* was funded by the Social Sciences and Humanities Research Council of Canada Research/Creation Grants in Fine Arts Award no. 848-2010-0019, 2011–15. The principal investigators were Solomon Nagler (coauthor of chapter 6), Kim Morgan (coauthor of chapter 7), and Martha Radice. The Situated Cinema as a project also drew on other sources of funding (see note 1) and inspiration including a summer school course taught by Evans and Rodmore at NSCAD University and the Dalhousie University School of Architecture in 2010, which produced a "periscopic" cinema.

4 The Situated Cinema itself was not framed as a "pop-up" intervention. Pop-up galleries, shops, restaurants, libraries, and the like have become a feature of many cities, especially those hit hard by recession, where the lack of funds to start a permanent venture are mirrored by the availability of vacant storefronts or other spaces to rent on a very short-term basis (Cochrane 2010; Rowan Moore 2013). Although they can be seen as a fun way to put otherwise empty spaces to use and are often marketed as exclusive and trendy precisely because they are ephemeral, pop-ups have also been criticized (and parodied) in the UK as an impoverished response to austerity, underemployment, and urban restructuring in favour of consumption and the so-called creative economy (Hatherley 2013).

5 The atmosphere of the first installation of the Situated Cinema outside the RAW Gallery is captured in the video of highlights of WNDX 2012 (available at http://www.wndx.org/highlights-2012/), which features brief comments from Solomon Nagler, Alexandre Larose, Alex MacKenzie, and Izabella Pruska-Oldenhof. Accessed 18 May 2016.

6 At least one artist has, however, created a bouncy castle as a certain critique of spectacle (Jones 2012). Thanks to Laurent Vernet for this reference and other insights in his astute reading of our text. We also thank Craig Rodmore for his useful comments and help with the illustrations.

BIBLIOGRAPHY

5468796 Architecture and Jae-Sung Chon. 2012. *Venice Catalogue.* Winnipeg, MB: 5468796 Architecture.

Adorno, Theodor W. 1974. *Minima Moralia.* Translated by E.F.N. Jephcott. London: Verso.

Agence QMI. 2012. "Plus d'alcool au Piknic Électronik." *Le Journal de Montréal,* 1 November.

Antwi, Phanuel, and Amber Dean. 2010. "Unfixing Imaginings of the City: Art, Gentrification, and Cultures of Surveillance." *Affinities: A Journal of Radical Theory, Culture, and Action.* 4 (2): 17–27.

Appadurai, Arjun. 1996. *Modernity at Large.* Minneapolis: University of Minnesota Press.

Archer, John. 2011. "Everyday Suburbia: Lives and Practices." *Public* 43: 21–30.

Arendt, Hannah. 2007. "The Conquest of Space and the Stature of Man." *The New Atlantis* 18: 43–55.

Artaud, Antonin. 1958. *The Theater and Its Double.* Translated by Mary Caroline Richards. New York: Grove.

Artifact Institute. 2015. "About the Artifact Institute." Fieldwork Residency Project. Accessed 22 June. http://fieldwork-hrm.org/wp/artifact-institute/.

Augé, Marc. 1995. *Non-Places: An Introduction to an Anthropology of Supermodernity.* Translated by John Howe. London: Verso.

Badger, Gina. 2012a. "Temagami Crescent." Blackwood Gallery, 23 April. Accessed 30 May 2015. http://blackwoodgallery.ca/exhibitions/2012/doortodoor4.html.

– 2012b. "Temagami Crescent." Gina Badger: Art + Research, 13 April. Accessed 30 May 2015. http://ginabadger.ca/2012/04/13/temagami-crescent/.

Baillargeon, Stéphane. 1993. "Vie et mort de l'art public." *Le Devoir,* 31 July.

Bain, Alison L. 2005. "Constructing an Artistic Identity." *Work, Employment, and Society* 19 (1): 25–46.

– 2013. *Creative Margins: Cultural Production in Canadian Suburbs*. Toronto: University of Toronto Press.

Bain, Alison L., and Heather McLean. 2013. "The Artistic Precariat." *Cambridge Journal of Regions, Economy, and Society* 6 (1): 93–111.

Bakhtin, Mikhail. 1984. *Rabelais and His World*. Translated by Hélène Iswolsky. Bloomington: Indiana University Press.

– 1990. *Art and Answerability: Early Philosophical Essays*. Edited by Michael Holquist and Vadim Liapunov. Austin: University of Texas Press.

Barber, Bruce. 2013. *Littoral Art and Communicative Action*. Edited by Marc James Léger. Champaign, IL: Common Ground.

Barrett, Alex. 2014. "The Sound of Silents: Is It Time to Revive the 'City Symphony' Film Genre?" *The Guardian*, 26 September. Accessed 21 May 2016. http://www.theguardian.com/cities/2014/sep/26/city-symphony-silent-films-genre-barbican.

Barthes, Roland. 1986. *The Rustle of Language*. New York: Hill & Wang.

Beebe, James. 1995. "Basic Concepts and Techniques of Rapid Appraisal." *Human Organization* 54: 42–51.

Bélanger, Anouk. 2005. "Montréal vernaculaire / Montréal spectaculaire : Dialectique de l'imaginaire urbain." *Sociologie et sociétés* 37 (1): 13–34.

Bellemare, Andrea. 2012. "Engineering Students' Exam Interrupted by Flash Mob." *CBC News*, 21 September. Accessed 12 December 2014. http://www.cbc.ca/newsblogs/yourcommunity/2012/09/engineering-students-exam-interrupted-by-flash-mob.html.

Bengtsen, Peter. 2013. "Beyond the Public Art Machine: A Critical Examination of Street Art as Public Art." *Konsthistorisk tidskrift/Journal of Art History* 82 (2): 63–80.

Bennett, Kelly. 2015. "Police Walk Line between 'Proactive Policing' and Privacy Downtown." *CBC News*, 4 March. Accessed 11 June 2015. www.cbc.ca/news/canada/hamilton/news/police-walk-line-between-proactive-policing-and-privacy-downtown-1.2980140.

Berardi, Franco Bifo. 2012. *Skizo-Mails*. Berlin: Errant Bodies.

Berger, Peter, and Thomas Luckmann. 1966. *The Social Construction of Reality*. New York: Anchor Books.

Berinstein, Florencia, Gloria Geller, Andrew Lochhead, and Ingrid Mayhofer. 2014. *Art as the New Steel? Changing and Challenging Perspectives on the*

James Street North Community, curated art exhibition. 9 May – 30 August. Hamilton, ON: Workers Art and Heritage Centre.

Bishop, Claire. 2004. "Antagonism and Relational Aesthetics." *October* 110: 51–79.

Blanchot, Maurice. 1987. "Everyday Speech." Translated by Susan Hanson. *Yale French Studies*, 73: 12–20.

– 1995. "Disorderly Words." In *The Blanchot Reader*, edited and translated by Michael Holland, 200–5. Cambridge, MA: Blackwell.

Blomley, Nicholas. 2005. "Flowers in the Bathtub: Boundary Crossings at the Public-Private Divide." *Geoforum* 36 (3): 281–96.

Blum, Alan. 2001. "Scenes." *Public: Art/Culture/Ideas* 22/23: 7–35.

– 2003. *The Imaginative Structure of the City.* Montreal & Kingston: McGill-Queen's University Press.

Boal, Augusto. 1985. *Theatre of the Oppressed.* Translated by Charles A. McBride and Maria-Odilia Leal McBride. New York: Theatre Communications Group.

Boivin, Julie. 2009. "Emerging Urban Aesthetics in Public Art: The Thresholds of Proximity." In *Public Art in Canada: Critical Perspectives*, edited by Annie Gérin and James S. McLean, 249–63. Toronto: University of Toronto Press.

Bonhomme, Jean-Pierre. 1993. "Sur le mont Royal, un groupe nettoie, l'autre pollue." *La Presse*, 25 May.

Boudreault-Fournier, Alexandrine. 2012. "Écho d'une rencontre virtuelle: Vers une ethnographie de la production audiovisuelle." *Anthropologica* 54 (1): 1–12.

– 2016. "Microtopia in Counterpoint: Relational Aesthetics and the Echo Project." *Cadernos de Arte e Antropologia* 5 (1): 135–54.

Bourdieu, Pierre. 1977. *Theory of Practice.* Cambridge: Cambridge University Press.

Bourdieu, Pierre, Alain Darbel, and Dominique Schnapper. 1969. *L'Amour de l'art, les musées d'art européens et leur public.* Paris: Les Éditions de minuit.

Bourriaud, Nicolas. 1998. *Esthétique relationnelle.* Dijon: Les presses du réel.

Boutros, Alexandra, and Will Straw. 2010. "Introduction." In *Circulation and the City: Essays on Urban Culture*, edited by Alexandra Boutros and Will Straw, 3–20. Montreal & Kingston: McGill-Queen's University Press.

Breitbart, Myrna. 2013. *Creative Economies in Post-Industrial Cities: Manufacturing a (Different) Scene.* Surrey, UK: Ashgate.

Brenner, Neil. 2013. "Theses on Urbanization." *Public Culture* 25 (1): 85–114.

Brigade SnW. 2008. "Arrêter le temps au Métro Berri-Uqam – Time Freeze." *YouTube* video, 1:53. Posted 7 April. Accessed 12 December 2014. https://www.youtube.com/watch?v=uilFI9gINeY.

Brighenti, Andrea Mubi. 2010. "At the Wall: Graffiti Writers, Urban Territoriality, and the Public Domain." *Space and Culture* 13 (3): 315–32.

Brown, David P. 2006. *Noise Orders: Jazz, Improvisation and Architecture.* Minneapolis: University of Minnesota Press.

Bruemmer, René. 2014. "Hippodrome Development Threatened as Agreement with Quebec Stalls." *Montreal Gazette*, 1 October. Accessed 18 June 2015. http://montrealgazette.com/news/local-news/ hippodrome-development-threatened-as-agreement-with-quebec-stalls.

Butler, Cornelia H. 2012. *From Conceptualism to Feminism: Lucy Lippard's Number Shows 1969–74.* London: Afterall.

Butler, Mark J. 2006. *Unlocking the Groove: Rhythm, Meter, and Musical Design in Electronic Dance Music.* Bloomington: Indiana University Press.

– 2012. *Electronica, Dance and Club Music.* Farnham, UK: Ashgate.

Caissie, Jean-Pierre. 2008. "Portrait d'une dislocation au Square Viger. Acteurs et notions de contrôle dans la gestion des espaces publics." In *Dis/location, projet d'articulation urbaine. Square Viger*, edited by Julie Boivin, Jean-Pierre Caissie, Jérôme Delgado, Raphaëlle de Groot, Marie-Suzanne Désilets, Louis Jacob, Fabien Loszach, Jean-François Prost and Armando Silvu, 3–14. Montréal: Dare-Dare.

Cameron, Sam. 2012. "Chinatown Revitalization: Laneway Strategy." *Laneways of Vancouver*, 26 July. Accessed 28 May 2016. https://lanewaysofvancouver. wordpress.com/.

– 2013. "Activating Vancouver's Laneways: Re:Imagining the Downtown Eastside's Under-Utilised Public Spaces." Unpublished MA diss., Royal Institute of Technology, Stockholm.

Carr, Stephen, Mark Francis, Leanne G. Rivlin, and Andrew M. Stone. 1992. *Public Space.* Cambridge: Cambridge University Press.

Cauchon, Paul. 2007. "Lancelot au pied de la montagne." *Le Devoir*, 23 July. Accessed 25 June 2015. www.ledevoir.com/societe/ actualites-en-societe/151126/macadam-lancelot-au-pied-de-la-montagne.

Cavell, Stanley. 2005. "Something Out of the Ordinary." In *Cavell on Film*, edited by William Rothman. Albany, NY: SUNY Press.

CBC News. 2014. "Supercrawl: 9 Visual Artist Installations Announced." *CBC News*, 6 August. Accessed 23 June 2015. www.cbc.ca/news/canada/hamilton/news/supercrawl-9-visual-artist-installations-announced-1.2728956

Center for Land Use Interpretation. 2015. "About the Center." Center for Land Use Interpretation. Accessed 25 June http://www.clui.org/section/about-center.

Cerwonka, Allaine, and Liisa H. Malkki. 2007. *Improvising Theory: Process and Temporality in Ethnographic Fieldwork*. Chicago: University of Chicago Press.

Chan, Emily. 2014. "Mystery Yarn-Bombers Leave Scarves around Ottawa." *CTV News*, 21 January. Accessed 1 March 2015. http://www.ctvnews.ca/canada/mystery-yarn-bomber-leaves-scarves-around-ottawa-1.1648920#.

Chan, Kenneth. 2013. "Telus Garden to Bring Pedestrianized Laneways to Vancouver." *Vancity Buzz*, 13 June. Accessed 28 May 2016. http://www.vancitybuzz.com/2013/06/telus-garden-project-unique-alley/.

Chtcheglov, Ivan. (1953)1982. "Formulary for a New Urbanism." In *Situationist International Anthology*, edited by Ken Knabb, 1–8. Berkeley: Bureau of Public Secrets.

City of Hamilton. 2013. *Transforming Hamilton through Culture: Cultural Plan 2013*. Hamilton, ON: Planning and Economic Development Department.

Clifford, James, and George E. Marcus. 1986. *Writing Culture: The Poetics and Politics of Ethnography*. Berkeley: University of California Press.

Cochrane, Kira. 2010. "Why Pop-Ups Pop Up Everywhere." *The Guardian*, 12 October. Accessed 21 May 2016. http://www.theguardian.com/lifeandstyle/2010/oct/12/pop-up-temporary-shops-restaurants.

Cohen, Abner. 1982. "A Polyethnic London Carnival as a Contested Cultural Performance." *Ethnic and Racial Studies* 5: 23–41.

Coleman, Nathaniel. 2013. "Utopian Prospect of Henri Lefebvre." *Space and Culture* 16 (3): 349–63.

Collier, David. 2012. *Hamilton Illustrated*. Hamilton, ON: Poplar.

Cook, Ian, and Mary Whowell. 2011. "Visibility and the Policing of Public Space." *Geography Compass* 5 (8): 610–22.

Corman, June, D.W. Livingston, Meg Luxton, and Wally Seccombe, eds. 2003. *Recasting Steel Labour: The Stelco Story*. Halifax, NS: Fernwood.

Crehan, Kate. 2011. *Community Art: An Anthropological Perspective*. Oxford: Berg.

Culhane, Dara. 2011. "Stories and Plays: Ethnography, Performance and Ethical Engagements." *Anthropologica* 53 (2): 229–43.

Dare-Dare. 2015. "Mission." *Dare-Dare.* Accessed 1 June. http://www.dare-dare. org/satellite/en/about-us/mission.

de Certeau, Michel. (1980) 1990. *L'invention du quotidien.* Vol. 1, *Arts de Faire.* Paris: Gallimard.

– 1984. *The Practice of Everyday Life.* Berkeley: University of California Press.

Dear, Michael, Jim Ketchum, Sarah Luria, and Douglas Richardson, eds. 2011. *GeoHumanities: Art, History, Text at the Edge of Place.* London: Routledge.

Debord, Guy. 1958. "Theory of the Derive." Translated by Ken Knabb. Originally published in *Les Lèvres Nues* 9. Accessed 31 May 2016. http://www.cddc. vt.edu/sionline/si/theory.html.

– 1994. *The Society of the Spectacle.* New York: Zone Books.

Deleuze, Gilles, and Felix Guattari. 1987. *A Thousand Plateaus: Capitalism and Schizophrenia.* Minneapolis: University of Minnesota Press.

Derrida, Jacques. 2000. "Hostipitality." Translated by Barry Stocker and Forbes Morlock. *Angelaki* 5 (3): 3–18.

Deutsche, Rosalyn. 1996. "Agoraphobia." In *Evictions: Art and Spatial Politics,* 269–327. Cambridge, MA: MIT Press.

Dion, Jean. 1993. "Pas de déchets au petit écran." *Le Devoir,* 25 May.

Doyon, Frédérique. 2012. "Dix ans de Piknic électronik, ça se fête en quatre nocturnes." *Le Devoir,* 28 June. Accessed 25 June 2015. www.ledevoir.com/culture/musique/353434/ dix-ans-de-piknic-electronik-ca-se-fete-en-quatre-nocturnes.

Drever, John Levack. 2002. "Soundscape Composition: The Convergence of Ethnography and Acousmatic Music." *Organised Sound* 7 (1): 21–7.

Drobnick, Jim, and Jennifer Fisher. 2012. "Editors' Introduction: Civic Spectacle." *Public* 45: 6–7.

Dunne, Anthony. 2001. *Hertzian Tales: Electronic Products, Aesthetic Experience, and Critical Design.* Boston: MIT Press.

Dworkin, Craig. 2013. *No Medium.* Cambridge, MA: MIT Press.

Edensor, Tim. 2010. "Walking in Rhythms: Place, Regulation, Style and the Flow of Experience." *Visual Studies* 25 (1): 69–79.

Eikels, Kai van. 2011. "What Parts of Us Can Do with Parts of Each Other (and When): Some Parts of This Text." *Performance Research: A Journal of the Performing Arts* 16 (3): 2–11.

– 2013. *Die Kunst des Kollektiven: Performance zwischen Theater, Politik und Sozio-Ökonomie*. Paderborn, DE: Fink.

Eylul Iscen, Ozgun. 2014. "In-Between Soundscapes of Vancouver: The Newcomer's Acoustic Experience of a City with a Sensory Repertoire of Another Place." *Organised Sound* 19 (2): 125–35.

Fabian, Johannes. 1983. *Time and the Other: How Anthropology Makes Its Object*. New York: Columbia University Press.

Feld, Steven, and Keith H. Basso, eds. 1996. *Senses of Place*. Santa Fe, NM: School of American Research Press.

Fikentscher, Kai. 2000. *You Better Work! Underground Dance Music in New York City*. Hanover, DE: Wesleyan University Press.

Financial Dictionary. 2015. "Game Theory." Investing Answers, 2001. Accessed 22 June. http://www.investinganswers.com/financial-dictionary/economics/game-theory-2160.

Florida, Richard. 2002. *The Rise of the Creative Class: And How It's Transforming Work, Leisure, Community, and Everyday Life*. New York: Basic Books.

– 2004. *Cities and the Creative Class*. New York: Routledge.

Fortin, Sylvie. 2009. "Apports possibles de l'ethnographie et de l'autoethnographie pour la recherche pratique en pratique artistique." In *La recherche création: Pour une compréhension de la recherche pratique artistique*, edited by Pierre Gosselin and Éric Le Coguiec, 97–109. Québec: Presses de l'Université du Québec.

Foster, Hal. 1995. "The Artist as Ethnographer?" In *The Traffic in Culture*, edited by George E. Marcus and Fred Myers, 300–15. Berkeley: University of California Press.

Foster, Susan Leigh. 2003. "Choreographies of Protest." *Theatre Journal* 55: 395–412.

Foucault, Michel (1986). "Of Other Spaces." Translated by Jay Misjowiec. *Diacritics* 16 (1): 22–7.

Franck, Karen A., and Quentin Stevens, eds. 2007. *Loose Space: Possibility and Diversity in Urban Life*. London: Routledge.

Fraser, Nancy. 1990. "Rethinking the Public Sphere: A Contribution to the Critique of Actually Existing Democracy." *Social Text* (25/26): 56–80.

Freud, Sigmund. (1905) 2003. *The Joke and Its Relation to the Unconscious*. Translated by Joyce Crick. New York: Penguin.

Gagnon, Monika Kin. 2006. "Tender Research: Field Notes from the Nikkei
    Internment Memorial Centre, New Denver, BC." *Canadian Journal of
    Communications* 31 (1): 215–25.
Gaitán, Juan A. 2013. "What Is the Public?" In *Ten Fundamental Questions of
    Curating*, edited by Jens Hoffman, 33–9. Milan: Mousse.
Garfinkel, Harold. 1967. *Studies in Ethnomethodology*. Englewood Cliffs, NJ:
    Prentice Hall.
Geledi, Sarah. 2012. "Hippodrome: A New Avant-Garde Neighbourhood
    by 2017." *Les Actualités*, 1 November. Accessed 22 June 2015.
    http://www.lesactualites.ca/01_anciensite/?site=CDN§ion=page&1=C1
    21031&2=C121031_hyppodrome.
Germain, Annick, Mabel Contin, Laurence Liégeois, and Martha Radice. 2008.
    "À propos du patrimoine urbain des communautés culturelles: nouveaux
    regards sur l'espace public." In *Les temps de l'espace public urbain:
    Construction, transformation et utilisation*, edited by Yona Jébrak and
    Barbara Julien, 123–43. Montréal: Éditions MultiMondes.
Germain, Rafaël. 2003. "Boum-boum. Les 25 ans des tam-tam du mont Royal."
    La Presse, 5 July.
Goffman, Erving. 1959. *Presentation of Self in Everyday Life*. New York: Anchor
    Books.
– 1963. *Behavior in Public Places: Notes on the Social Organization of Gatherings*.
    New York: Free Press.
Gondry, Michel (director and producer). 2008. *Be Kind Rewind*. Paris: Partizan.
Gosselin, Pierre. 2009. "La recherche en pratique artistique: spécificité et
    paramètres pour le développement de méthodologies." In *La recherche
    création: Pour une compréhension de la recherche en pratique artistique*,
    edited by Pierre Gosselin and Éric Le Coguiec, 21–31. Québec: Presses de
    l'Université du Québec.
Grafmeyer, Yves, and Jean-Yves Authier. 2008. *Sociologie urbaine*. 2nd ed. Paris:
    Armand Colin.
Graham, Dan. 1993. "Cinema (1981)." In *Rock My Religion, 1965–1990*, edited by
    Brian Wallis, 168–79. Cambridge: MIT Press.
Grimshaw, Anna, Elspeth Owen, and Amanda Ravetz. 2010. "Making Do: The
    Materials of Art and Anthropology." In *Between Art and Anthropology:
    Contemporary Ethnographic Practice*, edited by Arnd Schneider and
    Christopher Wright, 147–62. Oxford: Berg.

Grossman, Alyssa R. 2010. "Chorographies of Memory: Everyday Sites and Practices of Remembrance Work in Post-Socialist, EU Accession-Era Bucharest." PhD diss., University of Manchester.

Gubbay, Aline. 1979. "Three Montreal Monuments: An Expression of Nationalism." Master's thesis, Concordia University.

Haacke, Hans. 1975. *Framing and Being Framed: 7 Works, 1970–75*. Halifax, NS: Press of the Nova Scotia College of Art and Design.

Habermas, Jürgen. 1974. "The Public Sphere: An Encyclopedia Article (1964)." *New German Critique* 3: 49–55.

– 1989. *The Structural Transformation of the Public Sphere: An Inquiry into a Category of Bourgeois Society*. Cambridge, MA: MIT Press.

Hachey, Isabelle. 1994. "Tam-tam, propre, propre." *Le Devoir*, 29 April.

Haiven, Max. 2012. "Halifax's *Nocturne* Versus (?) the Spectacle of Neoliberal Civics." *Public* 23 (45): 78–93.

Hall, Tim. 2007. "Artful Cities." *Geography Compass* 1 (6): 1376–92.

Handfield, Catherine. 2008. "Les tam-tam on 30 ans… leur mystère aussi." *La Presse*, 11 May.

Hannula, Mika. 2006. *The Politics of Small Gestures: Chances and Challenges for Contemporary Art*. Istanbul: art-ist.

Hatherley, Owen. 2013. "Pop-Ups Are Papering over Our Crumbling Social Structures." *The Guardian*, 28 June. Accessed 21 May 2016. http://www.theguardian.com/commentisfree/2013/jun/28/pop-ups-crumbling-social-structures.

Hawkins, Gay. 2006. *The Ethics of Waste: How We Relate to Rubbish*. Toronto: Rowman & Littlefield.

Heinich, Nathalie. 1996. "L'art contemporain exposé aux rejets : Contribution à une sociologie des valeurs." *Hermès* 20: 193–204.

– 1997. "Outsider Art and Insider Artists: Gauging Public Reactions to Contemporary Public Art." In *Outsider Art: Contesting Boundaries in Contemporary Culture*, edited by Vera L. Zolberg and Joni Maya Cherbo, 118–27. Cambridge: Cambridge University Press.

Helmreich, Stefan. 2007. "An Anthropologist Underwater: Immersive Soundscapes, Submarine Cyborgs, and Transductive Ethnography." *American Ethnologist* 24 (4): 621–41.

Hennion, Antoine. 1993. *La passion musicale: Une sociologie de la médiation*. Paris: A.-M. Métailié.

– 2005. "Public de l'œuvre, œuvre du public?" *L'Inouï, Revue de l'IRCAM* 1: 64–8.

Hirschkop, Ken. 1999. *Mikhail Bakhtin: An Aesthetic for Democracy*. Oxford: Oxford University Press.

Hoek, Lotte. 2010. "Unstable Celluloid: Film Projection and the Cinema Audience in Bangladesh." *BioScope: South Asian Screen Studies* 1 (1): 49–66.

Holte, Michael Ned. 2006. "The Administrative Sublime, or The Center for Land Use Interpretation." *Afterall* 13, n.p. Accessed 31 May 2016. http://www.afterall.org/journal/issue.13/administrative.sublime.or.center.land.use.interpre.

Horowitz, Gregg M. 1996. "Public Art/Public Space: The Spectacle of the Tilted Arc Controversy." *The Journal of Aesthetics and Art Criticism* 54 (1): 8–14.

Howes, David, Kim Morgan, Martha Radice, and David Szanto. 2013. "The Sensory City Workshop: Sensing the City through Touch and Taste." Montreal: Centre for Sensory Studies Working Paper Series, Concordia University. Accessed 28 May 2016. http://www.centreforsensorystudies.org/the-sensory-city-workshop-sensing-the-city-through-touch-and-taste/.

Hutchinson, Brian. 2013. "Forgotten 'Country Lane' Experiment Could Be Answer to Vancouver's Desire for More Green Space." *National Post*, 2 July. Accessed 28 May 2016. http://news.nationalpost.com/2013/07/02/forgotten-country-lane-experiment-could-be-answer-to-vancouvers-desire-for-more-green-space/.

Idle No More. 2015. "The Vision." *IdleNoMore*. Accessed 1 March 2015. http://www.idlenomore.ca/vision.

Imai, Heide. 2008. "Senses on the Move: Multisensory Encounters with Street Vendors in the Japanese Urban Alleyway Roji." *Senses and Society* 3 (3): 329–38.

– 2010. "Sensing Tokyo's Alleyways: Everyday Life and Sensory Encounters in the Alleyways of a City in Transition." In *Everyday Life in Asia: Social Perspectives on the Senses*, edited by Devorah Kalekin-Fishman and Kelvin E.Y. Low, 63–84. Surrey, UK: Ashgate.

– 2013. "The Liminal Nature of Alleyways: Understanding the Alleyway Roji as a 'Boundary' Between Past and Present." *Cities* 34: 58–66.

Inagaki, Tatsuo. 2010. "Fieldwork as Artistic Practice." In *Between Art and Anthropology: Contemporary Ethnographic Practice*, edited by Arnd Schneider and Christopher Wright, 75–81. Oxford: Berg.

Ingold, Tim. 2013. *Making: Anthropology, Archaeology, Art and Architecture.* London: Routledge.

Jackson, Phil. 2004. *Inside Clubbing: Sensual Experiences in the Art of Being Human.* London: Bloomsbury.

Jacob, Mary Jane. 1999. "On Locating the Public in Public Art." In *Sur l'expérience de la ville: Interventions en milieu urbain,* edited by Marie Fraser, 101–5. Montréal: Optica.

Jacobs, Jane. 1961. *The Death and Life of Great American Cities.* New York: Vintage Books.

Johnstone, Keith. 1981. *Impro: Improvisation and the Theatre.* New York: Routledge.

Jonas, Marieluise and Heike Rahmann. 2012. "Interstitial Natures: The Alternative Production of Space." In *Opportunistic Urban Design: Book of Proceedings of the 5th International Urban Design Conference,* 50–7. Nerang, AU: AST Management.

Jones, Jonathan. 2012. "Jeremy Deller's Bouncy Castle Softens the Image of Stonehenge." *The Guardian,* 2 August. Accessed 21 May 2016. http://www.theguardian.com/artanddesign/jonathanjonesblog/2012/aug/02/jeremy-deller-stonehenge-bouncy-castle.

Jorgensen, Anna, and Marian Tylecote. 2007. "Ambivalent Landscapes: Wilderness in the Urban Interstices." *Landscape Research* 32 (4): 443–62.

Karrholm, Mattias. 2011. "Waiting Places as Temporal Interstices and Agents of Change." *Internet Journal for Cultural Sciences* 18. Accessed 28 May 2016. http://www.inst.at/trans/18Nr/II-1/kaerrholm_sandin18.htm.

Kazubowski-Houston, Magdalena. 2010. *Staging Strife: Lessons from Performing Ethnography with Polish Roma Women.* Montreal & Kingston: McGill-Queen's University Press.

Kester, Grant H. 2004. *Conversation Pieces: Community and Communication in Modern Art.* Berkeley: University of California Press.

King, Ronald. 2011. "Le dernier homme debout." *La Presse,* 1 August. Accessed 25 June 2015. www.lapresse.ca/debats/chroniques/ronald-king/201107/31/01-4422440-le-dernier-homme-debout.php.

Kirby, Kathleen M. 1996. *Indifferent Boundaries: Spatial Concepts of Human Subjectivity.* New York: Guilford.

Kitchen, Peter, Allison Williams, and Dylan Simone. 2012. "Measuring Social Capital in Hamilton, Ontario." *Social Indicators Research* 108: 215–38.

Knabb, Ken, ed. 1995. *Situationist International Anthology.* Berkeley: Bureau of
Public Secrets.

Kraven, Karen. 2011. "Apartment Hunting." Blackwood Gallery, 12 December.
Accessed 30 May 2015. http://blackwoodgallery.ca/exhibitions/2011/
doortodoor3.html.

Kristeva, Julia. 1991. *Strangers to Ourselves.* Translated by Leon S. Roudiez.
New York: Columbia University Press.

Kwon, Miwon. 2002. *One Place After Another: Site-Specific Art and Locational
Identity.* Cambridge, MA: MIT Press.

La Presse. 2001. "Les combats du dimanche près de la place des tam-tams."
La Presse, 16 September.

Labelle, Brandon. 2011. *Acoustic Territories: Sound Culture and Everyday Life.*
New York: Continuum.

Lacy, Suzanne, ed. 1995. *Mapping the Terrain: New Genre Public Art.* Seattle:
Bay Press.

Lamarche, Bernard. 2003. "Nouvel événement au parc Jean-Drapeau. Que
diriez-vous d'un beau dimanche après-midi... électronique." *Le Devoir,* 30
June. Accessed 25 June 2015. www.ledevoir.com/non-classe/30900/nouvel-
evenement-au-parc-jean-drapeau-que-diriez-vous-d-un-beau-dimanche-
apres-midi-electronique.

Larkin, Brian. 2004. "Degraded Images, Distorted Sounds: Nigerian Video and
the Infrastructure of Piracy." *Public Culture* 16 (2): 289–314.

Latour, Bruno. 2005. *Re-assembling the Social: An Introduction to Actor-
Network Theory.* Oxford: Oxford University Press.

Lean, David (director). 1945. *Brief Encounter.* Produced by Noel Coward.
London: Cineguild.

Lefebvre, Henri. 1991. *The Production of Space.* Translated by Donald
Nicholson-Smith. Oxford: Blackwell.

– 1996. "Right to the City." In *Writings on Cities,* translated and edited by
Eleonore Kofman and Elizabeth Lebas, 118–21. Massachussets: Blackwell.

– 2003. *The Urban Revolution.* Minneapolis: University of Minnesota Press.

– 2004. *Rhythmanalysis: Space, Time and Everyday Life.* London: Continuum.

Lefebvre, Henri, Catherine Régulier, and Mohamed Zayani. 1999. "The
Rhythmanalytical Project." *Rethinking Marxism* 11 (1): 5–13.

Levesque, Luc. 2002. "The 'Terrain Vague' as Material – Some Observations."
SYN: Atelier d'exploration urbaine. Accessed 28 May 2016. http://www.
amarrages.com/textes_terrain.html.

Levine, Robert N. 1997. *A Geography of Time: On Tempo, Culture, and the Pace of Life*. New York: Basic Books.

Lewis, Nathaniel, and Betsy Donald. 2010. "A New Rubric for 'Creative City' Potential in Canada's Smaller Cities." *Urban Studies* 47 (1): 29–54.

Ley, David. 2003. "Artists, Aestheticization, and the Field of Gentrification." *Urban Studies* 40 (12): 2527–44.

Liinamaa, Saara. 2014. "Contemporary Art's 'Urban Question' and Practices of Experimentation." *Third Text* 28 (6): 529–44.

Lloyd, Richard. 2006. *Neo-Bohemia: Art and Commerce in the Postindustrial City*. New York: Routledge.

Lofland, Lyn H. 1998. *The Public Realm: Exploring the City's Quintessential Social Territory*. Hawthorne, NY: Aldine de Gruyter.

Lossau, Julia, and Quentin Stevens, eds. 2015. *The Uses of Art in Public Space*. New York: Routledge.

Loubier, Patrice. 2001. "Avoir lieu, disparaître : sur quelques passages entre art et réalité." In *Les Commensaux: Quand l'art se fait circonstances / When art becomes circumstance*, edited by Patrice Loubier and Anne-Marie Ninacs, 18–29. Montréal: Centre des arts actuels Skol.

Low, Setha M. 2000. *On the Plaza: The Politics of Public Space and Culture*. Austin: University of Texas Press.

Low, Setha M., and Neil Smith. 2006. *The Politics of Public Space*. New York: Routledge.

Low, Setha M., Dana H. Taplin, and Mike Lamb. 2005. "Battery Park City: An Ethnographic Field Study of the Community Impact of 9/11." *Urban Affairs Review* 40 (5): 655–82.

Luka, Nik. 2012. "Hippodrome neighbourhood images." Private collection.

Lynch, Kevin. 1960. *The Image of the City*. Cambridge: MIT Press.

MacDougall, David. 2005. *The Corporeal Image: Film, Ethnography, and the Senses*. Princeton, NJ: Princeton University Press.

Madanipour, Ali. 2004 "Marginal Public Spaces in European Cities." *Journal of Urban Design* 9 (3): 267–86.

Maranda, Michael. 2009. *Waging Culture: A Report on the Socio-Economic Status of Canadian Visual Artists*. Toronto: Art Gallery of York University.

Marcus, George E. 2010. "Contemporary Fieldwork Aesthetics in Art and Anthropology: Experiments in Collaboration and Intervention." *Visual Anthropology* 23: 263–77.

Marks, Laura U. 1998. "Video Haptics and Erotics." *Screen* 39 (4): 331–48.

Markusen, Ann. 2006. "Urban Development and the Politics of a Creative
     Class: Evidence from the Study of Artists." *Environment and Planning A*
     38 (10): 1921–40.
Martin, Michael. 2002. "The Case for Residential Back-Alleys: A North
     American Perspective." *Journal of Housing and the Built Environment* 17:
     145–71.
Massey, Doreen, and Gillian Rose. 2003. *Personal Views: Public Art Research
     Project*. Milton Keynes, UK: Artpoint Trust.
Matthias, Sebastian. 2015. "groove feeling – somatischer Sound und
     partizipative Performance." In *Sound und Performance. Positionen ·
     Methoden · Analysen*, edited by Wolf-Dieter Ernst, Anno Mungen, Nora
     Niethammer, and Berenika Szymanski. Würzburg, DE: Königshausen &
     Neumann. Vol. 27 in the series Thurnauer Schriften zum Musiktheater.
Mauss, Marcel. 1923–24. "Essai sur le don. Forme et raison de l'échange dans
     les sociétés archaïques." *L'Année sociologique, nouvelle série* 1 (1923–24):
     30–186.
– 1978. *Soziologie und Anthropologie*. Vol. 2. Edited by Wolf Lepenies and
     Henning Ritter. Frankfurt: UllsteinVerlag.
– 1990. *The Gift: The Form and Reason for Exchange in Archaic Societies*.
     Translated by W.D. Halls. New York: W.W. Norton.
McBride, Jason. 2012. "Catch Ya Later, Toronto." *Grid*, 14 November.
McCormack, Derek P. 2008. "Thinking-Space and Research-Creation."
     Inflexions 1 (1). Accessed 28 May 2016. http://www.inflexions.org/n1_
     mccormackhtml.html.
McGreal, Ryan. 2008. "A Work in Progress: James Street
     North in Transition." *Raise The Hammer*, 11 September.
     Accessed 29 October 2014. http://raisethehammer.org/
     article/765/a_work_in_progress:_james_north_in_transition.
Menger, Pierre-Michel. 1999. "Artistic Labour Markets and Careers." *Annual
     Review of Sociology* 25 (1): 541–74.
Merrifield, Andy. 2008. "Lefebvre and Debord: A Faustian Fusion." In *Space,
     Difference, Everyday Life: Reading Henri Lefebvre*, edited by Kanishka
     Goonewardena, Stefan Kipfer, Richard Milgrom, and Christian Schmid,
     176–89. New York: Routledge.
– 2011. "The Right to the City and Beyond." *City* 15 (3/4): 473–81.
– 2013. "The Urban Question Under Planetary Urbanization." *International
     Journal of Urban and Regional Research* 37 (3): 909–22.

Micallef, Shawn. 2013. "Take to the Streets! Why We Need Street Festivals to Know Our Civic Selves." In *Rites of Way: The Politics and Poetics of Public Space*, edited by Mark Kingwell and Patrick Turmel, 101–12. Waterloo, ON: Wilfred Laurier University Press.

MontrealFM1023. 2012. "Montreal KPOP Gangnam Style Flashmob 2012.10.13. v2." *YouTube* video, 11:30. Posted 17 October. Accessed 12 December 2014. https://www.youtube.com/watch?v=w8q7RBsxUEU.

Moore, Rowan. 2013. "The Pop-Up Designs Changing the City Landscape." *The Observer*, 3 August. Accessed 21 May 2016. http://www.theguardian.com/artanddesign/2013/aug/03/pop-up-designs-architecture-london.

Moore, Ryan. 2013. "The Beat of the City: Lefebvre and Rhythmanalysis." *Situations: Project of the Radical Imagination* 5 (1): 61–77.

Morehouse, Barbara J. 2004. "Theoretical Approaches to Border Spaces and Identity." In *Challenged Borderlands: Transcending Political and Cultural Boundaries*, edited by Vera Pavlakovich-Kochi, Barbara J. Morehouse and Doris Wastl-Walter, 19–39. Aldershot, UK: Ashgate.

Muse, John. 2010. "Flash Mobs and the Diffusion of Audience." *Theater* 40 (3): 8–23.

Nagler, Solomon. 2010. "Nonstick Cinema: On Leaving Out the Theatre." In *Sites for Seeing: Out of the Cineplex and Into the Marshlands*. Sackville, NB: Struts Gallery. Exhibition Catalogue.

Negarestani, Reza. 2011. "Rainbows and Rationalism: The Fate of the Terrestial Manifesto of Art." In ILLUMNInations: 54t*h International Art Exhibition; The Venice Biennale Catalogue*, edited by Bice Curiger and Giovanni Carmine. Venice: Marsilio Editori.

Németh, Jeremy. 2010. "Security in Public Space: An Empirical Assessment of Three US Cities." *Environment and Planning A* 42 (10): 2487–507.

Newman, Janet. 2007. "Re-mapping the Public: Public Libraries and the Public Sphere." *Cultural Studies* 21 (6): 887–909.

Norton, Jacqueline, and Paul Shaker. 2009. *Building a Creative Catalyst Feasibility Study*. Report PED08280(a). Hamilton, ON: Department of Planning and Economic Development.

November, Valérie, Eduardo Camacho-Hübner, and Bruno Latour. 2010. "Entering a Risky Territory: Space in the Age of Digital Navigation." *Environment and Planning D: Society and Space*, 28 (4): 581–99.

Nowacek, Nancy. 2012. "Not From Here." Nancy Nowacek. Accessed 30 May 2015. http://nancynowacek.com/not-from-here.

O'Doherty, Brian. 1999. *Inside the White Cube: The Ideology of the Gallery Space*. Berkeley: University of California Press.

O'Rourke, Karen. 2013. *Walking and Mapping: Artists as Cartographers*. Boston: MIT Press.

O'Shaughnessy, Brian. 1995. "Proprioception and the Body Image." In *The Body and the Self*, edited by José Luis Bermúdez, Anthony J. Marcel, and Naomi M. Eilan, 175–204. Cambridge, MA: MIT Press.

Olaveson, Tim, and Melanie Takahashi. 2003. "Music, Dance and Raving Bodies: Raving a Spirituality in the Central Canadian Rave Scene." *Journal of Ritual Studies* 17 (2): 72–96.

Pacey, Arnold. 1991. "Technology: Practice and Culture." In *Controlling Technology*, edited by Eric Katz, Andrew Light, William B. Thompson, 53–63. Buffalo: Prometheus Books.

Paquin, Gilles. 1993. "Blitz auprès des amateurs de tam-tam." *La Presse*, 31 May.

Peck, Jamie. 2005. "Struggling with the Creative Class." *International Journal of Urban and Regional Research* 29 (4): 740–70.

Pelchat, Martin. 1994. "La Ville, la police et les percussionnistes vont 'encadrer' les Tam-Jam au pied du mont Royal." *La Presse*, 29 April.

Pérez-Gómez, Alberto. 1994. "Chora: The Space of Architectural Representation." In *Chora: Intervals in the Philosophy of Architecture 1*, 1–34. Montreal & Kingston: McGill-Queen's University Press.

Phillips, Patricia. 1989. "Temporality and Public Art." *Art Journal* 48 (4): 331–5.

– (1989) 2004. "Out of Order: The Public Art Machine." In *The City Cultures Reader*, edited by Malcolm Miles, Tim Hall, and Iain Borden, 190–6. London: Routledge.

Phillips-Silver, Jessica, C. Athena Aktipis, and Gregory A. Bryant 2010. "The Ecology of Entrainment: Foundations of Coordinated Rhythmic Movement." *Music Perception* 28 (1): 3–14.

Piknic Électronik. 2014. "Mission." Piknic Électronik. Accessed 8 February 2015. http://www.piknicelectronik.com/en/about/mission.

Pink, Sarah. 2009. *Doing Sensory Ethnography*. Los Angeles: Sage.

Pogue, David. 2009. "The MP3 Experiment." Pogue's Posts: The Latest in Technology from David Pogue (column). *New York Times*, 28 May. Accessed 12 December 2014. http://www.nytimes.com/2009/05/28/technology/personaltech/28pogue-email.html.

Poussart, Marie-Anne. 1993. "La police vivement accueillie au tam-tam du dimanche." *La Presse*, 16 August.

Prager, Karen J. 1995. *The Psychology of Intimacy*. New York: The Gilford Press.

Pressing, Jeff. 2002. "Black Atlantic Rhythm: Its Computational and Transcultural Foundations." *Music Perception* 19: 285–310.

Qayyum, Tazeen. 2012. "Threading Encounters." Blackwood Gallery, 23 April. Accessed 30 May 2015. http://blackwoodgallery.ca/exhibitions/2012/doortodoor4.html.

Quagliotto, Nathalie. 2013. "Gallery Intervention." Blackwood Gallery, 29 April. Accessed 30 May 2015. http://blackwoodgallery.ca/exhibitions/2013/doortodoor6.html.

Quinn, Bernadette. 2005. "Arts Festivals and the City." *Urban Studies*, 42 (5/6): 927–43.

Rail, Christianne (project manager). 2012. *Development of the Hippodrome de Montréal Area – Preparatory Document – Forum of Experts – December 9,10, and 11, 2012*. Montreal: City of Montreal.

Rallis, Nicole, and Layla Mashkoor (directors and producers). 2012. *This Is Hamilton ... After the Steel Rush*, filmed by Mark Hoyne. Hamilton, ON: Tiger in a Suit.

Rancière, Jacques. 2006. *Die Aufteilung des Sinnlichen. Die Politik der Kunst und ihre Paradoxien*. Edited and translated by Maria Muhle. Berlin: b_books.

– 2009. *Aesthetics and Its Discontents*. Translated by Steven Corcoran. Cambridge: Polity.

– 2010. *Dissensus: On Politics and Aesthetics*. Translated and edited by Steven Corcoran. London: Bloomsbury.

Reggio, Godfrey (director and producer). 1983. *Koyaanisqatsi*. Planegg, DE: Koch Media.

Reiss, Steven A. 1991. *City Games: The Evolution of American Urban Society and the Rise of Sports*. Chicago: University of Illinois Press.

Remy, Jean. 1972. "Urbanisation de la ville et production d'un régime d'échanges." *Sociologie et sociétés* 4 (1): 101–19.

– 1987. "La limite et l'interstice: La structuration spatiale comme ressource sociale." In *La Theorie de l'espace humain: Transformations globales et structures locales*, edited by Pierre Pellegrino, 219–27. Geneva, CH: CRAAL-FNSRS, UNESCO.

Renaud, Philippe. 2010. "Piknic Électronik. La huitième saison s'annonce mémorable." *La Presse*, 21 May.

Rieti, John. 2014. "Humans of Supercrawl." *CBC News*, 14 September. Accessed 11 June 2015. http://www.cbc.ca/news/canada/hamilton/photos/ humans-of-supercrawl-1.2765532.

Robertson, Lisa. 2006. *Occasional Work and Seven Walks from the Office for Soft Architecture*. Toronto: Coach House.

Rodman, Margaret. 1992. "Empowering Place: Multilocality and Multivocality." *American Anthropologist* 94 (3): 640–56.

Rodmore, Craig, ed. 2013. *Demountable Cinema / Cinéma démontable*. Winnipeg, MB: WNDX. *Situated Cinema* Catalogue.

Rogoff, Irit. 2005. "Looking Away: Participations in Visual Culture." In *After Criticism: New Responses to Art and Performance*, edited by Gavin Butt, 117–34. Malden, MA: Blackwell.

Rosenfeld, Arno. 2014. "If You Think the Clock Tower Was Impressive." *The Ubyssey*, 7 February. Accessed 1 March 2015. http://ubyssey.ca/blog/ engineers-san-francisco-car-001/.

Rotenberg, Robert, and Gary McDonough, eds. 1993. *The Cultural Meaning of Urban Space*. Westport, CT: Bergin & Garvey.

Ruttman, Walter (director). 1927. *Berlin Symphony of a Great City*. Produced by Karl Freund. Berlin: Deutsche Vereins-Film and Les Productions Fox Europa.

Sage, Vanessa E. 2013. "Visions of James Street North." PhD diss., McMaster University.

Sansi, Roger. 2015. *Art, Anthropology and the Gift*. London: Bloomsbury.

Sassen, Saskia. 2006. "Public Interventions: The Shifting Meaning of the Urban Condition." *Open* 11,18–26. Accessed 24 June 2015. http://www.skor.nl/_ files/Files/OPEN11_P18-26.pdf.

Schafer, R. Murray. 1977. *The Soundscape: Our Sonic Environment and the Tuning of the World*. Rochester, VT: Destiny Books.

Schechner, Richard. 1985. *Between Theater and Anthropology*. Philadelphia: University of Pennsylvania Press.

Schiller, Marc. 2009. "'New York Street Advertising Takeover' Brings Art to Over 120 Illegal Billboards in NYC." *Wooster Collective*, 26 April. Accessed 1 March 2015. http://www.woostercollective.com/post/ new-york-street-advertising-takeover-brings-art-to-over-120-illegal-billboa.

Schneider, Arnd, and Christopher Wright, eds. 2006. *Contemporary Art and Anthropology*. New York: Berg.

– 2010. *Between Art and Anthropology: Contemporary Ethnographic Practice.* Oxford: Berg.

– 2013. *Anthropology and Art Practice.* London: Bloomsbury.

Sennett, Richard. 1974. *The Fall of Public Man.* New York: Norton.

Seno, Ethel, ed. 2010. *Trespass: A History of Uncommissioned Urban Art.* Cologne: Taschen.

Serlio, Sebastiano. 1982. *Sebastiano Serlio on Architecture, Volume 1: Books I–V of "Tutte l'opere d'architettura et prospetiva."* Translated by Vaughan Hart and Peter Hicks. New Haven: Yale University Press.

Shapiro, Ben (director and producer). 2012. *Gregory Crewdson: Brief Encounters.* New York: Zeitgeist films.

Sharp, Joanne. 2007. "The Life and Death of Five Spaces: Public Art and Community Regeneration in Glasgow." *Cultural Geographies* 14 (2): 274–92.

Shepard, Mark. 2010. "On Hertzian Space and Urban Architecture." *Vague Terrain: Digital Art/Culture/Technology.* http://vagueterrain.net/journal16/mark-shepard/01 (site discontinued).

Shor, Mikhael. 2005. "Payoff." In *Dictionary of Game Theory Terms*, last modified 15 August. Accessed 22 June 2015. http://www.gametheory.net/dictionary/Payoff.html.

Silver, Daniel, and Terry N. Clark. 2015. "The Power of Scenes: Quantities of Amenities and Qualities of Places." *Cultural Studies* 29 (3): 425–49.

Simmel, Georg. (1903) 1950. "The Metropolis and Mental Life." In *The Sociology of Georg Simmel*, translated and edited by Kurt H. Wolff, 409–24. New York: Free Press.

– 1950. *The Sociology of Georg Simmel.* Translated and edited by Kurt H. Wolff. New York: Free Press.

Simonsen, Kirsten. 2005. "Bodies, Sensations, Space and Time: The Contribution from Henri Lefebvre." *Geografiska Annaler. Series B, Human Geography* 87 (1): 1–14.

Simpson, Bob. 2009. "Messages from the Field." *Anthropology Today* 25 (5): 1–3.

Skulenite. 2011. "'One Test More' – Engineering Musical Flashmob!" *YouTube* video, 4:24. Posted 25 September. Accessed 12 December 2014. https://www.youtube.com/watch?v=8majjGwwDZY.

– 2012. "'The Worst Test' – An Engineering Flash Mob." *YouTube* video, 4:19. Posted 15 September. Accessed 12 December 2014. https://www.youtube.com/watch?v=1lyHQLyZUuM.

Sloan, Johanne. 2007. "At Home on the Street: Public Art in Montreal and Toronto." In *Urban Enigmas: Montreal, Toronto, and the Problem of Comparing Cities*, edited by Johanne Sloan, 213–38. Montreal & Kingston: McGill-Queen's University Press.

Smith, Monica L. 2008. "Urban Empty Spaces: Contentious Places for Consensus-Building." *Archaeological Dialogues* 15 (2): 216–31.

Société du parc Jean-Drapeau. 2015. "About Us: Mission of the Parc Jean-Drapeau." Société du parc Jean-Drapeau. Accessed 14 February. http://www.parcjeandrapeau.com/en/about-us/.

Soja, Edward W. 2003. "Writing the City Spatially." *City* 7 (3): 269–80.

Solnit, Rebecca. 2000. *Wanderlust: A History of Walking*. New York: Viking Penguin.

SOS: Soul of the Street. 2011. "SOS: Soul of the Street." Factory Media Centre, 9 September. Accessed 11 June 2015. http://d4design.ca/factorymedia/index. php?option=com_k2&view=item&id=12:sos-soul-of-the-street-september-9-to-october-14-2011&Itemid=382.

Spolin, Viola. 1999. *Improvisation for the Theater: A Handbook of Teaching and Directing Techniques*. Evanston, IL: Northwestern University Press.

Ssorin-Chaikov, Nikolai. 2013. "Ethnographic Conceptualism." *Laboratorium* (2): 5–18.

Staeheli, Lynn A., and Don Mitchell. 2007. "Locating the Public in Research and Practice." *Progress in Human Geography* 31 (6): 792–811.

Stallabrass, Julian. 2004. *Art Incorporated: The Story of Contemporary Art*. Oxford: Oxford University Press.

Stamp, Robert M. 1991. "First Peoples on the Land." In *Early Days in Richmond Hill: A History of the Community to 1930*. Richmond Hill, ON: Richmond Hill Public Library Board. Accessed 30 May 2015. http://edrh.rhpl. richmondhill.on.ca/default.asp?ID=s2.4.

Steinberg, Neil. 1992. *If at All Possible, Involve a Cow: The Book of College Pranks*. New York: St Martin's.

Sterne, Jonathan. 2003. *The Audible Past: Cultural Origins of Sound Reproduction*. Durham, NC: Duke University Press.

– 2012. "Sonic Imaginations." In *The Sound Studies Reader*, edited by Jonathan Sterne, 1–17. London: Routledge.

Straw, Will. 2015. "Some Things a Scene Might Be: Postface." *Cultural Studies* 29 (3): 476–85.

Streeck, Jürgen, and Mark L. Knapp. 1992. "Interaction of Visual and Verbal Features." In *Advances in Nonverbal Communication: Sociocultural, Clinical, Esthetic, and Literary Perspectives*, edited by Fernando Poyatos, 3–23. Amsterdam: John Benjamins.

Sullivan, Graeme. 2010. *Art Practice as Research: Inquiry in Visual Arts.* London: Sage.

Taplin, Dana H., Suzanne Scheld, and Setha M. Low. 2002. "Rapid Ethnographic Assessment in Urban Parks: A Case Study of Independence National Historic Park." *Human Organization* 61 (1): 80–93.

Thompson, James. 2011. *Performance Affects: Applied Theatre and the End of Effect.* New York: Palgrave MacMillan.

Thompson, Nato, and Gregory Sholette, eds. 2004. *The Interventionists: User's Manual for the Creative Disruption of Everyday Life.* North Adams, MA: MASS MOCA Publications.

Thorns, David. 2002. *The Transformation of Cities: Urban Theory and Urban Life.* Basingstoke, UK: Palgrave.

Tingey, John. 2010. *The Englishman Who Posted Himself and Other Curious Objects.* New York: Princeton Architectural Press.

Todd, Charlie. 2004. "The MP3 Experiment." *Improv Everywhere*, 11 December. Accessed 12 December 2014. http://improveverywhere.com/2004/12/11/the-mp3-experiment/.

– 2005. "The MP3 Experiment 2.0." *Improv Everywhere*, 16 October. Accessed 12 December 2014. http://improveverywhere.com/2005/10/16/the-mp3-experiment-2-0/.

– 2006. "The MP3 Experiment III." *Improv Everywhere*, 17 June. Accessed 12 December 2014. http://improveverywhere.com/2006/06/17/the-mp3-experiment-iii/.

– 2007. "The MP3 Experiment Four." *Improv Everywhere*, 22 August. Accessed 12 December 2014. http://improveverywhere.com/2007/08/22/the-mp3-experiment-four/.

– 2008a. "Frozen Grand Central." *Improv Everywhere*, 31 January. Accessed 12 December 2014. http://improveverywhere.com/2008/01/31/frozen-grand-central/.

– 2008b. "The MP3 Experiment 5." *Improv Everywhere*, 20 October. Accessed 1 October 2009. http://improveverywhere.com/2008/10/20/the-mp3-experiment-5/.

– 2008c. "The MP3 Experiment Toronto." *Improv Everywhere*, 20 October. Accessed 12 December 2014. http://improveverywhere.com/2008/10/20/the-mp3-experiment-toronto/.

– 2008d. "MP3 NYC – Thanks!" *Improv Everywhere*, 27 September. Accessed 12 December 2014. http://improveverywhere.com/2008/09/27/mp3-nyc-thanks/.

– 2009. "The MP3 Experiment Six." *Improv Everywhere*, 15 June. Accessed 12 December 2014. http://improveverywhere.com/2009/06/15/the-mp3-experiment-six/.

– 2011a. "The MP3 Experiment Eight." *Improv Everywhere*, 25 July. Accessed 12 December 2014. http://improveverywhere.com/2011/07/25/the-mp3-experiment-eight/.

– 2011b. "Carousel Horse Race Prank by Improv Everywhere." *Urban Prankster*. 27 June. Accessed 12 December 2014. http://urbanprankster.com/.

– 2012a. "Meet a Black Person." *Improv Everywhere*, 6 February. Accessed 12 December 2014. http://improveverywhere.com/2012/02/06/meet-a-black-person/.

– 2012b. "The MP3 Experiment Nine." *Improv Everywhere*, 30 July. Accessed 12 December 2014. http://improveverywhere.com/2012/07/30/the-mp3-experiment-nine/.

– 2013. "The MP3 Experiment Ten." *Improv Everywhere*, July 22. Accessed 12 December 2014. http://improveverywhere.com/2013/07/22/the-mp3-experiment-ten/.

– 2014a. "FAQ." *Improv Everywhere*. Accessed 12 December 2014. http://improveverywhere.com/faq/.

– 2014b. "The MP3 Experiment Eleven." *Improv Everywhere*. 30 September. Accessed 12 December 2014. http://improveverywhere.com/2014/09/30/the-mp3-experiment-eleven/.

– 2015. "The No Pants Subway Rides." *Improv Everywhere*. Accessed 1 March 2015. http://improveverywhere.com/missions/the-no-pants-subway-ride/.

Toles, George. 2001. *A House Made of Light*. Detroit: Wayne State University Press.

Tonkiss, Fran. 2003. "The Ethics of Indifference: Community and Solitude in the City." *International Journal of Cultural Studies* 6 (3): 297–311.

Tonnelat, Stephane. 2008. "'Out of frame': The (In)Visible Life of Urban Interstices – A Case Study in Charenton-le-pont, Paris, France." *Ethnography* 9 (3): 291–324.

Tornatore, Giuseppe (director). 1988. *Nuovo Cinema Paradiso*. Produced by Franco Cristaldi and Giovanna Romagnoli. Paris: Les Films Ariane.

Tsukamoto, Yoshiharu. 2003. "Pet Architecture and how to Use it." *Sarai Reader* 3: 249–54.

Ukeles, Mierle Laderman. 1969. "Manifesto for Maintenance Art, 1969! Proposal for an Exhibition." Feldman Gallery. Accessed 22 June 2015. www.feldmangallery.com/media/pdfs/Ukeles_MANIFESTO.pdf.

Vanolo, Alberto. 2013. "Alternative Capitalism and Creative Economy: The Case of Christiania." *International Journal of Urban and Regional Research* 37 (5): 1785–98.

Vazquez, Alexandra T. 2013. *Listening in Detail: Performances of Cuban Music*. Durham, NC: Duke University Press.

Vernet, Laurent. 2014. "La vie sociale des œuvres d'art dans les espaces publics: une étude des publics au square Saint-Louis." *Environnement urbain / Urban Environment* 8: a1–a13. Accessed 2 October 2016. http://www.vrm.ca/wp-content/uploads/EUE8_Vernet.pdf.

– 2015. "The Social Life of Artworks in Public Spaces: A Study of the Publics in the Quartier International de Montréal." In *The Uses of Art in Public Space*, edited by Julia Lossau and Quentin Stevens, 149–66. New York: Routledge.

Vertov, Dziga (director). 1929. *Man with a Movie Camera*. Moscow: VUFKU.

Vidler, Anthony. 2002. *Warped Space: Art, Architecture, and Anxiety in Modern Culture*. Boston: MIT Press.

Ville de Montréal, Public Art Bureau. 2015. "Man, Three Discs." *Art Public: Ville de Montréal*. Accessed 22 June. http://artpublic.ville.montreal.qc.ca/en/oeuvre/trois-disques/.

Virilio, Paul. 1998. "'Is the Author Dead?' An Interview with Paul Virilio." In *The Virilio Reader*, edited by James Der Derian, 16–21. Hoboken, NJ: Wiley-Blackwell.

– 2009. *The Aesthetics of Disappearance*. Los Angeles: Semiotext(e).

Vitruvius Pollio, Marcus. 1960. *The Ten Books on Architecture*. Translated by Morris H. Morgan. New York: Dover.

Waitt, Gordon. 2008. "Urban Festivals: Geographies of Hype, Helplessness and Hope." *Geography Compass* 2 (2): 513–37.

Wakefield, Sarah, Susan Elliot, and Donald Cole. 2007. "Social Capital, Environmental Health, and Collective Action: A Hamilton, Ontario Case Study." *The Canadian Geographer* 51 (4): 428–43.

Warner, Michael. 2002. "Publics and Counterpublics." *Public Culture* 14 (1): 49–90.

Wasik, Bill. 2006. "My Crowd: Or, Phase 5: A Report from the Inventor of the Flash Mob." *Harper's Magazine*, March: 56–66.

Wayland, Sarah. 2012. "The Impact of Street Traffic on Residents: Some Research Findings." *Raise The Hammer*, 7 June. Accessed 29 October 2014. https://www.raisethehammer.org/article/1620/the_impact_of_street_traffic_on_residents:_some_research_findings.

Weaver, John. 1982. *Hamilton: An Illustrated History*. Toronto: Lorimer.

– 2010. "Hamilton." In *Canadian Encyclopedia*. Historica Canada, 1985. Accessed 5 November 2014. http://www.thecanadianencyclopedia.ca/en/article/hamilton/.

Wees, Nick. 2013. "Sound Composition and Creative Action at the Margins of Urban Space." Unpublished manuscript.

Westerkamp, Hildegard. 2002. "Linking Soundscape Composition and Acoustic Ecology." *Organised Sound* 7 (1): 51–6.

White, Richard. 2013. "Hamilton's James Street North: A Hidden Gem." *Raise The Hammer*, 9 July. Accessed 29 October 2014. https://www.raisethehammer.org/article/1899/hamiltons_james_street_north:_a_hidden_gem.

Whyte, William Hollingsworth (director). 1988. *The Social Life of Small Urban Spaces*. New York: Municipal Art Society of New York.

Whyte, William Hollingsworth. 1980. *The Social Life of Small Urban Spaces*. Washington, DC: Conservation Foundation.

Widmaier, Tobias. 2004. "Groove." In *Handwörterbuch der musikalischen Terminologie*, edited by Albrecht Riethmüller, 227–34. Stuttgart, DE: Franz Steiner Verlag.

Wiebe, Ashley Katherine. 2013. "Hand-Knit Scarves for Those Who Need Extra Warmth." *Global News*, 8 December. Accessed 1 March 2015. http://globalnews.ca/news/1017315/hand-woven-scarves-for-those-who-need-it-like-it/.

Wiles, David. 2003. *A Short History of Western Performance Space*. Cambridge: Cambridge University Press.

Winner, Langdon. 1980. "Do Artifacts Have Politics?" *Daedalus* 109 (1): 121–36.

Wirth, Louis. 1938. "Urbanism as a Way of Life." *American Journal of Sociology* 44 (1): 1–24.

WNDX. 2012. *WNDX Festival of Moving Image: Film Screenings, Performances, Artist Talks September 26-30, 2012*. Winnipeg: WNDX. Festival Program.

Wolfson, Shannon. 2009. "Construction Signs Warn of Zombies." *KXAN News* [Austin, TX]. Accessed 12 March 2012. http://kxan.com/news/road_signs_ warn_of_zombies (article no longer available).

Woodruff, Russell. 1997. "Artifacts, Neutrality, and the Ambiguity of 'Use.'" In *Research in Philosophy and Technology* 16: 119–30.

WorldTruthNow. 2012. "Idle No More Toronto Flash Mob Shuts Down Dundas Square." *YouTube* video, 1:19. Posted 21 December. Accessed 1 March 2015. https://www.youtube.com/watch?v=mG4bBu234ko.

Wynne, John. 2010. "Hearing Faces, Seeing Voices: Sound Art, Experimentalism and the Ethnographic Gaze." In *Between Art and Anthropology: Contemporary Ethnographic Practice*, edited by Arnd Schneider and Christopher Wright, 49–65. Oxford: Berg.

Zebracki, Martin. 2012. "Engaging Geographies of Public Art: Indwellers, the 'Butt Plug Gnome' and Their Locale." *Social & Cultural Geography* 13 (7): 735–58.

– 2013. "Beyond Public Artopia: Public Art as Perceived by Its Publics." *GeoJournal* 78 (2): 303–17.

Zukin, Sharon. 1995. *Cultures of Cities*. Cambridge, MA: Blackwell.

– 2010. *Naked City: The Death and Life of Authentic Urban Places*. Oxford: Oxford University Press.

CONTRIBUTORS

ALISON L. BAIN is associate professor of geography at York University in Toronto. An urban social geographer who studies contemporary urban and suburban culture, she examines the contradictory relationships between cultural workers, cities, and suburbs with particular attention to questions of identity formation, artistic practice, and urban change.

ROBERT BEAN is an artist and writer living in Halifax, Nova Scotia. He is a professor at NSCAD University. Bean has published books and articles on contemporary art and cultural history, and has been awarded grants from the Social Sciences and Humanities Research Council and Canada Council for the Arts.

LAWRENCE BIRD (MAA, MCIP) has a hybrid practice in architecture and visual arts. He works on infill urban design projects in Winnipeg, as he has done previously in Montreal and London, UK. His visual artwork has been exhibited recently at Inter/Access Gallery, Toronto, and Espace Architecture La Cambre Horta, Brussels.

ALEXANDRINE BOUDREAULT-FOURNIER is assistant professor at the University of Victoria. She teaches audiovisual anthropology. Her research projects focus on sound, media, and infrastructure in Cuba. She directed *Golden Scars*, a film funded by the National Film Board of Canada, and *Fabrik Funk*, an ethno-fiction about funk in São Paulo.

BRENDEN HARVEY has a master's degree in social anthropology from Dalhousie University, Halifax. His research interests include urban green space, internet culture, neighbourhood development, and social class. Since 2015 he has been working in the field of community improvement as a social policy research analyst for the City of Calgary.

WES JOHNSTON is an artist, writer, and cultural worker based in Halifax, Nova Scotia. Wes received a BFA from NSCAD University (2009) and has since been involved in artist-run culture in Halifax while participating in projects, residencies, and exhibitions at home and abroad.

LÉOLA LE BLANC is a media artist living in Dartmouth, Nova Scotia. She uses mobile technology to create historical, nonlinear narratives in site-specific public projects (*DAMMSel Day, iObject, Perpétuel*). Le Blanc has been artist-in-residence at the Banff New Media Institute and the Centre for Art Tapes in Halifax.

BRIAN LILLEY teaches architecture at Dalhousie University and practices on Canada's Atlantic coast. His interests include ecological, artistic, and computational strategies influencing design. His built projects advocate the well-being of communities through capacity-building. Recently, he has been involved in diverse material workshop projects, including community gardens and ceramic prototyping.

BARBARA LOUNDER is a visual artist and a professor at NSCAD University in Halifax, Nova Scotia. She has a BFA from Queen's University and an MFA from NSCAD University. She has presented her artwork in Canada and internationally. Her creative interests include walking-based and collaborative art.

MARY ELIZABETH LUKA is a Banting postdoctoral fellow at York University. She specializes in creative and strategic policy, planning and practice, and is an award-winning digital media producer-director. Her academic research draws on the concept of creative citizenship to investigate how civic, culture, and business sectors are networked in the digital age.

SEBASTIAN MATTHIAS is a choreographer whose works have been performed in North America, Europe, and Asia. The artistic research practice within his dance projects inspires his academic research into groove and contemporary dance, in the graduate program in urban publics and performance at HafenCityUniversity, Hamburg, Germany.

CHRISTOF MIGONE is an artist, curator, teacher, and writer. Between 2008 and 2013 he was the director/curator of the Blackwood Gallery at the University of Toronto. He lives in Toronto and is an assistant professor in the Department of Visual Arts at the University of Western Ontario.

ELLEN MOFFAT is a media artist who uses sound, image, and text projects to investigate sound and space, language, resonance, and social relations. Her production ranges from multichannel installations, to electroacoustic instruments, to performance as independent, collaborative and interdisciplinary work. She is a professional affiliate of the University of Saskatchewan.

KIM MORGAN is a visual artist working in multimedia. Her work addresses the impact of technology on the human body, our perceptions of time and space, and the shifting boundaries between the private and the public. Morgan is an associate professor at NSCAD University, Halifax, Nova Scotia.

SOLOMON NAGLER is a filmmaker whose works have been featured in film festivals across the globe. He also makes 16mm celluloid installations that engage with experimental architecture in galleries and public space. He is a professor of film production at NSCAD University in Halifax.

MARTHA RADICE is an urban anthropologist whose research interests include public space, public art and public culture, urban sociality and sociability, and neighbourhoods and community. She has recently published articles about cosmopolitanism, conviviality, and the publicness of public art. She is associate professor of social anthropology at Dalhousie University, Halifax.

NICOLE RALLIS has completed an interdisciplinary master of arts in globalization studies from McMaster University, and holds a joint honours degree in history and politics from Trent University. Her master's thesis employed documentary film methods to explore postindustrial transition in Hamilton, Ontario.

SUSANNE SHAWYER is a dramaturge and assistant professor of theatre history at Elon University. She researches dramaturgies of protest and the history of applied theatre in the United States and Canada.

SHANNON TURNER holds an honours degree in social anthropology from Dalhousie University and is working toward a master's degree in visual anthropology from Aarhus University. Her research interests include gender, queer identities, art, consciousness, and the theory and practice of cultural production and critique using visual forms.

LAURENT VERNET holds an MA in art history from Concordia University, and a PhD in urban studies from the Institut national de la recherche scientifique. Since 2009, he has been working at the City of Montréal's Public Art Bureau, where he now holds the position of commissioner.

NICK WEES is a graduate student in anthropology at the University of Victoria. His research interests include creativity and everyday life, sensory experience, marginality, urban settings, food, and the arts. He has a background in music, sound art, and experimental art practices and participates in local and national seed-saving efforts.